The Face of the Sea

The Face of the Sea

Lessons Learned in the Pacific Theater

ROBERT B. RUSSELL

SEA SPRAY BOOKS

Contents

DEDICATION

To the undecorated men of the United States Navy who did the things that brought success

FOREWORD

Sailors are known for spinning yarns and my father was a master. My siblings & I grew up listening to many tall tales, from the time he blew up a cast-iron bathtub while playing naval war-games as a child, to the "green smoke" episode from his service in the Pacific. Since childhood I have been trying to capture all the family stories and on my twelfth birthday, I received a lovely blank book in which to record them. I started by interviewing my father about that exploding bathtub and moved on to the rest. Little did I know that this interview would break the dam and release a torrent of writing which became The Face of the Sea.

In fact, my father had started working on The Face of the Sea as soon as he returned from the Pacific theater. The organizational problems, the waste of life and materiel that he observed during his five years of service continued to eat at him. Over and over, he began to tell his story, but was unable to find a way past the opening chapters.

Decades passed and perhaps provided the distance my father needed to gain perspective, research, and argue his case. As a teenager reading The Face of the Sea, I loved the story, but couldn't grasp the significance of his message. Re-reading it as an adult, I realized that the relevance of his critique reaches beyond a military application to business and all large organizations.

In the late eighties my father's criticism of the Navy was far too acute and he was unable to publish The Face of the Sea. At the time of his death in 1988 he was working hard on it, corresponding with his surviving shipmates and even the writer Walter Lord about the finer points of naval writing. It fascinated him that although many shared his memories, some were vastly different and some of the highlights—such as encountering the rogue, or "mammoth" wave—were not remembered at all by others.

This is not surprising as memory is a fragile thing, particularly in times of extreme stress. The Face of the Sea should therefore not necessarily be read as a historical documentation of the war in the Pacific (as my father wrote, even the official documents are not to be trusted), but as a tale of a blistering coming of age, wisdom gained, and a warning for future generations.

As a lawyer, he knew well how to argue a point, and although the preface may seem dry, his storytelling skill transcends time and cultural barriers. I remember apologizing to a Japanese colleague of my father's for any offending references to "Japs", but he smiled at me and told me how much he had enjoyed my father's "poetic memories of his youth." Thus, although some of his expressions may seem dated, I felt it important to leave his voice and poetry intact.

My father's position as an outsider looking in, combined with the roles he held, gave him a unique and broadly informed viewpoint and his critique is surely as valid today as it was then. Due to his work as a patent lawyer—especially in the field of radar—he had a keen understanding of naval technology development and his comments on drone warfare seem particularly prescient.

It is my hope that his legacy lives on through The Face of the Sea and that although a further 35 years has passed, his message has not lost its relevance.

Sarah Russell Spray, December 1, 2021

PREFACE

It is now nearly fifty years since Hitler unleashed the dogs of war on the world—long enough for a completely new generation of people to have assumed the leadership of the world. In order for these new leaders and the people who elect them to make sound judgments based on prior experiences, they should be made aware of certain aspects of history, which have been either forgotten or distorted in the intervening years. Thus, contrary to today's general understanding, the approach of war is far more difficult to detect than one might suppose. For example, people today seem to think that the menace of Hitler was so obviously evil and serious that the need to engage in war to stop him should have been clear to everyone at that time. In truth, however, most people in America at the time were of the opposite view and remained that way even for several years after the outbreak of war in Europe. The insidious part is that, although the general view in America changed dramatically after Pearl Harbor (December 7, 1941), people who lived through it then tend to forget that they did not see it coming, and today they give an impression that it could have been easily detected. This distorts the presentation of the history and fails to warn the future generations that the general tendency of people, then and now, is to put 'a blind eye' toward the approach of unpleasant things such as war. The problem is that this leads to unpreparedness and is one reason why lightning-quick military aggression ('Blitzkrieg') has often been successful in the past. There are, unfortunately, many examples of it in history. In fact, the Germans used it successfully against France in the war of 1870, and nearly succeeded with it against the allies in 1914 and 1939.

Along with a need for the public to be constantly mindful of the possibility of war, there is also a need to be aware that historically the professional military establishments of peace-loving nations, such as our own, are run essentially as 'civil service bureaucracies in which seniority, not talent[1] controls promotion and things proceed "slowly, cautiously, unimaginatively, and, at times, stupidly[2]." The result of both of these peace-time conditions is that serious lack of preparedness for war prevails and incompetence in the military establishment goes undetected both by politicians and the general public.

The U.S. Navy has suffered from this malady for many years. For example, during the presidency of Theodore Roosevelt, the Navy's gunnery efficiency was extremely low, but, typically, the command pretended otherwise. The inefficiency would have gone undetected but for the foresight and courage of a young commander named W. S. Sims. Sims took the unprecedented step (contrary to Naval Regulations) of writing a personal letter directly to the president, over the heads of his superiors in which he pointed out the weaknesses of the Navy's gunnery. The incident is described by Fletcher Pratt, in his 'Compact History of the United States Navy'[3]

"Sims pointed out that during the Spanish War our ships had made only five per cent hits out of the shots fired, and this was not only a wretched record on any computation, but one that would doom us to defeat in a contest with a major opponent.

Was it true? Roosevelt ordered firing tests under the conditions used by the British Navy, with reports to him personally. Their gunnery had recently been rejuvenated by the direct firing method of Sir Percy M. Scott, and they were getting eighty per cent hits under target conditions, while the U.S. Fleet could do no better than thirteen per cent in the trials the President ordered. Roosevelt immediately cabled for Sims, and by executive order placed him in charge of all Navy target practice for eighteen months, with word to 'cut off his head' if he had not achieved something by that time."

"Sims did; and it was well that he did, for the Japanese crisis arose just when he completed his work.[4]"

Pratt also continues with the following relevant comment:

"Promotion exclusively by seniority had brought to the head of the list a group of aging admirals, whose mere presence threatened another period of officer stagnation, and who were so conservative that only President Roosevelt's personal intervention had prevented them from having Sims court-martialed for insubordination over the gunnery business."

In Silent Victory' (pages 1-41), Blair also cites numerous case histories showing how this tendency toward inaccurate evaluation and unpreparedness has recurred throughout the history of the U.S.Navy.

That the U. S. has recently spent some $500 billion to create a 600 ship

Navy does not automatically mean that we are truly prepared to fight a real war. Thus, prior to World War II, the Navy made virtually identical peacetime allegations of preparedness. In actual fact, however, the U.S. Navy was hopelessly behind the Japanese in many ways, and it went undetected. The incompetence appeared in many technical areas, the most obvious of which was the failure on the part of the vast majority of the naval command to recognize that the anti-aircraft guns on the ships could not prevent air attacks on ships and that the ships themselves could not withstand bombing from the air (despite General Billy Mitchell's clear warning backed up by credible, convincing test evidence). This led to an unfortunate pre-war emphasis of Naval construction on battleships instead of carriers, and a failure to develop high speed Naval aircraft.

Less publicized was that, despite the lesson of Pearl Harbor, the Navy continued during the war to construct and/or deploy some ten new fast battleships at tremendous cost, instead of building useful ships such as submarines, and that, predictably, these mammoth battleships never sank an enemy ship and were never used effectively in the war effort (with one minor exception).

Still another equally serious misevaluation of weapons during World War II which has hitherto escaped public view relates to the command's misconception of the effectiveness of and/or need for destroyers to screen the aircraft carriers. Prior to World War II, the Naval command believed both that the 5′ guns of the destroyers could effectively repel air attack, and that the sonars and depth charges of the destroyers were capable of sinking submarines. These beliefs came from the same cause that Commander Sims, mentioned above, objected to, namely, inaccurate and overly optimistic test reports praising the weapons, which the command considered to be good. As a result, the command was unaware that neither the guns nor the depth charges of the destroyers were anywhere near as effective as had been supposed. One might expect that, soon after the war started, this inadequacy would have been rapidly detected and that the command would have responded appropriately. Actually, however, as will be revealed in this book, despite much evidence that both of these beliefs of the command were erroneous, the command adhered to them throughout the war, and based important command decisions thereon, to the serious detriment of the war effort and the needless loss of many lives.

The destroyer misevaluation issue has many different aspects which will be discussed below in this book, but the most dramatic way to illustrate the harm to the war effort caused by it is to compare the construction programs respectively for destroyers and submarines during World War II and the respective relative accomplishments of the two types of ship. During World War II, the Navy built some 800 new destroyers, as compared to some 140 new submarines with the cost per submarine being less than one half of that of a destroyer. The destroyers, however, were only partially effective. They helped deter attack but were never able to prevent either air or submarine attack against the ships they were intended to protect. With a few minor exceptions, the destroyers sank no enemy ships. At the end of the war, they were able to sink a significant number of enemy submarines, but this occurred only when the destroyers were employed in groups typically of four or more, together with an aircraft carrier (i.e., "hunter-killer" groups). The main contribution of the destroyers to the fast carrier operations was picking up downed aviators and rescuing personnel from the sunken carriers. By contrast, the Navy's 140 submarines under a different form of leadership than that in the surface fleet, by early 1945, had sunk over 5,000,000 tons of enemy ships and had reduced the Japanese merchant marine fleet to 2/3rds of that needed to sustain the civilian economy with nothing left over for their war effort[5].

If the Navy had built submarines instead of a minor percentage of the much more expensive and less useful destroyers, the submarines could have obliterated the Japanese merchant marine and concluded the war long before the atom bomb. If the Navy had refrained from building only one of the useless battleships, and had spent that money instead on building an equivalent number of submarines (estimated at over 50 submarines for one battleship), that alone could have done the job.

Whether or not these allegations of previously unpublished misevaluations and the harm to the war effort resulting therefrom are accurate, would be of little interest or importance today so many years after the fact, except that the time has come to start thinking about the next war. If analyzing those situations can shed light on weaknesses of the naval system and indicate a way to improve it, that analysis will be worthwhile.

In addition, the need to make such an analysis is indicated by a growing body of evidence that the Navy today is still mired in the same type of error-inducing thought pattern as it was in prior times. Paradoxically, the most notable example of serious weakness in today's Navy is the very same evidence to which the Navy points as demonstrating its strength, i.e., the Navy's fleet of some 600 ships including four mammoth task groups. Each of these task groups is centered on a reactivated World War II battleship and a nuclear carrier, and each cost the nation over $100 billion. The Navy justifies these vast (economy crippling) expenditures by a myriad of claims reminiscent of those of pre-World War II, including allegations that they can effectively defend these ships against missile attack (despite the recent debacle of the USS STARK in the Persian Gulf).

The sad, cold fact, however, is that, even if the Navy's claims that they can defend the ships were accurate, which many experts doubt, the Navy itself admits that their 'saturation' defense weapons can sustain an effective rate of fire for only a few minutes. Thus, each of those huge task groups can be obliterated by a concerted attack lasting more than a few minutes, made by supersonic jet bombers, at mast-head altitude, carrying missiles armed with small atomic warheads. Such an attack can be made successfully by sub-stantially less than 50 such bombers per task group attacking en masse. As Admiral Rickover testified before Congress, the U.S. fleet as presently consti-tuted would remain afloat for less than one half hour after the start of a real war[6]. Any one of the superpowers of the world, and even some of the oil-rich (and possibly 'trigger happy') lesser powers, can mount such bomber-mis-sile attacks. Accordingly, although both the administration and the general public are much impressed by these colossal Naval displays, and think that such size and quantity must represent high-scale preparedness for war, the present day Naval construction program has been, in fact, a waste, if prepar-ing to fight a real war is the objective. As a result, there exists today an urgent need to alert the public to the fact that, even though the possibility of war may seem remote, that possibility may, in fact, be much closer than one thinks. In addition, even though the Navy may seem to be well prepared and may assure everyone that they are thinking progressively now, unlike in former times, in fact, the earmarks of 'peace-time rot' are strong in today's Navy, the nation's first line of defense.

A major motivation, therefore, for writing this book was to present real life case histories illustrating first, why people tend to ignore the approach of war even when clear evidence of its imminence is presented to them, and second, why inherent features of the naval system as it was in World War II and as it still is today, cause the command to make and to retain misevaluations. Although the book is laid out in the form of a general narrative of the author's experiences, a large proportion of the incidents have been selected to illustrate both the weakness of the system and the conditions which cause it. Initially, the prewar failure of most Americans to heed the obvious signs of approaching war are described together with the surrounding factors which contributed to it. Thereafter, the book proceeds through a naval officer's training for the type of blind obedience and total loyalty required for combat, as well as the criteria employed for the promotion of officers, and how these factors combine to influence the thinking of the officers in a way which both stifles innovation and deters the passage of accurate information from the ranks to the command. That these aspects of the system resulted in serious loss is illustrated by analyzing how the war was fought both in the North Atlantic before the war and thereafter in the Pacific, how the command came to misevaluate the weapons, why the misevaluations continued to the end of the war, and why accurate evaluation information did not find its way to those who were responsible for making the decisions. In the course of this presentation, each of the major battles in the Pacific (Coral Sea, Midway, Savo Island, Cape Esperance, Santa Cruz, Guadalcanal, Tassafaronga, Philippine Sea, Leyte Gulf, and Okinawa destroyer picket line) is discussed in detail both as to its significant facts and how the misevaluations of the weapons affected the outcome.

A substantial portion of the book is devoted to explaining the technology. The reason for this is not that the technology of World War II has present day relevance, but to equip the reader independently to evaluate the allegations, which today's Navy vehemently deny, that the command did not receive accurate information, and erred significantly due to misevaluation. Also, although the technology of World War II is irrelevant to today's issues, the naval system which caused the problems in World War II is still the same, and, therefore, the study of how that system creates the error is well worth the effort today.

While major portions of the book are relevant to the analysis of the weaknesses of the naval system, and a brief recommendation for change is made at the conclusion, it would be erroneous to fail to mention the strengths of the system, of which there are many. Therefore, the book also describes naval life, naval customs and lore, as well as the aspects of the battles in which persons who lived through them rightfully took great pride. Also, in order to give the reader a non-sugar coated feel for how it really was to live in the naval system, the book describes the trials and errors of a young officer struggling to become an effective leader, the politics, the back biting and the in-fighting among the officers and men in the struggle for promotion, interspersed with vignettes depicting the men at work and play, the food, the smells, various funny things that happened, the storms, the broken bones, the men overboard, the blood and gore, the destruction and smashed equipment, the oil soaked survivors, and the tensions sometimes offset by the euphoria of the perpetual sameness of life, the beauty of the tropical surroundings, the natural phenomena, the sky, the stars, and even the multifaceted face of the sea itself.

The names of the ships described, and the officers having sufficient rank to make disguising them impractical, are real. Great care has been taken, however, when real names have been used, to limit anything negative to that which is either innocuous or necessary solely for historical accuracy. In a number of cases where both the system and the individuals are depicted in an unfavorable light, the names and places have been altered in order to avoid personal offense. Such incidents are deemed necessary for inclusion in the book, however, in the interest or accurate portrayal of the system and how it can go wrong.

The timeframe of the book is that of World War II, and, therefore, when the present tense is used it usually refers to the period 1939-1945 unless the text makes clear that modern times are intended.

(Note: In order to provide the reader with a quick comparison between this account and the official histories, reference is made in the text to the frequently differing versions of the same events as written by the major Naval historians. In the interest of brevity, footnotes indicate historian's surname together with the number of the relevant page of his work. The full title of the historian's work can be found in the Appendix.)

I. PRELIMINARIES

INTRODUCTION—THE LEGACY OF WORLD WAR I

There was little in the environment in the United States in the mid-1930's to lead people to think that a war might be coming or that the United States might have to be involved in it.

Young people growing up between the wars were very much aware of World War I. They were eager to learn more about it, and to hear the tales of heroism and sacrifice. As a consequence, the literature and films of the time were strongly oriented toward war subjects. Among the more prominent titles were "Hell's Angels", "What Price Glory", "Sergeant York", "All Quiet on the Western Front", "A Farewell to Arms", "Mata Hari", "Beau Geste", and "Mare Nostrum", to name but a few. On the other hand, while references to the war were everywhere, the older generation—especially those who fought in France, did not talk about it. They appeared to regard it as having been so horrible that they did not want to be reminded of it.

Nonetheless, there was other tangible evidence which gave the young an insight into how our fathers felt. For example, many people had relatives or acquaintances who had been gassed, shell-shocked, or wounded in the war. Another reminder was the pictorial Rotogravure sections of the Sunday newspapers, which people used to save from past years. A typical rainy-day pastime for young people in the pre-television era was to pour through the World War I issues of the Rotogravure. The pictures of the battlefields were gruesome enough, but the most shocking part was the number of pictures of young men "killed in action." Actually, the numbers of Americans lost in battle had been small compared to those of the French and English, but this was not pointed out. The newspapers simply presented page after page of portraits, usually about eight or ten per page, of good-looking young men who had died. To a young person's view during the period following World War I, it represented an appallingly large number of men who had sacrificed their lives for their country. The provincial manner in which it was presented left one thinking that America had more or less single-handedly won the war.

Although the older generation was tense and close-lipped about World War I, there was no diminution of the surge of faith and pride in America. The songs of World War I were still being sung, such as "Over There—The Yanks are Coming!", "Give My Regards to Broadway", "Pack Up Your Troubles in Your Old Kit Bag", "It's a Long Way to Tipperary", "Keep the Home Fires Burning", etc. This is not to say that anyone was bloodthirsty or interested in actually fighting a war. In fact, it was just the reverse. There was tremendous admiration of the way the "Doughboys" had marched off into the jaws of death full of spirit and confidence, but no one thought about repeating it. People had the idea that it was to be the final time that such a thing would ever have to be done. The "Doughboys" had fought to "make the world safe for democracy," and people held the "grand illusion" that World War I had been the "war to end all wars."

The generation which grew up between the wars, therefore, believed that a great war had been won, and that America had made a significant contribution to a permanent solution. They felt that America had shown the world her strength and that she could exist thereafter without any dependency on the rest of the world. Isolationism was the prevailing view.

As a result, the fall of the Weimar Republic in Germany, Hitler's rise to power, the burning of the Reichstag, the occupation of the Sudetenland, and Hitler's claims that Germany had been wronged in World War I, did not impress people then as much as people today might think they should have. This is where hindsight plays a major role. At the time, both abhorring war and holding a strong belief in isolationism, it was easy to convince oneself that whatever was happening in Germany was Europe's business, not America's. Incredible as it may seem, many people even sympathized with Hitler. Very few people saw any need to prepare for war, and this attitude undoubtedly affected the thinking of the professional military in America. In addition, in view of the well-known fact that Hitler was spending tremendous sums of money on public works, highways, and armaments, without having any visible means of raising funds with which to pay for them, many people thought that Germany would soon go bankrupt.

Many other factors also contributed to America's lack of preparedness for war. The arms limitations treaties deterred rearmament and the great depression of the early 1930 curtailed military expenditures. Perhaps the most dominant factors, however, were the extreme isolationism and a popular notion that the way not to have a war was to have nothing to do with it. It was as though ignoring it would make it go away. There were, however, a few people who did appreciate that it could happen again, and who were in high enough places to do something about it. Fortunately, President Franklin Roosevelt was one of those few. From around 1938 on, he started an unpublicized program (parts of which I will describe below) of vast rearmament, while, at the same time, for campaign purposes he was promising the American mothers that he would never send their sons 'to fight a war overseas.'

Accordingly, when viewing the background of this account of World War II, one sees America as a sleeping giant, contentedly ignorant of his weaknesses, naively believing that it he could avoid involvement in the turmoils of the world, and without appreciation of the obligation owed to the great nations of Europe which had stemmed the tide of German aggression in the 1914-1918 war.

THE CRASH OF THE CYMBAL

I first came to realize that a Second World War might happen, on a warm July night in Munich Germany in 1937. My brother and I had been spectators at the Olympic Games in 1936 and had been very favorably impressed by everything we had seen in Germany. Although we had heard a few rumblings of complaint from older people we saw nothing wrong. In fact, we thought that Hitler was doing an excellent job. Contrary to what we had been led to believe about the impending bankruptcy of the German economy, everything seemed to be booming. We became particularly enthusiastic after leaving Berlin and going to Bavaria where everything was "gemütlich." As a result, when we were offered another chance to travel to Germany the next summer, we leaped at it.

After arriving in Germany on the second trip, however, although the general level of activity was still as intense, we found that the spell of enchantment had disappeared. Waiters in restaurants were surly. If one asked for salt, one would be told that salt was not needed because it was already in the food. The bread was made of rice.

In 1936, Hitler had decreed that the German people should be friendly and hospitable to the foreign spectators at the Olympics, but in 1937 no such edict had been issued. Instead of being calm and affable, as they had been in 1936, the German people were tense and hostile. For example, we noticed several times when we waved at passing trains, instead of waving back; they would shake their fists at us.

Bicycling through Europe in 1937: RBR (right) and his brother, Jimmy – RBR Personal Collection

Once in Augsburg, on the way to Munich, we inadvertently started riding down a one-way street the wrong way. I was in the lead and, hearing a crash, looked around to see my brother sprawled on the ground. His assailant, a large angry woman was stomping off, shouting in a deep Wagnerian contralto, "Das ist verboten!" and shaking her fist.

Another incident occurred in Munich. One evening we were looking for a place to eat and thought we would try the Ratskeller. The menu was posted outside, so we propped our bicycles against the curb and went over to take a look at it. Before we could reach the building, a man kicked the bikes into the street, and we returned to meet another shaking fist and angry "Das ist verboten!"

These were small things, of course, but they left us mystified by what could motivate people to act in such a way. Also, small as they were, in retrospect they now seem analogous to the traces one hears at the start of a symphony of a theme, which later becomes dominant.

People today would undoubtedly find it hard to believe the intensity of the Hitler mania at the time. No one said "Good morning" anymore. The usual, and virtually only greeting was "Heil Hitler" coupled with the Hitler salute, and everyone, Americans included, were expected to do it. The old fashioned "Grüss Gott" of Bavaria was almost never heard (it has, of course, returned long since). There was a place in Munich, near the Siegestor, where a couple of early Nazis had been shot. It had been made into a sort of shrine. Two guards were stationed there and if a person did not give the Hitler salute when passing by, he would be arrested. The Hitler salute was to stand and raise one's right arm forward, hand stretched in a straight line, at a 45-degree angle upward. Hitler himself did not usually give the Nazi salute, but instead, merely flipped his hand up and back.

Then there was the "Horst Wessel Lied", the Nazi song which was actually much more of a national anthem than "Deutschland Über Alles". From listening to the way national anthems are sung today, people cannot imagine how the Germans thundered out the words of the "Horst Wessel Lied", the lyrics of which dealt with closing the ranks of the Nazi militia called the SA and marching spiritedly and eagerly to war behind the Nazi flag. Not only were the words shocking, but the way the Germans sang them signified a thirst for aggression on a very sinister scale.

The incident which finally made me realize that World War II might actually become a reality happened one evening in Munich. We had wandered out of the Hofbräuhaus at about 11:00 PM and were walking toward the Rathaus when we saw a crowd of about 500 people standing in the square in front of the Rathaus. Also, we could hear music coming from the direction of the old "Tor", or gate at the foot of the square. Actually, there was no tune to the music. It was merely cymbals going CRASH–CRASH –CRASH in a sort of deadly rhythm. At the end of the street, through the old "Tor", soon appeared a column of brown-shirted young men led by the cymbals, marching, each with a shovel, held like a rifle, on the shoulder. They were about 15 or 16 years old. As they marched steadily up through the square, the crowd parted to let them pass. I could see that the crowd was mainly parents, friends, and sweethearts. As the column came on through, the boys had their eyes fixed forward, and I began to watch to see if any of them might look toward the crowd. I was casting my eye over the entire column the way one looks at an entire ballet chorus at once to see if a foot or hand moves off time. All heads were solidly fixed. Not one eye moved. They marched straight on through to the deadly beat of the cymbals and thence on down the street for several hundred yards never looking to the right or left.

I turned to Jimmy, "Good God! Do you know what this means? We're going to have to do the whole damned thing over again!"

I often wished that more Americans could have been there because, while it made me see the light, America as a whole remained totally oblivious to it.

JOIN THE MARCHING RANKS—IN YOU GERMANY WILL LIVE

Other experiences on that same trip to Europe added to my conviction that war was coming. Since we were already feeling the hostility, my brother and I decided to leave Germany as soon as possible. We were, of course, on a limited budget, traveling by bicycle and sleeping in youth hostels. In every youth hostel in Germany in those days, Hitler had ordered that they post a copy of a speech which he had delivered at Nuremberg to the youth of Germany several months earlier. This speech was short but very impressive. The following is an abbreviated, free translation of it:

"It is clear that Germany has many enemies and equally clear that, because of this, Germany will again be at war. When this will happen is uncertain, but it will happen, and it can happen soon. Therefore, it is the duty of all Germans to shoulder the burden of preparation for war as a personal task. Germany must be strong. We must have the greatest army in the world. Our Navy must be on all seas. All Germans must work and sacrifice. Labor cannot strike. Labor must work. Capital cannot profit. Capital must pay.

And you the youth, you must play your part. You must join the marching ranks and work with all your energies and spirit. Today Germany is marching, and Germany is marching in you. Tomorrow Germany will march again, and in you Germany will live."

This speech, the Horst Wessel Lied, the marching youths, the saluting and "Heil Hitlers", and the tensions one could feel everywhere among the people, left us with no doubt about what was happening. As we approached the border of France, we heard from other young Americans that the Germans were stopping people at the bridge at Strasbourg for extended periods and investigating them for espionage. We had nothing to worry about on that score, but were afraid that the Germans might not see it that way. Apparently the surest way to avoid being stopped was to join a German youth bicycling club, the Radfahrverein, the members of which were being encouraged to travel into France at the time, and with a "triptik" (authority to travel), cross the Rhine at a small town as far as possible from Strasbourg.

Following this advice, we spent a day in Stuttgart shuttling back and forth between the U. S. Consulate, and the Radfahrverein. As it turned out, to become members, we had to provide evidence of residence in Germany. The Consul came to our rescue and assured the Radfahrverein that we were residents. We too had to assure them that we intended to return to Germany after our trip to France. This did the trick, and, with our "triptiks" in hand, we headed for the French border at a small town north of Strasbourg named Rastatt, where there was a ferry across the Rhine.

At Rastatt, the German border was guarded by a single sentry. He was affable, for a change, and engaged in conversation with my brother, whose German was good enough to keep up a "small talk" conversation. Gradually, however, the conversation drifted around to our bicycles, and the guard became curious as to where in Germany we had been able to buy two English bicycles. My brother tried to pretend that we had bought them second hand in Stuttgart, but this was a mistake because the guard was from Stuttgart and was very incredulous about there being a second hand bicycle shop there having any English bicycles to sell. My brother kept insisting, and the guard kept on looking skeptical. Luckily the ferry showed up, we went aboard, and departed toward France, and to freedom, with the German guard still standing there shaking his head. He obviously did not believe our story about the bicycles, but luckily he never thought to challenge anything else. We entered France with great pleasure and relief, and no remorse whatsoever about breaking our promise to return.

THE SPECTER OF DEATH

One further experience during that same trip to Europe in 1937 gave us important conditioning for World War II. It occurred immediately after we left Germany. Since our plans had been disrupted by our rapid exodus from Germany, and we were now becoming increasingly concerned about the possibility of war, we decided to visit the battlefields of World War I instead of Paris. Although we had gained superficial impressions of the war, as mentioned above, and had studied biased versions of it at school, we really knew little about it. What we saw truly opened our eyes.

Our first introduction to the battlefields was at Apremont and St. Mihiel, south of Verdun where we bought maps and brief histories and started talking to people. Apremont was where the American Army made its first appearance as an independent unit. We crossed the river at St. Mihiel and bicycled up to the top of the bluffs on the eastern side at the exact place where the Americans had entered the fighting in 1918.

The terrain was fantastically desolate. All one could see was gray and brambles. No cultivation was visible, only rough and desolate wasteland. A description of it written by an American at the time presents a most ghastly scene of mud, rats, shell holes, bodies, broken equipment, horrible smell, and stretching for miles as far as the eye could see. We were told that a better place to see the battlefield was 20 miles north at Verdun, and especially at the forts of Douaumont and Vaux to the cast of Verdun.

Douaumont is at the top of a rise which slopes gradually to the east for about four miles. The terrain was still amazingly bleak. While nature must have worked some improvement in the twenty years since the war, the land was still totally ruined. Twenty years is supposed to be a long time—Rip Van Winkle slept for twenty years. But yet, all one could see for miles was gray desolation—all hummocked. Even in surrounding areas where farming had recommenced, we were told that unexploded shells were killing between fifteen and twenty farmers every year.

The fort of Douaumont was barely visible, nothing but rubble. Down in the underground passageways it was the same, only broken bricks and concrete. There were photographs of whole towns so completely wiped out that only in an aerial photograph with the sun at a low angle could one see the vestiges of previous structures.

Seeing it still in such desolation after such a long period was impressive enough, but perhaps the most shocking part was to read the history. Here was a battlefield of over 1,000,000 dead. The major part of the fighting occurred earlier in the war, in 1916, when the German army had advanced to the north of Verdun to within about 50 miles from Paris. The German lines were extended, and Verdun represented a threat to their communications and supply. This caused them to launch a concentrated attack on Verdun. The odds were very heavy against the French because the Germans had six rail heads leading to Verdun, whereas the French had only one they called the 'Voie Sacre', and since it was within the range of the German artillery, it soon became passable only on foot or by mule train.

The battle was fought in an exceedingly gruesome manner. The Germans would open the day with a massive bombardment, which the French nick-named the "rideau de fer" (the iron curtain), for an hour or so, and then they would attack with infantry. At this point, the French, who had been hiding in the underground passages of the forts would come out, set up their machine guns and start firing away at the advancing Germans.

Day after day, this took place. The accounts refer to 40,000 to 60,000 men being killed in a single day. Each night the Germans would retreat, the French would bring up more men and ammunition, and the whole thing would start over again the next day.

Ever since World War I, the professional military institutions, military historians, and all students of warfare have pointed to the stupidity of the leadership, which led to such a holocaust. Little did anyone think that the lesson had not been learned and that both MacArthur[7] and Nimitz (see below p. 340) would be guilty of the same blunder in World War II.

After leaving Verdun, we travelled on through France and began to notice the World War I monuments in the small towns. This too was shocking because the lists of those who had given their lives for 'La Patrie' were so long, often representing as much as half of the eligible men of a town.

These experiences, of course, left us with an intense repugnance to the whole idea of war and they brought an entirely new dimension to our thinking. We could not erase from our minds the thought of these tremendous sacrifices by the French and the English for a cause which really was our own, and it completely changed our view about America's obligation to contribute to the elimination of aggression by a predatory nation, which we now saw recurring. These views were not shared by our contemporaries at home, most of whom had no idea that the French and English had sacrificed to such an extent, and very few of whom thought that America had any obligation to participate with other nations for security against aggression.

"HITLER IS A CAVITY IN THE TOOTH OF CIVILIZATION, HE IS EATING AWAY MORE AND MORE, AND SHOULD BE DRILLED!"

From these experiences in Europe in 1937, I was not only convinced that Germany was on its way to war but also that America would be, and should be, involved. Beyond this, I knew that I too wanted to be personally involved. The contemplation of all of those men killed in action in prior wars—although horrifying to me also made me feel that, if they did it for me, I was going to do it for those who follow me. I was not, however, inviting death. My idea was to do what I could do as best I could, but to do it sensibly, and survive if possible. For this reason, I had no hesitation to join the Navy. Not only did I fancy that my chances of survival would be better in the Navy, but I also liked the idea of having a bunk to sleep in, and if death were in store for me, I preferred the sea anyway. I joined the N.R.O.T.C. at Harvard, over my father's strong objection — he thought it was a total waste of four good college courses.

In addition, I began reading war histories (especially about the British Navy and Admiral Nelson) studying war technology and telling everyone around that I believed war was coming.

I was virtually alone, however, in my views and after Germany had invaded Poland and Britain had declared war against Germany in 1939, a strong movement called 'America First' gained popularity in the United States. While my views had not created much argument initially, after 1940 (Dunkirk etc,) the discussions often became very heated even though only a few sided with me. For example, On April 23, 1941, there was an 'America First' rally at

Harvard attended by 3000 students. I decided to picket it, but was able to bring together only 14 people who agreed with me. We did, however, succeed in having our picketing effort written up in the Boston papers. I saved the newspaper clipping.

HARVARD MILITANTS, PACIFISTS CLASH TODAY

this war as a personal task. Join the marching ranks! Then our m-)tto will be 'Onward America'! The American spirit will be marching in us, and in us America will* live.'

A statement of position issued by the peace-strikers explained: "Acting together we will tell the college communities and the nation as a whole that we want and mean to have peace. Some of us are pacifists; others are not. Some of us are for aid to Britain; others are opposed. All of us are united in our opposition to military intervention in the war—to convoys and an A. E. F."

Their rally will be led by Tudor Gardiner of Boston, a student and by several members of the faculty.

Peace, it probably will not be wonderful at the Harvard-Radcliffe "strike" against war today. The student peace-strikers will be picketed by strikers against the peace strike.

The two factions have announced plans to hold demonstrations today, the pacifists in Sanders Theater at 11 A. M., the militants outside.

Sponsoring the demonstration for all-out peace are the American Student Union, the Harvard Committee Against Military Intervention and the Harvard Conference for Democracy in Education. Their followers, participating in a national undergraduate gesture against war participation, will walk out of classes

today in protest against increasing sentiment for American convoys.

They will parade with posters bearing their views.

Their student critics will also parade with posters.

Led by Robert B. Russell, '41, of New York, the militants issued a manifesto yesterday which set forth: 'Soon we will be in the war. Now is the time to roll up our sleeves and get ready for the fight. In the future we must have no squalling from labor. Labor must work. We must have no kicks from capital. Capital must pay.

"We must have an army greater than any other in the world. Our navy must be on all seas. In the future any American must shoulder

*The resemblance to Hitler's speech was intentional.

BOSTON   TRAVELER,   WEDNESDAY,   APRIL   23,   1941

PICKETING HARVARD PEACE RALLY— Carrying placards voicing their opposition to almost everything having to do with war, this group of students is shown picketing the Harvard peace rally at Sanders Theater in Cambridge today.

Clipping of Boston Traveler article describing RBR's picketing of the Harvard peace-strikers' demonstration. RBR Personal Collection

I took to writing pamphlets and distributing them in Harvard Square. One of them was, in fact, quoted in the above-mentioned article. In writing it I intentionally lifted Hitler's words from his speech to the German youths because I, personally, thought they were excellent. I only thought that they should be used for a good cause, not Hitler's.

In another of my pamphlets, I started with the sentence, 'Hitler is a cavity in the tooth of civilization, he is eating away more and more, and should be drilled.' In addition to distributing it publicly I also handed it around to my friends who wrote comments on it and gave it back to me. One of the better comments was as follows:

"Dear Bubbles: What are you going to use to fill the cavity? Gold or Amalgam?"

"ALL NIGHT IN AND BEANS FOR BREAKFAST"

My first sea duty was as a Midshipman while I was still in the R.O.T.C. at Harvard, on the old Battleship WYOMING on a cruise to Havana in the summer of 1940. A midshipman is a trainee. He is neither an officer nor an enlisted man. In fact, the whole idea is to indoctrinate the Midshipman to the crew's quarters, to the food, the work, and the duties from the crew's point of view. We, therefore, slept in hammocks, which we rolled up each morning, and stowed during the day. We lived out of a tiny locker (about 16" x 16" x 18" deep), ate at the crew's mess, polished brass, holystoned the decks, stood watches, and did everything exactly as the crew did. We also were supposed to be learning as much about everything as we could and, therefore, unlike the crew, we were given constantly changing watch assignments so as to cover as many areas of the ship as possible (i.e. engine rooms, boiler rooms, generator rooms, radio rooms, bridge, gunnery, etc.) Every third night, we were given all night in and beans for breakfast which, forever afterward, became the expression of supreme contentment.

THE STONE AND THE BRASS

An important part of our Midshipman's training was the holystoning and the brass polishing. A holystone is a square block of tan colored soft stone that looks like sandstone, with a cup-shaped depression in its upper surface. You put a broomstick in the depression and use the stick to scrub the stone back and forth on a deck which has been doused with water. The operation involves 20 or 30 "Gobs" (the Navy slang for an ordinary, enlisted seaman) lined up in a row with their holystones aligned on a single plank. When the Boatswain gives the order, everyone starts out, each with his arms crossed and locked onto his own stick, and with everyone counting out loud, scrubbing back and forth in unison on the same plank. Then at a signal, all shift to the next plank.

An important part is that the decks need very little holystoning, but the idea is that you do it because you are ordered to do it. The same goes for the brass polishing. The whole exercise is to put the Midshipmen through the stunt of holystoning or brass polishing—especially when it does not need to be done. It strongly influences one's attitude.

I found out later in the war that an acceptance of orders and regimen is essential among men thrown into the battle context, and in times of crisis, when things in the leader's opinion need to be done, they must be done quickly, and without any argument. Anything short of prompt, total compliance results in chaos.

At the time, however, I thought that the holystoning and the brass polishing, when they were unnecessary, was not only nonsense (as it was) but damaging to morale (as it really was not). It was not until later, under stress and privation, that I began to see the point. While such training is essential for combat, the negative effect of it is to condition one never to question the wisdom or common sense of what is being done, and since this conditioning is basic to the training system, any junior officer soon learns that officers who criticize the command are not promoted. It leads to a Navy-wide acceptance of foolish ways to do things as will be described many times in this narrative, not only among the midshipmen holystoning decks, but unfortunately at all levels of command.

RUSSELL   TATTON   DOUGLAS   CUNNINGHAM WESSELHOEFT

RBR and fellow midshipman circa 1940. RBR Personal Files

"FELT SLIGHT BUMP"

At the end of the Midshipman cruise, we came into New York harbor and anchored at Staten Island (near where the Staten Island ferry docks). During the anchoring procedure, we Midshipmen were lined up at Quarters on deck in our white liberty uniforms.

Things on the ship, however, were apparently not going as they should. We could feel the thump of the engines and propellers running at high speed and see great streams of dirty colored propeller wash flowing along both sides of the ship towards the bow. Obviously, the ship was trying to go astern but nothing was happening. There was also a great deal of confusion, shouting, and men running back and forth—not among us Midshipmen—but principally among the ship's officers and the bridge people.

Obviously, the Wyoming had gone aground.

Going aground is a major incident on a ship of the U.S. Navy. Since I had spent much time in small boats as a child, and had gone aground literally hundreds of times, I could not see why it was such a "big deal." All one does is try to pull her off using the engines and failing that, one waits for the tide to turn, and floats her off. Not so in the Navy.

The underlying source of the problem in the Navy, not only with grounding but also with many other things, is promotion. Promotion is the only thing most Naval officers really think about. The pressure is tremendous. It is analogous to the pressure we see today when our teenage children apply for entrance to top ranking colleges. There are only a few places and many applicants, and the entire future seems to hinge on success. So too in the Navy. There are not many places for even the relatively low rank of Commander. Less than one half of any given Annapolis class will make it to Commander. Many less will make it to Captain, and only a small percent will make it to Admiral. But yet, to retire after twenty years as, say a Lieutenant, age 43, on 1/2 pay, leaves a bleak future for a person who, by his education, has been led to aspire to heights of leadership. At that age, for such a person to start a new career is hard. To do what? Be the dogcatcher in Hicksville? It, therefore, is a fact that the entire officer corps of the Regular Navy lives and breathes focused on promotion. For example, the most important publication to come in the mail is the Naval Register. Every time it is published, all the officers read it nervously to see who made it and who did not. Another aspect is the "Fitness Report". Every six months and at any change of duty, every Commanding Officer has to fill out a "Fitness Report" for every officer under his command. These reports are used for purposes of evaluating promotion. They set forth the numerous criteria on which an officer must be graded, such as "Attention to detail", "Ability to understand and carry out orders", "Seamanship", "Loyalty", etc. The problem which the extreme stress over promotion creates relating to the Fitness Report, is that the commanding officers become extremely uncomfortable about giving any grade less than perfect. This is because, if some CO's are tough graders, and others are soft, the good officers will tend to lose out. The result is that the usual fit-ness report of any officer will show all marks uniformly "down the right hand side" (meaning all top marks—the marking system in the Navy is based on 4.0 being the top mark, which accounts for the Navy expression "This is 4.0" as meaning perfection), and it is well recognized that giving a mark in any col-umn which is only one grade less than perfect is equivalent to the "kiss of death".

What has all this to do with the grounding of the Wyoming? Perfectly simple. The grounding of a ship must be reported and explained. The explanation has to include who was responsible for it and why the error occurred. The Captain, of course, is ultimately responsible, but usually one or more others are also at fault, and in the report, the Captain will state who else is at fault in order to excuse himself or at least to minimize his culpability, and this shift-ing the blame goes on down the line, until the lowest signalman striker can expect to be involved. There is an old creed in the Navy, "loyalty up—loyalty down" which comes into play at such times. Everyone below is expected to support the cover-up of those above him, and the superiors to cover-up for the juniors. They band together because everyone's chance of promotion is jeopardized. (This creed has more serious ramifications, which I will discuss below).

The result of these tensions is that on any Navy ship, after giving the order to "back her down" and the expected motion of the ship to the rear does not take place, all hell breaks loose. Not only the Captain, but everyone near the chain of command who has responsibility for the navigation and the ship handling, immediately sees the whole thing as drastically affecting the cen-tral point of his life, i.e. PROMOTION.

The following quotation from Potter demonstrates how grounding a ship can ruin an officer's chances for promotion:

"Spruance asked King to promote Moore to Rear Admiral, but King would not hear of it. Moore had once run a cruiser aground and that was a blunder that King would not forgive."[8]

It so happened that, on that particular occasion on the Wyoming, after about ten frantic minutes with all four engines racing in reverse, the Wyoming miraculously eased slowly off the mud bank which had been holding her.

At that time, the Engineering Officer of the Wyoming was Lt. Cdr. Glen R. (Roy) Hartwig, USN, more about whom I will be writing shortly in this account. He and I were having a chat some years later about the old Wyoming, he having mentioned his tour of duty on her as Engineering Officer. I told him I had taken a cruise on her, and it turned out that we had been aboard both at the same time. I mentioned that I recalled a moment when we had anchored off Staten Island that the Wyoming seemed to have gone aground, and asked him "Whatever happened about that? Did they have an investigation and all that?"

He answered that once the hysteria had passed, and the Wyoming was safely off the mud bank with no apparent damage, they all sat around silently for a while. Finally, the Captain called the Quartermaster striker (i.e. the lowest ranking person on the bridge) who keeps the Quartermaster's log in which all things such as orders to the helm, signals, messages, and 'bells' to the engine room, are logged, and told him to record in his log "10:28 AM—felt slight bump-." Nothing else appeared about it in any official log, paper or report of any kind, and, as far as I know, no one (other than Hartwig to me) ever even breathed a word about it since.

Apropos of the Navy's paranoia over the grounding of a ship, Potter recorded the following conversation between Admiral Nimitz and General Vandegrift:

"Late in the evening over a drink, Nimitz said 'You know, Vandegrift, when this war is over we are going to write a new set of Navy Regulations, so just keep it in the back of your mind because I will want to know some of the things you think ought to be changed.'"

Vandegrift replied, "I know one right now. Leave out all reference that he who runs his ship aground will face a fate worse than death. Out here too many commanders have been far too leery about risking their ships."[9]

SALUTE THE UNIFORM NOT THE MAN

Another aspect of Naval life in which I had already become immersed as a midshipman comes under the heading "R.H.I.P." which means "Rank Has Its Privileges". One's indoctrination in RHIP starts as soon as one signs up. It includes learning the uniforms, the insignia, the titles, and ways to address seniors and juniors, the saluting, where to stand, etc. In addition, one learns the privileges, prerogatives, or other benefits to which the respective ranks are entitled. A typical example has to do with flags displayed on the yard arms of the ships when the fleet is in port. Officers of high rank, their chiefs of staff, and the commanding officers of the ships are entitled to have certain flags hoisted to indicate their presence on or absence from their ships. This is why admirals are referred to as having "flag rank", and why the ship on which the Task Force commander has his headquarters is called the "flagship". Admirals are also provided with a fancy "barge" (i.e. a long, speedboat type of launch with a plush stateroom forward, white paint, tassels, much polished brass, spotless white seat covers, a crew of three plus a mess attendant, etc.). Of course, the lesser ranks have their proportionately lesser privileges, and all are rigidly observed. For example, a Vice Admiral cannot have a Captain for his Chief of Staff even if he requests it. Instead, he must have a Rear Admiral[10]. Hundreds of these trappings of rank and station exist, not only for shipboard but also for shore duty. For example, an officer on shore duty has to reach a given rank before he is allowed to have a leather couch in his office. The whole panorama of these figments of RHIP becomes a major part of the thinking of the entire officer's corps, and undoubtedly has much to do with intensifying the agitation over promotion.

One can look at RHIP as representing the pageantry of the Navy, and as a reward for excellence. A closer inspection, however, reveals that one normally gains promotion by conforming, by creating no enemies, and by making no mistakes. This is because there is very little to compare between the performances of officers, especially during peacetime. As long as they do what they are supposed to do, they are all equal. Once in a while an officer will do something to attract attention and be commended. For example, when Lt. Cdr. Hartwig, mentioned above, was in Guantanamo before the war, he was given a commendation for the excellent way he had hung the Chinese lanterns at the admiral's gala ball. There are, of course, other awards such as the "E" for engineering efficiency which will be described more in detail below. They are eagerly sought after because they enhance the chances of promotion. In fact, Hartwig also won one of those. On the other hand, commendations are not necessary. Most officers are uniformly graded 4.0 and promotion follows on the basis of seniority, whose "skirts are cleanest", and who has offended the least number of people. Then after one has been promoted, one gains respect by virtue of having the rank. This accounts for the saying sometimes heard, 'I salute the uniform, not the man.'

In much the same way as training blindly to obey tends to suppress common sense among the subordinates, RHIP has harmful effects among the seniors. Once they reach high rank, RHIP has the effect of making them so secure that there is no longer any goad of competition. This leads to complacency and inertia, the harmful effects of which will be described from time to time as this narrative unfolds.

LT. GUNDERSON

My next sea duty was on an Eagle boat out of Boston harbor in the Spring of 1941 while I was still a Midshipman. Eagle boats are strange little ships of about 100′ in length and built exactly like a box. In fact, they were made by the Ford Motor Company at the end of World War I, completely out of flat steel plates riveted together. Therefore, everything was flat and angular, without any curves to be seen.

The engineering plant was steam, the boilers were coal fired, and the firerooms were pressurized exactly as on the larger ships of the era of World War I. So even though it was very small and awkward looking, the Eagle boat was a good training ship because it had, in capsule form, virtually everything one would find on larger ships, even though somewhat antiquated.

Eagle Boat – USS EAGLE PE-2 US Naval Archives

Our routine on this cruise was to leave Boston and steam up and down the coast for three or four days and then return to port for a night.

I enjoyed the night watches most. As Midshipmen, we were assigned to the duties of JOD (Junior Officer of the Deck), which involved making routine inspections of the ship, log entries, and other simple jobs around the bridge and elsewhere on the ship. The part that was fun was spotting various navigational aids such as flashing beacons, bell buoys, lighthouses, etc. and then plotting the position of the ship in relation thereto. For reasons mentioned above, the Captain and the Officers of the Deck were always especially anxious to know the exact position of the ship, and constant verification was appreciated.

The method of communication to the engine room on the Eagle boat was by voice tube.

My assignment was to stand the JOD watch under the Executive Officer, Lt. Gunderson, as Officer of the Deck.

Mr. Gunderson was a small man with a very quick manner. He was about 40 years old and had been "passed over" twice, meaning that he had not been selected twice for promotion to Lt. Cdr. when his name came up. As mentioned above, promotion is paramount, and, conversely, being passed over is a tragedy for a Naval officer. It immediately changes his whole life. But not only is his life affected; his wife also finds herself immediately separated socially from the other women at the base with whom she once was socially equal. The children are likewise affected. The expected increases in family income are absent. The duties for him remain the same, except now younger men will be giving orders to him. Being passed over twice is a disaster.

Mr. Gunderson was a martinet. Everything we did was inspected by him with ultimate precision, and no flyspeck went without bitter comment. You could not report to him "Everything is all set, Sir!" Instead, you had to say what the condition was. If he asked you a question and you answered, "I do not know, Sir," he would hit the roof. The answer you were supposed to give was "I will find out, Sir." If you asked him for permission to go ashore, he would say, "I don't give a damn where you go. You can go straight up if you like. If you want to leave the ship you can." etc. etc.

We Midshipmen had no feeling for the torment inside Mr. Gunderson, which undoubtedly made him as he was. All we knew was that he seemed to be totally picayune, ridiculously strict, and stupid as well. In short, we "hated his bloody guts."

On one particular night, we were approaching the Isle of Shoals. The night plan indicated that we would continue northeast until Star Island was abeam, at which point we would reduce speed, reverse course, and head back toward Cape Ann.

I was at the pelorus (a device on the wing of the bridge equipped with a sight and means for determining the bearing of an object) reading out the bearing of Star Island as it gradually approached the beam. Mr. Gunderson was inside the wheelhouse waiting for me to sing out.

Finally, Star Island was abeam. "Star Island abeam, Sir!"

Gunderson reacted instantaneously. "RIGHT STANDARD RUDDER" and then to the voice tube, "ENGINE ROOM" At the other end of the voice tube was one of the other Midshipmen on the cruise. Instead of saying "Engine Room Aye!" as he was supposed to do, he said "Yeah?"

Gunderson exploded. "LISTEN YOU WISE GUY, WHEN I SAY SOMETHING DOWN THIS VOICE TUBE, YOU REPEAT EXACTLY WHAT I SAY, EXACTLY AS I SAY IT, GODAMMIT, SAVVY?"

Up through the voice tube, we on the bridge then heard the following:

"Listen you wise guy, when I say something down this voice tube, you repeat exactly what I say, exactly as I say it Godammit, savvy?"

"BULLETS FOR BRITAIN", MR. ROOSEVELT PREPARES FOR WAR

My parents were furious with me because Lib and I had decided to marry immediately after my graduation from Harvard in June 1941. My father said he'd be damned if he was going to support me, and my mother thought that the whole idea was nonsense.

In order to carry out our plan, therefore, I had to have a job, and for this purpose I went around to a tennis playing friend of mine, Don Carpenter, who also happened to be the president of Remington Arms in Bridgeport. He was a bit skeptical about hiring me because people had begun trying to obtain jobs at Remington in order to escape the draft. I explained that I would be a Commissioned Officer in the Naval Reserve, would be called up for training in a couple of months, and that I had no intention of using a job at Remington as an excuse to avoid military duty. He accepted me on the spot.

Lib and I were then were married, took a small flat in Bridgeport, and I went to work at Remington.

Having been quite familiar with Mr. Roosevelt's campaign promises during the presidential election of 1940, that he would never send American boys "overseas to war," I was rather abruptly surprised to find at Remington that they were training large numbers of foremen to occupy jobs in munitions plants elsewhere in the United States. Remington put me immediately into the administrative side of the training program, a fact which is of no significance except that on that job, I soon became aware of the actual numbers, and found that 400 foremen were being trained each week. The program took three weeks for a pupil to complete and, therefore, we had 1,200 foremen in the process of training at any one time. The proportions were staggering. I knew that American munitions plants were making "bullets for Britain", but munitions plants capable of using over 20,000 foremen (one year's output of the training program) bespoke of preparations for war on a far greater scale than I, and I am sure the average American, had previously supposed possible. American involvement on such a scale indicated direct participation, which, in turn, meant, that overseas activity would be inevitable.

HORATIO ALGER PAYS OFF

On Saturday afternoon, August 23, 1941, I was playing golf on the 16th hole of the old Fairfield Country Club course. I saw Lib driving down the beach road parallel to the golf course. She then stopped, got out of the car, and came running over to where we were. "You've got your orders to report to the Navy!" she gasped. She was very upset, as anyone can appreciate. Conversely, as few may appreciate, I was excited. I felt that this was my time. This was what it was all about. I was on my way.

We went home immediately, and I began preparing to go to Boston, where I had to report. My orders were "proceed and report" orders, which meant that I was allowed four days plus travel time to arrive at the reporting office.

The way it worked out, with a physical examination included, I did not have to report until Monday September 1st.

Although I could have taken more time, I finished up at Remington very quickly, packed and left for Boston on Thursday. Then on Friday morning in Boston, I began to think about reporting. Years before, I had read a Horatio Alger story about a rich father who wanted to test his son. The son was very keen to go with his father on an ocean liner to Europe. When he (the son) awoke on the day the steamer was to depart, his father had certain jobs for him to do. Thereafter, during the day, at the point when he completed each job, another job was given him. Finally, his last job brought him to the ship. If he had not done each job as fast as he could, he would not have made it. Although the story was as corny as "The Little Engine That Could", there is no question but that I actually thought about that story at that time. When I told Lib I was going to report, she was furious—and I cannot reasonably blame her—but yet, I was very keen.

I reported.

Since my ship, the USS RUSSELL (more about which presently), was at that time out on patrol, I reported to the personnel office of the First Naval District. A Commander Hooper was the Commanding Officer. He greeted me, put me on temporary duty in his office, and turned me over to Mary Mooney, his secretary to fill out my reporting papers. Then in a few minutes, it being around 4:00 PM on a Friday, he put on his hat and coat, and started for the door. Mary, bless her soul, caught his eye. "By the way Commander, how about signing Mr. Russell's reporting papers?" She had not actually completed them, but he put his signature at the bottom of the page and departed. She then completed them, and I was officially logged in.

I had no idea at the time what a difference it was going to make, but later in the war, it turned out that promotion was based on the average between the date of one's commission and one's reporting date. By reporting on that Friday, instead of the following Monday as I could have done, I was promoted to JG (Lieutenant Junior Grade) ahead of those who reported on the Monday; to full Lieutenant also; and so on. Totally apart from the money, which was substantial, the difference resulted in opportunities for better job assignments and more responsibility. So Horatio Alger was right after all!

After several weeks of temporary duty in Commander Hooper's office, we received word that the RUSSELL would be arriving in port the next day. Commander Hooper asked me to come into his office.

"Russell, I want you to know that I like what you have been doing here. In fact, I would like to offer you a job here. What do you say? I am pretty sure I can arrange it if you would like me to."

He knew that I had just been married, and undoubtedly was being sympathetic.

My mind, however, was very "one track" at that moment, I wanted to be in the fleet. Also, I had a premonition that my being assigned to a ship having my own surname, was a good omen. Anyway, I did not hesitate. I thanked him, but said I was not interested. As I walked out of his office, however, I felt a heavy burden. First, I knew it was not fair to Lib. Second, I was aware that there would be times when I would regret the decision—as indeed there were many.

RUSSELL OF THE RUSSELL

It was a cold, gray September morning, when Lib and I got up at 6:00am, had a silent breakfast, put my cruise box in the back of the station wagon and started out for the Navy Yard from our small flat in Cambridge, Mass. to report for duty on the USS RUSSELL (DD414). On the way we picked up Charlie Woodman, a college and NROTC classmate, who had also been assigned to the RUSSELL at the same time. We then proceeded through Cambridge, crossed Prison Point to Charlestown, then down a narrow, dingy street past the honkey-tonks and brothels which lined the entrance to the Navy Yard, through the gate, presented papers to the sentry, passed into the Navy Yard under the bowsprit of Old Ironsides, around a small sunken dry dock, and up to the gangway of the RUSSELL moored in the first slip beyond Old Ironsides. (In fact, it was the exact same slip where the USS CASSIN YOUNG (DD793) is moored today in Boston's National Historical Park). Going aboard, we met the Executive Officer, John Dimmick (Lt. USN) who assigned us each to a stateroom and introduced us around to the officers with the duty, the others having gone ashore.

It is appropriate at this point to describe the ship that was to be my home for the next 21 months.

USS RUSSELL (DD–414) USN *Ref*: NH 107278

First, however, I should say that there was no connection between the officer for whom the RUSSELL was named (Destroyers are named after officers) and my family. I found out later that he held various minor commands during the Civil War, rose in the ranks later and was promoted to Rear Admiral in 1886. My assignment to the RUSSELL was totally coincidental.

The wardroom extended athwartships the full beam of the ship, had a leather transom (couch) at each end, doorways leading aft at each side, and a central companionway also leading aft, up to the captain's cabin, the radio shack and above that to the Commodore's cabin and then to bridge. Forward from the wardroom was a central passageway with five officer's staterooms on each side. Mine was the second one forward on the starboard side. It included a hanging locker (closet), a desk-drawer combination, with a fold-out desk surface, and a combination locking safe in it. I also had a wash basin with a mirror cabinet above, an armchair, and a built-in bunk with a ventilation blower over it. The deck was maroon "battleship" linoleum. I unpacked my cruise box with mixed feelings of pride, excitement, and wonder. Next ahead for me lay the task of learning my ship.

The RUSSELL was a Sims class (one stack) 1500-ton destroyer. Although small compared to a carrier or battleship, she was far from tiny. She was longer than a football field, and her superstructure stood higher than a five-story building.

She had a main battery of four, five-inch guns capable of firing a 57 lb projectile accurately to over 15,000 yds (7 1/2 miles). She had two centrally located torpedo mounts having four 21" torpedoes each, enough to sink a Battleship. She had about 50 depth charges—sufficient to sink a fleet of Submarines (or so we thought); ten 50 cal. machine guns later replaced by 20mm anti-aircraft guns, and assorted small arms, including 45 caliber submachine "Tommy" guns, carbines, Springfields, 38 caliber and 45 caliber automatic pistols (one of the latter was issued to each officer) weapons enough to equip a sizeable boarding or landing party. On the other hand, she had very little protection. The gun mounts looked like they were protected by turrets, but, in fact, they were only covered with a thin shell to protect the men from the elements, not from bullets. The skin of the ship was a mere 1/4-inch steel plating, but she did have reinforcing at the bow for ramming purposes.

The RUSSELL's engineering comprised two firerooms forward having two boilers each located under the stack, and two engine rooms aft, one for each shaft of her twin screws. The shafts were driven by steam turbines built to operate under high pressure (600 psi), and superheated (500 F) steam and capable of developing 30,000 horsepower. In view of the fact that World War I Battleships had less horsepower, and the Queen Mary, a ship 60 times larger than the RUSSELL, had only 7 times the horsepower, it is evident that she was a very high powered ship for her size.

She carried 400 tons of fuel oil, enough to last her about ten days of cruising under maximum economy conditions, but only enough for about four or five days during high speed fleet operations under combat conditions.

Her peacetime complement of officers and men was about 150, but during the war it was increased to about 250.

When I reported on board, the Captain was Lt. Cdr. Glen R. Hartwig, mentioned above as having served previously on the battleship Wyoming. He was of the Annapolis class of 1928. Lt. Dimmick was Exec.; Lt. Lee Pancake, Engineering; Lt. Wm Barnes, Gunnery; Lt Charles Hart, First Lieutenant; Lt. Jg. John Caster, Damage Control; Lt. Jg. John Carter, Paymaster; and Lt. Jg

(USNR) John Durst, Communications. There were also three Ensigns, "Finn" Toivonen, Wm. Bargeloh, and Herbert Silberman recent graduates of the Officer's training school on the USS PRAIRIE STATE.

The RUSSELL remained in Boston for several days, and the day before her scheduled departure, Captain Hartwig returned from shore leave. After being introduced to him in the wardroom, he asked a few background questions and then:

"What I'd really like to know—you being a local boy—is whether you are familiar with Boston Harbor."

I did not hesitate—"Yes Sir!" (In the Navy the emphasis is on the "Sir"). Actually, although I had steamed in and out of Boston on the Eagle boat half a dozen times, I had not, in fact, made any detailed study of it. On the other hand, my experiences with Lt. Gunderson, had taught me always to answer positively. The result was not quite what I had expected.

"Good, I will need you on the bridge tomorrow morning when we get under way, to identify buoys and give me accurate courses to steer!"

Although this immediate reaction of the Captain's came as a shock to me, there was no way that I could say "Hey Captain*, I didn't mean I know Boston harbor that well..." My only choice was to carry through with it. Later in the evening, I went up to the bridge, found the chart of Boston harbor, and spent the small hours of the morning learning every buoy, island name, and all other points of interest.

(* In the Navy on board ship, the Commanding Officer is addressed as "Captain" regardless of his rank. Similarly, the Squadron Commander is called Commodore even though his actual rank may be different. Lt. Commanders are addressed as "Commander", but all more junior officers are merely addressed as "Mr." One has to learn these things quickly or suffer being blasted for making a mistake.)

BEDLAM ON THE BRIDGE

The next morning when we got under way, I was introduced to a scene which can be described only as "Bedlam on the Bridge."

I have already explained the Naval officers' fear of making a mistake, which might jeopardize their chances of promotion, such as running a ship aground. This paranoia, however, also applied to any other act which might be observed by officers above in the chain of command who might be sitting on a future selection board. Therefore, any maneuvers in harbor, which could easily be seen, for example by the Commandant of the Navy Yard from his office window, or maneuvers at sea which would be observed by officers of higher rank, always created high tension.

Although, he became much more relaxed later, when I reported on board, Captain Hartwig was still very "up-tight" on the bridge while getting under way, docking or maneuvering, not only for the foregoing reasons, but also because he had had little prior experience in destroyers. Naval officers actually receive little "hands on" training in ship handling. This may be hard to believe to persons outside of the Navy, but the explanation is simple. Since there is so much tension about it and the ultimate responsibility is the Commanding Officer's, it is a rare Commanding Officer who will let anyone else do it. Thus, although all Junior Officers (engineers included) are required to stand deck watches and become qualified as "Officer of the Deck" (OD), and at least nominally, be able to run the ship, give orders to the helm, etc., in any case of maneuvering, piloting, coming alongside, etc, the Captain always takes over, and the Officer of the Deck virtually never has a chance to try his own hand at it. So, it was a fact that on the RUSSELL, when I reported on board, Hartwig was not only short on ship handling experience, but scared to death of the possible consequences of even a small mistake that could be observed by a higher ranking officer. The same lack of experience also applied to the other officers on board. None had had appreciable ship handling, and later, when each, in turn, eventually obtained a command of his own, he came to the tasks of ship handling and piloting as a relative neophyte.

The scene on the bridge that morning was, as a consequence, ridiculous. A Junior Officer was stationed at each alidade to take the bearings of various buoys, a Quartermaster was stationed at the fathometer to read the soundings, and another Junior Officer was stationed behind the helm to read out the headings of the ship, and each had orders to sing out continuously what each was observing. Another Junior Officer had orders to relay the information to Mr. Dimmick in the chart house.

Once we got under way, everyone was shouting at once and the Captain was running here and there telling people either to do something or not to do it but instead to do something else, and barking orders to the helm and to the engine room and changes thereto in rapid fire succession.

It was an incredible scene. Bargeloh later told me that the previous Captain, a Commander Pollock, had been a good ship handler, but that this was ridiculous, and that morale had suffered. While Hartwig did eventually become much better, the bridge scene during getting underway and docking always remained loaded with tension, and was, in fact, similar on many other ships on which I served.

By contrast, the bridge scene on a merchant ship is totally different. Later in the war, I had occasion to pilot a number of merchant ships through the secretly charted mine fields at Noumea, New Caledonia, and at Espiritu Santo, New Hebrides. Typically on a merchant ship, the helmsman can be given an order such as "Do you see that white rock over there?" "Yes" "OK then, steer for it," and then for the next few minutes, no one on the bridge will say a word until, perhaps a new course, or a change of speed is needed. A merchant ship will often be brought into harbor and anchored with as few as half a dozen orders.

(The Navy way, however, led to the famous time when, after finally bringing the ship in and having the lines safely secured to the dock, the Captain bellowed down the voice tube to the engine room, "SECURE THE MAIN ENGINES!", and the answer came back, "SECURE THE MAIN ENGINES HELL! WE STILL HAVE 12 BELLS TO ANSWER!")

CONTRABAND TO ENGLAND

After a few harrowing moments identifying buoys and landmarks for the

Captain, we passed Deer Island, and along with three other ships of our squadron, nosed slowly out to sea through the eastern channel past the Graves light. The day was calm and the water an oily gray. All ships increased speed to 15 kts on a southeasterly course.

I was at last at sea, headed out, embarked on a destiny, which I had felt ever since that night in Munich, steaming toward the eastern horizon beyond which there was a war. The silhouette of the skyline of Boston gradually dropped lower and lower on the horizon astern until it disappeared, and ship-board life started. Sometime around mid-day we rendezvoused with a convoy of six merchant ships. This seemed normal enough at first, until we came close and saw that, on their main decks were stacked P-38 fighter planes. The P-38 was the American fighter that had two engines and split fuselages and split tails. It was very distinctive. No other airplane looked like it at all.

This was electrifying news. Here we were, convoying P-38s, obviously, blatantly contraband, to England! The amazing thing to me was that no one on the ships even bothered to cover the P-38's with tarpaulins. There they were, wide open for anyone, including a German U-boat Commander with his periscope, to see.

As I mentioned above, I had been surprised by the amount of munitions activity I had seen at Remington Arms. This shocked me even more.

My family were staunch Republicans, and Roosevelt's socialist views had not been well received in our home. As a consequence, I had been conditioned to expect that he had been insincere about his promises never to send American boys to war overseas. On the other hand, while I held these negative views of Mr. Roosevelt, I was very much in favor of what I had learned both at Remington Arms about his energetic enhancement of our munitions production capacity, and now, what I was learning about our convoying contraband to Europe. Even so, I still felt there was something wrong about his keeping the American people ignorant of what he was doing. I had been brought up to believe that democracy is the best form of government and that the leaders are supposed to be faithfully following the will of the people regardless of their own private views. But here I was witnessing the reverse, and strongly in agreement with it.

Not only did I learn that America was actively engaging in contraband, but also that the German U-boat Commanders had been given orders to sink American ships. These orders had been issued by Hitler at about the same time as my assignment to the RUSSELL. They resulted from what became known as "The GREER incident."

The US destroyer GREER was at sea off Iceland and made sonar contact with a submarine. In the sub-arctic ocean, the water conditions are such that sometimes sonar contact can be made at several thousand yards. (In the Pacific, contact is rarely made at over 1000yds). The GREER spotted this submarine at a range of about 2,000 yds and began tracking her. Also, they radioed to Iceland to find out if there were any friendly submarines in the area. The British in Iceland replied that the sub must be German and asked the GREER to indicate the sub's exact position, which the GREER did and continued to do while the British began trying to bomb it from the air. The German Commander did not take kindly to the GREER's participation in these activities and let several torpedoes go at her. The GREER had been careful to remain pointed directly toward the sub so as to present the least vulnerable part of the ship and as small a target as possible to the sub. In any event, the torpedoes missed. At this point, the GREER radioed to Washington that she was being attacked by a German sub. Shortly thereafter, the GREER pulled away and returned to Iceland.

The American people were then informed that the Germans had launched an unprovoked attack on one of our destroyers, which had been engaged only in preserving our neutrality.

Other incidents similar to the GREER incident, occurred in rapid succession. One of our Destroyers, the KEARNY, while convoying contraband south of Iceland, was hit by a torpedo amidships. She did not sink but was able to reach port in Iceland. Another destroyer, the REUBEN JAMES (a "4-piper" of World War I vintage), was less fortunate. She was hit and sunk in a con-

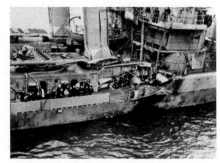

USS KEARNY October 1941 USN Ref NH 52254

voy 350 miles ahead of us. After these attacks, we were given orders to "shoot to kill", which is also noted by Blair.[11]

Although keeping a diary was forbidden, there were many violators of the rule. I did not start mine until February 1945, at which time I put down everything from the beginning, as I could remember it at the time.

I described the atmosphere on board ship at that time, in my 1945 "diary" as follows:

"After the Greer incident we were at war in fact, if not by declaration. Shipboard life was rigorous, and we were at General Quarters often. All ships travelled darkened at night and held wartime routine, dumping trash, pumping bilges in the evening and blowing tubes only at night, and holding dawn General Quarters. We all knew it was serious. Scuttlebutt (i.e., rumor) had it that the Reuben James had been hit in the Chief's quarters in the bow of the ship, which affected our ship by causing a general exodus by the Chiefs from that part of the ship. One would find the Chiefs sleeping everywhere but in their own quarters. The Chiefs had always felt had a certain claustrophobia anyway as their quarters were way forward and down several decks. Nothing could make a Chief move so fast as the siren because the siren in the Navy is used as the signal for "collision", and the Chiefs, due to the location of their quarters were particularly interested in collision. I'll never forget the time old MacIsaacs (Chief Electrician's Mate) tore through the wardroom in his "long handled skivvies", hurdled the table and went straight up the companionway opposite like a bolt of lightning. Actually, I think the Reuben James had been hit further aft, but that made little difference to the Chiefs."

We were fired upon at least once that I knew about. It happened while I was on watch with Mr. Pancake as the OOD. Mr. Pancake and I were both on the starboard wing of the bridge. He looked down. "Hey, look at that!" Running alongside of us about 20' out, parallel to the ship, was a white line of bubbles. It all happened so fast that it was over before we had a chance to become frightened. We rang the General Alarm, went to GQ and spent the next hour or so dropping depth charges around without results.

On another occasion our ship was sent out with several other Destroyers to help protect a convoy of 40 ships, only to find when the RUSSELL finally reached them, that less than 20 remained afloat.

The American people never were really informed that America was already at war with Germany in the fall of 1941, at least three months before Pearl Harbor.

ONE HAND FOR THE SHIP, ONE FOR YOURSELF

The North Atlantic in late fall and winter, in a destroyer especially, is incredibly bad. On an average day, the ship would roll continuously over 20 degrees to each side. I mean for days on end without a roll of less than 20 degrees. To give an idea of what a 20-degree roll means, a 10 degree roll is enough to cause the dishes on a table to slide onto the floor. Rolls of over 40 degrees were not uncommon. We, therefore, would continue from day to day without a normal meal at the table, eating only sandwiches and fried things like chicken legs. The galley was equipped with a deep fryer mounted on gimbals (pivots which allow things to hang and thereby stay level while the ship rolls). This made it easy to fry things, but difficult to cook by any other normal method. Therefore, the food consisted of fried pork chops, fried chicken, fried steak, and then for a change, fried spam. We had bread, of course, cheese, canned vegetables and fruits, and powdered milk.

The wardroom was provided with sockets in the floor (deck) and brackets in the ceiling (overhead) to receive vertical stanchions between each chair on each side of the Officer's mess table, and the way one ate one's meal was to hold the food in both hands, and hold one's self with an arm hooked around a stanchion.

On every trip out into the wintry Atlantic half a dozen men would end up injured arms, legs, wrists, ankles, etc.

On a destroyer of the Sims class, there is no way for the men to go between the after crew's quarters and the forward part of the ship without going on deck, so the men quartered aft were always getting soaked to the skin. Several were lost overboard, not from the RUSSELL, but from other ships of our squadron.

Anywhere one went on the ship, one had to hang onto something.

An old expression in the Navy is "one hand for the ship and one for yourself."

I never knew which hand was for me and which for the ship, but at least I knew that I always had to be hanging onto something, even while in my bunk. A hammock would have been a good thing to sleep in, but Destroyers are not suitable for hammocks. There is not enough room. We officers slept in bunks equipped with side rails. The side rails would keep one from falling out but not from shifting sideways in the bunk with each roll. The only way I could sleep was to tilt my bunk on its side at an angle of 45 degrees (using chains secured to the overhead) and sleep wedged in the V formed between the bunk and the side of the ship.

Storm lashes shipping off Iceland, 15 January 1942 USN Ref: 80-G-13353

Everything had to be secured. For example, things in drawers had to be wedged tight or else they would roll and clang about. Even the clothes hanging in the closet had to be bound. I found this out the hard way. I had a nice "bridge coat", a heavy-weight Navy blue overcoat with brass buttons, to wear on dress occasions, or for going ashore. After several months, it wore out simply hanging in the closet without being lashed.

WATCH IN THREE

Inasmuch as we were essentially at war, the ship was maintained in what was called "Condition 3", which meant that approximately 1/3rd of the crew were at battle stations at all times, and all doors, hatches, etc. were "dogged" down with only the emergency hatches open. In this way, the ship could go more rapidly to GQ (i.e. to full readiness for battle, with all guns manned, all doors and hatches closed).

It also meant that additional officers and men had to be provided for regular watches at the gunnery control. Since the usual peacetime complement did not provide for these extra personnel on watch, we were essentially under-manned, and as a result, Charlie Woodman and I immediately found ourselves standing JOOD watches on a "watch in three" basis, i.e. four hours on and eight hours off.

The routine would be as follows. Assuming, for example, that one had the 12 to 4 watch, one would eat an early lunch and then stand the afternoon watch. Thereafter, one might do some paperwork or study something before dinner at 6:00 PM. At 7:00 PM, one would then go to bed, and, if there were no GQ's during the night, one might sleep for 4 1/2 hours, then get up, have a cup of coffee, and go on watch. At about 4:15 AM, one would be relieved and per-haps flop in one's bunk fully clothed for an hour or so, at which time "dawn GQ" would be called.

(Under war conditions, all Navy ships regularly went to GQ one hour before sunrise until sunrise. This was a hold-over from earlier wars. The idea was to be ready to do battle if an enemy ship happened to be within sight at dawn. After radar became available, dawn GQ was totally unnecessary but yet we continued to do it, a typical characteristic of the Navy; i.e., no one either in the ranks or at the top is willing to suggest that something which had been ordered by the command could be in error. It was this characteristic of failure accurately to appraise an existing unnecessary condition or form of weakness, which undoubtedly accounted for the Navy's prewar unprepared-ness in major ways and remained as an underlying deterrent to the adoption of improvement throughout the war. It is still the same in the present-day Navy.)

After dawn GQ, usually around 7:00 AM, one would have breakfast, and at about 8:00 AM be facing one's daytime tasks, which would include "turn to" (i.e. cleaning up), maintenance, and many routine assignments depending upon one's specialty. I was in communications, as I will describe more in detail presently, and usually had decoding, filing, and hundreds of other minor matters to tend to, besides trying to learn how to use a lot of complicated equipment. However, by this time, one would have had only about 5 1/2 hours sleep and would also be looking for a chance to catch an hour or so more sleep before starting the whole process over again.

In order to rotate the most undesirable watch, the midwatch (i.e., midnight to 4:00 AM), we used what is called a "Dogwatch". This meant that the 4:00 PM to 8:00 PM watch would be split so that one officer would stand only the first two hours, and the next officer in the rotation would stand from 6:00 PM to 8:00 PM. This would cause a shift in the rotation so that every third day each officer in sequence would have "all night in and beans for breakfast".

I did not see much difference. Whichever way it was done, "watch in three" was a tough grind. It seemed like there was never time enough to do anything, only enough to grab a bit of sleep here and there, and then stand watch again.

"IT GOES ON LIKE THIS FOR A WHILE, AND THEN IT GETS WORSE"

I had sailed in small boats and was used to bouncing in a chop, so I did not expect to be seasick. I was not, however, prepared either for the severity of the weather (the continuous—endless deep rolls), or for the grease laden food. As for the weather, in the Atlantic, the direction of the wind will make major shifts every several days or so. In the Pacific, it will blow in the same direction all year long and the waves become very large and spread out, but not uncomfortable. In the Atlantic, the waves are much shorter between crests and steeper, and, after a wind change, the waves of the former wind will continue to come through the waves of the new wind direction. The result is that nothing is predictable. The ship will roll and then lurch and pitch and stagger as the waves from different directions hit her at unexpected times.

In addition, the storms seem to be endless or at least at the end of a storm it seems as though the next storm is already on you.

The food was digestible for the first few days, but soon became virtually unbearable. I asked Bargeloh whether it was always like this, and he told me, "It goes on like this for a while, and then it gets worse!"

"WE ALL DID IT, YOU GOTTA DO IT TOO"

One night, three or four days out on my first trip, it finally caught up with me. I was standing JOOD watch under Mr. Pancake and began feeling extremely seasick. I took a bucket and sat back by the flag bag at the rear of the bridge, trying to be sick, but without success. All I knew was that I felt so sick I would have welcomed death, but even that option was not available.

Finally, in desperation, I went to Mr.Pancake.

"Maybe if I could lie down for a few minutes below it would help."

"Nonsense, we all did it; you gotta stand your watch too!"

"KEEP YOUR BOWELS OPEN AND NEVER VOLUNTEER"

Soon after we joined our first convoy on my first trip out, the Captain and the Communications Officer, Mr. Durst, were fumbling over the signal book put out by the British Navy for merchant ships, entitled "Mersigs". Even though we had not yet reached the area of bad weather, Mr. Durst had already become quite seasick. In fact, soon thereafter, he went below and was hopelessly seasick for the remainder of the trip, i.e. about 15 days. Upon Mr. Durst's departure from the bridge, the Captain tossed me the book:

"Hey, see if you can make any sense out of this stupid thing!"

We had the immediate problem of trying to understand the specific signal which was flying on the Convoy Commander's flag hoist, but a more fundamental problem was that there was no way to make quick reference to anything in the book. (I have never understood how the British themselves were able to use the book.)

That night, I squandered a few of my precious hours of sleep to study the book in depth. What it needed was a detailed index and then a system of tabs keyed to the index so that one could find whatever one might be looking for in an instant. I obtained some gummed tabs from the Yeoman's office, made the index, and appeared the next morning ready to solve the "Mersigs" riddle.

It worked. Thereafter, whenever a new signal would come out, I could find and interpret it within a few seconds. The Captain was very pleased with this, but he did not simply leave it at that. I soon found myself losing more of my precious hours of sleep (and all the while not feeling too well myself) to go to the bridge to interpret the Mersigs book whenever a new signal came out.

Inasmuch as Mr. Durst was virtually incapacitated by chronic seasickness, I was appointed Assistant Communications Officer. Shortly after we returned to Casco Bay at the end of my first trip out, Mr. Durst was relieved for medical reasons and the Captain asked me if I thought I could handle the C & S (Communications and Supply) Division under Mr. Dimmicks's supervision. I said I thought I could, and the Captain gave me the job.

One of the benefits (or detriments depending on how one looks at it) of being on a small ship, is that, only on a small ship would it have been possible for a raw Ensign to be appointed Communications Officer within four weeks of reporting on board. On the other hand, Destroyers are ships of the battle fleet, and, therefore, they must have practically all of the same communications equipment, circuits, codes and other communications functions as the larger ships, only there are less personnel (especially officers) to handle them. Thus, the Communications Officer on a destroyer has to do, and take responsibility for (but with a lot less help) all of the same things that much more senior officers with more support have to do on larger ships.

This was when I learned the wisdom of the old Navy saying, "Keep your bowels open and never volunteer!"

"NEVER WANT ANYTHING TOO MUCH, YOU

MAY GET IT"

I had been extremely keen for increased responsibility and promotion and felt very proud of myself for becoming C&S Officer so rapidly. The backlash was not long in coming.

First, the personnel under me included:

a) Radiomen-(one Chief, one 1st Class, two 2nd Class, one 3rd Class, and three strikers—total 8 men)

b) Signalmen-(one Chief, one 1st Class, one 2nd Class, one 3rd Class and three strikers- total 7 men)

c) Quartermasters (One Chief, three strikers- total 4 men)

d) Commissary (one Chief, five cooks, three strikers- total 9 men)

e) Mess attendants (total 9 men)

f) Miscellaneous men such as Laundry, Ships Stores, Yeomen, Accounting, total about 10 men.

Every one of these men knew much more about his job than I did, particularly the Chiefs, and there was no way that these men were going to pay much attention to what I might say.

The equipment I had charge of included:

a) radios both for receiving VLF and for sending and receiving by Morse code. Also, we had equipment for short range voice transmission and reception;

b) navigation equipment

c) sonar

d) fathometer

e) coding machine

f) signal flags, blinkers, emergency flares, etc

g) safe for keeping all codes and other secret documents,

h) various other equipment under "miscellaneous" above.

Here again, I knew virtually nothing about any of them, and had little prospect of being able to obtain sufficient working knowledge of any of them to do my job properly, let alone being seasick and having to stand "watch in three".

Another backlash was in the wardroom. Not only were my contemporaries sour about my sudden vaulting over them to the status of a Division Head, but even among the more senior officers right up to the Executive Officer, I could feel a distinct chill. Undoubtedly, they could remember spending years of frustration as junior officers, doing virtually menial tasks, and here was this new officer, not even an Annapolis graduate at that, doing a few things to please the Captain and being made a Division Head in four weeks.

I soon had an experience that made me aware that all would not be "peaches and cream". One area of particular vulnerability for an officer with my new job was the safe and the secret documents in it. The Communications Officer has custody of all such documents and together with the Executive Officer, must submit a "sighting report" every three months or so, indicating that all such documents are on hand. Both he and the Executive Officer must sign the list and swear that they actually saw each document. There is a great deal of tension over the absolute, inviolate integrity of the secrecy of all such documents. In fact, procedures for sinking or burning them in the event of abandon ship are meticulously practiced. There were weighted canvas bags in which the documents could be thrown overboard in situations when burning was impossible, but our instructions were that burning was the only sure way. Communications Officers are conditioned and trained to regard the duty of secure disposal of the secret documents as sacred—far more important than the personal safety of the officer.

Many of the documents would be secret codes, or secret minefield charts, or secret war plans which no one except the Communications Officer or the Captain would use. Others, however, relating to secret, confidential or restricted equipment, such as instructions for the operation and maintenance of certain gunnery controls, or the sonar, and later the radar, might be used by various people around the ship. When this was done, a sign-out procedure was followed. In particular, there was one book about Gunnery Exercises for which there was no valid excuse for confidential status, and which was in frequent use by many people. Very soon after I became Communications Officer, this Gunnery Exercise book was "found" unattended on the wardroom table and turned over to the Executive Officer. It created a big flap. The book had not been "signed out" and no one would admit to putting it there. How it got there was a mystery to me. I was called on the carpet and reprimanded. Thankfully the reprimand was only oral. No report was written.

So now, I found myself with the tremendous tasks of learning the entire gamut of the technology of the C&S Division, establishing myself as a leader of some 50 men who had no reason other than rank to accept my leadership, a hostile wardroom, and—to cap it off—precious little time, the exhaustion of the long watches and little sleep, the constant—constant—constant deep rolling of the ship, and the smell from the galley of grease—grease—grease. I had only myself to blame. As my father used to say, "Never want anything too much, you may get it!"

"THIS TASTES JUST LIKE MOOSE DUNG, BUT I LIKE IT!"

In the logging camps in the Maine forests, there used to be a rule that if you complained about the food, you had to do the cooking. And then there was the time this fellow who was doing the cooking wanted to get rid of the job, so he went out in the woods, found some moose dung, and served it the next morning for breakfast. The first fellow to try it said, "Hey, this tastes just like moose dung"—and then caught himself just in time—"But I like it!"

I was on watch one evening with Mr. Dimmick and ventured to ask whether something might be done to improve the food. He replied without hesitation, "Yes, I am sure there is, and, in fact, you are just the one to do it. From now on, you are our new Mess Treasurer!"

The Mess Treasurer supervises the officer's mess and the mess attendants. He buys the food, and keeps the books of the mess, etc. The Officer's mess is separate from the ship's. We would, in effect, "buy" many staple items from the general issue at a low price, but we also bought special things. The Chief's quarters did much the same thing. They lived off the general issue for the bulk of their food, but had extra things as well, for which they all chipped in.

Although the last thing I needed at that point was another burden, there were advantages in being Mess Treasurer, none the least was that the food did improve. Although I never was able to balance the books at the end of the month and always had to chip in (or take out) a few dollars to make it balance, I was able to do the job without much discomfort, and, in fact, remained Mess Treasurer for most of the time I served on the RUSSELL. I also did the same subsequently on other ships.

AT THE END OF THE LONG TABLE

Despite the fact that we were effectively at war with the Germans, everyone on the RUSSELL (at least in the wardroom) was surprisingly well disposed toward them, equally surprisingly anti-British, and, to a man, ardent "America Firsters". Captain Hartwig had had a short stretch of peace-time duty with the German Navy and he raved about it. In addition, the fact that the German subs were firing at us seemed fully justified. No one wanted it or liked it, but still, no one saw it as anything more than what they themselves would do in the same situation. (Of course, I saw this latter point the same way too.) As for the British, they had fired on the RUSSELL one night as the RUSSELL was entering port in Iceland. The RUSSELL had apparently made an error in the recognition signal, which Mr. Durst vehemently denied. In any event, the whole ship was furious at the British "for firing on us without cause". Also, the men had had fights with the British sailors ashore in Iceland. Another thing which had caused a lot of irritation was the Mersigs Signal book. The Navy simply dismissed it as "stupid" and made no effort to find out how to use it.

I was an Anglophile, however, and I suspected that the recognition signal error had been the RUSSELL's. Also, I had no trouble with Mersigs, and, in any event, I thought that America should be in the war alongside the British then, and on a declared basis.

So here I was, not only in "over my head" as the new C&S Division head, but aware of the chill that the promotion had created, and that someone was "gunning" for me enough to "find" a confidential book unattended. Furthermore, as Mess Treasurer my seat was at the end of the long table opposite the Captain who sat at the head. (Captain Hartwig always ate with us unlike some Captains who join the mess only occasionally). I found myself facing a dozen or so officers all looking down the long table and telling me how wrong I was.

GRAY HAIRS AT 23

While I was very much in favor of America entering the war, and wanted to participate, I do not mean for a moment that I was not scared. Destroyers are very vulnerable. They have no armor plate at all, except at the bow. The skin of the ship is made up of 1/4-inch welded steel plates which makes them, in Kipling's words, the "egg-shells of the sea". Thus a 50-caliber armor piercing bullet will go right through a destroyer and if it happens to hit one of the boilers with their 600-psi steam pressure at 500 degrees F, one such bullet can sink the ship.

(The following quote from the Boston Globe of 4/9/85 from the obituary of one Joseph Elsberry is relevant:

"His squadron once sank a German destroyer without bombs. His team of fighters sank the destroyer in Trieste Harbor in Italy, using only 50-caliber guns on June 23, 1944. The sinking was denied by the Germans, but later confirmed by films of the attack.")

I can remember going to bed, hearing the rushing, slapping water—literally only 1/4 inch away along the side of the ship, and thinking about what I would do, or try to do, if the next instant the water were to come rushing in. It was known that a man could survive only a few minutes in the cold North Atlantic without any protection, but that he had a chance for a while if clothed. I had a sheepskin-lined leather jacket which I kept near me and a Persian lamb hat, both of which I had in mind taking into the water if and when the time came. Usually, after we had joined up with the merchant ships on a convoy, there would be fairly frequent submarine alerts, and depth charge attacks. In addition, we had drills. The Captain was intent on improving the speed with which the ship could go to GQ. Also, he had frequent loading drills for the gunnery crews.

The alarm klaxon for the drills was the "Chemical Alarm" (so named for reasons related to drills for defense against gas attack. We had gas masks on board, but drills for gas attack were no longer practiced). The Chemical Alarm was rung by the Officer of the Deck by hand, twelve rings.

The General Alarm consisted of 24 rings of the same klaxon, but it was done automatically by a timer.

For this reason, when the alarm went off, the cadence was slightly different between the Chemical and the General Alarms, but it was difficult for neophytes like Charlie Woodman and me to tell whether it was only a drill (i.e. the Chemical Alarm) or the real thing (i.e. the General Alarm).

We soon learned a way to distinguish between the two. "Finn" Toivonen was a great hulk of a man. He was blond and ruddy complexioned. His eyes had a Mongolian cast—typical of people of Finnish extraction—and he had a large round head with a wrinkle of fat at the back where the cranium joins the neck. He was a former football player and could move like a flash when necessary, but who mostly did very little. Between watches, he would usually be sleeping soundly on one of the wardroom transoms (stuffed leather couches at each end of the wardroom). When the alarm went off, if it was the Chemical Alarm, Finn would simply continue sleeping for 6 or 8 rings, then gradually roll over and start putting on his shoes. If it was the General Alarm, he would be off the transom at the second ring, charging up through the escape hatch, with Charlie Woodman and me bringing up the rear.

By this time, I also knew that my wife Lib was pregnant, and while I still felt my obligation to all of those guys who died in prior wars, and still do, I was highly concerned that my own demise might happen a good deal sooner than I wanted or thought necessary. As a result, I acquired a small cluster of white hairs on either side of my head.

It wasn't until about 20 years later that the remainder started turning. That is, of course, the hairs that did not fall out.

THE GREYHOUND AND THE WOLF

The usual convoy to which we were assigned had the cargo ships lined up in two or three columns, spaced about 3,000 yds apart and with about 1,000 yds between ships in each column. The destroyers (usually five or six in those days) would be stationed along a slightly bent line across the front of the formation separated from each other by about 3,000 yds, and also ahead of the leading cargo ship by about 3,000 yds as well.

Submerged submarines operated solely by battery power and were capable of making only about 5 kts. sustained speed underwater (slightly faster in short bursts). Thus, if the cargo ships could steam faster than 5 kts., the destroyers' chance of protecting the ships was substantially better because it would mean that the sub would have to attack from the front and penetrate the destroyer's sonar screen before reaching good torpedo range. Such penetration happened from time to time, but usually, the sub was detected and the attack would be broken up by depth charge attack, not sinking the sub, as I will explain below, but at least preventing him from attacking.

Unfortunately, many cargo ships at the time were capable of steaming only at about 5 kts. Also, there were never enough destroyers. The maximum feasible spacing between destroyers was 3,000 yds. because the sonar was good for only about 1,500 yds (not even that in the Pacific). This meant that good destroyer protection would require a complete ring of destroyers around the convoy spaced no more than 3,000 yds apart, which could not be done without at least a dozen destroyers. There were simply not enough destroyers available. In fact, a convoy would be lucky to have six.

Protecting a 10-kt. convoy with six destroyers was reasonably comfortable. During the day, the submarines would have to submerge, and the destroyers needed only to protect the van. The entire convoy would also follow a zigzag course to make the submarine attack more difficult. Zigzagging would reduce forward progress, but zig-zagging plans had been devised which lost as little as 6% of forward progress, while still quite effectively confusing the submarines.

At night, the problem was more complex because the submarines could then surface and attack at much higher speeds of up to 18 kts. Radar was just coming in at that time, but we did not have it yet when I was on convoy duty in the North Atlantic.

The Germans found that night surface attack was much more effective if done with several submarines at a time, called "wolf packs". In fact, the "wolf packs" attacked in much the same way that wolves do; i.e. by nipping at the flanks. If destroyers were taken from the forward screen to protect the rear, then the Germans would attack from ahead. During a wolf pack attack, as soon as a destroyer detected a sub, the sub would submerge and be safe, as I will explain shortly. Of course, a destroyer might chase the sub and try to contact it on sonar, but could not take much time hunting for subs without leaving the convoy exposed to attack by other subs, and, as soon as the destroyers would leave, the submerged sub would resurface and move around at high speed to a new position for attack.

One may ask how all of this could be done at night by subs without radar. The answer is simple. Ships at sea can always be seen with binoculars at night up to around 8,000 yds, depending upon the height of eye. This is true even on the darkest of nights with no moon and under heavy clouds. Of course, fog and heavy rain totally preclude vision, but it is a commonly held fallacy that nights can be so dark that ships cannot be seen. I once read, for example, in C. S. Forester's, "Captain Horatio Hornblower" series, about how at dawn, Hornblower had been surprised to find an enemy ship only one mile away. I can attest to the fact that other than being in a dense fog, such does not really make sense.

On the other hand, to be able to see at night, one's eyes must be truly accustomed to the dark. It takes at least 1/2 hour after last looking at a light, for one's eyes to be able to see well at night. Second, one cannot use the point of maximum vision. I do not know why, all I know is that one has to look around the object, not at it. Third, the binoculars must be rock steady. This can only be done by propping them on the wing of the bridge on three points of contact. This is difficult to do with the ship rolling, but it can be done and is absolutely essential. Unless a telescopic lens is so held, the image one sees through it will move too rapidly for identification. Curiously, the vibration of the ship which is simply up and down (not tilting) causes no problem as long as the support is a three-point contact.

So much for technique. Now for what one sees. For some reason, which I never quite understood, ships are always darker at night than the sea. This is so even for a white-painted hospital ship. Thus, there simply is no camouflage, which can effectively hide the silhouette of a ship's hull against the sea. However, ships are not always darker than the sky background, but they are either darker or lighter than the sky background about 95% of the time. Another visible feature is the wake. The bow wave and stern wash of a ship are always visible.

The bow wave is, of course, white and will be specked with phosphorous. The stern wash is white and luminous near to the ship but as it recedes it turns into a flat slick. The distance astern to which the wash remains visible depends upon the condition of the sea and how fast the ship is traveling, but it will always be visible behind a 5-kt. cargo ship on a calm night for at least five miles. Of course, spilled oil or refuse in the wake enhanced the opportunity for detection. In addition, hydrophones were used by the subs to detect the presence and bearing of the convoys.

Accordingly, the Wolf Packs had no trouble spotting the convoys. They would then take their time, study the zig-zag plan long enough to figure it out, and plan an attack to coincide with one of the sharper zigs of the zig-zag plan, at which point, one flank would be more exposed.

Moving in for the kill, they would easily spot the cargo ships and destroyers while still at a relatively safe distance, determine the patrol pattern of the destroyer at the stern of the formation, wait until the destroyer moved to one side and then close in on the other side. Having achieved position alongside the formation, the sub would start firing torpedoes at the cargo ships usually from the surface, at least at the start. The lookouts on the ships, of course, might see the sub, but the sub's silhouette is much smaller than a ship's, and since the sub would be coming up from the rear, its stern wake at least would not be seen. In addition, only a few people such as the OD had binoculars, and spotting subs without the techniques described above, was substantially less likely. It was much easier for the sub to spot the ships. If the sub was spotted, the destroyers in those pre-radar days would turn on their searchlights in hopes of making a hit on the sub before it could submerge, but the chances of success by so doing were slim indeed. I read accounts of the British doing it, but I was aware of none by American ships until much later in the war.

As a result, the U-boats had a decided advantage, and Wolf Pack hunting was highly successful especially on 5 kt. convoys. 10 kt convoys had a better chance.

(People today, 1987, may not appreciate the proportions of what was going on. The U-boats were sinking on average over 400,000 tons of allied ships per month during this period, and it was only due to the fact that American industry could build ships faster than that, that we were able to keep Britain supplied.[12] Today, however, America depends largely on imported steel, and the steel industry of America is relatively impotent compared to during World War II.)

(A second interjection worth noting is the curious fact that the United States submarines did not adopt these very successful tactics of the Germans until 1944[13], but when they did, they single handedly, in one year, reduced the Japanese merchant marine capacity from around 5,000,000 tons to less than 2,000,000 tons, a level which was only 2/3 the amount required to sustain the civilian economy of Japan—to say nothing of their war effort.[14])

On our first trip out, a ship of our squadron, the HUGHES (DD410), spotted a U-boat astern of the formation and gave chase. Later on, during that same night, the RUSSELL had sonar contact with a sub ahead of the formation and dropped enough depth charges to discourage the attack. We were never sure whether there were two subs, or the one spotted astern had sped around the formation in time to make an attack from ahead.

The U-boats, however, had no way effectively to attack high speed ships such as the British Queens, which steamed safely without escort through submarine infested waters throughout the war.

"OK JOHN, I'VE GOT IT"

An old jingle in the Navy goes, "When in trouble, when in doubt, run in circles, scream and shout, 'relieve the deck.'"

"Relieving the deck" means to take over as Officer of the Deck (i.e. OOD or usually shortened to OD in common parlance.).

The OD is, in effect, in command of the ship. His orders take precedence over any other officer's except the Captain's. Thus, while one is OD, one can give even the Executive Officer an order. Obviously, such orders to senior officers based on OD status are not given by junior officers very often, but it can and does happen, as I will relate later in this narrative.

Taking full charge of and being responsible for the ship is a serious step and requires the officer to be on top of many things.

Obviously, he must know the cruising condition of the ship, any night orders of the Captain, the course and speed of the formation, the position of all ships of the screen, the location of the convoy commander as well as the screen commander, the position of all ships of the convoy, the zig-zag plan, exactly where in the plan the convoy is at the moment, and any patrol procedures for the destroyers which may differ from the convoy's zig-zags.

In addition, he is required by Navy Regulations to know a large amount of general information, such as (1) the range and bearing to the nearest land, (2) the names and whereabouts on the ship of all prisoners-at-large (men under disciplinary detention who are permitted freedom), (3) the soundings of all peak tanks (destroyers have half a dozen tanks, as for example at the extreme bow of the ship, which are supposed to remain empty), (4) the condition of the engine and firerooms (i.e. the engines and boilers in use), (5) the condition of the galley fires, etc.

Further, on certain watches specific reports to the Captain must be made such as the latitude and longitude of the ship, the winding of the chronometers, the muster of all P.A.L.s (prisoners at large), etc. at 8:00pm.

Beyond this, for an officer to be properly qualified to "stand top watch" he must know certain basics of ship handling such as the cardinal rule that one never gives an order to the helm without looking first to the side toward which the ship will turn, even if one was over on that side of the ship a minute before. He also must know how to use a "mooring board" (more accurately, a "mooring and maneuvering board" but commonly shortened) to calculate the course and speed required to approach a ship under way or cross a formation without hitting other ships. He needs to know how to use the stadimeter to take mast height sightings to determine the distance to the ship next ahead in column. In addition, he must have a thorough working knowledge of the entire ship. For example, he must know the locations of all outlets of all communication systems and what phone or voice tube to use to call whom, and the emergency system to use in case of breakdown. He should know the locations of all emergency equipment, the water systems (fire and bilge) and the electrical and steam systems. He also needs to know how all the weapons work. Damage control is another area with which he must be familiar. For example, he should know from the ship's inclining experiment the maximum safe roll, the normal period of roll, and the point at which the ship may become in danger of capsizing due to flooding below decks. In addition, during a normal watch there will usually be as many as 70 men standing watch all over the ship in the engine rooms, boiler rooms, generator room, gunnery control, at the guns (1/3 manned), depth charges, radio, radar, sonar, and lookouts, and the OD must know where they are and what they are supposed to be doing. Normally he will not be called upon to use more than a small fraction of this knowledge while standing a given watch, but he needs to know it to be able to act intelligently in an emergency.

He, of course, has to know how everything on the bridge works (i.e. the engine room annunciator, the revolution indicators, the voice radio communications systems, flag hoists, flashing lights, the helm, the gyro compass, the magnetic compass, and the emergency procedures for each in case of failure of the primary system. In particular, on a destroyer, he must know how the sonar works and whether the sonar operator is searching properly. He must be able to distinguish a "Doppler shifted" sonar echo from an echo from a temperature gradient. In addition to all this, he must monitor the lookouts and signalmen and keep an eye on the destroyer screen and the convoy commander, he must be sure that the Quartermaster is faithfully logging everything that happens, and, finally after he has been relieved of the watch, he must enter in the ship's log a complete report of what happened on the watch and sign it.

So, when an officer comes up to relieve the deck, gives a faint half-salute, and sleepily says "OK, John, I've got it," do not be deceived. This can happen only because both he and "John" know that he has done it so many times and already knows so much of the above from his training and his previous watches that the answers to only a few questions, if any, will usually suffice. Likewise, do not be surprised if "John", who has just been relieved, opens the logbook, and simply enters "Steaming as before."

40 MEN OVER THE HILL

For me, finding myself already at war was not a problem because I believed in it. However, to anyone who thought that America should not be in it at all, the idea of going out in the North Atlantic, living in a virtual cement mixer, getting shot at, standing watch-in-three, GQ at night, drills and greasy food, made no sense at all.

It was, therefore, no wonder that every, time we put into port, and gave the crew liberty, large numbers went "over the hill". Several times, over 40 men from the squadron failed to report on time after a single liberty, and some were A.W.O.L. Most of them were apprehended and either sent to jail or back to the ship for punishment.

In one spectacular case, Meltzer, one of our Boatswains mates 2nd Class went over the hill and was eventually found boarding a train in Buffalo, NY. It was said that several of the military patrol tried to take him into custody to no avail. They enlisted the aid of the local police, and eventually it took six of them to down him. This story followed Meltzer and from then on, he was some sort of hero on the RUSSELL.

I have heard people say that, compared to the Vietnam war, we, in World War II were lucky because we were fighting for a great cause, whereas no one really believed in the War in Vietnam and that this difference explains why there were so many draft dodgers and deserters in the Vietnam situation. Actually, the very same thing as Vietnam took place in the early stages of World War II due to the fact that most people in America were thinking that America should not be involved in the war in any way. The men who went over the hill in the fall of 1941 were only responding in much the same way as those in the more recent Vietnam situation and for largely the same reasons. The only difference was that, in 1941, the world was really facing a crisis though few appreciated it. After Pearl Harbor, this problem virtually disappeared.

NEVER BE A GOOD JOE

When I had been training at an earlier time in the R.O.T.C. at Harvard, one of the regular Navy officers who was responsible for teaching us how to be good officers, laid great stress upon being tight-lipped, and never being friendly with the enlisted men. His attitude struck me as being totally "stuffed shirt". I saw no reason why enlisted men would not respond reasonably to reasonable treatment. Beyond this, I saw the distinction between enlisted men and officers as an unnecessary holdover of the class distinctions of times gone by.

Therefore, when I reported to the RUSSELL, I was immediately friendly with everyone I met—officers and men—and they reciprocated, or so I thought. Later, however, as I mentioned, my rapid promotion to Division Head, my radical pro-war views, and my Anglophilia, caused me certain stresses in the wardroom. Also, among the men, particularly among the chiefs, no one paid much attention to me when it came to discussing the technology. These negatives, however, did not deter me. I was continually having cups of "java" with the men, talking small talk, etc., and I felt I had developed friendly, personal relationships with many people, officers and men alike.

One of the most critical functions of the Communications Division on a ship of the fleet is the accurate and complete monitoring of what is called the "Fox Schedule". This is the long range (VLF frequency) radio broadcast which comes out in Morse code and is transmitted to all ships and stations continuously from Naval Headquarters. Orders to all ships and personnel come out on the Fox schedule. In many cases, the messages would be classified and therefore encoded. Any secret message can be important, but the most important message which came out frequently on the Fox Schedule, but at irregular intervals, was the change of the recognition signal (the signal a ship uses to identify itself at night or when first sighting another ship). I mentioned this above in relation to the incident when the British in Iceland fired on the RUSSELL for not having the correct recognition signal. Obviously, to have the correct recognition signal can be a matter of life or death for the entire ship.

Now, on the RUSSELL, we were not getting these changes to the recognition signal with complete regularity, and, right after I took over as Communications Officer, I found out by checking with another ship that we had the wrong recognition signal. Luckily, I found it out before anyone else did. I then called all the radiomen together and they all agreed that we should do everything we could to improve things. I felt particularly good about my approach—no stress—no need to be stern or tight-lipped or aloof. As I always knew, reasonable men will respond reasonably. I even felt like writing my former R.O.T.C professor and telling him about it.

Only a few days later, I found out by the same method that we had missed a change of the recognition signal again.

This time I stormed up to the "Radio Shack" to find two men asleep on the deck, comic books strewn around, and the "Fox Schedule" blaring away with a coded message, and no one taking it down.

This was serious. I immediately got hold of Chief Costa and told him to correct the situation. Next, I went down to my cabin and wrote up a list of specific instructions for the Radio Shack such as (1) no one to sleep in Radio Shack, (2) no comic books in Radio Shack, (3) at least one man at all times monitoring the "Fox Schedule", (4) no one to go to the head without being relieved of the watch, etc. I then posted my list in a prominent place for all in the Radio Shack to see.

Several hours later, I came back, and my list was gone. I then called all the radiomen together including those who were trying to get some sleep. No one knew what had happened to the list. I told them I was only trying to do what I could to get this thing done the right way, for their safety as well as mine and everyone else's.

By this time, however, I had begun to see that Mr.Roosevelt was not the only one fighting an undeclared war.

I began checking the Fox Schedule myself to see if there were any gaps in it, but this was of no use because it is normal for there to be periods when the only transmission is the call sign of the sending station (NSS) over and over. Thus, while I could see gaps in the recordings, the radiomen assured me that there had been no messages at those times, and I had no immediate way of checking up on it.

I did, however, check the Radio Shack more frequently to make sure that the monitoring was continuous. This led to mounting tension between me and the radio men which culminated in an incident sometime later in early 1942. I had gone on a routine check to the Radio Shack and found the Fox Schedule broadcasting a coded message and no one at the typewriter, in fact, no one to be seen at all. I began yelling and pretty soon Chief Costa showed up. Next, in came the 1st Class, Bleyer, who then sat down at the typewriter and started recording the Fox Schedule. Bleyer allowed as to how he had been to the head. Costa said he had relieved Bleyer, that he had been there when I arrived, and had not missed any part of the schedule. Bleyer, in true loyalty-up-loyalty-down fashion confirmed what Costa had said. I blew up, called them "lying sons-a-bitches", went to the Captain, and demanded an immediate "Deck Court" (a "Deck Court" is a disciplinary proceeding which the commanding officer of a ship can hold). As soon as it could be arranged, Costa and Bleyer were called on "the mat", and, under oath, told their story about how Bleyer needed to go to the head, how he had asked Costa to relieve him, how Costa had taken over recording the schedule, how he was recording it when I came in, how Bleyer then returned and took over the schedule from Costa. Each corroborated the other perfectly. The Captain then turned to me. "Mr. Russell, what do you have to say?"

I was stunned by the fact that Costa and Bleyer actually would try to pull off a lie like that. I simply said, "Captain, IT STINKS!" I then told what had happened and how I had saved the portion of the Fox Schedule which had been recorded and would compare it to the real schedule from another ship. I further emphasized that no small part of their offense was their lying under oath.

The Captain took it under advisement until the evidence came in proving that, indeed, a portion of the coded Fox schedule had been missed. Both Costa and Bleyer were demoted (i.e. "broken") one grade.

These men were highly qualified radiomen, and the incident was so far from characteristic of them as to suggest that they may have planned it as a form of retaliation against me for what seemed to them to be my needless but constant interference with their business. If so, it nearly worked. If the Fox schedule had not actually started transmitting a coded message shortly after Costa left the Radio Shack, so that there was hard evidence that a portion had been missed, such a plan might have worked. Captain Hartwig would never have given out a serious fine for an innocuous lapse. In fact, even so he was not as concerned about missing a portion of the schedule as he was about their lying under oath.

After this incident a new era started in the C&S Division on the RUSSELL. Regardless of whether the incident had been planned or merely a result of sloppiness, it seriously deepened the rift between me and the radiomen. I knew that most, and possibly all, of the men would sympathize with Costa and Bleyer, but I had no way of knowing who they might be or the degree thereof. In any event, widespread hostility was clear. Although I was aware, at the time, of officers like Caster who could command respect and still remain low key, and I, in fact, achieved it later in the war, at the time I was incapable of doing it. Therefore, it appeared to me that I had no other course than to adopt the pattern recommended by my professor in NROTC. I became tight-lipped and aloof. I was no longer "Bob" but "Mr. Russell"; I no longer had cups of "java" with the men; I visited not only the Radio Shack but other C&S areas as well, frequently, and looked but did not talk.

Other changes were made. In those days, after the rapid increase of per-sonnel in the Navy had started, some officers had started promoting men without their being really qualified. There were instruction courses and examinations for each grade, but some Division Officers were not insisting their men pass them. Not so in the C&S Division on the RUSSELL from then on. I heard a lot of grumbling about "How come we have to take these exams when no one else does?" etc.

I held daily "Quarters" with the men standing at attention (another custom which was not being practiced by other Division Officers at the time). In a word, I had become very hard (unquestionably too hard) and very "regular" in a short span of time.

(And then there was the time that this Regular Navy Officer ran his home the same way he ran the ship, called his wife "the Exec", etc. And once, when a window was broken, held "Captain's mast". The first boy was called in. "Did you do it?" "No Sir." "Do you know who did?" "No Sir." "OK, dismissed." Sec-ond boy, "Did you do it?" "No Sir." "Do you know who did?" "No Sir." Third boy, "Did you do it?" "Yes Sir." "Well, before I impose sentence, do you have anything to say?" "Yes Sir." "What is it?" "Yes Sir, I want a transfer out of this chicken s–t outfit.")

There was a period when virtually everyone in the C&S Division wanted a transfer. Whether or not things would have improved without my change of manner is an open question. In any event, the recognition signal was never missed again, the hostility gradually subsided, I gradually relaxed, and things started to run properly. The C&S quarters were neat and clean. Promotions were given only when deserved. It took a while, but morale eventually became high.

ROBERT THE RED-ASSED ENSIGN

In the fall of 1941, an "ALNAV" letter was sent to all ships and stations pointing out that there was an urgent need for improvement in all technologies, that the Navy's policy was to be alert to new ideas, and when received, to move rapidly forward to their adoption. All personnel of whatever rank or grade were accordingly urged to submit ideas to the Navy Buships (Bureau of Ships) for screening.

One of my jobs as Communications Officer was also to serve as ASW Officer (ASW stands for antisubmarine warfare). A new piece of equipment called an "Antisubmarine Recorder" had just been installed on the RUSSELL when I first came aboard. It was a device, invented by the British, used to indicate the distance between the ship and a submarine, continuously recording it on a slowly advancing sheet of paper so that one could see at a glance how rapidly the ship and the submarine were approaching each other. The device was also very helpful, if you knew how to use it, in determining the course of the submarine and the proper time to let the depth charges go.

Along with the Recorder, we had been given various publications on ASW techniques as well as a British book with a yellow cover outlining the experiences of the British in ASW against the Germans in the war to date. The book soon became known as the "Yellow Peril". The U.S. Navy's reaction to the "Yellow Peril" was similar to their reaction to "Mersigs" mentioned above, i.e. to more or less dismiss it as stupid without considering it adequately.

On the other hand, inasmuch as I was given the assignment of operating the Recorder and using it to determine when to fire the depth charges, I studied the "Yellow Peril" carefully. I learned that, contrary to the accepted view in the Navy at the time, a depth charge attack by a destroyer against a submarine had virtually no chance of sinking the sub. By the time I made this study, we had already carried out numerous depth charge attacks and everyone who witnessed them thought we were at least damaging the submarines. A depth charge explosion is a very impressive thing. If the depth setting is less than 50 feet, a tremendous geyser of white spray shoots high into the air. If the depth setting is deeper, the explosion sends up a large frothy bubble. In addition, the sound is very impressive. It goes off with a sharp metallic ring, and the surface of the water all around stands up with shimmering dark blue tiny droplets. Everything below decks on a destroyer, even 1000 yds away from the explosion is jolted as if hit by a hammer. Glass gauges in the engine rooms are frequently shattered and electrical circuit breakers can be tripped. Since a depth charge explosion is shocking enough to witness from a surface ship, it is no wonder that the Navy thought that the submarine would have little chance of survival below the surface. In fact, in the Navy's prewar "war games" whenever a destroyer made sonar contact with a submarine, the sub was automatically scratched off as "sunk"[15]. These factors had previously led me to be much impressed when I had witnessed the depth charge attacks made by the RUSSELL, especially when a black substance would float to the surface after the attack and Captain Hartwig would report it as evidence of damage to the sub.

The Yellow Peril, however, was based on a wealth of recent, actual war experience of the British against the Germans, and it presented an extremely convincing analysis. It explained that all Doppler shifted sonar signals are not necessarily submarines, and that the black substance which floats to the surface after an attack is "exudate" from the TNT in the depth charge. (A "Doppler shifted" signal is a signal in which the echo has a different tone than the transmission. The difference in tone comes from the motion of the echo producing target. Normally a Doppler shifted echo will be a submarine, but a school of fish can also cause it). The Yellow Peril also made clear that only if you see wreckage such as mattresses, fuel oil, sticks of wood, life jackets, and can hear "breaking up noises" on the sonar etc, can you claim to have hit a sub.

In order to support the analysis, the Yellow Peril described both war experience and elaborate tests proving that the lethal radius of a 600 lb. depth charge (the largest we had) was only about 12 feet. The smaller, 300 lb.

charge, had a lethal radius of only about 8'. This was very much shorter than the U.S. command had led us to believe. Next, the book described the geometry of a typical depth charge pattern and showed that one could fit a typical submarine within the pattern, free of the lethal range of any of the charges such that, even if the pattern were placed perfectly, and the charges were set at the same depth as the sub, there would be less than a 10% chance of making a hit. The book also compared the abilities of a sub and a destroyer to turn quickly. Here the sub was clearly superior, having a turning circle at full rudder of less than half of that of the destroyer, and being capable of turning at twice the angular rate. Next, the limitations of the sonar were discussed. As a ship approached a submerged sub, sonar contact was lost at around 400 yds and, since destroyers are about 350' long, and the sonar had to be near the bow whereas the depth charges had to be at the stern, contact would be lost with the sub at over 500 yds from the depth charges. Also, the sonar could not function (due to water noise) if the ship were traveling at faster than 15 kts (500 yds/min). Thus, it would be over 60 seconds between the loss of contact with the sub and reaching a point over the sub, and another 10 to 30 seconds (depending upon the depth of the sub) before the charges would go off. In that space of time, the sub could easily turn so as to be completely outside of the depth charge pattern and the destroyer would have had no indication that the sub had even started turning. Even if the sub started turning sufficiently before the destroyer lost contact with it for the turn to be detected, the destroyer could not turn fast enough to stay with the sub, and the sub would inevitably escape. When one adds to this the fact that we had no way of determining the depth of the sub, the hopelessness of the astern method of submarine attack became clear.

The stark, cold fact was that, unless the sub commander was exceedingly stupid, the destroyer had no chance of hitting a sub with the astern depth charge attack method.

This was indeed shocking news. The Navy had asked for suggestions for improvement from the fleet, and this struck me as an ideal area to explore. I began to analyze what would be needed to improve the chances of success.

The main problem with the astern method came from losing sonar contact with the sub, and the ensuing long delay between loss of contact and dropping the depth charges. Another problem came from the fact that once the depth charges went off, they caused so much turbulence in the water that the sound waves of the sonar could not penetrate through the same area for 15 to 20 minutes. The Yellow Peril explained how the German subs had taken advantage of this by sneaking behind the "shadow" of the exploded depth charge pattern and escaping from the destroyer on the opposite side. Accordingly, it was clear that considerable improvement could be achieved if contact with the sub could be maintained while the destroyer remained at a distance (the way the GREER had done) and, if the depth charges were not exploded except upon actually striking the sub, or being within lethal range. By 1941, we had already developed magnetically detonated mines, so the idea of magnetically detonating a depth charge seemed perfectly feasible. Of course, exploding the depth charge upon contact would have been the easiest and surest way. If we had had enough destroyers, we could have stationed several at a distance to keep in sonar contact with the sub while coaching another destroyer onto the sub (as we did later with the Hunter Killer groups). We were, however, very short of destroyers at the time. What was needed, if a single destroyer was to do it, was a gun something like an Army mortar which could be aimed and fired so as to lob the charges out in front of the destroyer accurately to a range of about 1000 yds. I spent a little time calculating the forces required and concluded that, if one of the 5" guns of a destroyer could fire a 54 lb 5" projectile 15,000 yds, there would be no problem firing an antisubmarine bomb of about the same weight a mere 1000 yds. With such a weapon, the destroyer would be able to stop, remain pointed at the sub (so as to present the least target and least vulnerable part of the ship to the sub), track the sub at leisure without fear of losing contact with him, and lob the bombs at him varying the range and bearing by short intervals, until hitting him.

The installation of such a gun would, of course, have required the removal of one of the 5" guns of the destroyer, preferably the no. 2 gun, but the usefulness of all four of the 5" guns on the destroyers was questionable. Destroyers in the North Atlantic were used mainly for ASW for which the only need for guns was when a submarine surfaced. At such times, however, three 5" guns would have been as good as four, as a practical matter. With the guns firing in automatic, a destroyer should be able to hit a sub with one gun. The fourth gun was only marginally useful, if that.

I thought I had an excellent idea and got one of the yeomen to type it up for me for submission in response to the ALNAV request for new ideas.

My letter, of course, as with all correspondence from the ship had to be forwarded via the chain of command, the first link of which was Captain Hartwig.

I was sitting in the wardroom and heard a thump overhead and then "HOLY MOSES! HEY! GET RUSSELL ON THE DOUBLE!" A messenger tumbled into the wardroom, "Mr. Russell, the Captain wants to see you. On the double, Sir."

So I went up to the Captain's cabin. He shut the door behind me. "Sit down. Now! Just how in the hell can you, a red-assed Ensign, have the audacity, the gall, to think that you, you of all people, could evaluate between the weapons on a Navy ship? This is the stupidest thing I have ever seen. What the hell am I supposed to do with it?"

One must appreciate that Captain Hartwig had recently submitted several submarine attack reports in which he had claimed (by observing black material which later turned out to have been exudate) to have sunk or damaged German subs, and that he had received a good deal of kudos from these reports. Therefore, the key point of my thesis, i.e. that the astern depth charge attack was hopeless, struck a sensitive nerve. I went through the problems of identification of a submarine, that fish reflect Doppler, etc. I showed him the geometry of the pattern, the evidence proving that the lethal radius of the depth charges was very small, and the improbability of hitting a sub even with a perfectly placed pattern, the quickness of the turning circle of the subs, and that the black material on the surface was exudate, while Hartwig fumed and sputtered and called the British stupid.

Finally, he said, "I don't care what they say, I refuse to send a letter like this from this ship." I, however, was not to be put off and pointed out that I was replying to an ALNAV, and, as far as I could see, he did not have the option to refuse. This time he sputtered some more but had no answer. Finally, he said, "OK, Godammit, here!" and he signed it as follows, "Forwarded, disapproved!"

I then sent it in to the BuShips and never heard another word about it again. All this happened in November 1941.

Although I did not appreciate it at the time, my proposal had placed Hartwig in an impossible bind. Since the top "brass" of the Navy evidently had not studied (or did not give credence to) the British experiences, and no one on the firing line was suggesting to the command that they were in error, the command still thought that the astern depth charge attack was effective. My suggestion was too much of a departure from Hartwig's then thinking for him to go along with it, but even if he had agreed with it, he could not have approved it without in effect, telling his superiors that their evaluation of the astern depth charge attack method was in error, to say nothing of casting suspicion on his own submarine attack reports.

Officers who wish to be promoted are wise to do as little as possible to cause friction or embarrassment and officers who are known to challenge the wisdom of their superiors have virtually no chance of success. Hartwig knew well what one does and what one does not do in the Navy, and, accordingly, there was no way that he was going to tell the command that they were following a false premise or do anything but veto my proposal.

(I would like to interject here that once, after the war, I had the good fortune of interviewing President Eisenhower while he was still President of Columbia University, and mentioned this problem. He said that the fear of saying or doing something which might run contrary to the views of the command was a major deterrent to progress in the services. He also said that when he was with MacArthur in the Philippines, MacArthur had tried to counteract it by establishing a policy that no one would be promoted to General rank unless he had had at least one good reprimand in his record).

Although I was unable to persuade Captain Hartwig to relay up the chain of command that they were misevaluating the effectiveness of the existing ASW equipment and the urgent need for this important and easily implementable change in the armament of the destroyers (it could have been designed and installed quickly if the command had wanted it, and it would have saved literally thousands of lives and billions of dollars), I succeeded at least to some extent with Hartwig himself. Never again did he pretend that the exudate was evidence of a damaged sub. Also, although we were occasionally fooled by schools of fish, we obtained a recording of the various sonar Doppler sounds and by listening to them over and over and practicing on our own equipment, we became quite proficient. In addition, Hartwig, himself, thereafter, studied the Yellow Peril, and the whole approach to the sonar and depth charge attack on the RUSSELL became quite different. We no longer had any illusions about sinking subs, but instead recognized that our value was in identifying the sub, and using our depth charges to drive him down deep to prevent torpedo attack until the convoy or other formation could move out of danger. Hartwig's initial scorn totally evaporated and he put me in charge of the depth charge attack procedures. From then on, I handled the Recorder, calculated what to do and when, after which the Captain ordered it.

Although we participated in probably over 100 depth charge attacks against real subs thereafter, in only one such attack did we ever actually damage a sub. I will describe it later in this narration. It occurred in the Pacific at around the time of Santa Cruz, (October 1942). We were lucky. Most destroyers of the battle fleet never hit one at all.

(The idea of a forward-throwing ASW weapon was not unique. Many others also proposed similar devices. The real reason why the command did not pursue it was that the top people continued to hold an exaggerated notion about the effectiveness of the astern form of depth charge attack and no one lower down was brash enough to disabuse them of it. On the other hand, even without encouragement from the top, various efforts were made by courageous individuals to build forward-throwing weapons. Toward the end of the war by the time when the United States had plenty of escort vessels, "Hunter Killer" groups were formed comprising four to six destroyer Escorts (DEs) and at least one Escort Carrier (CVEs). These groups were sent out into the North Atlantic with the specific mission of finding and sinking German subs. They would locate an enemy sub, track it from a safe distance, and then direct one of the destroyer Escorts to an attack position while the others maintained sonar contact. The Hunter Killer groups were highly successful and finally broke the back of the German U-boat menace. During the war, the Navy experimented with several of the ahead-throwing antisubmarine weapons then being developed. One was called the "hedgehog". It was installed on some of the smaller escort vessels. Its range was only 200 yds and it was incapable of firing before losing sonar contact, but, even with this disadvantage, if coached into position by other ships, the ships which had it were scoring fairly well at the end of the war. Yet another form of forward-throwing weapon having a slightly longer range was tried. The principle drawback of these weapons was that they did not have sufficient range. Neither of them was installed on destroyers of the Fast Carrier fleet. It was not until long after World War II, at around the time of the Korean War, that the Navy finally got around to replacing the no. 2 5" gun on the destroyers with a forward-throwing weapon capable of lobbing an antisubmarine bomb accurately forward at a range of about 1000 yds. It was highly effective against World War II types of submarines. Of course, by the time of the Korean War, submarines had become much more capable of deep submergence and evasion, and the time when the weapon would have been really useful had passed.

Although I had had personal misgivings about some of what I had observed in the Navy prior to this incident, this was the first time I had a clear view of the mechanism inherent in the naval system by which the command can acquire and retain misevaluation. It also demonstrated why, even when the Navy sincerely wishes to seek out and adopt suggestions for improvement, the system prevents it.

"READY TWO"

The RUSSELL's main battery comprised four 5" guns in separate shielded gun mounts, two forward of the bridge and two aft of the after deck house. They fired a 54 lb. projectile at a maximum range of about 15,000yds (7 1/2 nautical miles). Projectiles of three different types could be fired as follows: (a) armor piercing shells to be used against ships, (b) anti-aircraft shells with timed fuses, or later in the war, with proximity fuses triggered by microwave reflections from the target, or (c) star shells, with timed fuses which, upon explosion, would display a very brightly burning flare suspended from a parachute, to illuminate the surface of the water at night. The illumination would last for about 5 minutes.

The controls for the 5" guns were designed so that each gun could be aimed automatically in azimuth and elevation from a central computer (analog, crude by 1986 standards but still a computer capable of solving complicated ballistic problems automatically) which was in turn controlled for stability by the ship's main gyro. The computer was mechanically rather than electronically operated, but it still worked well. It represented a major improvement over the gunnery of World War 1. The accuracy was good against slowly moving targets, but contrary to the belief of the command, it was not effective against aircraft.

When the controls were in "automatic", the range, bearing, course and speed of the target, as well as other ballistic information would be "cranked" (literally) into the computer which would automatically set the fuses and point the guns in the correct direction and keep them so pointing despite the roll of the ship. After firing had commenced, the gunnery officer could enter corrections based on his observations of the results through the optical system of the Mk 37 director.

Each gun also could be fired in "manual" and had a pointer and a trainer with manual (as well as servo) controls, ready to aim and fire the gun independently of the central control. In the practice drills, firing by manual as well as by automatic was always carried out.

Loading was done in part manually and in part automatically. The powder was so-called "smokeless powder". It too was new since World War I. It was a kind of explosive made up of molded plastic briquettes enclosed in brass cartridges. The briquettes had holes running through them like a honeycomb so that the force of the detonation would reach all parts of the powder instantaneously. The detonation was not literally smokeless, but the smoke was minor compared to the smoke from the guns of prior wars.

The breach of the gun was opened automatically after each shell had been fired and a blast of compressed air would clear out the bore. Next, the loading crew would put a powder cartridge and shell in the tray, and actuate a hydraulic ram which, would shove the cartridge and shell together into the barrel, with the shell coming up against the lands and grooves of the rifling on the inner surface of the barrel of the gun. The shells were provided with a ring of soft metal which would conform to the rifling and serve both to hold the shell in fixed position before firing, and as a lubricant when the shell was fired.

The brass powder cartridges came in reusable containers. After firing, the cartridge was ejected automatically into the asbestos gloves of the "hotshellman" who would then drop the empty cartridge through a scuttle in the deck of the gun mount.

All of these operations were carried out as fast as possible, and in order to improve speed, loading drills were conducted using dummy gun breaches set up on the main deck, every day as well as at virtually every dawn GQ. A firing rate of about 15 rounds per minute was normal (most ships claimed higher rates). The sequence became highly repetitive with all members of the loading crew doing their jobs instinctively and by rote, and on the older 5" guns of the type we had on the Wyoming, the gunner in charge of the loading crew would sing out, as the breach was slammed shut, "Ready one", "Ready two", "Ready three", and so on, as the case might be.

This gave rise to the story about how an old gunner, after serving for many years and reaching retirement, settled in a little village in upstate Vermont. One winter night not long thereafter, he was sitting in the General Store in front of the pot-bellied stove with his coonskin hat in his lap telling the assembled multitude about his times at sea, the battles, and all of his heroic deeds. After a while, some of the local kids decided to test his reactions, placed a 5" salute (firecracker) under his chair, and set it off. When it detonated, the old gunner reacted instantaneously, jumped up, opened the stove door, shoved the hat into the stove, slammed the door shut, and yelled, "Ready two!"

"HOT, STRAIGHT, AND NORMAL"

In addition to the depth charges and the 5" guns, the RUSSELL was equipped with eight 21" torpedoes arranged in two mounts of four torpedoes each located amidships on top of the deck house, and pivoted so that they could be fired to either side of the ship.

A torpedo is, in effect, a complicated, self-propelled, self-guided missile equipped to go under water. In order to do this, it must have a propulsion plant. It must have controls to keep it at the correct depth in the water and pointed in the right direction. It must carry an effective warhead and a means to fire the warhead at the appropriate moment.

For propulsion, torpedoes are driven by counter rotating sets of propellers (counter rotating so as to neutralize the torque which one set alone would have) driven by turbines powered by the combustion products of alcohol and compressed air.

(The Japanese torpedoes at the time used compressed oxygen instead of air and were far more effective than ours. Air, of course, is 78% nitrogen, an inert element that contributes nothing to combustion. Thus, our torpedoes were being held back by the nitrogen in the compressed air, whereas the Japanese torpedoes used only pure oxygen, and, therefore, had far greater speed and range.[16]

When a torpedo is fired, a trip actuates the propulsion system, simultaneously introducing and igniting the alcohol and the compressed air. Water is also injected into the combustion stream and instantaneously converted into steam which in turn drives the turbines for propulsion. Our torpedoes could be set to travel at 45 kts for about 4500 yds. or at slower speeds for longer distances. If the ignition system failed to ignite the alcohol for some reason, the torpedo would run "cold" on the compressed air alone, but at only half speed and for much shorter distance.

The guidance system is operated by a small gyroscope which is also actuated at the time of firing. The direction of the torpedo is controlled by means of vertically disposed vanes (like rudders) located at the rear, behind the propellers, which are operated by small servo-mechanisms acting in response to signals from the gyro. The attitude and depth of the torpedo are controlled by horizontally disposed vanes operated in response to signals from a water pressure sensor and also from the gyro.

The warhead (i.e., about 500 lbs of TNT) is arranged to fire either on contact or by a detonator adapted to respond to magnetic changes due to the proximity of a ship. These latter detonators, however, which had been highly touted before the war, turned out to be ineffectual. At the end of the war, we were using only contact detonators. The warhead is armed by a number of turns of the screws and takes 10 or so seconds to move the exploder up to the firing pin, the delay being gauged to be sure that the torpedo is well clear of the firing ship before becoming armed.

A torpedo has virtually everything in it, in terms of propulsion and control that a ship has, all crammed into a casing some 21" in diameter and 12' in length (not including the war head). It is, therefore, an extremely complicated, highly sophisticated, precisely engineered, and expensive weapon in which many things require precise adjustment, and which can malfunction. In addition, a torpedo can be a dangerous instrument against the ship that fires it. Thus, if the direction system is not properly adjusted or malfunctions so as to cause the torpedo to turn rather than run straight, the torpedo will simply make a circle and hit the firing ship. In fact, a British Cruiser was sunk by one of her own torpedoes in this way. This was a hazard even when firing unarmed torpedoes in practice because an unarmed torpedo traveling at 45 kts. underwater, can poke a substantial and dangerous hole into the skin of a destroyer. Accordingly, an entire section of the Gunnery Department of a destroyer, consisting of some dozen ratings headed up by a Chief, is assigned to deal exclusively with the care, adjustment and firing of the torpedoes.

On the RUSSELL, while I was on her, we were never called upon to fire the torpedoes in anger, although some of the ships of our squadron did later on, in the actions around Guadalcanal. We fired them, however, many times in practice (recovering them afterward, of course) and, at the time of firing, it was always a tense moment until the Chief Torpedoman would sing out to the bridge, "Hot, straight, and normal, Sir," to signify to the Captain the proper functioning of the torpedo.

"E" FOR EFFICIENCY

I do not mean to knock Hartwig as much as I appear to be doing in several of these yarns. Actually, I think he was a victim of the system in certain ways, and I do mean to knock the system. It happens that the actions of several officers depicted herein, such as Gunderson's, Hartwig's, and some of the others, simply illustrate the points.

Hartwig was very strong on engineering and efficiency. It paid off very handsomely for us later in the war. I, therefore, would be remiss if I failed to make clear my gratitude to him and my admiration of his abilities especially in fuel conservation while underway and in engineering.

In the Navy, engineering efficiency is heavily emphasized. They have an annual competition among ships of various classes for an award of "most efficient". A ship which wins it can display a big "E" on its smokestack. More importantly, the engineering officer of a ship which wins an "E" will stand a better chance for promotion.

Actually, Hartwig had won this several times in his career. In addition, the

RUSSELL had won the "E" for Sims class destroyers for the year which preceded my reporting on board, and Lt. Pancake, who was responsible for it, had gained a reputation of being a remarkably good engineering officer.

The way the award is determined is by comparing the records of ships, including fuel consumption, materials purchased and expended. Other criteria are also used, such as the "down time" for repair or maintenance of the engines, pumps, condensers, evaporators, generators, boilers, etc., as well as performance data taken during special trials.

As a result, all year long the engineering officers on all ships watch everything with minute care, go around turning off lights, grumbling about the hot showers, etc. It becomes a way of life.

For example, even after we were at war and the competition for the "E" had been suspended for the duration; Hartwig was still obsessed with saving fuel. In particular, he was constantly checking the quality of the smoke issuing from the stack. The reason he was so interested in this is that the fuel combustion in the firebox of the boilers is at peak efficiency only when the smoke is a light-yellow haze. If there is too much air, the smoke will be white, and if too little air, combustion is incomplete, and the smoke will be black. In either case fuel is wasted through improper combustion.

An important aspect of engine room efficiency is to avoid change of engine speed as much as possible. Any change of speed causes a chain reaction in the engine room. First, the throttleman must adjust the speed of the engines. This causes a change in the steam consumption, which in turn, causes a change in the steam pressure, requiring in turn a change in both fuel and air to the firebox, and in turn a change in fuel and air supply pressures and so on. The whole sequence has to be finely tuned to produce and maintain the efficient yellow haze smoke. A change of even a few rpm will throw off the whole balance which may take 10 to 15 minutes to restore. In the meantime, extra fuel will be wasted.

Therefore, Hartwig would become irritated with any Officer of the Deck for changing speed except at widely spaced intervals. It was far better in his view to be a little out of station with respect to the convoy than to be constantly changing speed. Hartwig's attitude made it permissible for the OD to "cheat" a little on the zig-zag plan. Thus, if the ship was behind station a few hundred yards, the OD could cut the corners of the zig-zags and catch up without changing engine speed, or conversely, he could go slightly wider on the corners, if needed, to move back. Hartwig liked this up to a point. Of course, if the OD cheated so much a to cause the Screen Commander to signal us "Posit" (meaning "get back into position") Hartwig would blow into a geyser of rage.

One of Hartwig's special points was never to exceed 25 kts. The fuel consumption vs. speed curve of a destroyer turns sharply upwardly at 25 kts. This is due to a phenomenon called "hull speed" which is defined as the speed at which the wave of translation of the ship exceeds the water line length. When a ship attempts to steam faster than hull speed, the stern drops and the ship is then, in effect, trying to go uphill, which accounts for the proportionally greater expenditure of fuel at speeds above hull speed. The formula for hull speed is 1.34 times the square root of the waterline length. It figures out to almost exactly 25 kts. for a destroyer.) Accordingly, every knot of extra speed above 25 kts requires a tremendous additional expenditure of fuel. The thumb rule is that the fuel consumption doubles for each knot above 25 kts. Thus, in any kind of detached duty when we might be ordered to steam at higher than flank speed (25 kts), Hartwig would, if he could get away with it, cheat again and steam at only 25 kts.

Another fetish of Hartwig's was the straightness of the track steered by the helmsman. A crooked track obviously wastes fuel. Thus, if Hartwig, upon glancing aft, could see a path with wide digressions in it, he would hit the roof. Helmsmen vary considerably in their ability to keep the ship on a straight course. The problem comes from the swing of the ship in the waves. If the bow starts to swing, say to the right, the helmsman will apply left rudder to counteract the swing. How much left rudder to give it is a matter of choice. At some point thereafter, the swing of the ship to the right will stop, say at 5 degrees off course, and start back. At this point, the helmsman has to decide when to take off the left rudder, and how much rudder to put on in the opposite direction to "meet her", i.e. to keep her head from swinging too far to the left. It becomes a constant matter of judgment on the part of the helmsman, and the problem is compounded by the waves, particularly in a following sea. If the sea is following, the ship will tend to yaw radically as it rides off a wave. Strong rudder is needed at that point, whereas much less rudder may be needed to counteract the swing back. A good helmsman learns how to compensate and to avoid "over control". He also usually looks ahead and at the sea most of the time. Of course, he continues to check the compass, but he is mainly studying the waves and trying to anticipate their effect. There is no question that a good helmsman can save a substantial amount of fuel. We had an especially good one on the RUSSELL, a sandy haired torpedoman, whose name escapes me. Captain Hartwig always used him for GQ and special sea detail.

Ways to save fuel also applied to other aspects of the ship. For example, after a week or so at sea, the ship would run out of stored fresh water, and the evaporators would have to be operated to condense sea water into fresh water for the boilers as well as for drinking purposes. Condensing sea water takes a lot of fuel, and as a result, the use of fresh water at sea was strictly limited. Heating sea water for showers also takes fuel, as does generating electricity for lights. Once we went to the Pacific, we never heated the shower water.

The anomaly is that these officers who, after the war started, had no compunction about firing hundreds of extra rounds in gunnery practice, to the cost to the American taxpayer of hundreds of thousands of dollars, were nevertheless continued to be complete misers when it came to the slightest thing that might save fuel.

I will describe later how this paid off for us and very likely saved our lives.

In passing it should be noted that the competition for the "E" undoubtedly did the Navy a great deal of good. Thus, while the U.S.Navy was embarrassingly ill prepared at the start of the war in some areas such as aircraft, torpedoes, gunnery, and ASW, where the tendency to submit erroneous reports of success in practice prevailed and the lack of true, battle condition trials lulled us into thinking that we were better than we really were, competition in engineering on ships of the Fleet produced first class results.

THE BALM OF THE SEA

When I was a child, I saw a silent film entitled, "Mare Nostrum", the memory of which recurred throughout the war. One scene at the beginning of the film showed two small boys playing with model square rigged sail boats. The models were fabulously equipped with tiny guns that actually fired bullets. I always dreamed about owning such a model. "Mare Nostrum" may have started my interest in the Navy.

The particular scene, however, from "Mare Nostrum" which came to mind hauntingly throughout the war showed a man at the railing of a ship under-way at night, looking down at the waves and the spume constantly passing by. In the scene, he stands there silently for quite a long time watching the wash of the wake. Next, one sees the lights and silhouette of the ship in the distance, in the middle of a circular view which is divided by graduated cross-hairs as one would see through the periscope of a submarine. Next one reads a caption, "Fire Torpedoes", and then one sees a thin white line of bubbles progressing rapidly across the surface of the water toward the ship. A huge vertical column of white then engulfs the side of the ship where the man was standing. The final scene is an underwater shot showing an image of the man sinking slowly through the water along with debris from the ship

I have always been fascinated by the sea and never tired of looking down at the waves and the spume constantly flowing along the sides of the ship. The sea is a paradox. It is at once terrible, frightening, imponderable, intriguing, beautiful, constantly changing, but always the same, often violent, but always calm and completely peaceful only a few feet below the surface, and some-times at the surface.

Kipling has a line in his poem "Boots" in which he cautions the marching sol-dier against counting the bullets in the bandoliers of the soldier marching next ahead, for fear of losing sanity. On board ship, the waves and spume sweep by in a similar endless monotone, but yet, I never felt any challenge from them, only a soothing influence similar to the balm which sleep brings to the hurt mind.

Steaming at sea in the North Atlantic in the fall of 1941, despite all of the drawbacks and pains, I felt at home.

Later on, as the weeks stretched into months, and then into years, and the miles away from home stretched from hundreds into thousands, the flow of the sea, the spume, the phosphorous at night, the stars, and the wind, con-tinued to supply the balm needed to make the pain bearable.

THE MAMMOTH WAVE

When two speedboats are running parallel at about the same speed, their wakes will spread and overlap. At the point of overlap, the waves will combine to make a sharp spike which will sometimes move rapidly ahead.

A similar thing takes place while steaming in formation with destroyers. Every so often one of these spikes will appear and so resemble a solid object moving through the water that the lookouts will mistake it for a periscope.

Not only do the relatively small waves of ships' wakes combine once in a while in this manner, to make a single much larger wave, but the still larger waves of the sea itself also will combine to make a mammoth, or "rogue" wave.

I had read about this phenomenon in accounts of ships at sea in storms depicting men suddenly seeing a huge wave, twice as high as any of the others, coming toward them, with everyone frozen in terror, grabbing anything solid, holding on—waiting—waiting—and then being engulfed -, rolling, tumbling in green sea water, spume, and then scrambling—trying to bring things together afterward, hopefully to still be afloat.

I had read about the phenomenon so many times that I was prepared to believe it. I did not expect, however, actually to experience it within a few miles of Boston.

In late November 1941, we brought a convoy of empty ships back from the "Neutrality" zone and were released to proceed independently to Boston while still about 100 miles from the coast. A strong (i.e. 30-40 kt) NW wind was blowing, the waves were high (i.e.15′ to 20′), and we were bucking directly into them, periodically taking green seas over the bow. I went off watch at midnight and went to bed.

People who have not lived on a ship for an extended period might not realize it, but even while lying in one's bunk, a person can pretty well feel what is going on elsewhere on the ship. One can feel the throb of the propellers, hear the whine of the fireroom blowers, hear the bulkhead doors closing, hear shouts on deck, hear the water hitting the ship, feel the motions of the ship as she bucks and weaves, and hear the clatter of shifting gear as well as the strains on the ship as the pressures shift. Whenever any of these things changes, even by a small amount, one can usually sense it and feel what is going on.

I was sleeping lightly when some shouting and clatter on deck woke me. Next, there was a long, seemingly peaceful moment in which the bow felt as though it was dropping but then continued to drop. This continued dropping was indeed strange. I sat bolt upright and grabbed for my shoes. Next, there was a shudder and the ship stopped dead as if she had hit a wall, with the bow still pointing down. Then came a tremendous rush of water overhead accompanied by clanking, cracking, buckling, and ripping noises. Then the bow pitched radically upwards and came crashing down again. Finally, the ship started to buck and weave against the NW wind and waves as before.

By this time, I was on my feet as were most of the others, trying to find out what had happened and to assess the damage. The people on watch described a phenomenal wave which had been as high as the level of eye on the bridge (i.e. 37 feet) and steep. They had seen it coming a minute or so before it hit, but could do nothing about it. They simply stood there in awe waiting until it hit. The bow of the ship had gone straight in and green water had engulfed the ship virtually to the bridge.

We were lucky because we were headed straight into it and our ship was long enough not to be rolled over backward. As it was, however, the green seas ripped up a number of the deck stanchions causing leaks all along the main deck, particularly in the chiefs' quarters (forward) and swept away a number of unarmed depth charges aft. Parts of the radio antennae and superstructure were swept away. Otherwise we seemed to have miraculously escaped.

Later that same day after reaching the security of the Boston Navy Yard and inspecting the damage, we found that a deep wrinkle had been created in the deck the whole way across the ship just aft of the no. 1 gun. This showed that the entire bow section of the ship had been bent upwardly by about 10" relative to the remainder of the ship. The fore-and-aft main stringers of the ship had simply bent. No cracks, however, could be found and no serious harm had been done. In fact, the RUSSELL continued from then on until the end of the war without any attempt to repair the wrinkle.

FOG-BOUND ON THE DAY OF INFAMY

Between trips out on the Neutrality Patrol, we would usually spend four or five days in Casco Bay, Maine refurbishing. It was not all relaxation, however, because a great deal needed to be done to prepare for the next trip. In addition, the gunnery and torpedo crews needed firing practice. Therefore, we would usually spend one of our all-too-few days in port, steaming offshore firing at towed targets. On one of these occasions, on December 6, 1941 to be exact, we had spent the day offshore and were returning to port when a dense fog rolled in from the sea completely enveloping us about a mile off the entrance of Casco Bay. We did not have radar at that time, and it was simply impossible to do anything except anchor and wait.

In the morning, I was in the wardroom when a messenger stumbled in yelling, "Mr. Russell, Mr. Russell, the Captain wants you on the bridge on the double!" (With Hartwig, it was always "on the double".)

When I arrived on deck, the Captain showed me a message which the radiomen had just given him, and asked, "What in the hell does this mean?"

The message read: "TO ALL SHIPS AND STATIONS, EXECUTE WAR PLAN NO. 3 AGAINST JAPAN. THIS IS NO DRILL. REPEAT THIS IS NO DRILL."

Forgetting for a moment Mr. Gunderson's training, I answered, "I haven't a clue, Captain."

Hartwig blew up, "For Christ's sake find out!" I did not know where to start because, up to this point in my Naval career, we had never had anything to do with war plans. There were, however, quite a few secret documents in the safe which I had not read, so I started looking there.

On my way down, I went into the radio shack and by this time newscasts were coming in about the Japanese attack on Pearl Harbor.

Eventually I found a book of war plans for the Atlantic but nothing about the Pacific and no War Plan no. 3. I then took what we had on war plans to the bridge and left it with the Captain.

"SIX WEEKS TO VICTORY"

After about 1/2 hour, the Captain called me and told me to assemble all of the officers in the wardroom.

I notified everyone, and with us all sitting there talking over what little we knew, the Captain came down and went to the head of the table. He was rubbing his hands and spoke excitedly, "Well, I guess you all know by now that the Japanese have attacked us at Pearl Harbor. We have been given orders to execute a war plan against the Japanese. We do not know exactly what that means because we don't have that plan on board, but we will get it. At least, I do know that we have been going through war games in the Pacific for the past twenty years with the Japanese as the potential enemy, and we know exactly what to do. So all I can say is that this is what we have prepared for and we'll show the yellow little bastards what it's all about. We'll be in Tokyo in six weeks."

Everyone got up with a feeling of elation. The fog lifted and we entered Casco Bay.

Not long afterward, we all listened on the radio to President Roosevelt's famous speech in Congress about how December 7, 1941 would go down in history as a "day of infamy". Later we heard the declaration of war by the United States against Germany and Japan.

2. PEARL HARBOR TO CORAL SEA

A BIZARRE COLLISION AT SEA

Everything changed dramatically after Pearl Harbor. The RUSSELL was assigned to a Task Force including the aircraft carrier YORKTOWN, the battleship NEW MEXICO, several cruisers, and the remainder of Des Ron 2 (our squadron of Sims Class destroyers), and headed south for Norfolk, Virginia. We were not told what they had in mind for us, but transfer to the Pacific seemed probable. On the way south, more or less directly off New York City, we witnessed a bizarre collision at sea.

A merchant ship named CALIFORNIA had been observed approaching the formation from the southeast, and rather than altering her course to avoid us, she had decided to steam through our formation. The ships in Naval formation are usually spaced quite widely apart (3000 yds or so) and one might think that a ship coming from another direction would be able to pass through without trouble. The CALIFORNIA, however, was evidently not particularly concerned about how she planned to do it, and all of a sudden, she had reached a "point of no return" with the Battleship NEW MEXICO. A strange thing about collisions at sea is that, before the event, no one who has not studied or experienced such phenomena can comprehend how they could possibly ever happen. One would expect that there would be ample time to take avoiding action immediately the danger is recognized but in fact, once an irretrievable mistake has been made, there may still be several minutes remaining to watch it take place without being able to do anything to stop it.

In this particular case, the CALIFORNIA found herself in front of the NEW MEXICO about 1/12 mile away and in a position in which no matter what either ship did by way of full rudder or full engines, the two ships were going to collide. On seeing what was going to happen, the Captain ordered the RUSSELL to go to GQ and I arrived on the bridge just in time to witness the collision. The respective engine rooms of the NEW MEXICO and the CAL-IFORNIA were backing down at flank speed, the horns were tooting frantically, and their respective rudders were thrown hard over. Then for the next minute or so, the two ships ground inexorably toward their meeting. Finally the NEW MEXICO nudged into the CALIFORNIA on the starboard side slightly forward of amidships. If the NEW MEXICO had not been backing down at flank speed for the preceding several minutes, she would have cut the CALIFORNIA in two. As it was, the cut in the side of the CALIFORNIA stopped a foot or two above the water line, and the NEW MEXICO backed away.

The CALIFORNIA then had a decision to make. Could she still proceed to Sandy Hook, or did she need help? It so happened that the wind was blowing hard from the north east, and with the cut on the starboard bow, with the CALIFORNIA steering Northwest, there was a risk that the waves crashing into the starboard side would wash into the cut. With things in this condition, the Captain of the CALIFORNIA showed what everyone: knew already by this time, namely that he was stupid. He decided to reject assistance and to head for Sandy Hook. Soon, the water striking the starboard bow of the CALIFORNIA, started entering the cut, the CALIFORNIA then settled down in the water to a point where the cut was below the water line. From then on, nothing could stop the inflow and the CALIFORNIA simply sank. We saw the collision, but merely read the details of the sinking years later in the published accounts of the inquest. In fact, since Charlie Hart had the deck and Charlie Woodman had been JOOD at the time, they were called upon for evidence at later date.

WE ARE FITTED WITH RADARS

Ever since the German battleship BISMARK had demonstrated the effectiveness of radar by using it to sink the British battle cruiser HOOD on May 24, 1941, there had been a crash program in the U.S. Navy to install radars on as many U.S. ships of the fleet as possible. Accordingly, during our stay in the Norfolk Naval shipyard, the RUSSELL and the rest of the ships of the squadron, were fitted with radar. By this time the carriers and cruisers had already received theirs. The radars at that time were adapted primarily for air search.

USS RUSSELL and USS SIMS at Norfolk VA, 16 December 1941 USN Ref: 19-N-26675N226676

Ours could detect aircraft out to about 150 miles, line-of-sight (i.e., in a straight line). It could also detect objects on the surface out to about 10,000 yds, and low flying aircraft out to about 15,000 yds. In order to pick up a plane at longer range the plane had to be flying at high altitude. The radars on the carriers were more powerful and their antennas were much higher. They could detect surface craft to about 25 miles and aircraft at high altitude to over 200 miles.

We sent a radioman over to the base to learn about the radar. In this instance, I was fortunate because no one in the C&S Division had any prior knowledge of the radar any more than I. At this same time, fire control radar was also being installed on a number of the heavy cruisers[17].

OFF TO PANAMA

On December 18th, 1941, the RUSSELL headed south from Norfolk in a Task Force comprising the carrier YORKTOWN, several Cruisers and five ships of Des Ron 2. While in Norfolk, Messrs Dimmick and Barnes were transferred, Mr Pancake became the "Exec", M. Hart took over Engineering, and at about this time a new officer, Lt. Baylor, came aboard.

Captain Hartwig was extremely eager to have the RUSSELL transferred to the Pacific fleet. He could visualize his classmates getting in on the dash to Tokyo, becoming heroes, etc., and receiving bonus points for promotion, while he was still stuck on the East Coast, far away from the glory. This had been particularly frustrating to him and he was delighted when we, at last, headed south for Panama. I was not aware of our destination, but it was perfectly obvious that we were headed for the Pacific.

SWEAT IN THE SCUPPERS

Having just been in the cold and wintry North Atlantic, the change to warm waters and sunshine of the Caribbean was highly welcome, but it had its drawbacks.

As Communications Officer, I was constantly required to decode secret messages. For this purpose, we used a secret coding machine called an "ECM" (Electric Coding Machine). It was essentially an electric typewriter of crude and huge construction compared to today's electronic typewriters. Everything operated by means of solenoids acting against springs. It made a great thumping sound whenever a key was struck so as to actuate the printing hammer to hit the print roll. The encoding was controlled by 10 wheels each of which jumbled the circuits between the keyboard and the printing hammers. Thus, when one pressed a letter on the keyboard, a different letter would be printed depending on the positions of the wheels, and each time, when one printed a letter, the wheels would be advanced to a new position. Thus, one would set the machine up with a prearranged wheel combination and type a plain language message, but out of the machine would come a tape with coded letters on it. Then the coded message would be transmitted. At the receiving station, an identical machine would be set up with the wheels in the same places. The coded message would be typed in and the original plain language message would come out. Periodically, variations in wheel settings would be sent out by other secret codes. Since the possible combinations totaled in the billions, the ECM was regarded as highly secure.

Naturally, I had to be extremely careful about not letting anyone even see the ECM or the wheels, and for security purposes a small lockable room was constructed specifically to house the ECM with just enough additional room for a person to operate it. The room was literally only the same width and about 6" longer than a telephone booth and was provided with no ventilation.

Soon after leaving Norfolk, we entered the Gulf Stream, the weather became warm, and, after passing Key West, it became hot.

In the coding room the temperature was around 95 F. I would strip to my underwear and type away. So much sweat would pour off me that a pool would form along the corner of the room and slosh back and forth as the ship rolled.

Why is this worth mentioning? It is only that, six weeks later under identical conditions (the conditions having been much the same during the entire interval), there was not a drop of sweat on me. The human body is highly adaptable. I think it can adapt to almost anything.

For example, I spoke earlier about being frightened in the North Atlantic. In time, that too disappeared under even more frightening conditions.

It is important to know that this adaptation process takes place. It teaches you that, if things are unbearable, wait a while. They will become bearable.

THE KETCHUP AND THE DRESS WHITE UNIFORM

After Key West, we entered the true tropics. The weather was fabulous; the wind blew steadily at 17 kts. from the northeast, the sea was mild. As the ship knifed easily through the seas, the flying fish would break; from the top of the bow-wave and glide along the surface outwardly to the side. Kipling's "On the Road to Mandalay, where the flying fishes play" etc., had always been a favorite of mine. Also, Coleridge's "We were the first to ever burst into that silent sea" came strongly to mind. Having also been steeped in sea tales of all kinds, such as Stevenson's, and Nordoff & Hall's, I was excited to find myself really on a ship at sea, really in the tropics, and really to be involved in what I believed was a sacred war, to a far greater extent than many of the characters in the books I had read.

USS Russell (DD-414)
Image courtesy of William Bargeloh

Arriving Havana, Cuba.

The USS RUSSELL (DD-414) arriving Havana – William Bargeloh Personal Collection

In addition, the prospect of going through the Panama Canal was exciting. I dug out some literature we had on board relating to the Canal, i.e.., the history, the physical arrangement of the locks, how it was built, how it operates, etc.

When we entered the Canal, I assumed that, in true Navy fashion, the crew would be lined up at Quarters in white uniforms, and the Officers as well, would be in dress whites. I, therefore, put on my whites and went into the wardroom for lunch.

Unfortunately, I had it wrong. Everyone else was in khaki. So I sat there through lunch in some embarrassment, but the climax came when one of the mess boys brought around the ketchup. As he approached me, he "tripped" and doused me with ketchup. Needless to say, it brought the house down. My whites (after laundering) were put in the bottom drawer, and other than once or twice on leave, were never used again.

THE WAR AGAINST THE RED SNAPPERS

Prior to reaching the Pacific side of the Canal (the entrance of which is actually farther east than the entrance on the Atlantic side); we had been warned that the Japanese submarines were gathering to attack U.S. shipping in the vicinity of the Canal. For that reason, we were particularly nervous as we headed into the Pacific.

Very soon after exiting, we picked up a sonar contact which was distinctly "up Doppler shifted". "Up Doppler" means that whatever it is, is coming toward you (this is why church bells ring higher when you are approaching than after you pass and are going away). Also, the sonar echoes were sharp sounding and narrow in bearing. The contact had all of the indications of a sub so we went to GQ and immediately made a depth charge attack. The contact happened to be a school of red snapper. My handling of the attack must have been accurate because, within several minutes a couple of tons of red snapper floated to the surface. As I said before, we had become fairly proficient with the sonar by then, but a tightly grouped school of fish can be hard to distinguish from a sub.

AFIRE WITH PHOSPHOROUS

From then on until the end of my service at sea, we had meals at the wardroom table without stanchions, except for several times in typhoons. The Pacific was, as advertised, beautiful, blue, and mainly peaceful.

As we headed north along the western coast of Mexico, we passed through an area known as the Gulf of Tehuantepec which is noted (at least in C.S.

Forester's Hornblower Saga series) for stormy weather. The night we went through it, however, the sea was glassy calm.

I came on watch at 4:00am, as JOOD under Mr. Pancake. My predecessor on watch, Bargeloh, told me that they had been seeing some spectacular phosphorescence. It was, in fact, still going on. At first, I saw luminescence, apparently stimulated by the bow of the RUSSELL, shooting outwardly, under the surface of the water, for many hundreds of yards in a kind of fan-like progression. Later, I saw it also coming from other ships in the formation. Several times, the entire surface of the ocean seemed to be luminous as far as the eye could see. Normal phosphorescence, of course, is only a few flecks of phosphorous here and there, usually in areas of turbulence, such as in the bow waves or in the stern wash.

(I have read more recently about large luminescent areas being observed from aircraft over the "Bermuda Triangle", but I have no idea if it was the same as what we saw. I never saw it again. It has been suggested that it is a self-stimulated reaction of tiny luminous plankton.)

THE PREMIER PLANE GUARD OF THE FLEET.

During World War II, in order to launch aircraft, a carrier needed to have a wind speed across her deck of at least 35 kts. Since the normal cruising speed of the Task Force was 15 kts. and the wind in the Pacific was usually around 17 kts., in order to launch, the carrier would have to turn into the wind and speed up to at least 18 kts., and in order to be safe, they usually increased speed to 20 kts.

Since there were fairly frequent mechanical and/or engine failures during carrier flight operations causing a plane to ditch, a destroyer called the "plane guard" was ordered to follow behind the carrier at a distance of about 700 yds. so as to be in position rapidly to rescue the flight crew. In addition to the plane guard, a second destroyer would be sent out ahead to provide a screen in cases where the carrier would have to leave the formation due to changing course for launching.

Captain Hartwig, at that time, was the junior destroyer Commanding Officer in the Squadron, and the RUSSELL was, therefore, stationed at the far end of the screen (on the left side of the formation), and since the ship at the end of the screen was the most logical choice for plane guard duty, we were constantly given that assignment.

Here is where Hartwig's fuel economy obsession paid off for us.

When the carrier was preparing for flight operations, the first signal would be two black balls, called, "shapes", hoisted at the carrier's yard arm. Then, after about two minutes, without further signal, the carrier would turn into the wind and start launching or recovering aircraft. Once the carrier had turned, the two destroyers designated to accompany her would have to hustle to assume their respective plane guard or screen positions, and this would use up extra fuel. If the wind was coming from dead ahead of the formation, and was strong enough, the carriers could launch without changing course, and the plane guard destroyer could reach station easily and quickly, but if the wind was from any other direction, as it was most of the time, then the plane guard destroyer would very likely find itself several thousand yards behind station, with the carrier steaming at 20 kts. or so. The destroyer would then have to put on at least flank speed (25 kts.) to catch up. The simple mathematics of the problem shows that, even if the destroyer were only 3000 yds behind, it would take him 15 minutes to catch up, by which time the flight operations might well be over, and the Admiral would be irritated by not having had a plane guard on station in the meantime. In addition, the main turbines of the destroyer (rather than the more efficient cruising turbines) would have to be used and extra boilers would have had to be lighted up. This would cause an expenditure of substantial extra fuel.

Hartwig's technique when flight operations were approaching was to cheat on his position in the screen, and to edge toward the expected plane guard position. Then, when the "shapes" went up, he would turn immediately and head directly across the formation toward the place where the carrier would be in about 10 minutes. He could predict this fairly accurately because the carrier would usually continue on its present course for about two minutes before turning, and, since the turning circle of the carrier and the direction and velocity of the wind were known, the launching course and speed of the carrier, as well as the probable location of the carrier in 10 minutes could all be calculated. In this way, immediately after the shapes went up, the RUSSELL would be heading directly across the formation to its new, plane guard station while the carrier would continue on for several minutes on the course of the Task Force, then turn and proceed to where the RUSSELL was already heading. Instead of expending fuel, sometimes we would even slow down to reach the new station, depending upon the direction of the wind. The saving in fuel was tremendous.

The problem with Hartwig's method was that it meant that the ship would be leaving its station in the screen without authority. None of the Captains of the other ships of the Squadron did it. Either they were afraid to start the maneuver without authority, or they did not see the advantage of it or figure out how to do it without being hit with a "posit" signal from the Admiral. Hartwig never submitted any report or recommendation on this to the command. Evidently he did not want to admit officially that he was doing it because if anything ever went wrong while the RUSSELL was out of station, such as a submarine penetrating the screen through the place where the RUSSELL should have been, Hartwig would have wanted to preserve the option of denying that his being out of station had been deliberate. Also, if he made an official report on it, the Squadron Commander for the same reason would very likely have ordered him to stop doing it.

In any event, none of the other destroyers did it, and the difference in fuel consumption was major. The RUSSELL was able to serve as plane guard on a regular basis without consuming any more fuel than the other ships of the Squadron, whereas, when any of the other ships were given the plane guard duty, their fuel consumption drastically increased.

The fuel condition of the destroyers in a Task Force is a major factor limiting the ability of the fleet to remain in the battle zone. Destroyers can normally steam for eight or ten days if allowed to use only one boiler and their cruising turbines, but in the battle zone, the full engineering plant had to be kept in readiness and the destroyers generally needed refueling every four days. The refueling would be done at sea with the destroyers coming alongside either a tanker, a battleship, or a carrier. Fueling at sea also had to be done at relatively slow speed which meant that the Task Force would have to withdraw from the combat area. Thus, if any destroyer were to take plane guard duty and expend, on flight operations alone, as much fuel as it would spend in a single day of normal cruising (which could easily be done by a destroyer steaming for a short time at high speed), that ship would require fuel one day sooner than the rest, and the whole Task Force would have to retire from combat because of that one ship.

Therefore, Hartwig's success with fuel conservation gave the RUSSELL the reputation of being the premier plane guard destroyer of the fleet.

Of course, all of this did not immediately come about on our first exposure to plane guard duty on the way north from Panama, but it started there.

The manner in which it benefitted us all personally (and may well have saved our lives) was that the RUSSELL was constantly kept with the carriers. This meant that we were virtually safe because no enemy, ship or aircraft would bother shooting at, torpedoing or bombing a destroyer if a prize target such as a carrier were nearby. Thus, many of the other ships of our Squadron (eventually the total came to nine) were sent off on other kinds of duty, such as the night surface actions around Guadalcanal, etc., and were sunk. The RUSSELL, however, although witnessing virtually everything of note as long as I was on her (until May 1943) was never in any real danger, and outside of being strafed during the battle of Santa Cruz, was not even fired upon, except the German torpedo I mentioned, and when the British fired upon us because we had given them the wrong recognition signal.

POP BARROW EVADES THE SHORE PATROL

We arrived in San Diego shortly after Christmas 1941, and immediately began preparations to put to sea again to "points unknown". Captain Hartwig had been briefed on the flagship and knew what we were going to do, but he said nothing to the officers except possibly the Exec, and no one else was told anything except that we would be in port for several days and that the crews should be given liberty.

"Pop" Barrow was the Chief Signalman. He was thin, bald, and tan, with heavy wrinkles on the sides of his face. His smile revealed the absence of front teeth.

His specialty was flag reading. At sea, communication between ships by flag hoist or blinker is essential because radio signals can be picked up by the enemy. Even short-range microwave voice radio can sometimes be picked up at a distance, and, therefore, it was used sparingly.

The difficult part about reading flags is that the direction of the wind across the deck of the ship may be such that the flags will be aligned with one's line of sight (pointing either toward you or away from you) or at a sharp angle making it difficult to see the flag at all. Also, sometimes the flags will be flapping rapidly in the wind such that certain flags such as "Fox" (F), "How" (H), "Uncle" (U), or "Victor", (V) which are all red and white, may be extremely difficult to distinguish. (Photo Ref 11)

"Pop" Barrow had exceptionally good eyes (if not teeth) and he also had developed an ability to keep the long-glass focused on the flag-bag of the flagship such that, as the flags were being pulled out, and bent onto the halyards, he would be able to catch a glimpse of them before they reached the full effect of the wind.

In order to illustrate how proficient Pop Barrow and his signal crew were, I should say a word about the flag hoist procedure.

Flag hoist signals normally emanate from the Flagship and comprise a number of flags arranged vertically on one or more halyards. The letters are a coded representation of a standard message which can be looked up on the signal code book. Sometimes, if the message is not in the code book, it has to be spelled out. The procedure is for the other ships in the command to hoist the same signal as the Flagship and, when all ships have it hoisted, if the signal is for information only, the Flagship will simply pull it down. If the signal is an order to carry out a maneuver, the instant when the signal is pulled down by the Flagship, is the command to execute the maneuver. The proficiency of a signalman is, therefore, measured by the speed with which he can first detect the signal, next, how quick he can bend it onto the halyard and hoist it, and thereafter, his alertness in singing out the instant of execution.

Pop Barrow was so good that even though we were the farthest ship in the screen from the Flagship, we normally had the hoist "two-blocked" (i.e., fully hoisted), before any of the other ships. In fact, one time, after the RUSSELL had executed a plane guard maneuver in an especially smart manner, and the Flagship began to hoist a congratulatory signal to us, i.e. "Well Done", Pop

Barrow having the flags for the signal already bent on, two-blocked it even before the Flagship had fully hoisted it, to the great amusement of everyone.

I did not find out until later, but, although Pop looked about 60 years old, he was actually only 38. Of course, at 23, 38 still seems quite old. In addition, Pop had been in a good deal of trouble over the years. His problem, as with many a sailor of his persuasion, was not so much the "cigareets and wild weemen" as the "demon rum". Pop was one of these fellows who does well at sea. The longer one could keep him at sea, the better he would become, but give him liberty, and boom! He would fight with anyone, including his best friend, and the shore patrol was merely an invitation for a brawl. With him liberty and AWOL were synonymous, yet he always "shipped over" at the end of a cruise (i.e. after a six year hitch).

He was such a good signalman that he rose to the rating of Chief three times only to be broken for infractions he caused ashore. He was Chief again when I joined the RUSSELL.

On our first night in San Diego, liberty and shore leave were ordered for one-half of the ship's company and officers respectively, and it so happened that Pop Barrow and I and Captain Hartwig, each dressed in Navy blues, went ashore in the same launch, arriving at the dock at about 8:30pm. We started up the street together, but soon, each went in his own separate direction. I was only interested in making telephone calls home, found a phone, and made long distance calls to Lib and the folks. Then at about 8:45pm I went into a bar, had a beer, and at about 9:00pm headed back to the dock.

When I arrived at the dock, the second launch was still there. I talked to the coxswain for a minute or two. He said he figured he'd be returning to the ship in a few minutes. During this time, I became aware that a person was sitting hunched over on a nearby bench. I went over to see who it was. This was at about 9:10pm.

Sure enough it was Pop Barrow. I put my hand on his shoulder and it felt hard. I shook him gently, but he was rigid. I had previously heard the expression, "stoned", but I had never imagined that it meant that a drunk could be literally hard and rigid like that. Moreover, I could not imagine that, in the short time of 40 minutes, Pop Barrow could have consumed enough liquor to do much to him. I asked the Coxswain to help me get Pop into the boat and eventually, with one of us on each side, we managed to lower him into it. On the way back to the ship, I tried massaging him and was able to limber him up a little. He did not regain consciousness until the next morning, but, although still heavily "hung over", he was rather proud of himself for having evaded the shore patrol. How he did it, however, indeed, how he got back to the dock, remained a mystery.

TOP WATCH STARTS A FIRE

Within several days we put to sea in the same Task Force with which we came through the Panama Canal, i.e. the carrier YORKTOWN, two cruisers, and DesDiv 3, five out of the nine ships of the Squadron. Soon after clearing Point Loma, we were joined by three large Matson liners, (the Lurline, Matsonia, and Monterey). We were not told, but we could see with binoculars (and Pop Barrow confirmed) that the decks of the liners were crowded with U.S. Marines (it was obvious from their haircuts). We were also not told where we were going, but after a day or so of steaming southwest, we had a fairly good idea.

For some time, in fact, ever since the Captain had put me in charge of the Sonar Recorder and depth charge attack procedures, I had been serving as de facto, if not official Officer of the Deck at General Quarters. The Captain, of course, was on the bridge at GQ and would generally take the "con" (having the "con" means that you are the officer who is directing the helm and giving orders to the engines). but periodically the Captain would give me the con for purposes of following the zigzag plan or the like. Therefore, I was constantly having practice at it. In addition, by the time we had left San Diego, I had already become familiar with much of the technology of the C&S Division and had completed (and been examined on) the Ship's General Information Course, and, therefore, I knew a large part of the things enumerated above needed to qualify me for top watch. Also, since I was giving and grading the exams for the enlisted men for their advancements in rating, (a good way to learn a subject), I was becoming proficient in their specialties as well. Therefore, within a month or so after leaving San Diego, I was qualified and started to stand top watch in the ordinary rotation, as well as assuming the billet of OOD at GQ (a billet I continued to hold from then until I left the RUS-SELL, and also later on the OWEN (DD563)).

Being qualified for top watch within five months was quite fast, and, again I faced the problem of having vaulted over the heads of other Junior Officers who had been aboard longer than I. This time, however, it seemed to make little, if any, difference. The other Junior Officers had already overcome their animosity toward me, and Pearl Harbor had at least improved my credibility as far as why we were at war. Therefore, with the exception of Lt. Baylor, my new promotion did not create any additional strain. With Lt. Baylor, however, it was quite different. It seemed to ignite in him a fire that burned with a steady white-hot intensity that never diminished as long as he and I remained on board together. I will write more about Mr. Baylor later.

NEVER ORDER A MAN TO DO A JOB WHICH YOU YOURSELF WOULD NOT DO

In the R.O.T.C. we had been instructed that a good officer will never order an enlisted man to do a job that the officer himself would not do. The principle is a good one, but when I thought about applying it, I realized that there were problems. How would an enlisted man know that the officer would have courage enough to do the job unless the enlisted man had seen the officer doing either that or a more dangerous job before? And even then, if the man had seen the officer do one brave thing, how would the enlisted man know that the officer still had the courage? Battle fatigue sets in after long periods of suffering serious risk. I simply came to the conclusion that, if there was a dangerous job to do, and no one was stepping up to do it voluntarily, I would do it myself.

And then there was the time one evening when the messenger came down while I was finishing dinner and told me the Captain wanted me on the bridge because the radar had gone on the "fritz".

I had no idea what could be wrong with it, but the Chief radioman and I took out the Operator's Manuals and started checking things one after the other. Luckily, near the beginning of the book, they cautioned the operator to check the antenna for loose wires or cord which could ground the antenna. I took my binoculars and, sure enough, there was a rope lashed between both the antenna and the antenna mount. I asked the Chief if such a rope was normal, and he said he didn't think so. Also, there was no indication of such a rope in the manual. It was, therefore, fairly obvious that the rope was grounding the antenna particularly because we had just been through a rain squall and the rope was wet.

The next question was how to get rid of the rope. The mast of a destroyer is about 90' high. It is equipped with welded bars that form a kind of ladder by which one can climb it. The mast is, therefore, not difficult to climb. The difficult part is the roll of the ship. Thus, as one goes up the mast, while at sea, one will swing from side to side well out over the water.

No one was volunteering, so it became clear that I would have to do it.

Lib had given me a good pocket knife with a single large blade, and my plan was simply to climb up to the base of the radar and cut the line away with my knife, making sure, of course, that the radar had been turned off before I went up.

I had no difficulty climbing but as the swings from side to side became larger due to the extra height, it became proportionally more difficult to hang on. By the time I reached the base of the radar, I had to wrap my arms around the mast and interlock my hands to keep from falling off. At this point, the offending rope was literally touching my nose, but I could not do anything about it. Holding on with one hand briefly, I was able to get the knife out of my pocket. Then I had the problem of opening out the blade, which I tried unsuccessfully to do with my teeth. I eventually solved it by reaching around the mast with both hands and opening the blade on the far side without being able to see it. Finally, with the knife open, and again holding on briefly with one hand, I was able to cut away the rope. Folding up the knife was easier and once I could hold on again with two hands, the crisis was over.

From then on until the end of the war (and also since then, whenever I have been on small boats cruising), I have always worn a sheath knife on my belt.

THE BIG PICNIC

On our way south and west into the Pacific, the atmosphere on the RUSSELL was one of excitement heading into war yes, but only against the Japanese. Everyone felt relaxed. So far, we had heard nothing about the fleet maneuvers and the expected big victories against Japan, but still, the general attitude was that of a big picnic. The weather was fabulous, the sea beautiful and easy. The dishes stayed put on the table, and the stanchions remained stowed. Also, we had taken on several additional junior officers so that now the rotation of watches was reduced to "watch in four", which is a good deal more bearable.

As we approached the equator, the Captain ordered a good old-fashioned line crossing ceremony with the crew "taking over the ship". King Neptune held a "Court Martial" of all of the officers, and ordered punishments, such as bean shaves, dunkings, crawling through a canvas sleeve filled with garbage, etc. My crime was "committing Anglophilia; being unable to distinguish between Angles and Angels." (Mr. Pancake wrote up these "charges". Mine was evidently stimulated by the arguments I had had with him and the others in the wardroom when I had sided with the British). King Neptune sentenced me to take station on the fo'c'sle with a pair of toilet paper rolls bound together to look through them (as binoculars), and to report to him when I saw the equator. I also was given a medal. It was made of sheet copper and cut in the form of a cross. (I still have it). On it were inscribed the words "For Drills". I supposed at the time that it referred to my having turned so "Reg" with the radiomen.

Not long after, we reached Pago-Pago, Samoa where we left the Marines. Being in communications was fortunate for me because I could always go ashore on the excuse that I needed to check the latest code change, and get the latest secret mine field charts, etc. I was keen to look around Pago-Pago having read Margaret Mead's "Coming of Age in Samoa", and another book entitled "Rain" in which the setting was Samoa. The tropical trees, turquoise water, and lazy, sun-soaked atmosphere of Pago-Pago were all in keeping with my expectations, but I saw no beautiful, sexy young girls trying to lure me away from the ship. The people seemed generally to be sickly and I saw two cases of rather shocking elephantiasis (huge, ulcerated legs). I also was able to walk around and found where Sadie Smith's (principal character in

"Rain") house was supposed to have been. I probably should have been more sensible than to expect anything. The house was simply an ordinary frame house with a fairly large porch. All of which, of course, shows that it is the story of the people, which is the really interesting part, not the place itself of the physical objects.

WE MAKE THE JAPANESE "SEE STARS"

We entered Pago-Pago around January 10, 1942 but only stayed there for a day or so. Soon we were at sea again heading northwest. I remember passing near the island where Robert Louis Stevenson died. Thereafter we moved to the north and crossed the equator at the 180th meridian. We were rather proud of this. Crossing at the 180th gives you the "Order of the Golden Dragon". (I did it again two more times later in the war.)

Then the Task Force linked up with another Task Force which had come down from Hawaii, including the carrier ENTERPRISE, and on or about January 20th, the two Task Forces carried out a raid on the Japanese-held Marshall and Gilbert Islands.

Considering that the RUSSELL had been in Casco Bay, Maine on Pearl Harbor day and the Captain had predicted our victorious entrance into Tokyo Harbor within six weeks, and, considering also that Hartwig had been extremely chagrined about being stuck in the Atlantic while his classmates were becoming heroes in the invasion of Japan, it is ironic that we, on the RUSSELL, were to participate in the first offensive effort of any kind against the Japanese, and that Hartwig's own ship would be the first ship of the Pacific Fleet (not counting the activity in the Philippines) to fire a bullet in anger at the Japanese after Pearl Harbor.

During the raid, the YORKTOWN sent an air strike against one of the Gilbert Islands and one of the planes had been forced, by engine trouble, to ditch to the west of the Task Force. The RUSSELL was sent to try to find the aviators. During this detached duty after we had observed an unidentified aircraft on the radar, suddenly Pop Barrow sang out "Captain, there's the airplane, and she's Nipponese!" We all then spotted her, a large four-motored Japanese Naval air-search "flying boat", moving very slowly (probably no faster than 60 mph), at a distance of about 12,000 yds, i.e. the extreme range of our 5" guns. The Captain immediately ordered Lt. Baylor in gunnery to "Open Fire!"

Within a few seconds, the guns blazed away for two or three salvos. Then, as we all waited anxiously to see the plane blown out of the sky, we saw instead a few small specs in the sky, and then descending in broad daylight, a nice spread of star shells (having no destructive power) in the vicinity of the Japanese patrol plane.

Everyone on the bridge immediately cracked up. We could not, of course, laugh out loud, but around behind the wheelhouse, out of the Captain's view, we were staggering around holding our sides, and stifling down the laughs.

The enemy plane must have been mightily perplexed. I can hear them now, "So desu-ka—Yankee Navy invent new weapon?" Whatever, the plane soon turned away and disappeared from view. Not long afterward, one of the fighter aircraft from the carrier came on the air having sighted the Patrol plane, and in the next few seconds we heard him shouting "I shot his ass off!" Then we saw a column of smoke on the horizon.

The RUSSELL's battle report of the incident stated, "Attacked by large four-engined enemy bomber sighted at 1035 bearing 290 range 10,000 yds. Opened fire. Although no hits were observed, plane could be seen later burning on horizon bearing 340 range 20,000 yds," and the official Navy report stated, "The TF 17 destroyers fired a few rounds of AA ammunition at a single four-engined bomber which attacked YORKTOWN".

Although the newspapers at home played it up, the raid by the Pacific Fleet against the Marshalls and Gilberts was strictly a token. The Japanese had nothing on those islands.

I should interject that anyone wanting to study World War II, or any war for that matter, should use the war diaries, the official battle accounts including the secret reports of the admirals, the news releases and the like, very cautiously. I was in charge of writing the war diary of all ships I was on and of the destroyer Squadron Staffs later. My procedure was to write up a draft using data from the logs and what I could remember and present it to the Commanding Officer. He would then edit it, give it to the yeoman to type up in final, and submit it to headquarters. It is a cold fact of life that many things were exaggerated if favorable or distorted or ignored if unfavorable. This is nothing new; of course, it has been standard procedure ever since Caesar wrote his "Gallic Wars".

THE TRANSPACIFIC SWELLS

After the raid on the Marshalls and Gilberts, we headed northeast toward Pearl Harbor.

North of the islands one comes to a wide stretch of deep water that runs for several thousand miles on an east-west line where the huge transpacific swells build up. Although these waves are actually over 30' high, their crests are not steep and they are spaced nearly a mile apart such that on a destroyer one hardly notices them at all. They can affect the larger ships, however, depending on the course and speed.

On this particular occasion, we were headed more-or-less into them and steaming at fairly high speed, i.e., 20 kts. Under these conditions the carriers would dig their bows down into the on-coming swells and take on green seas nearly up to their flight decks. In fact, part of the YORKTOWN's forward flight deck was damaged by one of these seas at that time. Thus, at least for once, the tables were turned and we on the destroyers were comfortable while the larger ships were pitching and tossing.

THE SPECTER OF DEFEAT

The wrecked destroyers USS DOWNES (DD-375) and USS CASSIN (DD-372) in Drydock One at the Pearl Harbor Navy Yard soon after the end of the Japanese attack – USN Ref: 80-G-19943

The RUSSELL entered Pearl Harbor on February 7, 1942.

We had been aware, of course, that ships had been sunk, but we had no idea it would be anything like as bad as it was. Our first inkling that the magnitude of the destruction had been far greater than we had expected came as we approached the harbor entrance. That two destroyers were outside on anti-submarine patrol was not abnormal, but the color of the ships was. They were black from their waterlines up to their main decks and covered with fuel oil stains. Also, outside of the harbor entrance was a huge oil slick and clumps of congealed fuel oil floating everywhere. Then, as we entered the channel, fuel oil blanketed the entire surface. Wreckage appeared everywhere. The remnants of two destroyers twisted, burned masts, superstructures, etc. on one side of the channel jutting out of the water at odd angles. Then we began to see the sunken Battleships within the harbor, the burned-out hangars on Ford Island, the wrecked dry-docks with bombed out ships in them. The fuel oil was about 4" deep everywhere in the harbor. Above all the smell was particularly horrible and overpowering, not simply the smell of bunker oil, but bunker oil and wreckage and the rot of the dead. It may not have been as bad as Verdun, but it was far more than enough for me.

We anchored north of Ford Island and sat down to a quiet lunch. I suppose the main thought in many of our minds was that the Navy had misevaluated the destructive power of aircraft against ships. Not many years before, an Air Force General named Billy Mitchell had vociferously extolled the virtues of airplanes over Battleships. In fact, he had even demonstrated their superiority in a live test, but he committed the faux pas of challenging the honesty of his opponents, for which he was court martialed and disgraced[18] Now, Billy Mitchell had been proven right. Here we saw again, but in a strikingly horrible context, the ill effects of the Navy's inability accurately to assess its weapons, its tendency to adhere to prior thought processes, and its pattern of resisting even obviously desirable change.

Immediately after Pearl Harbor, however, those in charge were removed, and a court martial followed. Everyone was talking about how the Navy had learned its lesson, and that changes would be made. Some changes were made only in obvious areas, such as increasing the emphasis on carriers. No basic changes, however, were made. Battleship construction, amazingly, remained at high priority although it was quite clear that battleships could not defend themselves against aircraft. Virtually everything else remained the same. No one suggested that there might be a more basic lesson to be learned or that the system might be at fault. Nor has anyone else since (as of 1987) made such a suggestion. The system is still basically the same.

GILLIE "SKINS" A GREEN MORAY

The general atmosphere in Honolulu was near hysteria. Anything Japanese was bad and people of Japanese origin were seriously persecuted, regardless of their U.S. citizenship or true loyalty to the U.S.A.

No longer were there girls in grass skirts doing Hula dances and stringing leis around the necks of sailors. Nor were the famous beaches of Waikiki adorned with suntanned bathers or surfboarders. The beaches were, instead, covered with rolls of barbed wire. In fact, there was a time immediately after Pearl Harbor when the Japanese could have easily invaded Hawaii and everyone there was still very much aware of it. By the time the RUSSELL arrived, although invasion might have been more difficult, the Japanese still might have been able to do it.

In those days, there lived in Honolulu a distant cousin of Lib's named Ather-ton Gillman, or "Gillie", and whenever I had shore leave, I would go up to his house in the suburbs in the direction of the Pali (not far from the Punaho School). Gillie was a huge, muscular man in his late 40's, graying and balding, but deeply tanned, curly gray hair sticking out of his shirt front, and strong as an ox. He had attended Harvard only briefly, (Gillie was not much interested in things intellectual) but he was at Harvard long enough to play football one season and was reputed to have been selected for Walter Camp's All America Team as a tackle.

Gillie seemed to live in a different world. He just figured that we would take care of the Japanese somehow and he went back to what he liked doing best anyway, i.e. fishing. Gillie had a small place on the shore across the Pali in Kailua, and instead of paying attention to his real estate business, he preferred catching langoustes.

A langouste (or spiny lobster) is like a North American lobster except that it has no enlarged front claws. It can otherwise be as large as a lobster, and the meat is delicious.

Gillie invited me to go fishing with him and his small son, Gillie Jr. (about 10 yrs old). Gillie's method of catching the langouste was to swim down and find one hiding around the rocks. Then simply grab its back, bring it to the surface, and toss in into a fish tank in the boat. When a langouste is caught by the back, he thrashes around, but not having front claws, he is less dangerous than a lobster. Gillie used goggles and flippers, but needed no scuba equipment. He was a strong swimmer and, by virtue of long practice, could stay down for about two minutes. One might say that Gillie fished "Japanese style".

Gillie, of course, knew where all of the most suitable rocks were, and we set out. He told me how to do it, where to look, etc., and to watch him a few times before attempting it. He also explained that a major problem is the green moray. A green moray is an eel, which can get quite large, i.e. about 5' long and about 6" in diameter. It also has a long, somewhat dished, snout and a correspondingly large mouth full of dangerous teeth.

Apparently, the moray will occupy the same kind of crevasse in a rock as a langouste, and one has to be careful while feeling around the crevasses to find a langouste, not to encounter a moray.

Gillie had a rubber-band powered spear gun to take care of the moray and also to spear-fish on occasion. The spear gun comprised a long metal shaft with a sharp, barbed spearhead at one end. The gun was held by means of an elongated wooden handle through which the butt end of the spear was inserted. The handle had attached to it a heavy rubber band in the form of a loop. The way the gun worked was to loop the rubber band over the butt end of the spear and then pull the handle down the shaft to stretch the rubber band. About half-way down the shaft there was a catch onto which the handle would be latched. In this condition, the gun would be ready and could be fired simply by pointing the spear at the target, holding the handle and, with the thumb, releasing the catch. The spear would then dart out like an arrow. Gillie, of course, had charge of the spear gun. It looked like a mighty lethal weapon to me.

When Gillie had arrived at the place he had selected for fishing (he knew this simply by looking at the shore line), he stopped the motor, let the boat come to rest and then, to my surprise, simply tumbled over backward into the water with the spear gun in hand. Gillie Jr. and I followed suit. I tried to swim down under the water without much success, but I could see Gillie about 15′ below poking around the rocks. We continued to do this for a while. I could not stay down even for a minute, just barely able to reach the rocks before having to surface. Gillie finally came up with a small langouste which he took back to the boat and put in the tank. We then moved to another place and started again. This time Gillie had not been down long when his head popped up and he said he was "going to take care of" a moray. Then in another few seconds Gillie surfaced and shouted, "Godammit, I only skinned him!" Gillie Jr. and I did not need to be told what this meant, and we fairly flew over the water to the boat. When I got on board, I looked around and here was Gillie swimming along with one hand and holding the spear away from him with the other hand. The moray was wrapped around the spear and thrashing away. Soon he got it alongside. I grabbed the spear end first and then took the butt end from Gillie, and, with the moray in the middle flipped the moray and the spear together into the tank.

After he came aboard and things calmed down, Gillie decided to kill the moray because the moray was quite capable of mutilating the langoustes in the tank. Gillie then retrieved the spear and, with it, held the moray flat against the edge of the tank while I was given the task of smashing the moray's head with a four-foot length of 2"x4".

Gillie said, "Morays never die until sunset, no matter what you do to them. All you can do is make sure they can't hurt you." I did that much at least.

I asked about eating the meat of the moray because my dad used to refer to "boiled eel and mashed potatoes" as a delicacy. Gillie said, "Only the Japanese eat eel." I love Japanese food so, as far as I am concerned, this must mean that the moray is delicious, but, to Gillie, it was inedible.

BLOODY MARY IS NOT THE GAL FOR ME

The RUSSELL left Pearl Harbor on February 16, 1942 and moved south in a Task Force with the carrier

YORKTOWN, in position to support several token raids (similar to the Marshalls and Gilberts raid) on Japanese held islands and installations in New

Guinea. At one point the Task Force was used to escort ships carrying the American Army Division to New Caledonia. The Americal Division was formed one-half from the "Yankee" Division (from Massachusetts) in which I had a number of friends (i.e. Jack Coolidge, Mack Marshall, Ted Browne, Cammie Burrage, my cousin Brin Russell and many others). I do not remember where the other half of the Americal Division came from, perhaps it was California.

Our first entry into port at New Caledonia was dramatic. On March 29th, we were detached from the Task Force to escort the tanker TIPPECANOE to Noumea and arrived there on April 2nd after having been at sea continuously for 45 days. That morning, after serving pancakes to the crew, we only had left in the ship's stores a few cases of spinach and lima beans, not enough for a meal for the crew. Also, even though we had entered port our problems were not automatically cured because there was no Naval base at Noumea at that time. The tanker, however, was able to give us enough to tide us over until we could rejoin the Task Force and receive provisions from some of the larger ships. We stayed in Noumea for about three days and had an opportunity to go ashore several times. New Caledonia is an interesting island. There is something about the concentration of chemicals in its soil that makes it impossible for rodents to live there. One might suppose that this would make it an ideal place to live, but nature always takes care of everything. There were plenty of other things in New Caledonia to make a person uncomfortable.

The name New Caledonia undoubtedly came from the appearance of the island from the sea. It has steep, smooth, gray-green hills rising up from the sea much as one sees in the Clyde estuary, or as the islands of Jura and Islay appear from the shores of Argyle.

The old harbor at Noumea comprises a small sheltered basin at the foot of the town, into which one or two cargo ships can fit. The basin interconnects over a shallow bar with a wide roadstead extending for about ten miles to the west, sheltered by a long island which runs parallel to the mainland. The fleet could not enter the old harbor but had to steam to the west around the island and then back up the roads to the approaches of Noumea. In years past, the French maintained a prison on the island along the lines of their famous (or infamous) prison on "Devil's Island" in South America. The buildings of the prison colony were still plainly visible.

When the Task Force first arrived, Noumea was still a sleepy little tropical town. It soon became a bustling metropolis with virtually a full-fledged Navy Yard, a floating dry-dock, masses of Army and Navy equipment, and thousands of people. But at least for a fleeting moment when we arrived, we could see how it was in the past.

The houses were generally white-walled and secluded with shutters closed and caked with dust as though it might have been twenty years since they had last been opened. I did, however, have a glimpse into several of the houses through open doors, and saw lovely, cool gardens filled with brightly colored flowers and heavy dark green fronds. The inner doorways had beaded walk-through curtains in them.

Proceeding up the street, we came to a building with a large sign over the doorway which read "Grand Hotel et du Pacifique". I presume there once had been two hotels in Noumea, the "Grand Hotel" and the "Hotel du Pacifique", and the name resulted from a merger.

Grand Hotel et du Pacifique – Photo Credit: France TV1

We immediately entered the hotel and had some drinks at the bar. Among the native laborers were some large, muscular, good looking, dark Polynesians. They applied something to their hair that made it orangish-red. Their principal occupation was loading coconuts and they moved very slowly. There also was a large group of Tonkinese doing different types of work, such as working on roads or in the fields in gangs. Years later, when I saw the musical hit "South Pacific", I was surprised that one of the heroines of the play was a Tonkinese girl. The Tonkinese I saw were totally unapproachable. They spoke no English, and precious little French. They chewed betel nut, as in the "Bloody Mary" song, but the effect was to completely discolor and ruin their teeth. Also, they were filthy. In addition, while I assume that there was prostitution because there always is, it certainly was not much in evidence. So for me, while I found it credible that the Frenchman in the play might fall in love with the U.S. Navy nurse, the other part about the beautiful, seductive Tonkinese girls was total nonsense.

COUSINS MEET

While ashore in Noumea, I wanted to see if I could find some of my friends in the Americal Division, and after walking around, came into an area where some of the soldiers were pitching their tents. I asked around, finally located a group from Massachusetts, went into a tent and asked, "Any of you fellows know a Lt. Jack Coolidge?"

"Naw! And we don't want to know him!" It turned out that Jack Coolidge, Mack Marshall and apparently all of the people I knew except Brinley Russell had remained with the other half of the Yankee Division which eventually ended up in Europe.

I found Brin by going to the "Rear Echelon" (i.e. the Personnel Office). They gave me his unit name and location, which happened to be several miles out of town. I was then able to hitch-hike out there, and when I peered into his face through the tent flap, he was a mightily surprised soldier.

We reminisced a bit. He took some snapshots and we parted with wishes of good luck.

Later on in the war, I ran into Brin again when he was on Guadalcanal. That time, I went ashore to get secret publications. I only had a few minutes but contacted the rear echelon as before, they told me where he was, and I got a friendly Jeep driver to run me out there and back. Brin had caught malaria and was, in fact, in an infirmary, all loaded up with atropine. The fighting on Guadalcanal at that time was quite intense, and as far as I could see, Brin was a good deal better off with malaria in the infirmary, than fighting the Japanese up on the hills. At least I could write home to the folks that I had seen him, and, although sick, he was being taken care of and otherwise OK.

THE CAPTAIN KEEPS US FIRMLY AT ANCHOR

The roadstead at Noumea where we anchored was a large expanse of water with plenty of room to anchor the entire fleet. Also, the wind, as always in the Pacific, blew steadily at about 17 kts. from the southeast (southern latitude trade winds). Thus, the ships would all ride at anchor aligned in more-or-less parallel fashion and spaced somewhat as though steaming at sea in the Task Force.

Now, one night Captain Hartwig had been over to the Senior Officer's club (needless to say, establishing a Senior Officer's club is one of the first functions of the Naval Construction Battalion at any new base). He came back to the ship well "tanked", stumbled through the wardroom, and smiled as he missed the railing of the ladder leading up to his stateroom (stairs are always called "ladders" in the Navy). Once in his stateroom, he glanced out of the porthole, and could see the YORKTOWN directly abeam about 4000 yds, away. The RUSSELL's usual station, however, while steaming in the Task Force was 5000 yds abeam of the carrier. By now we had checked the distance to the carrier so often that any officer could tell at a glance, at least roughly, how far away the carrier was simply by the size of her image. So, seeing the carrier through the port hole like this, the Captain was immediately alarmed, and called the bridge.

Our in-port procedure was to have only one man (either a Quartermaster or Signalman striker) standing watch on the bridge to receive flashing light messages. The striker on watch that night was Schwarz. He answered the phone:

"Bridge Aye!"

"Bridge, this is the Captain!"

"Aye Aye sir!"

"Ask the OD what's the range to the carrier!"

"Range to the carrier, Aye Aye sir!"

Now at this point, Schwarz did not know what to do. The OD was in his bunk and would not know the range anyway, so Schwarz simply took a look at the carrier and picked up the phone:

"Range to the carrier 4000 yds. sir!"

"I thought so. Tell the OD to move out 1000 yds!"

"Move out 1000 yds. Aye Aye sir!"

Schwarz hung up wondering what was going to happen next. Nothing did, of course, and soon the Captain was sleeping contentedly, satisfied that he had put the ship back on station.

A NEW FORM OF NAVAL WARFARE, BATTLE BETWEEN AIRCRAFT CARRIERS

During the period in which the U.S. Army and Navy were building up in New Caledonia, the Japanese were moving steadily south into New Guinea (Rabaul), and in the Solomans (Bougainville and Guadalcanal), capturing what they regarded as "unsinkable carriers" (i.e. island airfields).

Our Task Force remained constantly at sea patrolling the Coral Sea. By this time, reports of our losses in the Philippines, Singapore and elsewhere were steadily coming in, and these, coupled with the shocking image of Pearl Harbor, had wrought a major change in the atmosphere on board ship. No longer was it a big picnic. Instead, everyone on board began to think more seriously about tightening discipline, and such things as one's life jacket and one's helmet, and the precise location of one's abandon ship station.

In view of the steady and evidently irresistible advance of the Japanese toward Australia and the now rapidly tarnishing image of American supremacy, the U.S. Navy was keen to find a place they could attack the enemy and report back some form of offensive action. This accounted for the strikes on the islands previously mentioned as well as the raid on the northeast shore of New Guinea, Salamaua and Lae. The latter raid was made by moving the carriers north into the Gulf of Papua near Port Moresby, New Guinea and on March 9th carrier planes were sent over the mountain ridge to attack the Japanese installations on the coast beyond. This was more daring than the two previous raids. Claims of sinkings were made, but still the raid accomplished little. The Japanese did not even bother to retaliate. For us in the fleet it was uneventful.

(I remember on the morning of the strike witnessing a large number of local thunderstorms, and a fantastic array of seven separate rainbows, all visible at the same time—believed to be a record!)

It is possible that the raid on Salamaua stimulated the Japanese. In any event, soon thereafter, reports started coming in from the coast watchers and submarines that the Japanese were moving army units down the islands and also bringing major Naval forces including carriers into the approaches of the Coral Sea. Since the U.S. could not afford to let the Japanese capture New Guinea, and this is exactly what they appeared to be about to do, it was obvious that the U.S. would have to take a firm stand in the Coral Sea. Thus, it followed that we would very likely witness the first battle in history involving aircraft carriers on both sides. This was a moment in history comparable to the time when the Monitor and the Merrimack fought in the American Civil War and introduced the ironclad ship into Naval Warfare.

In view of this it will be useful to describe the opposing fleets and how the commands were proposing to attack and defend their respective fleets using these new weapons.

The first and most important thing in a carrier battle, as in any battle, is to locate, identify and assess the strength of the enemy. For this purpose, both we and the Japanese had Submarines deployed not only to torpedo enemy shipping but also for reconnaissance. The submarines using their periscopes, would observe enemy fleet activity, and, as soon as it was safe for them to do so, surface and radio the information to fleet headquarters. Coast watchers were another source of information. The people who did the coast-watching were, in many cases, Americans put ashore from Submarines in isolated areas. Other times they were ordinary locals who were anti-Japanese. In either case, they would attempt to hide in the jungles and survive off the land. The principal problem the coast watchers had was that when they sent radio messages, the locations of their transmitters would be detected by the Japanese by Radio Direction Finders ("RDF"), and, therefore, immediately after making any transmission, the coast watcher would have to go into deep and extended hiding, and, if possible, move to a new location. Many unrewarded heroic incidents occurred among the coast watchers.

Other forms of reconnaissance included high altitude, long range Army bombers and Naval search planes from shore bases. The Naval long range search planes flew very slowly, and could, of course, be shot down easily by the much faster carrier-based aircraft, and, therefore, they were not much good for searching for aircraft carriers.

Finally, the carriers themselves had their own planes which could be sent out on search missions. Generally, on the U.S. carriers, the SBD's (Scout Bomber Douglas) did double duty as dive bombers and search planes. As dive bombers their radius, at that time, was about 250 miles. When equipped with extra fuel tanks in place of bombs, an SBD had a search radius of about 400 miles. The radius of the F4F fighters was substantially less, i.e. about 200 miles maximum.

The object was to locate the enemy as quickly as possible and to attack him, hopefully, before he could locate and launch an attack on you.

For attack purposes, the carriers employed dive bombers and torpedo bombers, and fighters to accompany and protect the bombers. When we first went into these early battles, the dive bombers were SBD'S, the torpedo bombers were TBD'S, and the fighters were F4F's. We were unaware at that time of the capabilities of the Japanese planes—more about that a little later.

In order to defend against an air attack, the carriers depended primarily upon the CAP (combat air patrol), fighter aircraft deployed above the Task Force. If unidentified planes (called "Bogies") were detected on the radar, the CAP, or portions of it, would be "vectored" out to intercept them. If they turned out to be enemy (called "bandits") the CAP would try to shoot them down, but if they succeeded in avoiding the CAP, the only remaining defenses were the AA (anti-aircraft) guns of the ships

During the early battles, the primary anti-aircraft guns were the 5" 38 caliber guns on the carriers, cruisers and destroyers, previously described. Again, at this stage of the war, we believed that they were highly effective against attacking aircraft.

Once a dive bomber or torpedo plane had penetrated through both the CAP and the AA barrage, the next question was how capable the ships were of withstanding bombing and torpedoing. I have already mentioned that the destroyers were vulnerable. Although the KEARNY had miraculously survived being torpedoed amidships (see photograph), in general, one good hit would put a destroyer out of action and could even sink a destroyer. The cruisers had more armor but even they were vulnerable especially to torpedo attack. The flight decks of the carriers were vulnerable in the sense that a well-placed bomb or shell hit could disarm the carrier by making flight operations impossible. The carriers were equipped with an armored deck below the hangar deck and about 10" of armor plating along the sides. The armored deck could be pierced by a well-directed armor piercing bomb and the side armor was incapable of withstanding a torpedo. Below the armored deck, however, the carriers were well compartmented and, therefore, if the watertight compartments were properly closed, it would take quite a few torpedoes to sink a carrier. The principal danger for the carriers was the 100 octane aviation gasoline (AVGAS). The AVGAS was stored below the armored deck where it was relatively safe. It was supplied to the planes on the hangar and flight decks through a network of pipes and hoses which would, of course, be shut off, drained and filled with CO^2, if there was a threat of bombing attack. AVGAS burns at a very high temperature and if an AVGAS fire is not promptly extinguished, it can ignite the steel of the ship and once that happens, nothing can be done to save her. Therefore, if during air attack, it became necessary to refuel aircraft on the flight or hangar decks, the carrier would be very vulnerable until the fueling could be completed and the pipes drained and filled with CO^2 again.

We did not know at that time how we compared to the Japanese. They had won a stunning victory at Pearl Harbor, but we were training aggressively to catch up. Thus, whenever we were at sea, the carriers would be constantly launching aircraft for simulated bombing and torpedo attacks on the formation, with the air squadrons attempting to bring in the dive bombers and the torpedo bombers as nearly simultaneously as possible so as to force the CAP to defend against both dive bombers and torpedo bombers simultaneously. The effect of this was to split the CAP and give the attacking planes a better chance to penetrate. During these exercises, the radar fighter directors would practice vectoring the fighters onto the attacking planes. In addition, the gunners would practice tracking them. At other times the carriers would launch "drones", i.e., small robot airplanes, in order to give the ships live firing practice.

Our attitude in the fleet, as we approached the first battle in history between aircraft carriers at sea was one of optimism. Our defeat at Pearl Harbor was attributed to our having been caught off guard. This time we were not off guard, and due to the lucky fact that the U.S. carriers had been away from Pearl Harbor on December 7, 1941, we still had carriers ready to fight. Moreover, we had radar, whereas the Japanese did not (and would not for another year). We still believed that we were better equipped and manned than the Japanese. In fact, Admiral Nimitz had published a directive to all commanders indicating his view that the United States fleet was superior, and that the U.S. should engage the Japanese in battle whenever possible, even when outnumbered[19].

Although the official point of view may have been "bullish", we in the fleet were not exactly of the same frame of mind. My own confidence had been shaken earlier when I came to realize that the command had misevaluated the effectiveness of the astern form of depth charge attack against Submarines, and, from what I had seen of the AA gunnery target practices against drones, I did not agree with the glowing reports of success which the ship repeatedly turned in to the command. Moreover, although we had no real idea of what was in store for us, we all knew that we were heading into a major confrontation. People around the ship had grown more serious. Of course, we stood our watches and did our routine jobs the same as before, but people talked less, and tempers flared more quickly.

THE BATTLE OF CORAL SEA

(a) The SIMS and NEOSHO Serve as Decoys

While the fleet was patrolling the Coral Sea, after the raids on Salamaua and Lac, reports began coming in, which I would decode each night and review with the Captain in his stateroom, indicating that the Japanese were amassing troop ships, carriers, cruisers and destroyers in the Rabaul area. Evidently, they were about to launch an invasion attempt in the direction of the southern tip of New Guinea. Two large carriers and one small one were sighted. At this point, Admiral Fletcher moved the Task Forces (TF 16 with the LEXINGTON and TF 17 with the YORKTOWN) up on the eastern side of the Coral Sea roughly 350 miles south southwest of Guadalcanal, and brought up the fleet tanker, NEOSHO, to top off the ships with fuel. We were not informed specifically, but it seemed probable that he had in mind some form of attack the next day.

During the fueling operations, Charlie Hart, the Chief Engineer, came on deck and apologetically reported to the Captain that one of our four main fuel pumps was out of order and that the ship could not possibly steam faster than 25 kts. Captain Hartwig thought about it for a while and finally sent a message to the Flagship explaining the condition. Within a few minutes, the RUSSELL was relieved from the Task Force and assigned to escort the NEOSHO.

That night, we watched the fleet steam off to the northeast in the direction of Guadalcanal where enemy activity had been reported, while we remained with the NEOSHO.

During the following morning, air strikes from the carriers caught the Japanese unprepared and sank a number of small ships in the Tulagi area. We, on the RUSSELL, could pick up transmissions on the MN radio circuit sufficiently to learn that a successful attack had been made. The fleet returned the next day to take on fuel again from the NEOSHO. By this time, the NEOSHO was floating high in the water (indicating lowness of fuel), and it was rumored that once she had completed this particular fueling operation, she would be sent back to the States. All hands on the RUSSELL were, therefore, much excited about the prospect of a leisurely cruise across the Pacific to the States in company with the NEOSHO. The problem with the pump, which I remember the Captain discussing with Messrs Pancake and Hart was that a bearing had burned out and the pump shaft had been scored. We had no spare shafts and the only way the pump could be repaired was either to build up the shaft or to improvise one. The easiest thing to do would have been simply to wait until we could find a repair ship. The engineers, however, set about improvising the repair and worked continuously on it through the night. Finally, the next day just as the fueling operation was nearing completion, Charlie Hart stumbled onto the bridge covered in grime and sweat and reported that the pump had been repaired. Captain Hartwig, paused briefly realizing that this might mean that we would be reassigned to the fleet, but also recognizing that he had no choice, scribbled on a piece of paper, and then, "OK Russell, here send this to the Flagship." The message he handed me reported that the pump was back on the line. Sure enough, the RUSSELL was promptly put back into the Task Force and the SIMS, another ship of our Squadron, which in the interim had developed pump trouble, took our place with the NEOSHO.

Not long afterward, the Task Forces formed up and started steaming west into the setting sun, while the SIMS and the NEOSHO, carrying our hastily written letters, disappeared over the horizon. That night, the Captain and I went over the latest secret messages which disclosed enemy fleet and invasion units moving down the western side of the Coral Sea, and it was obvious that Fletcher was moving the fleet into position to launch a strike against that force the following morning. We discussed it. The Captain was cursing the luck of the SIMS. Personally, I had mixed feelings. I felt I was getting what I asked for—i.e. I would be where the real fighting was going to take place. On the other hand, I was not altogether sure, now, that I was so happy about it. I had just learned via the Fox Schedule, that Lib had given birth to a healthy 5 1/2 lb. baby boy, to be named RBR Jr. I would be lying if I tried to pretend that I would not have opted to stay with the NEOSHO, if I had had any choice in the matter.

That night, (May 6th 1942) undoubtedly stimulated by Fletcher's attack on Tulagi, the Japanese carrier fleet moved over to the eastern part of the Coral Sea to look for us while we moved by them to the south and west to be in position to hit the Japanese invasion forces on the western side of the Coral Sea. In the morning, May 7th, the Japanese sent out search planes to the south and east looking for us, while at the same time, Fletcher search planes were sent out to the north and west. Not realizing that the enemy carriers had passed to the north of us, we missed them. The Japanese search planes, however, located the SIMS and NEOSHO, heading east. Apparently the NEOSHO looked like a carrier to the Japanese search pilot because the Japanese Admiral sent a large strike force to the southeast against them. The SIMS was obliterated (on the second attack) with the loss of all but 13 men. The NEOSHO did not sink but was virtually completely destroyed. Actually, she was sunk four days later by our own ships. 109 men were eventually saved from the NEOSHO.

The loss of the SIMS, of course, came as a great shock to us on the RUSSELL. We knew her and her crew well, having nested with her many times. That we came so close to being in her place—and would have been if the machinists mates on the RUSSELL had not worked so hard through the night. The fact that we would have liked to have been with the NEOSHO was disquieting in one way, but helpful in another way. It made one think that fate is fate, and not to try to interfere with it.

Fletcher had not planned it that way, but the SIMS and NEOSHO served, in effect, as decoys to draw the enemy away from our Task Forces.

While all of this was going on with the SIMS and NEOSHO, Fletcher's Task Forces to the west found and attacked the Japanese invasion forces. Several ships and one small carrier, the Shoho, were sunk. Fletcher let it go at that because he had received word about the attacks on the SIMS and NEOSHO, and decided to turn back to the East in search of the enemy carriers which had been reported as the Shokaku and Zuikaku.

Although historians have treated Fletcher's move to the west early on May 7th and his concentration on the Shoho as a mistake[20], he had cleverly drawn the enemy carriers to the east by attacking Tulagi first, he had then dodged them while hitting their western prong so as to blunt their invasion plans, and now he was returning to hit the enemy carriers from the other direction. It had the makings of a brilliant "divide and conquer" master stroke comparable to Jackson's at Port Republic and Cross Keys. But for one failure, which I am about to describe, it could have been that master stroke.

(b) Between the Scenes at Coral Sea

Although Fletcher knew from the distress messages from the SIMS and NEOSHO that they had been hit, he was not sure what type of attacking planes had done the damage because the SIMS and NEOSHO did not have a chance to describe whether the attackers had been carrier based aircraft, and since MacArthur's Army search aircraft from Australia had not located the enemy carriers in the Coral Sea, Fletcher concluded that the SIMS and NEOSHO had been attacked by shore based bombers. Not being sure where the enemy carrier fleet was, he started steaming north and, soon, unbeknownst to either, the two fleets were less than 100 miles apart and closing fast.

Toward evening, after recovering all search aircraft, the LEXINGTON's radar picked up a large group of "bogies" about 30 to 40 miles out, circling. It was clear that they were enemy planes because all of ours were accounted for. Accordingly, fighters were sent up. Soon they made contact with the enemy planes and chased them away. The visibility was bad, and the Task Forces were continuously dodging through local thunder showers. Eventually, we heard the fighter director call in the planes, and we even saw a section of two of them fly past us. By this time, it was nearly dark. I was standing on the port wing of the bridge talking to Crutchfield, the Chief Commissary Steward, (who also had become proficient in operating the radar and had assumed the GQ station of radar operator), having just been relieved of the watch. Several planes were coming around the landing circle in a clockwise direction. This was odd because our planes are required to circle counter-clockwise. Furthermore, these planes had a peculiar amber colored wing-tip light. I cannot claim that I actually suspected they were enemy, but it seems amazing to me now that I did not. It is a fact, however, that even when one is trying to be alert, if something happens which one thinks is out of the realm of possibility, one's mind simply will refuse to believe the obvious. There was something, though, that held our attention on those planes, not intently, but casually, along with the conversation. The Captain in his chair up forward on the bridge was also watching them and when the plane's lights flashed on and off several times, the Captain asked Terrill, the signalman, what the flashes meant. Terrill answered, "Looks like 'slant sign', Captain." Hartwig then, slapping his thigh laughed, "How about slant eyes?"

In less than a minute after the light flashing episode, the planes flew directly over the RUSSELL. Crutchfield and I looked up and sure enough the shape of the wing was that of the Japanese dive bomber "Val". I let out a whoop, "Captain, those are Jap Vals!" The Captain was quiet for a moment. "Go to General Quarters. Dammit, Russell, maybe they are Japs, but I won't fire on them if there's the slightest chance that they are our boys."

We did not open fire, but in a minute or so, the rest of the Task Force did, and tracers were flying all over the sky. Not only were there Jap planes in the air but also Americans and we heard the pathetic cry of one of our aviators on the radio, "Hey, that's me you're shooting at."

Bedlam reigned for a few moments. Our own planes pulled away and the Japs, who, at first apparently thought we were their own force, departed, our planes returned, and we landed most of them. Several of our planes, however, never got back. The last we heard from one of them on the radio was that he had us in sight and was coming in. At that time, however, there were no planes in the air around our formation. He very likely had the Jap carriers in sight.

After things subsided, the LEXINGTON reported a slowly moving radar contact about 25 miles away. In view of the mix-up which had just occurred between ours and the enemy's planes, and the fact that one of our pilots had reported sighting us when there were no aircraft in the air around us, there was not the slightest doubt in anyone's mind that the LEXINGTON's radar contact was the enemy carrier Task Force. The LEXINGTON continued to report this contact for about half an hour. It was to the north of us and was slowly moving east. We headed away, to the west, and then later to the south for the remainder of the night.

This was the proper moment for a night surface attack. In fact, in the British Navy, admirals who failed to attack under comparable circumstances were court-martialed and hung (e.g. the famous cases of Admirals Calder and Byng). Here are the facts. First, the value of cruisers and destroyers was minor compared to carriers. That was the lesson of Pearl Harbor. Second, in order to neutralize a carrier, all one had to do was land a few shell hits on its flight deck. Third, we had radar, and, as yet, no radars had been observed on Japanese ships. Although we found out later that the Japanese, due to the superiority of their torpedoes, outclassed us in close range night surface warfare, at Coral Sea we still thought we were better in all ways, even at short range. Actually, at long range, our fire control radar (which the cruisers had at the time) turned out to be highly effective and could have been at Coral Sea if it had been used. In any event, a few good shell hits on the flight decks of the Japanese carriers would have been worth more to the U.S. war effort than all of our cruisers and destroyers combined. We could have split into several groups and, using our radars, coordinated attacks simultaneously from different directions. Because the Japanese did not have radar, and we had good radar, at least on the cruisers, there is no doubt that we could have closed to effective gunfire range of the cruisers (12,000 yds.) well outside of their visible range, illuminated them with star shells, and made enough hits on their carrier flight decks to neutralize their air power. Also it is probable that our cruisers and destroyers could have escaped unharmed.

At the very least, Fletcher should have sent a Cruiser to dog the enemy so that their exact position would have been known to facilitate an accurate surprise air attack at dawn.

Nimitz defended Fletcher's decision on the ground that Fletcher could not afford to weaken his screen of destroyers and cruisers[21]. In view of the fact, known at the time, that the British super-liners Queen Mary and Queen Elizabeth were steaming at high speed, without a screen, unharmed, through submarine infested waters, it was clear that our carriers could do likewise without a destroyer screen. And furthermore, the alternative of sending at least a Cruiser with its superior search and fire control radar to dog the enemy could have been done without significantly weakening the screen.

Nimitz's defense of Fletcher prevailed. No one in the upper echelons of the command appreciated (or was bold enough to argue with Nimitz) that Fletcher had failed to make the most of his radar advantage, or that the carriers could have steamed safely at 30 kts without a destroyer screen.

(c) The Air Strikes (May 8, 1942)

The next morning, as soon as it was light enough, air searches were launched. It was a beautiful, clear day where we were. This was a mixed blessing, however. It was beautiful and clear for the enemy planes to attack us, whereas, to the north it was cloudy. At around 8:00 AM, our search planes reported sighting an enemy carrier Task Force about 175 miles away to the northeast. Signals went up immediately ordering an attack, and the carriers wheeled around into the wind to launch.

Anyone who has ever served on the ships of the fleet and witnessed the launching of an air strike will know the true position occupied by the Naval aviators in World War II. We on the ships were doing a job that had to be done to assist the carriers in reaching the battlefield, but the airplanes did the attacking, they bore the burden. That morning as they were forming up and passing over us in a steady chain of sections and squadrons in wedge formations, we could not keep back our feelings of appreciation. We waved like fools even though they could not see or hear us.

By 9:00 AM, the strike was on its way and we were left to steam back and forth, monitor the radio circuits, wait for their return, and prepare for what might happen. During this period the ship was kept at GQ, but all hands were allowed to stand "at ease". I was OD and remained occupied with keeping the ship on station relative to the YORKTOWN. This took my full concentration because she would often turn without any signal.

At around 10:15 AM, we heard that our turn had come. One of our search planes had sighted a large group of enemy planes headed toward us, about 100 miles out, coming in high. The fleet split into two groups, one each respectively with the LEXINGTON and the YORKTOWN, (we were with the YORKTOWN), launched all remaining planes, and went into anti-aircraft formation with the cruisers and destroyers in a relatively tight circle surrounding the carrier. All AVGAS pipes on the carriers were emptied and replaced with CO_2 under pressure to minimize the fire hazard, and all ships went to GQ with watertight compartments closed, ammunition up and in readiness, all boilers on the line, and everyone wearing life jackets and battle helmets. The fighter protection of the Task Force consisted of a CAP of about 25 fighters overhead and about 16 SBD dive bombers stationed low around the formation to intercept the enemy torpedo bombers. Soon we heard on the radio one of the aviators yelling "Hey Rube!" (i.e. the call for the fighters to gather) indicating that the Japs had been sighted and were coming in. All ships went up to 30 kts. As I have mentioned, the carriers, in those days turned without signal, and simply expected the smaller ships to stay with them. At this point the Captain took the con and I concentrated on watching the carrier and letting the Captain know when I had detected the slightest indication that she was starting a turn. This was critical because the loss of only a few seconds would result in a major loss of position.

Next, we heard for the first time, the sound of the large ships going into action against attacking planes. It starts out with a few separate bursts, then works up to a great rhythmic thumping, rumbling and crashing. I was extremely busy at the alidade tracking the YORKTOWN, but glanced quickly at the LEXINGTON in the other formation where the first attack was already coming in and saw two little black torpedo planes coming in low and fast. When I say fast, I mean substantially faster than any of the U.S. torpedo bombers we had seen during practices. Our torpedo bombers at that time launched their torpedoes at about 100 kts. These enemy bombers were launching at about 150 kts and were much faster than even the SBD's who were supposed to be protecting us from them. The first enemy plane dropped his torpedo just as I caught sight of him, and in another instant, he was streaking in flame, careening in a steep wing-over and crashing into the side of the LEXINGTON aft of the stack. I looked back at the YORKTOWN. A dive bomber was coming down on her. We commenced firing.

Although we had fired depth charges at German Subs and had had torpedoes fired at us in the North Atlantic, such warfare was more or less impersonal. Here we were witnessing the enemy attacking us, dropping bombs on our men and torpedoes into our ships, firing with their machine guns directly into our decks, killing our men and we were killing him or doing our best to do so. Seeing this did something to me I neither expected nor planned for. I suddenly found myself engulfed in a seizure of hated and desire to kill. The sight and sound of the carnage turned me from a relatively mild, live-and-let-live individual to a near maniac with a blood-thirsty compulsion to destroy anything to do with the enemy. Although people in a peacetime setting, quite properly decry and condemn such compulsions, it is clear to me from having been through it that, first, it cannot be prevented; it is a result of war. Second, it is necessary; it completely eliminates fear, and makes it possible for a man to carry on aggressively in the face of death. Fortunately, it subsides rapidly when the stress is over.

At the time the Japanese dive bombers started their attack, we were making 30 kts. and going into tight turns to keep parallel to the carrier. Captain Hartwig and I were racing together from wing to wing of the bridge, guns blazing away with dust and smoke choking the air. I heard an explosion, and, looking aft, saw a huge geyser go up about 50 yds off our starboard quarter. We later concluded from the fact that no enemy bombers had been seen overhead at any time that it had been a stray 5" shell from one of the ships on the other side of the formation, but at the time, I thought it was an enemy bomb. The Captain then ordered a tight turn to the left, and while he and I were running forward on the starboard wing, the two forward guns slewed up against the stops (which keep them from firing directly into the bridge), and let go a full salvo. The gun flash was so near to the bridge that it burst the plates sending rivet heads in every direction and knocking the Submarine Recorder off the bulkhead. The Captain and I were thrown to our knees. At the same time, the ship heeled way down to starboard. The heel came from the turning of the ship, but I did not realize it at the time. I was on my knees; I felt myself and I was OK. I was sure, however, that in the next moment we would be swimming. Then, much to my surprise, the ship righted itself, and Hartwig and I were back at it again as though nothing had happened, I trying to follow the carrier, and he ordering the guns to be fired whenever targets came within range.

During all of this, little Schwarz, the Quartermaster striker, had somehow sneaked a tommy gun out of the arsenal, and was walking around with it at his shoulder aiming it at dive bombers. Amid the din of the RUSSELL's salvos, Schwarz kept repeating in an excited voice to the Captain, "Can I shoot, Sir? Can I shoot, Sir?" Eventually, permission was given, and Schwarz got much satisfaction out of unloading his magazine at the enemy planes. They were about 5000 yds outside of the range of his gun, but he did not know it, and even seemed quite proud that several of the dive bombers had been knocked down.

In a little while the raid subsided, the enemy planes withdrew, and the battle mania to which I referred abated. In the distance, we could see our anti-torpedo-plane patrol having a dogfight with enemy planes. The carrier had steadied down by this time, and I went over to the port wing to watch the dogfight. Two planes were skirting close to the water while two others were above them and making machine gun runs on the lower ones. We naturally assumed that the Americans were on top because that is the way it always was in the movies, and, as the dominant planes shot one of the lower ones down, a rousing cheer went up on the RUSSELL. Lt. Pancake was heard to remark, "Don't cheer boys, they're dying over there," as he twisted his pipe stem sideways between his teeth. Next the two dominant planes began attacking the one remaining lower plane, which suddenly banked and started coming directly toward us. The Captain, thinking it was a Jap about to make a suicide run on us, exposed the broadside to him, and ordered the guns to open fire. The plane continued to come on through the black shell bursts and headed directly toward our port side. We were making hits on him with the Oerlikon guns the whole way, and just as he came abeam about 200 yds. out, he careened and crashed into the water. Then for an instant, we beheld a sickening sight. In the wreckage, the large, red, white, and blue striped tail of an American SBD stood up for a moment and then sank out of sight. It seemed likely that the aviator had been hit by the Japanese and was desperately trying to come close enough to us to be picked up. The way he did it, however, left us no choice. The identifying insignia of an aircraft cannot be seen when the aircraft is coming directly toward you. Also the shape of the SBD as seen from directly ahead, was very similar to that of the Japanese Zero.

The Task Forces steamed out of the attack apparently in good shape. The

LEXINGTON had a small fire up forward on the port side, which seemed to be under control, and all ships were making 25 kts. The LEXINGTON had taken at least two torpedoes and several bomb hits in addition to having one of the attackers crash into her. The YORKTOWN had also received a bomb hit or two, but did not appear to be in any difficulty. Therefore, the Task Forces continued on, apparently in satisfactory condition.

In the meantime, the air strike from our carriers had found the enemy and had at least damaged both of their large carriers. While standing near the MN circuit, I heard Dixon's famous message "Scratch One Flattop."

In an hour or so, the survivors of our air strike against the enemy began to return. Quite a few had been so heavily damaged that they were forced to ditch because the risk of crash landing on the carriers was too high. We learned from the pilots we picked up how the Japanese planes had been flying circles around our planes.

The pilots remarked about the "showboating" and rashness of the Japanese pilots. One F4F pilot told about how a Jap Zero pulled into a loop right in front of him, and gave him a free chance to shoot the Jap down, which the American did. Other stories, however, were not so favorable. We picked up an American torpedo bomber pilot named Swanson. His plane had been badly shot up by the Japanese Zeros. His gunner had been hit by machine gun fire and said to him at the last minute, "Swanny they got me. I can't go on." Still sticks in my memory. Swanny, however, was able to limp back to the Task Force, ditch in front of us and be picked up.

THE LEXINGTON SENDS A SIGNAL WHICH CAUSES AN UNFORTUNATE CLASH WITH POP BARROW

Several hours after the enemy attack, and after our own planes had returned, the two Task Forces were steaming four or five miles apart while preparing to launch aircraft again. Suddenly the LEXINGTON slowed down and turned out of column. As the RUSSELL, in the YORKTOWN Task Force, was the nearest ship to the LEXINGTON, we were responsible for relaying any flag hoist or other signals from the LEXINGTON to Admiral Fletcher on the YORK-TOWN. A flag hoist appeared on the LEXINGTON's yard arm. Pop Barrow leveled his spyglass onto it and immediately sang out three letters. I do not remember the exact letters but I do remember that the first one he sang out was "F" or "Fox" as we called it. Soon all of the other ships of the YORK-TOWN Task Force were flying it. I went to the signal book to see its meaning and found that it meant something like "I am discharging coal." I took up my glasses to see if I could tell whether Pop had it right.

The problem was that the wind was blowing directly away from us toward the LEXINGTON, and the only thing visible was a series of narrow blurs flapping to each side of the halyard. The upper flag was definitely red and white, but there are four red and white flags F, H, U, and V, and it could have been any one of them. I then went back to the signal book and found that, if the signal began with an H or "How" as we called it, it would mean "I have just suffered a serious internal explosion." This seemed to me to be far more logical. Also, it was the kind of signal that the LEXINGTON would not want to put out on any radio circuit for fear that the enemy might pick it up and be encouraged to make another attack on us. I took up my glasses again, and due to several fortuitous random shifts of wind, was able to see that the first flag of the hoist was indeed an H. My next problem, however, was what to do about it.

As the reader will recall, I had not been well received by the professional Chiefs. It was imperative that I handle this situation tactfully.

"Hey Pop! I wonder if you have that signal right? Are you sure that that first flag is not an H instead of a F?"

"Naw. It's an F all right!"

"Look up the meaning, Pop. That signal you have up there doesn't make any sense."

"I don't have to look up any signal. I can see it!"

I was beginning to feel uneasy. I had given Pop a way to back out, and he had refused it. But the Task Force and the Admiral were not being given important information, and as both Communications Officer and Officer of the Deck, I was doubly responsible.

"Pop, I really think it is an H!"

"Look, I'm the Chief Signalman on this bridge, and I read the signals. I see an F!"

I had to act.

"You may be the Chief Signalman, but I am the OD on this bridge. TAKE THAT GODDAM SIGNAL DOWN IMMEDIATELY AND RUN IT UP WITH AN H AS THE FIRST FLAG!"

Pop looked at the Captain. I did not wait.

"Terrill, you heard what I said, take it down!" Terrill obliged, and put up the signal with an H first.

The situation was very tense. My signal was now flying and all ships in the YORKTOWN Task Force changed their hoists to conform. The Captain was nonplussed. According to Naval protocol, he should back the officer, but he had great faith in Pop Barrow. Most important to Hartwig was that the signal be correct because, if it were not, it would redound upon him personally. Hartwig, however, was not about to try to read the signal himself, and, having no idea which signal was correct, all he could do was stand there in silence. I remained frozen with my binoculars fixed on the LEXINGTON. No one spoke. Pop Barrow went aft and sat down on the flag bag. Gradually the angle between the RUSSELL and the LEXINGTON shifted enough for us to see the flags clearly and my signal was established as the correct one. Pop Barrow, however, did not get over it.

This clash with Pop Barrow was indeed unfortunate. I was fond of him and held him in high esteem. Also, although toothless, bald and scarred, he was, as I have said, a master of his craft. The entire crew held him in a unique form of veneration sometimes reserved on ships for such ancient sea dogs. The incident led to serious repercussions among the men.

THE LEXINGTON BURNS DUE TO FIRES FROM HER OWN AVGAS AND THEN SINKS

The problem with the LEXINGTON was that her AVGAS lines had been ruptured due either to enemy shrapnel or to the suicide crash. AVGAS lines are supposed to be kept filled with CO_2 when not in use, for safety reasons, and one can determine whether they have been ruptured by checking to see if the CO_2 still remains under pressure in the lines. From talking to survivors later, we learned that this procedure had not been carried out thoroughly enough and the result was that when the AVGAS was pumped into the lines to fuel the aircraft preparatory to launching, the AVGAS spilled out below decks and exploded upon ignition, knocking out the engine and fire rooms. The LEXINGTON sheared out of line and commenced circling aimlessly. Not long after, we could see that a major fire was raging aboard her.

Destroyers alongside USS LEXINGTON (CV-2) to assist in the carrier's abandonment –
USN Ref: 80-G-7403

The Task Forces stayed together for a little while, but then separated in order to permit the YORKTOWN to keep launching and recovering the fighter cover. This continued all afternoon and we could see the LEXINGTON on the horizon with a great column of black smoke jetting upward from her. Every now and then someone would say that he thought the smoke was getting less, but we knew it wasn't. It kept getting worse, and finally we heard that they were abandoning ship. After that, we closed her again to screen and help take on board survivors. She was really burning by the time we got up to her, huge billows of flame and smoke covering the whole forward part of the ship, and the flight deck covered with a mass of men lowering themselves into the water and some jumping overboard.

A destroyer alongside USS LEXINGTON (CV-2) as the carrier is abandoned during the afternoon of 8 May 1942 – USN Ref: 80-G-7398

After the LEXINGTON sank, since Admiral Fletcher was not sure that the enemy carriers had been put out of action, and especially since the Army search planes from Australia had reported a carrier Task Force 150 miles to the north of us, we retreated from the Coral Sea at high speed. Actually, the Army had sighted us but they had had the position wrong.

AFTERMATH OF CORAL SEA

To find ourselves running south in the night with many oil-soaked survivors on board and leaving the Coral Sea to the enemy was far different than we had expected. The defeat at Pearl Harbor had shown us that the Japanese were capable, but even after Pearl Harbor, we still believed that our carriers and aircraft were superior to those of the Japanese.

Taking survivors off LEXINGTON – USN Ref: 80-G-7392

The picture of the triumphant race to Tokyo still persisted. Coral Sea completely erased that illusion. We now knew that the enemy's aircraft could fly faster, were more maneuverable and had longer range than ours. In addition, we had seen them flying right through our supposedly invincible AA gunfire. To be sure, a few had been shot down, but it was quite clear that our AA fire was not going to stop an air attack. Not only had our weapons been overestimated, but, in the course of the battle, we had failed to exploit the value of our radars by not dogging the enemy on the night of May 7th. These things were unsettling. It was clear that the Japanese were waging the war aggressively and had twice as many carriers as we. These things brought home the hard and clear fact that we were going to have to fight a long and difficult war.

DON'T GO AFT OR YOU WILL BE THROWN OVERBOARD

I was never sure that what I am about to describe resulted from my exaggerated application of discipline following my run-ins with the radio men or from my clash with Pop Barrow. It could have been a combination of both. In any event, not long after Coral Sea, Mess Attendant Bryant came into my cabin with his eyes standing out like a couple of white marbles on a black platter.

"Mister Russell—Mister Russell—I gotta tell you something…"

"Yeah Bryant, what's up?"

"Well sir, well sir, someone told me, he told me—that you'd better watch out—never go aft, no sir, never go aft."

"What the hell are you talking about Bryant? Never go aft my eye!"

"That's what they say—that's what they say."

"What's this all about? Are you trying to tell me that if I go aft, I'm going to be thrown overboard?"

"Yessir that's just what they say!"

"Who is this that's saying these things?"

"I don't know sir—I just know they says it."

"OK, Bryant—thank you—don't worry about it." He shut the door.

A destroyer is a small community of some 250 men. A person has to live with everyone else. There was no way to hide from or ignore a thing like this. I saw no choice but immediately to accept the challenge in the only way that it would mean anything to the crew, i.e. totally alone and without reliance on weapons or rank. I stood up, looked into the mirror, put on my hat, and started aft. There were two things certain in my mind. First, I was not going to let anyone get behind me, and second, if I was going overside, I was not going to be alone because that was the only way I could be sure that they would call out "man overboard".

I walked aft on the port side as is customary. It was after dinner in the early twilight and men were about on deck. I saw someone move quickly aft of the after deckhouse just as I appeared on deck. Walking slowly, I looked directly into each man's eyes. Rounding the after deck house I found myself facing five or six men only about eight feet away. I stopped and stared at them. They glowered back. I knew them all by name. Only one of them was in my division. Behind me were the life lines and then the sea. My heart was pounding and the adrenaline surging through my arteries. There is no question but that the war had already had a deep effect on me. Perhaps it was the strain of the North Atlantic, or the horror of Pearl Harbor, or the death and destruction I had just witnessed at Coral Sea. Whatever it was, I know that inside me at that moment, I was actually eager for someone to try something. No one moved. I waited a while and then moved farther aft. Finally, at a place where I could not be seen from the bridge, I turned around and faced a second group, that time with only the depth charges behind me. For a time, everyone in the group was glowering at me. Eventually, however, several got up and moved over to the companionway down to the crew's quarters, and I walked slowly up the starboard side.

There was no question in my mind but that Bryant's information, if not precisely accurate, was very close, and that I was encountering a serious level of animosity. I was – and am today – grateful for his courage. Also, I think it was equally clear that my response, if it did nothing else, showed that I was not afraid to face them alone. I had no illusions that my gesture was going to make the men dislike me any the less. My objective was only to let them know that I had guts, a necessary first step in gaining the respect of men. Also, it was clear that this one visit aft would not accomplish much, and, therefore, I made my nightly trip around the fantail a matter of routine for several weeks, until I no longer encountered groups of men glowering at me.

I should say in passing that I had previously read many times of Army Officers in World War I being found on the field of battle shot in the back. I had also read of Naval Officers being reported "missing at sea" during normal steaming in calm weather. In fact, one of my own classmates at NROTC was reported as "missing at sea" during World War II. It does happen.

LIFE AT SEA

By this time, except for very brief stops at Samoa, Hawaii, and New Caledonia, we had been continuously at sea for over five months since leaving San Diego. At one point, in fact, the Task Force was continuously at sea for 107 days. Very few voyages in history, even in the times of Drake and Magellan, have exceeded that duration. During such times, of course, we were constantly fueling at sea and receiving supplies from larger ships as well as mail occasionally via fleet tankers. Here are some of the elements from our life at sea which have remained with me:

The Euphoria

When one remains at sea for an extended period, life seems to change completely. The first thing to change is the flies. After about a week at sea, one suddenly realizes that there are no more flies or mosquitoes. Another thing that disappears is the hurt of homesickness. This takes longer. I felt very homesick for quite a while, but in about a month or so I began to realize that it had vanished. A kind of euphoria set in, as though I was almost dreaming, and I found that I had to whip myself to keep from falling deeper into it. I speak, of course, strictly of the Pacific. The North Atlantic is something else. The battles did not change it. In fact, they made the numbness worse.

The lack of exercise was severe. Standing watches, decoding messages, and doing routine paperwork, was all essentially sedentary work. Although standing OD at GQ for 20 or more hours during the battles, (or even standing an ordinary four hour watch) can be exhausting, exhaustion is not the equivalent of exercise, and I began to crave exercise. The only options on the RUSSELL were jogging (more-or-less in place), calisthenics, and a punching bag, which I frequently used.

On most American ships, everyone was badly out of shape. (Later in the War, the Chief Petty Officers of the British cruiser, Achilles, challenged the Chiefs of the RUSSELL to "games on the fantail". I was invited as a guest observer. It was most embarrassing. The British won every game except one game in which one's abilities to throw and catch a ball accurately were tested.)

The Boatswain's Pipe

Routine procedures such as reveille, "chowdown", "turn-to", "special sea detail", "clean sweepdown", etc., were broadcast on the ship's PA system. The announcement was initiated by a call of the Boatswain's pipe followed by a verbal order, as for example, "Now hear this, go to your stations all you special sea detail."—(the special sea detail comprised the specialized crew members on the bridge, in the engine rooms, and on deck for getting under way, mooring, going alongside, anchoring, etc.) or—"Now hear this, sweepers man your brooms—a clean sweepdown fore and aft—empty all trash cans," etc., usually repeated once.

The Nasal Twang

The voice, tone, accent and inflections of the broadcasts on the ship's PA system were nasal, and harsh and spoken with hard a's and r's, and for good reason too. The idea was to be clearly heard and understood. The same applied to the voice radio broadcasts between ships on the TBS and MN radio circuits on the bridge. I believe that the need to be heard and understood and the twang used to assure it, accounts for the phenomenon that, for example, in a crowded restaurant abroad with hundreds of people talking, one can often distinctly hear an American talking at the far end of the room, with his nasal twang and his hard a's and r's. It may be unattractive in that context, but it was very useful in the Navy for the same reason that it is unattractive in the restaurant. It can be heard over other noises. Conversely, the highly attractive and mild inflection of the English accent with its soft a's and r's is simply lost in a noisy context.

The Haircuts

We had no specifically assigned or trained barbers on board the RUSSELL, but there were always a few sailors who would set up shop on the fantail (or on the bridge for the Captain) on a calm day, and cut hair for a small fee.

The Laundry

Destroyers were fitted out with commercial laundry equipment and two men were assigned to laundry duty. Therefore, everyone on board could count on having clean clothes at all times. One time, however, a practical joker threw a bat of fiberglass insulation into the wash. The result was disastrous. When a garment has been washed with fiberglass in the water, it gives the wearer an extremely painful and persistent rash, and that same garment will continue to do so after many washings. The best thing to do is throw it away.

Later in the war, I spent several weeks on a Merchant Ship and learned to wash my clothes the way Merchant mariners do. They put the clothes in a bucket with soap in the water, insert a hose from a steam line into the bucket, and meter a vigorous stream of steam into the water. The steam bubbles and bangs as it condenses while agitating the clothes and achieves a thorough wash in a 10 or 15 minutes without any mechanical or moving parts.

Critical Speed

I have already mentioned that when one is at sea for an extended period, one begins to hear, feel and recognize what is going on elsewhere on the ship. This is particularly true about changes of course and speed. When the ship is on a given course, it will roll, heel, pitch, bounce, lurch, etc. in a more-or-less given repetitive manner, which will differ from the motions felt on a significantly different course. Therefore, one can usually tell merely from the feel of the ship whenever a significant course change has been made. Similarly, the vibrations of the propellers can be felt, and when a significant speed change is made, one can feel the quickening or slowing down of the beat. A refinement of this, however, relates to resonance. As a child, I had read that soldiers are required not to march in step across bridges for fear of establishing a resonance in the structure which might damage the bridge. I also had seen a shocking film of the destruction of a suspension bridge in the Pacific Northwest in the early 1930's during a storm due to resonance between the structure of the bridge and the storm. Everything apparently has resonance, including ships. As a result, when the beat of the propellers comes into resonance with the natural frequency of the structure of the ship, everything shakes exaggeratedly. This is called the "critical speed". On the RUSSELL, the critical speed was unfortunately 144 r.p.m or exactly 15 kts., the speed at which the Task Force always cruised during normal Fleet operations (the maximum feasible speed for sonar). This made things quite uncomfortable for long periods, especially on the bridge where the vibration was so bad that one could not rest a coffee cup on anything. This made the procedure of "cheating on the zigzag plan" described above (p. 85) particularly useful. It permitted steaming at 141 r.p.m. at which speed the resonance was very much less. There also were minor resonant points at lower and higher harmonically related speeds. These too could be felt but to a lesser degree. Thus, not only did one know when a major speed change occurred, but one also knew it when a small change of even a few r.p.m. took place near one of the resonant speeds. This became very useful to me later on in the war when I became a Squadron Operations Officer and no longer had to stand watch but was "on call" instead. Any significant speed change would mean that something was happening on deck. Many times on my way to the bridge, I would meet the messenger coming to call me.

Messenger Boys of the Fleet

One of the functions of the destroyers was to take mail, personnel, and other things around the fleet. On a normal day at sea with the Task Force, a destroyer would be sent on such errands several times. The procedure was simple. The destroyer would take position astern of the receiving ship, the then move up on a parallel course to a position about 20 yds abeam. A line throwing gun would then be used to send a light messenger line over to the other ship.

The messenger line would then be used to lead a heavier line over to the other ship. Once the heavier line was secured to both ships, a breeches buoy would be mounted on it on a pulley with lines to pull it across between the ships. The passage of the breeches buoy was very quick. What took time was to move around the fleet, especially overtaking from astern. The delay could be minimized if the destroyer were to turn smartly to a position close under the stern of the other ship and thereby

Example of using a breeches buoy. Photo Credit: AP Photo

avoid having to make a long overhaul. The RUSSELL frequently served in this manner.

The Curse of Censorship

One of the worst after-effects of the hysteria following Pearl Harbor was the institution of censorship of mail. I suppose it really was necessary; not that we were very likely to have a spy on board, but primarily to keep the crew from writing home about where the ship had been and what it did. Such information could be picked up by real spies in the U.S. from inadvertent disclosure by the families and could be useful to the enemy in breaking our codes.

Anyway, we were required to censor the mail. Most of us hated it. To read the intimate details between the men and their loved ones was totally repulsive. Few officers ever actually did it. We simply scanned hurriedly over what they wrote to catch a place, name, or time or the like.

Professional Gamblers

One thing, however, about the censorship of the mail did provide a measure of amusement. It related to gambling. Gambling is prohibited on ships. It cannot, of course, be stopped; but the rule against it is a good one. Men in the Naval context are quick tempered enough without any further causes of friction, and gambling leads to little else. The way that censorship figured in it was that whenever the Captain permitted the paymaster to hold a pay-day, within a week or so, three or four individuals would send large money orders home (far greater than their pay), and the rest would send little or nothing. In addition, it was invariably the same three or four individuals who acquired all the money. We made no effort to prosecute the professionals because it seemed improper to use the information gained by the censorship for such a purpose, but the Captain did, at least, try to protect the amateurs by limiting cash distributions at sea to $10.00.

In order to discourage gambling, John Caster had a policy in his Division of grabbing the pot whenever he came upon a group of men gambling. He would simply take the money and contribute it to the "Ship's Service Fund", a fund which was used to buy things for the crew or pay for movies or outings ashore and the like. His technique did not, of course, stop the gambling but I expect it helped. I adopted it.

The Food

The food was good. There were a lot of people who complained, but some people will complain about anything, and, of course, institutional food can never be as good as home cooking. Nevertheless, the ingredients were excellent, and the cooking was well done in both the crew's and officer's messes. I am, of course, speaking only of the Pacific. In the North Atlantic, as I have said, due to the weather which interfered with cooking, the food was terrible.

There is an old Navy Regulation that makes it mandatory for at least one officer to sample the crew's mess each day, and the custom on the ships on which I served, was for the sampling to be done by the officer who was about to relieve the deck for the 1200 to 1600 watch. We, therefore, each of us, sampled it in rotation. It was usually as good as or better than the officers!

The only problem with the food was storage. The amount of food that could be kept refrigerated was limited. Thus, the only milk we had was either canned or powdered. If powdered milk is made carefully with the exact proportions and stored for a day or so under refrigeration, it can be quite good. I eventually grew to like both forms, and, in fact, even today, I am quite happy to have Carnation milk in my coffee. The eggs were preserved by "water glass" (Editor's Note: a method of preservation using a solution of sodium silicate) and although entirely edible, their yolks were redder than normal and they did have somewhat of a "taste". Powdered eggs were also available. Again, if the powdered eggs were made with care, they were virtually as good as the real thing (scrambled, of course). The same thing can be said for the powdered potatoes. We had plenty of steak, lamb chops, pork chops, bacon, ham and preserved meats such as franks, corned beef, chipped beef, and spam.

The men might say that the officers had steak when they did not. Such a statement would not be accurate. The men had steak as much as the officers, but cooking steak on a large scale and keeping it hot on steam tables tends to ruin steak. The men had steak, but it was not appetizing. Vegetables and fruits all had to be canned. We would take on board as many cases of potatoes and onions as could be stored topside, and so usually, for a month or two, we would have fresh onions and potatoes. In fact, the onions would sprout greens, and a person could snip them off and have a snack of fresh greens on occasion, which I used to do. In addition, once in a while a flying fish would be blown up onto the fo'c'sle and the lucky finder could have fresh fish for a meal. All-in-all, there is no question but that we were fed very well.

Ice Cream

One thing we lacked on the RUSSELL and really craved was ice cream. Most of us were big ice cream eaters at home in a temperate climate, but to be here in the tropics, in perpetual summer, and not to have ice cream at all, was next to unbearable. Most of the larger ships had ice cream making machines and, by using a powdered ice cream mix, they could make excellent ice cream. Therefore, whenever we went alongside for fuel or provisions, we would always beg for ice cream. It was such a precious commodity that we had to keep it under lock-and-key. In fact, since I was both C&S Division Head and Wardroom Mess Treasurer, I retained custody of the key to the freezer compartment.

One time Captain Hartwig came down to breakfast in a foul mood and barked to the mess boy, "What's for breakfast, as if I don't already know!" "How about pancakes, Sir?" "Naw!" "How about eggs and bacon?" "Naw! I'm sick of them!" "How about sausages?" "Naw." "Well Captain, what would you really like?" "Warmsby, there's only one thing I'd really like and that's ice cream, but, what the hell, get me some eggs and bacon." When the Captain said this, I saw Warmsby look at me. He and I both knew that there was still a quart of vanilla saved over from the last time we served ice cream to the crew. So, I winked at him, followed him out into the Officers' Galley, and gave him the key. Then a few minutes later, in streamed all the Mess Attendants in a line with Warmsby in the lead holding up a big dish of ice cream on a silver tray.

The Heat

The weather was very hot. The sun was directly overhead, and near the equator the water temperature was 94 degrees F. Below decks was even hotter, perpetually. One can always dress warmly against the cold but there is no escape from the heat. Prickly heat rash is the problem. I do not fully understand what prickly heat is. It produces a rash which is easy enough to explain but the pain from prickly heat is not on the surface as with any other rash. The pain is down deep and feels like hundreds of pins sticking in several inches. One can put powder or salve on it, but nothing really works except to cool off. I found that if I could somehow cool off—I mean be really cold for a few minutes each day, then I could last for the remainder of the day without suffering from prickly heat. In search for a way to cool off, I found I could do it by taking a shower at night and then, while still wet and in my underwear, stand in the "air castle" (a place along the main deck amidships) where there was always a breeze. In this way, even though the breeze was warm, the evaporation would make me cool, and I would stand there happily shivering for the necessary few minutes.

The Navy Attitude

It does not take long after joining the Navy for a typical American farm boy to become a full-fledged Navy "Gob", with all the mannerisms, the walk, and the talk of his shipmates.

When Gene Free came to the RUSSELL, he had not been away from the farm for more than a few weeks. He was assigned to me and I made him a signalman striker.

One night not too long afterward, I had the 8 to 12 evening watch and Free was also on watch. The night was balmy. The ship was cutting through the waves and rolling gently. I was moving back and forth checking the ship's position, checking the zig-zag plan against the clock, checking the sonar and radar operators, checking the lookouts to make sure they were alert. Everything, however, was very quiet—only the "pings" and echoes of the sonar and the background ships noises (mainly the blowers) could be heard. Free was on the starboard wing, and Schwarz was standing look-out watch on the gun platform below. The following conversation ensued.

Free: "Look-out?"

Schwarz: "Look-out, Aye!"

Free: "Y'know what?"

Schwarz: "Huh?"

Free: "Y'know what I'm gonna do?"

Schwarz: "Yeah, whuzzat?"

Free: "Well, when I get out of this man's Navy, I'm gonna take an oar. I'm gonna put that oar on my shoulder, and I'm gonna walk. And when I get so far from the sea that someone will come up to me and say, "Hey Bub, what's that on your shoulder?" I'm gonna stick that oar into the ground and stay there for the rest of my life."

(Whether Free knew his Classics or whether this was the archetypical yearning of a man from the land so far at sea, I will never know.)

On another occasion, a new recruit came aboard and was assigned as a Quartermaster striker under Schwarz, and I overheard Schwarz telling him the following: "OK, now, if you're going to stand watch with me up here on the bridge, you gotta get this one thing straight. There's the right way, the wrong way, the Navy way, and my way, and on my watch, we do it my way, savvy?!"

Foul Language

Some sailors will utter an obscenity every third word until it becomes nauseating to hear. I found that the degree of foul language on a ship varies in inverse proportion to the fitness of the ship to do its job. When foul language is rampant, the quarters are filthy, the men are filthy, and everyone is blaming everyone else for things not going as they should.

I heard a lot of it and eventually cracked down. I drew a line between God-dammits, Jesus Christs, etc. and references to bodily organs and functions.

One time after the war, I was talking to a French friend and told him about my policy of condoning Goddammits but prohibiting reference to sexual organs. He was horrified. He saw no harm in what I prohibited, but was shocked by what I permitted!

Mascots ("Benny Cotton")

The men at sea may appear to be a tough lot, but they are really soft-hearted to the core. For example, one of the most popular tattoos was in the form of a flowered cross with "Mother" written on it.

To want a mascot was also very much a part of a sailor's nature. Some ship's Captains did not permit pets, others did. Whenever pets were allowed on board, their comings and goings and antics usually occupied a large part of the conversation.

Almost the same as a pet, was the occasional very young sailor. I know that people today will say that older sailors paying attention to younger sailors is homosexualism but I think that is a lot of nonsense. Sailors (and any men in similar circumstances) particularly in combat, are often sensitive with raw, tender emotions. They want to hug a little kid who may be homesick. To me that has nothing to do with homosexuality.

We had a little black kid who came aboard in Pearl named Benny Cotton. It seemed that Benny had no idea what his name really was, who his parents really were, or what his real age was. That was part of the problem. He had no business being in the Navy at all at his age (he was really only about 10) but not knowing how old he was, he had said he was 18, and no one could prove him wrong. He became the pet of the ship.

I remember one of his pass-times was to fly his airplane in the air castle. He had made a little airplane out of two sticks of wood nailed at right angles, and a sailor had whittled a little propeller for him and tacked it to the front so it could spin. Then Benny would stand in the air castle with the airplane held up and the propeller spinning and fly it around as though in a dogfight.

One time I came into the radio shack and found Benny Cotton standing beside the Fox Schedule recorder.

RBR: "Benny Cotton! What in the name of goodness are you doing here?"

Benny: "Gettin' the dope! Mr. Russell, gettin' the dope!"

Like as not on a typical evening, one would see a sailor sitting with his arm around Benny, telling him a goodnight story.

It was a sad day when Captain Hartwig went over to the base and told them that sending Benny to sea had been an obvious mistake. The crew loved him. Possibly he was more loved on-board ship than he might have been at home. Anyway, he was sent home, wherever that was.

The Liquor

I have heard all kinds of stories since WWII about the widespread use of liquor on board the U.S. Navy ships during WWII, and I do not doubt that some of them are true. I moved around the ships I was on a great deal and participated in bag inspections from time to time, and I never saw any liquor. Undoubtedly some was hidden, but a small quantity would not have lasted long. We were at sea for long periods. It would have been consumed within a few days. Any large cache of it would have been noticed. I have heard of stills being operated, but I am incredulous. A still has to have fermented sour mash which can be smelled at a distance. A still also takes up a fair amount of room. The Officers each had a personal combination-locked safe in their staterooms in which they could have easily stored a bottle or two, and this is what I am told was a common practice on larger ships. All I can say is that at least during the early part of the war, when we were going through the more or less frightening days of Coral Sea, Midway and Santa Cruz, I saw none of it on the ships on which I served. Later in the war when things became more relaxed, I was aware of it.

To illustrate the attitude in those early days, several times on the RUSSELL, Captain Hartwig called me into his cabin after we had had the deck continuously for 20 hours or so, and ordered the ship's doctor to administer to him and me "for medicinal reasons", a couple of highballs each of bourbon. The fact that he felt obliged to go through the charade of having the doctor prescribe it as medicine, indicates the attitude. If liquor was present at all, it was very minor.

Whether it would be advisable to have liquor on board Navy ships as they do in the British Navy is questionable. Having been through it, I am inclined to agree with Kipling's lines from "Gunga Din" in which he says, "But when it comes to slaughter, you will do your work on water."

This is not to say that the pure grain alcohol, which we carried on board for various purposes where wood alcohol was not suitable, never found its way into those thirsty mouths. I will relate later how the wing of the RUSSELL's bridge was damaged by banging it into the flight deck of the aircraft carrier Hornet while we were taking off wounded men from her during the Battle of Santa Cruz. Shortly thereafter, we were sent to a repair ship. A party of acetylene torch cutters, metal smiths, and welders came aboard, repaired our bridge, and we were ready to rejoin the Fleet the next day. The Captain ordered the special sea detail to go their stations to get under way.

"Boatswain!"

"Boatswain, Aye."

"This is the Captain! Heave up to short stay!"

"Heave up to short stay. Aye, aye, Sir."

"All set aft?"

"All set aft. Aye, aye, Sir." "All set in the wheelhouse?" "All set in the wh — Hey—wait a minute Captain. Something's wrong with the magnetic compass. It's dry as a bone—– why those sons-abitches yard workers have opened up the compass and drunk off all the alcohol it floats on!"

Another time, when we first put to sea on one of my later ships, I had occasion to be in on the training of the damage control party. Our procedure was to muster at dawn G.Q. by calling out the names of the sailors in the damage control party in alphabetical order. On this particular morning, one sailor did not respond to the call of his name.

"Smith. Smith!"

No answer.

"Where the hell is Smith?"

"Don't know, Sir."

"Hey! you Jones, you're an electrician's mate same as Smith. Is your bunk near his?"

"His bunk is next to mine, Sir."

"OK, go down and get him the hell up here on the double!"

A minute or so later, "Smith's not in his bunk, Sir!"

"Hey, Smith! SMITH!"

"Wait a minute, Sir. There's a guy lying here on the deck. Hey, Mr. Russell, it's Smith. Can't seem to wake him." He appeared to be in a coma. I bent down close to his nose and mouth to see if he was breathing.

"Well, I'll be Goddammed—the sonov-a-bitch is stinking drunk."

We found out later by examining his requisition slips for supplies from the Navy yard, that he had stocked up enough pure grain electrical contact cleaning alcohol to clean the electrical contacts of a battleship for a year.

I am told that the pure grain alcohol used in torpedo propulsion also found similar use from time to time, but I was never invited to any of those parties.

Fads

Men at sea on a ship will quickly fall into a fad. We had many. I can only remember a few. There were beards. Every so often a beard fad would hit a ship and everyone would be growing beards. It might last six months and then as soon as it came it would disappear and everyone would again be clean-shaven.

I remember the rings fad. Someone discovered that a 50 cent piece could be hammered on its edges so that the metal would widen, and with continued hammering the metal would form a broad silver ring. The center would then be removed by drilling and the edges could be filed smooth leaving an attractive silver ring, which could be sold for $5.00, i.e., ten times the cost of the raw material.

The fad took off like wildfire, and, at its height, all day long, all one could hear would be the "tap-tap-tap" of the crew making rings everywhere on the ship.

Songs were similar to fads. Any new hit would sweep the ship. I remember when Irving Berlin's "I'm Dreaming of a White Christmas" came out. It was particularly appropriate because most of us were literally dreaming about walking across a frozen lawn, or snow, or ice, or slush, not only the white snow, but also all the less attractive things we normally hated in winter, but had not seen for so long. "White Christmas" really swept us.

Women on Board Ship

Here again, I may be naive, but, with one exception, I never saw any evidence of any women being on board any ship on which I served other than having the Officers' or Chief's wives or sweethearts to dinner while in port (which was a common practice).

The exception occurred soon after putting to sea in the OWEN, DD 563, a ship I was on later in the war. The Engineering Officer reported that the pumps were unable to draw oil from one of the fuel tanks. Later, we put into a Navy Yard, investigated, and found the entrance to the fuel line clogged by a pair of ladies nylon underpants. How they got there remained a mystery, but it did give rise to much amusing speculation.

The Officers

I have already described Caster and several of the others. My narrative would not be complete without more about Captain Hartwig and Bill Bargeloh.

Captain Hartwig was of medium height (about 5' 10") and somewhat large around the middle. He was fair-haired and of ruddy complexion. His eyes were so light blue that one could qualify him as being "white cued". The cast of his face, his voice and his manner were Germanic (consistent with his heritage), remarkably similar to the modern American TV actor, Jack Klugman (alias "Quincy"). He had fine hands, was neat, precise, and fancied himself artistic.

Beyond this, he was somewhat of a "tough guy". His favorite sayings were "You gotta look out for number one", and "Never give a sucker a break". He, like most of his generation, was a worshiper of Red Grange, the famous football player, and this admiration accounted for his referring to our ship, the RUSSELL, as the "Galloping Ghost of the Iceland Coast" (Red Grange had been known as the "Galloping Ghost").

As further indicating his nature, one of Captain Hartwig's yarns was about the time he turned over the Engineering Department to his relief at the end of his tour of duty as engineering Officer of the Battleship Wyoming. All Division Heads are responsible for "Title B" equipment (for example, as Communications Division Head on the RUSSELL, I was personally responsible for items such as my binoculars, and my 45 automatic pistol). One had to sign for such Title B items on taking over and have one's relief sign for them when turning over to him otherwise one was charged personally for them. In Engineering, one of the pieces of Title B equipment in the machine shop was a milling attachment for the lathe. Equipment of this sort was carried on all ships so that any ship could fabricate its own spare parts from raw materials in an emergency. When Hartwig had taken over Engineering on the Wyoming, he had signed for a bag labeled "Milling Attachment" without examining the contents, but later on he had opened up the bag and found in it only nuts and bolts. So when Hartwig turned over the Engineering Department to his relief, he did exactly the same, and his relief had signed for it without looking into the bag. This was a cause for great mirth on Hartwig's part.

One of Captain Hartwig's greatest pleasures was playing "Acey Deucey", a game similar to Backgammon, played on a Backgammon board. He used to play it incessantly with Finn Toivonen. They played for the "championship" of the Iceland Coast, for Reykjavik, for the Panama Canal, for each of the Hawaiian Islands, etc. I played cribbage with him once in a while, but never got into the Acey Deucey.

One may find hard to believe the fact that, even though living on the same ship, in the same Wardroom, day in-day out, one does not automatically become close to—or know well—another officer. One can easily pass by another officer many times coming off or going on watch, work separately on one's own assigned tasks, and eat at the same mess—even side by side—without saying much to a fellow officer or learning much about him or from him. Once in a while, a common chord may be struck which one may explore with another officer. I had this with Bargeloh. He enjoyed certain poetry which I too liked and we had fun going through our respective repertoires together. It was from him that I learned the poem "Back and side go bare—go bare" by William Stevenson as well as other poems and songs. Bargeloh was from Parkersburgh, West Virginia. He was lean. Smoked cigarettes incessantly, was not strong or aggressive, and was strangely prone to invoking Hartwig's ire. Why this should have been was a mystery to me. He was intelligent, but yet Hartwig's blustery manner seemed to paralyze Bargeloh. This tended to hold Bargeloh back while Hartwig was on board, but after Hartwig was detached, Bargeloh blossomed.

To illustrate how one can live closely with other men and learn very little, a young Naval Academy officer named Bob Brown came aboard in Pearl before we headed toward the South Pacific. He and I often stood watch in sequence. He was slightly built of quiet demeanor and bright, it all ways a first-rate officer. He was in gunnery. I do not believe that he and I ever talked to each other about ourselves, and very little about our tasks on the ship. Another similar case was that of Charlie Woodman. He and I came aboard together. We had been friendly in college meeting frequently at dinner parties, dances, gatherings, etc. He had always been pleasant, easy to talk to, and, although not a close friend, someone I liked. On board ship, it was no different. In fact, there was perhaps even less contact between us on board ship than at college. I still felt very friendly toward him, but we almost never spoke to each other.

My contacts with Lee Pancake, Charlie Hart, John Caster, Baylor, Herb Silberman, and the others were perhaps even less, although I often talked to Caster on the subject of Naval customs and lore, and to Silberman about New York City where we both grew up.

In sum, it is a simple fact that we were at war. There was serious business at hand, watches to stand, and a lot to do between watches to say nothing of catching some sleep. Socializing, if at all, was minor. Perhaps the major time for personal contact was on watch. It was at such times that I came to know Bargeloh, who used to stand JOD under me.

While on watch, there obviously were many routine matters constantly to tend to, but they became so repetitive that one could often converse at the same time. For example, following the zigzag plan never interrupted the conversation.

Since anti-submarine screening for the Task Force was one of our major functions during ordinary cruising, a very close monitor of the sonar had to be maintained. While standing watch, however, on the wing of the bridge one could hear the "pings" of the sonar in the background reverberating and varying in tone regularly as the sonar operator would swing in 5 degree increments through the forward sector. If the sonar operator were to fail to shift the head between pings, one would immediately be aware of it (due to lack of change of tone). The conversation would instantly stop, and one would step into the pilot house to see what was happening at the sonar. Even more dramatic would be the reaction to a Doppler-shifted echo. Regardless of where one was on the bridge or what one might be doing (conversing or otherwise). A Doppler-shifted echo would cause the OD immediately to check with the sonar. If a second such echo were heard, he would jump to the voice tube to the Captain's emergency cabin (where the Captain slept at sea) and say, "Doppler-shifted echo, Captain! Permission to go to G.Q?" Even without permission, if he was sufficiently convinced, the OD could ring the general alarm on his own initiative and start the anti-submarine attack procedures.

A conversation on watch could easily be interrupted in such a manner and resumed several hours or even days later.

"Steady Bearing Sir!"

When the bearing between two approaching ships is steady, it means that the two ships are on a collision course. For this reason, when another ship comes into view, the Captain will always want to know not only the bearing but also whether the bearing is moving and which way. Therefore, Officers soon learn to check the bearing of any newly sighted ship for motion and to report both the bearing and the motion at the same time. Reporting only the bearing will usually evoke a blast from the Captain. On the other hand, although reporting "Ship approaching, steady bearing sir!" may not stimulate the Captain's anger, it will bring him rapidly out of his emergency cabin.

Comfort and Dangers

During the times we were away, the people at home had a mistaken idea about how uncomfortable we were. Obviously, the war brought severe discomfort to many people in other branches of the services, but with us, provided we did not get hit, it was mainly a lazy summer cruise on a sea of forgetfulness. This was true even for those of us in the Navy who were involved in the battles. Of course, all hell would break loose once in a while for a few minutes, but it was soon over, and nothing exciting would happen again for days on end.

My father, assuming that I was in agony, quoted me in a letter the famous words to Aneas from his father, "Forsan et haec olim meminisse juvabit" ("Someday the memory of even these things will be pleasing to you"). He had no idea that most of the time it was pleasing to me even then.

Of course, the danger was very near at hand. We had recently miraculously escaped, when, at the last minute, the SIMS took our place with the NEOSHO. Many other similar close calls happened later which I will describe. My attitude was that if we were going to "get it", it would be over quickly. I was never going to give up. I was somehow going to fight my way up, but if in the end unable, then so be it and it would be as in Mare Nostrum, infinitely more desirable than in the stinking mud, rats and debris of a shell hole as at Verdun. The only true trauma came from being forced into a dangerous situation needlessly as, for example, at the whim of a superior officer or due to the stupidity of the Command. This happened to me several times later in the war, especially at Okinawa, as I will relate, and it was extremely hard to take.

The Sun

When I was younger, I did not tan much and usually suffered from sunburn during summer. Therefore, in the tropics, I kept covered up. The sun, however, was so intense that after a year or so, I noticed that I had acquired a deep tan all over. Eventually with one exception, I became inured to the sun. The exception was the lips, and whenever we had fueling at sea, or an air strike day, when I would have to be on deck as O.D. for an extended period, my lips would burn.

At first, I did as everyone else and wore sunglasses to protect my eyes from the glare of the reflection on the water. I found, however, that sunglasses exhausted my eyes and I took to protecting them merely by squinting. Also, since I would spend a major part of my time on deck looking through my binoculars (and I mean literally over one-half of the time), and since the UV does not come through the binoculars, I was better off without sun glasses. As I was virtually living with my binoculars on, I found that there was a tremendous difference between very accurately adjusted binoculars and binoculars that were only very slightly out of line. If they are out of line, the eyes can adjust so as to see the image properly with both eyes, but so doing puts a strain on the eye muscles. Soon one gets a headache. If the adjustment is perfect, one can look through them all day long without problem.

The Smells

Odors are hard to describe. There is no scale against which to compare them. Also they change, and if the tiniest nuance is altered, a completely different memory may be brought back. On a U. S. Naval ship there is a kaleidoscope of scents which merge and change in a myriad of various ways. Recently, I had occasion to visit a World War II destroyer, the CASSIN YOUNG, at the Boston National Historical Park. Being aboard ship again brought back vast panoply of aromas I had forgotten. Perhaps the most prominent smell below decks is that of the Navy-issue paint which, although dry, still dominates the atmosphere, combined with the musk of the insulating coverings on certain pipes and bulkheads. Along with these are smells picked up from topside by the ventilating blowers with traces of fumes from oil in the blower bearings and a vestige of the smells of the hatch gaskets, the greases on the hatch dogs, and the dark brown, sticky compound (called monkeyshit) used to seal the cable joints. This potpourri of below decks odors will be found anywhere on the ship often enhanced, depending upon where one is, by whiffs of the mess hall, the crew's dishwashing machine, the disinfectant used for swabbing decks, the linoleum and the wax used on it, the men themselves, their bunks and hanging clothes, the heads, the showers, the soap, etc. Passing along the main deck one will catch a suggestion of the onions or perhaps a rotting potato in the crates, or the cooking smells of the galley as well as the rancid grease in the exhaust duct of the galley blower. The open doors of the machine shop with its pungent cut-metal smell, the ship's laundry and its detergent, the boatswain's locker with its tarred hemp lines, the fuel trunks and raw bunker oil fumes, the fire room and engine room hatches emitting their lube oil and steam smells blended with a touch of ozone from the generators, will each contribute its timpani to the orchestra of smells. In addition, the stack gases which often swirl down along the main deck will provide distinct smells of their own differing markedly depending upon whether the fire rooms are making black smoke (not enough air), white smoke (too much air), or light haze (correct mixture). Then there is the smell of the spilled, dried coffee on the Silex coffee machine in the wardroom, and the cigarette, cigar, and pipe smoke including the dead or smoldering ashes thereof, anywhere on the ship. On the bridge sometimes with the wind dead astern, one may have to stand one's watch choking and weeping in the stack gases which envelope the bridge. Finally, there is the fragrant relief of the spray-laden air of the sea itself, the purifying tonic, the elixir of the sailor's life, the gift of God, and along with it sometimes, a hint of distant land.

Sunrise Sunset

As I mentioned, at sea we always went to GQ one hour before sunrise and remained there until sunrise. We, therefore, watched Homer's "rosy fingers of dawn" come up many hundreds of times. I will write later about the "green flash of dawn", which I witnessed several times. Generally, however, the sunsets were more colorful.

My routine was to go up on the bridge after dinner, light up a cigar, and watch the sun go down. The Task Force would be smoothly cutting through the easy swell. The silhouettes of the ships now turning darker against the western horizon. In the background would be the ever-present noise of the blowers, and the pings of the sonar. Everything else would be quiet except for Pop Barrow singing out the night signals, and the halyards running in the blocks. Then as the sun would drop lower, and the small round clouds turning quite black would stud the sky in an unbroken chain toward the sinking sun, the world would drift into oblivion, and we into our thoughts.

CONVICTED AS A DRAFT DODGER

After leaving the Coral Sea and on the way back to Pearl, we received mail from a tanker. Among my letters was one from the Draft Board in Westport, Conn. written to me in January. It had taken five months to catch up to me. In it, the Draft Board had issued a summons for my arrest for failure to report for selective service and a notification that unless I complied within a short time, I would be convicted as a draft dodger.

I replied that I had no intention whatever of complying with their orders nor would I pay any heed to their conviction. I also told them they were welcome to catch me, if they could, but it might be difficult because I was on the U. S. S. RUSSELL (DD414) somewhere in the Pacific Ocean.

INFLATION SFTRIKES AT NUKUALOFA

During this passage back to Pearl after Coral Sea, the Task Force made a one day stop at Nukualofa, Tongatapu, the principal port of the Tonga Islands.

Afternoon liberty was decreed for the crew, but I asked for permission to go ashore in the morning to check the secret publications. Permission was granted and I asked around among the other Officers if anyone wanted to come along with me. Herb Silberman was the only taker and we set off in the gig at 8:00am.

Nukulalofa was a nice little tropical British town. Everything was clean. The streets along the main square were lined with palm trees reminiscent of Hamilton in Bermuda but on a smaller scale. The people were nicely dressed and clean.

I thought it would be fun to hire some bikes and ride across the island. Herb agreed. We then found a bike rental shop and paid $2.00 each for the day's rental.

RBR 1942 – RBR Personal Collection

All was well and we started out along the main highway leading out of town. For several miles we encountered people coming in town in horse-drawn carts, all dressed up, on their way to market. Invariably, they greeted us with smiles and "Good Morning" etc. As the road continued and narrowed somewhat, we started passing through plantations and small farms. At one point, several little lean razor-backed pigs ran across our track. Herb asked me what kind of animal it was. I could understand why he asked because they were the least pig-like pigs I had ever seen. They were more like half-starved dogs, lean, long-legged, and hairy—but they had the unmistakable cloven hoofs, snout, ears and curly tail of a pig. Herb was incredulous, but became satisfied when I said they were swine.

Farther out in the island, we came to a group of buildings with several teenage girls in red uniforms with white banded sleeves seated out front on a porch. Since it seemed obviously to be a school, we stopped and asked about it. The English headmistress came out, introduced herself and then took us all around explaining what they did and showing us the facilities.

There were two remarkable features. First, the low pressure, calm, friendliness of everyone—not just at the school but everywhere in the town, up and down the road, etc. The other thing became particularly apparent when we went into one of the classrooms filled with pupils. There was a mild fragrance in the air, something like the scent of a gardenia. I asked the Headmistress about it. She took us into the corridor and explained, "These people are remarkably clean and place great stress upon the complete absence of body odor. Therefore, they bathe often and rub onto themselves a lotion the scent of which you smell. You might not think that you yourselves are particularly unclean, but I assure you that to them you would be."

Herb and I were taken aback by this little speech, but it certainly left us with a nice impression of the people.

Later in the morning, Herb and I returned to the town, and looked around. We went into the Law Court briefly, and there, in complete conformity with British custom, the judge and barristers were all wearing traditional robes and wigs.

Eventually we ran out of things to do. I went to the Naval Communications Office to do my business, and we started to return our bikes. By this time, the crews had been on liberty for about one hour. The rental shop owner saw us coming and asked anxiously if we were returning our bikes. We could see a line of sailors waiting at the bike shop, and, since we had had enough biking anyway, we were happy to let him have them.

During the short span of five hours, the rental price for bikes had risen to $20.00 per hour.

3. MIDWAY

PRELIMINARIES

After leaving Tongatapu, the Task Force went immediately to Pearl Harbor, arriving on May 27, 1942. On our way north from Tonga to Hawaii, we began decoding secret messages indicating that large quantities of U.S. Naval and Military materials were being concentrated around Pearl Harbor. Also, virtually upon her arrival in Pearl, the YORKTOWN was put in dry-dock for repairs on a crash basis, and all ships were rapidly provisioned and rearmed. Liberty hours were shortened, and the Captain was called to CincPac headquarters for special briefings. No one was telling us what was up, but it was obvious that something serious was in the wind. This became even more apparent when, after only three days in port, the YORKTOWN was hurriedly sent back to sea together with the ENTERPRISE and HORNET, and all three were sent to positions several hundred miles north of the island of Midway.

The Captain had been very secretive up to this point, but, once we were at sea, due to the fact that I needed to be familiar with the operation order for communications purposes, he explained the situation to me. The thing that amazed me most was that the cryptanalysts at Pearl Harbor had succeeded in breaking the Japanese codes. In fact, this was the reason for the extreme emphasis on secrecy. It was absolutely essential that the Japanese remain unaware that we could decode their messages. The information of immediate interest, however, was that the Japanese were planning an invasion of Midway Island. The cryptanalysts had even been able to find out the exact time they expected to land, and the composition and deployment of their forces. Although it was extremely important to have such information, in this case, it was not particularly reassuring because the numbers of ships the Japanese were bringing and the strength of their forces was so much greater than ours. At this time the U.S. had only five large carriers, of which two, the SARATOGA and the WASP, were not available. Thus, we could muster only the ENTERPRISE, the HORNET, and the recently damaged YORKTOWN. Although, there were six U. S. battleships on the West Coast, Admiral Nimitz chose not to deploy them. Accordingly, the fleet which the U.S. sent out to defend Midway consisted of three carriers, eight cruisers and about 16 destroyers. The Japanese, however, were bringing a strike force of four of their largest fast carriers, two battleships, and a large number of cruisers and destroyers. Their invasion force comprised many transports, a battleship, a large number of additional cruisers, destroyers, and one carrier. In addition, as we had just learned at Coral Sea, their planes could fly rings around ours, attack at higher speeds, and sustain combat at longer range. Also, their torpedoes were vastly superior to ours. This meant that we were both outnumbered and outclassed. While it bore heavily on my mind, I did not mention it to anyone.

RENDEZVOUS OF TASK FORCES 16 AND 17 NORTHEAST OF MIDWAY JUNE 2ND

On June 2, 1942, Task Forces 16 and 17 rendezvoused 250 miles northeast of Midway Island. The ENTERPRISE and HORNET were in Task Force 16 and the YORKTOWN in 17. The RUSSELL was in the screen of Task Force 17. At this time reports came in that the Japanese had attacked U.S. bases in the Aleutians. This was evidently a ruse to draw our forces away from Midway. We made a feint to the North, but soon returned toward Midway. Of course, if we had not broken their codes, the ruse might have worked.

JUNE 3RD. ENEMY INVASION FORCE SIGHTED 700 MILES SW OF MIDWAY.

Search planes sighted the Japanese invasion force on the morning of June 3rd 700 miles southwest of Midway. Army B-17's and Navy PBY's from Hawaii tried to attack this force with little if any result. We on the ships heard only about the sightings.

JUNE 4TH, ENEMY CARRIERS SIGHTED 180 MILES NW OF MIDWAY

Soon after dawn, at 6:00 AM, on June 4th, a large group of enemy airplanes was sighted by a U. S. Navy PBY flying boat, 180 miles northwest of Midway. We heard this report on the radio at the time. From the positions given, the U. S. carriers were about 190 miles from the Japanese strike force, well within the range of the enemy's planes and even within that of our dive bombers and torpedo planes but bordering on the extreme range of our fighters

All airplanes available (about 60) at Midway were immediately sent up either to defend the island or to attack the enemy carriers. Most of these planes were of obsolete design, slow, and no match for the Japanese. Very few returned. When they tried to attack the enemy carriers, they totally failed. The air power at Midway was thus virtually wiped out. The B-17's from Hawaii also tried unsuccessfully to attack the enemy carriers. One unfortunate aspect of these attacks on the enemy carriers was that the pilots did not report the position of the enemy carriers on any of the radio circuits the fleet was monitoring. Admiral Fletcher, therefore, had no updated information about the enemy's position since the time of the 6:00am sighting.

Unlike the attacks of our planes from Midway and Hawaii against the enemy carriers, the Japanese attack on Midway by the planes previously sighted had been devastating, rendering the Island virtually helpless.

8:00—ENTERPRISE AND HORNET LAUNCH AIR STRIKES FIRST—YORKTOWN LATER

Despite the fact that the enemy's attack on Midway had crippled the island, it did one good thing for us. It led the enemy's attention away from our carriers. In fact, the enemy was so intent upon striking the Island that they had not taken care to search thoroughly to the northeast. In addition, their attacking the island brought about further delays required to recover, refuel, and reload their airplanes from the strike against the island. This was fortunate, but it was imperative that we make the most of our luck. So far, there had been no indication that the enemy knew of our presence. Fletcher did not act immediately, however, but waited until around 7:30am to start launching an air strike, and even then, only the ENTERPRISE and HORNET launched. Also, the order for them to proceed was delayed. They did not head off toward the enemy until around 8:00am. In the meantime, an enemy pontoon-type reconnaissance plane (the kind usually carried by the cruisers) had spotted us shortly after 7:30am. In fact, using its own high powered telescopic rangefinder, one of the cruisers of Task Force 16 had been able to see the enemy plane. Due to the fact that the enemy plane was a hydroplane, it had obviously come from one of the enemy's Cruisers and presumably it had reported us to the enemy command. Now we were in for it. Surely, the enemy would recognize the urgency for him to act promptly and send everything he had against us, and, even if our air strikes might hit some, or even all, of his carriers, there would have been no way we could win the battle by simply trading carriers with the enemy.

After this, things went from bad to worse. During the interval between the 6:00am sighting and the dispatch of our first air strike at 8:00am, the enemy fleet had moved radically north, and by the time our planes arrived where they thought the enemy was, he had been able to move far enough away from that location to escape view. As a result, our planes missed him and went on farther south. Then they began to face the prospect of running out of fuel before they could return to their carriers. Some of them went on to Midway where they hoped to take on enough fuel for the return trip. One group, however, decided to risk running out of fuel and have another shot at locating the enemy fleet. This was perhaps one of the most courageous and important decisions of the battle. In the meantime, however, several of the torpedo bomber squadrons from our carriers separately found the enemy and attacked. The Japanese Zeros were much too fast for them and virtually annihilated them. No hits were scored. Only one pilot survived, Ensign George Gay who had the good fortune, while in the water hiding under his aircraft seat cushion, to witness important portions of the battle thereafter.

Back at the U.S. carriers, we were squirming. After the enemy's cruiser scouting plane had sighted us, the urgency of our attacking the enemy carriers with all we could muster was perfectly obvious. Fletcher, however, delayed. Finally, at 9:00am, some three hours after the initial contact report of the enemy carriers, he ordered the YORKTOWN to launch her strike, but still he had no better idea of the enemy's whereabouts than the earlier strike which had missed them. Then miracles started happening. The above mentioned dive bomber group from the ENTERPRISE, which had decided to make a second attempt to find the enemy carriers on its way back toward the ENTERPRISE, sighted the enemy formation at around 10:00am. and immediately moved in for an attack from the southwest. At about the same time, the YORKTOWN's dive bombers on the way out sighted the enemy from the northeast and likewise started an attack. The Japanese, in the interim had finally decided to launch a major strike against our carriers and the first planes of that strike were moving off their flight decks at around 10:20am, at the very moment when the dive bombers of both the ENTERPRISE and the YORKTOWN peeled into their dives and came thundering down onto them. The enemy fighters had been occupied with fending off the attacks of the YORKTOWN's torpedo Squadron 8 (almost completely annihilated as mentioned above) and had not seen the dive bombers coming in overhead, again illustrating the importance of their not having radar. Our simultaneous attacks by both groups in the "nick of time" could not have been done better by a Hollywood film director.

Three of the Japanese carriers were put out of action within minutes. One of their carriers, the HIRYU, escaped to the north. The elimination of these three carriers before their launch was the vital blow of the battle. It eliminated some 250 of the enemy's aircraft. In view of the fact that later that same day, it took less than 50 of the enemy's planes to put the YORKTOWN out of action, it is plain that none of our carriers could have survived the enemy's attack which we had succeeded in stifling in a mere matter of seconds. From the radio circuits on the RUSSELL we had learned about the early sightings. We also surmised that something must have gone wrong with the air attacks from the ENTERPRISE and the HORNET because we had heard nothing from them on the aircraft voice radio circuits at the time they should have reached the enemy. We also were squirming with impatience over Fletcher's apparent inability to see the urgent need to launch long before he did. Then, in the midst of these feelings of anxiety merging into despondency, all of a sudden, we heard scattered snatches of the American aviators whooping it up and hollering as their bombs hit the enemy carrier's flight decks. It was an incredible, unbelievable, fantastic sensation.

YORKTOWN'S OWN AIRPLANES LEAD THE ENEMY TO HER AND SHE SUFFERS A DIVE BOMB ATTACK

The battle was not over yet, however. The HIRYU still remained healthy and highly lethal. Immediately after our dive bombers had made their attack on the three enemy carriers mentioned above, the HIRYU launched planes to tail our returning planes, and having located the YORKTOWN by this method, the HIRYU launched a dive bomber strike against the YORKTOWN.

AIR ATTACK, THE YORKTOWN HIT

The HIRYU's strike came in high and was picked up on radar at about 50,000 yds. The CAP was vectored onto them, and we could see a "merged plot" at about 20,000 yds. Then we could see a long vertical stream of the smoke of a plane going down in flames. No one cheered. We knew better this time. Then with our binoculars we could see an intense dogfight going on at high altitude.

The Task Force increased speed to 25 kts. and the YORKTOWN began turning radically without signal as she had done in Coral Sea, to try to throw the dive bombers off their aim, while we, on the destroyers and cruisers did our best to parallel her.

Everyone had long been at battle stations, helmets and lifejackets on, tense and alert. All hands topside were craning their necks to catch a glimpse of the enemy coming in and to be the first to yell out. One of the cruisers on the other side of the formation spotted them first and we heard the "kerthump" of the first AA burst, followed by the great thunderous rhythm of the large ships opening up. Next, in the general area of the AA bursts we could see the dive bombers, streaking down on the YORKTOWN in steep very fast dives. The RUSSELL opened fire, and, as in Coral Sea, the Captain and I were rushing around from wing to wing of the bridge as the RUSSELL turned to follow the crazy maneuvers of the YORKTOWN, all the while with the guns blazing away, the Captain screaming to be heard above the noise, dust and smoke saturating the air, shell bursts and tracers filling the sky, and the surface of the water speckled with the explosions of spent shells. Suddenly a huge belch of orange flame flared out of the YORKTOWN's open after-hangar deck door. The enemy planes kept coming down and she took another hit, this time near the stack, and then still another further forward.

USS YORKTOWN (CV-5) hit amid anti-aircraft fire – USN Ref: 80-G-414423

Only about seven enemy dive bombers got through the CAP, but at least two good hits were scored. The YORKTOWN went into an aimless turn and then stopped altogether with a thick column of black smoke rising from her.

We who had seen the LEXINGTON at Coral Sea were sick. The YORKTOWN seemed to be in much worse condition than the LEXINGTON had been, and our hopes were dim. The important thing on the YORKTOWN, however, was that the AVGAS had not, in fact, been hit, and the CO^2 system was functioning adequately to protect her from accidental ignition. Actually, the YORKTOWN had not been badly damaged. The problem was that the second hit had landed in the engine room vents. The engine rooms then filled with smoke, making them untenable, and also cutting off the air for the boilers. This rendered the YORKTOWN temporarily immobile. The fire caused by the first bomb was not serious. Most of the smoke that seemed so bad to us out on the screen, was simply coming out of her stack. We could not determine that however, because it was drifting down around the ship before being blown away. It looked as though the whole hangar deck was on fire.

The enemy dive-bombing attack had come in at 12:25 pm, nearly two hours after our important dive bombing of the enemy carriers. On the other hand, since we had just been attacked, it meant that there was no longer any doubt that at least one potent enemy carrier still remained afloat and healthy. Thus, as we circled around the motionless, burning, and very conspicuous YORK-TOWN, we did it with the anxiety and expectation of further attacks.

USS Yorktown (CV-5) dead in the water after being hit by Japanese bombs on 4 June 1942 – USN Ref: 80-G-32301

Gradually, the smoke from the YORKTOWN began to diminish. At around 2:00 pm, the signal for 5 Kts went up. Everyone cheered. The RUSSELL moved up and took her station in the screen. In another few minutes, up went 10 kts, and just in time, enemy torpedo bombers were reported approaching the formation. This information seemed to do something to the YORKTOWN, and, with the smell of battle in her nostrils, she began to surge ahead, now 12kts, then 15, and then 17. Up went several fighters. About this time, we could see the enemy torpedo bombers, thin, sleek; not like ours which have much more body, but lean and dangerous looking. They were visible way out on the port beam, across the formation from us, streaking along very close to the water, coming in like "bats out of hell".

Our fighters did their best, following the enemy right into our own anti-aircraft barrage, but they could not prevent the attack. Out of the dozen or so attackers, at least 8 got through. Two of these planted their torpedoes in the port side of the YORKTOWN somewhat forward of amidships, and then they hedge-hopped over the fo'c'sle of the YORKTOWN and just as quickly disappeared out of the formation. At the moment when the torpedoes hit, the YORKTOWN was in a hard turn to the right. Two immense columns of white spray and smoke shot up from her in rapid succession, as she heeled to port due to the turn.

This took place at 2:48pm. The cruiser ASTORIA ceased fire at 2:54. That a torpedo bombing attack could have been made two- and one-half hours after the dive bombing attack, adequately proved that at least one healthy enemy carrier remained lurking in the distance.

THE ABANDONMENT OF THE YORKTOWN

Exactly what went on at this moment on the YORKTOWN is not clear. It was the subject of much confusion at the time as well as dispute since then. Perhaps the most important fact bearing on the state of mind of those who were aboard her is that the remaining enemy carrier had just been sighted by our search planes. In fact, the contact report of her location came in almost at the same time as the torpedo attack against the YORKTOWN took place. Thus, still another attack could be expected. In fact, anyone who had witnessed the air attack drills of our fleet, knew that the objective in carrier based attacks is to have the dive bombers and the torpedo bombers come in as simultaneously as possible so as to divide the enemy's fighter protection. Thus, immediately after the torpedo attack on the YORKTOWN, everyone expected a massive dive-bombing attack.

(Curiously, none of the historians of the battle has emphasized this point. I can only say from having been there that it was a very real concern of mine and everyone around me. In fact, within the next few minutes, there were two radar reports of "bogies" which sent all ships into air raid alert. What happened and why the men on the YORKTOWN responded the way they did can only be understood properly if this fact is kept in mind.)

I will describe below the technical details relating to the condition of the YORKTOWN and some of the discrepancies between what actually happened and the various official accounts of it, but first, I will describe it as we saw it from the RUSSELL out in the destroyer screen.

USS YORKTOWN (CV-5) *being abandoned by her crew after she was hit by two Japanese Type 91 aerial torpedoes, 4 June 1942. USS BALCH (DD-363) on right* – USN Ref: 80-G-17062

Immediately after the torpedo hits, the YORKTOWN stopped dead in the water and took on a 16 degree list. Very soon thereafter, i.e. within only one or two minutes, we could see men abandoning her, dumping over life rafts, and climbing down ropes. At around 2:55, the RUSSELL closed in to the YORKTOWN'S starboard bow to start picking up the swimmers. The official reports say that an "abandon ship" signal was hoisted at her yard arm. We saw none and none can be seen in any of the contemporaneous photographs. Field acknowledges[22] that before any decision to abandon the YORKTOWN was made, "up forward, men were abandoning ship."

After the RUSSELL arrived near the YORKTOWN, but not being able to come close enough to the men in the water to bring them aboard, the Captain ordered the gig to be lowered, and sent Meltzer, the boatswain's mate 1st class (of Buffalo train station fame) as coxswain. Meltzer had not been long in the boat when a new enemy air raid was reported, and the RUSSELL was ordered to haul back out to the screen. Meltzer was still within hailing distance and we shouted to him to remain, to pick up as many as he could, and that we would be back for him. The RUSSELL then returned to the screen. The RUSSELL's quartermaster log shows that she returned to the screen at 3:14pm[23] Since the ASTORIA was still firing at the departing Japanese torpedo bombers at 2:54pm, and it would have taken the RUSSELL at least 20 minutes simply to go in drop the gig and immediately return, it is clear that the abandonment started almost immediately after the torpedo hits.

After the RUSSELL had returned to the screen, she milled around as before, and, when the air raid proved to have been a false alarm, she went back in again close in to the YORKTOWN's starboard bow.

On arriving near the YORKTOWN, we sighted Meltzer in the gig. He had taken too many men on board at first and had swamped her. Then, he had succeeded in getting most of them to go back into the water, and, miraculously came chugging up to the RUSSELL with the gig virtually awash. I cannot explain it, but somehow the motor kept running. He pulled up on the starboard side, and the gig was hoisted onto the starboard davits.

Then for about ten minutes, we remained only about 200 yds from the YORKTOWN, letting the survivors try to swim to us. Swimming with life jackets in oil covered water is next to impossible. Nothing happened. The men in the water were not very far away but could reach the ship only with great difficulty. Moreover, the few that could manage it were so exhausted and heavy with their life jackets soaked with water and oil, that they could not climb up the cargo nets to come aboard. We tried throwing them heaving lines (having a heavy lead-filled "monkey fist" at the end to facilitate throwing), but if our aim was not extremely accurate, the line would sink before the swimmer could reach it.

Destroyers stand by to pick up survivors as USS YORKTOWN (CV-5) is abandoned during the afternoon of 2 June 1942. (USS RUSSELL 2nd from left) – USN Ref: 80-G-21694

Up on the bridge, the Captain was growing more and more impatient in view of the extreme tension of the threat of a new air attack. I conceived the idea that the rescue could be accelerated by dragging a long line astern of the whaleboat and have it sweep in an arc so that the men in the water could grab onto the rope. As the tension mounted, I decided to suggest it to the Captain. He shrugged and said "Naw!" Evidently, he still had the fate of the gig in mind. After a couple of more tense, motionless minutes, with very few survivors reaching the ship, and everyone growing still more uneasy, I went back to the Captain. "Captain, I'm sure I could drag a rope behind the whaleboat and make it work!" The Captain gave a quick wave of his hand and in irritation, "OK then Godammit, go and see if you can do it."

I was off like a shot down the ladder and, as I passed the radio shack yelled, "Come on you guys, we're going out in the whale boat." At the same time, I sent a deckhand to the Boatswain's locker for a big coil of 1" rope. Next, I jumped into the whaleboat on the port davits with two of the radiomen (Bass and Austin) right behind me.

(This was the first real sign that the radiomen had accepted me as a leader. Not only had there been animosity but also, it must be remembered that we were leaving the ship in a small boat in the middle of battle at a time when the decision of that battle was still in doubt and at the exact moment when another attack from the enemy was expected. We did not know what to expect, and we could clearly foresee the possibility of having to fend our way in the boat with more survivors than she could handle, and to try to reach the islands somehow under holocaust conditions. That these men elected to come with me at that time, gave my morale a great lift.

Meltzer came along in the boat also as coxswain and he brought with him, Stashkovich, the engineer from the gig to run the motor. We were lowered into the water and within about three minutes of the Captain's permission, we were on our way. I firmly secured one end of the rope to the stern cleat of the whaleboat and began paying out the other end while ordering Meltzer to head toward the YORKTOWN. Several survivors nearby grabbed the end of the rope and the force of pulling them along made the rope come taut. Then as I paid out the rope with the swimmers at the end serving as a kind of sea anchor, we started turning the whaleboat in a broad circle to the left. In this way, the rope swept across the water while the swimmers, by the hundreds, grabbed it. Then we turned back toward the RUSSELL and started pulling them slowly in. Within less than ten minutes, we had brought a load of 200 or so swimmers alongside. Cargo nets had been lowered over the railing and by then, deck hands on the nets were waiting to hand-haul the survivors onto the deck. Although the whaleboat had come close to numerous men swimming, I had not taken any of them into the whaleboat. It was faster to pull them alongside instead, and not take the time required to lift them into the boat.

On my first trip out, I took a mental note of how far up the water was on the side of the YORKTOWN. She was listing enough to expose the armor belt on the starboard side, and the place where the armor belt curved down to the water's edge was about 20' forward of the hangar deck door. I could see that she was rolling gently only a few degrees and that her period of roll was reasonably short. This was a good sign because it meant that she was in no danger of capsizing. Also, on the second trip out, I checked the same place on the waterline again, and it was steady. Thus, it was clear that the YORK-TOWN was not sinking.

During the second trip out, as I approached the YORKTOWN, I saw some men in the water waving frantically and yelling that a man was drowning in the water where they were. I told Meltzer to head toward them. At about this same time, we came near the exposed armor belt from which a Naval Commander and his mess attendant had just embarked together in a rubber life raft. As the mess attendant started rowing, the Commander yelled to me to come over and pick them up. I shouted back that a man was drowning, and we would pick the Commander up later if necessary, The Commander then screamed at me, "I order you to come at once and pick us up!" I replied, "I'm picking up people who need to be picked up. I'll be back for you later after everyone who is in danger has been picked up." He then yelled, "What is your name? I demand that you state your name at once!" I said, "I am Russell of the RUSSELL. Do as you like!", and I went on to pick up the man in distress.

This particular man in distress was a peculiar case. Since he appeared to be drowning, I ordered Bass and Austin to bring him aboard the whaleboat. Then, when we pulled him out of the water, he was hard—just like Pop Barrow had been that night in San Diego. I put Bass and Austin to work rubbing him. As far as we could tell, he was unconscious but when the whaleboat came alongside the RUSSELL with the second load of several hundred swimmers on the tow-rope, the man suddenly came to life and sprang up the cargo net like a shot without assistance.

While we were alongside the RUSSELL with everyone on the ship peering down at us from the bridge and gunnels, Meltzer announced that the tow line had become fouled in the propeller and that the boat could not go out again. I saw the line near the propeller, and, in order to assess how bad it was and what might be done, I had Bass hold my legs so I could plunge my head and shoulders into the water at the stern of the whaleboat and take a look at it. Underwater, I could see that the line was not fouled in the propeller but merely caught in the propeller guard. I came up and told Meltzer it was OK and said for him to take her out again. Meltzer said "No!" I said, "What the hell do you mean 'No'? I say it is OK. Take her out!" Meltzer again said "No!" I did not hesitate but putting my right foot into the stern of the boat and driving from it, caught Meltzer under the chin with my left elbow and hurtled him forward so that he landed flat on his back on the engine cover in the midships compartment of the boat. Then I yelled to Stash, the engineer, "All ahead full!" Stash complied and out we went again, with me at the tiller. Next, I told Meltzer to get back up, take the helm, and do what I told him the next time. He complied.

What I did was strictly taboo in the Navy. Annapolis men are supposed to be able to obtain compliance with their orders without any form of physical enforcement or threats. On the other hand, while my manner of obtaining Meltzer's cooperation was a matter of some dismay to the Regular Officers who witnessed it, the effect on the crew was quite the reverse. From that moment on, the attitude of the men on the RUSSELL toward me changed decidedly for the better.

As we headed out on the next trip, I heard the General alarm on the RUSSELL ringing. Obviously, the expected enemy dive bomber attack had been picked up on the radar, and I assumed that the RUSSELL would return again to the screen as she had before. We still had swimmers to gather, however, and so I continued to swing the line around. Then in a few minutes, since the RUSSELL remained dead in the water, it became clear that the alert had been a second false alarm. Thereafter, we made several more trips with the rope until we had cleared up the entire area around the RUSSELL. Then we brought the whaleboat back to the ship, and were hoisted aboard, after which the RUSSELL pulled back out to the screen. The whole operation from the time the Captain gave me the approval, until we were headed back out to the screen the final time, had taken only about 35 minutes.

CHARGED WITH INSUBORDINATION

During this time, while I was performing my act with Meltzer (before an audience of several hundred men peering down from the bridge and the ship's railings), and while I was otherwise pulling men in on the rope, the above mentioned Commander from the YORKTOWN and his mess attendant had paddled their way to the RUSSELL (without so much as a drop of water or oil on them), and were comfortably resting in the Division Commander's cabin. The Captain called me in and told me that the Commander had spoken to him about my refusal to take him into the whaleboat, that the Commander was very upset about it, and was lodging a complaint against me demanding a court martial. Captain Hartwig also seemed to be disturbed. I could not believe it. I simply said, "Let him demand it and good luck to him. He will be the laughingstock of the Navy when I describe him and his mess boy, dry as a bone and primly rowing, while men nearby were drowning." Evidently, the Commander came to realize how ridiculous his charge was because I never heard another word about it.

"ONE OF THEM HARVARD JAPS"

During the evening, the officers from the YORKTOWN were telling us about what happened on the YORKTOWN. This is when we learned that no one knew whether there had been an actual order to abandon ship. Most of them said that all they knew was that everyone was abandoning ship and that they, therefore, did it too.

One of the officers was telling us about how he had been on the foredeck of the YORKTOWN when the enemy torpedo bombers had skimmed over them only about 20 feet up, and just at that moment, the officer had looked directly eye-to-eye with the rear gunner of the Japanese plane—at which point the Japanese gunner had thumbed his nose at the Officer on the YORK-TOWN. Finn Toivonen's voice then came loud and clear from the back of the wardroom, "Hey, Captain, that must have been one of them Harvard Japs!"

"PERMISSION TO COME ABOARD, SIR?"

At another point in the discussion, Bargeloh was telling the assembled group in the wardroom how the first YORKTOWN sailor who had been able to struggle up the cargo net, covered with fuel oil, soaked with sea water and exhausted, brought himself up to his full height, faced aft, saluted the colors and asked, "Permission to come aboard, Sir??"

HIRYU LOCATED AND BOMBED

Although we were aware that three of the enemy's carriers had been successfully dive-bombed, we also knew that another enemy carrier although located was still active and highly dangerous. Therefore, we could not relax. Strangely, the attacks we expected from this other carrier never materialized. In actual fact, the Japanese had plenty of time to do it, but held off in order to rest their crews. Then, at almost exactly 5:00 pm, just as the Japanese were about to launch a major strike against us, the dive bombers from the ENTERPRISE and HORNET found them and completed the job of putting the HIRYU out of action.

Again, we heard snatches of the dive bomber pilot's conversations on the voice radio as they hit the HIRYU and watched her start burning. This was indeed a stirring moment because it meant that we were now very likely in the clear, and the victory was ours. The HORNET and the ENTERPRISE still had 80 some odd healthy aircraft with which we could dominate any of the ships of the enemy fleet, and safely defend Midway.

"THE ENEMY IS STILL COMING ON"

During the afternoon, before the HIRYU had been hit, we remained in air raid alert and kept milling around the YORKTOWN, while several of the other destroyers continued to pick up survivors close aboard her. We continued to be highly concerned about the threat of further air attacks, and, but for this threat, we would have gone alongside the YORKTOWN not only to evacuate her men, but also to perhaps try to start salvage. Instead, nothing was done for the YORKTOWN, and she continued to float peacefully, rocking gently one or two degrees to each side. The official accounts speak about the destroyers going alongside to take off the people[24], raging fires[25], bulkheads bursting, and a list to port of 27 degrees[26]. None of it is true. There were no fires visible. When the salvage crew went back some 40 hours later, they found a small fire in a rag locker forward nothing worth mentioning. No bulkheads were bursting. The list was only 16 degrees as the photographic evidence proves beyond doubt.

Scene on the flight deck of USS Yorktown (CV-5) shortly after she was hit by two Japanese aerial torpedoes 4 June 1942 – USN Ref: 80-G-14834

16 degrees is a good list. Coffee cups will not stay on a table which is tilted 16 degrees, but yet it was not a dangerous list. The short period of her roll, which anyone there at the time could see, meant that she was in no danger of capsizing. Her engine rooms were intact, and five of her eight firerooms were still undamaged. In addition, her emergency generator was operational[27]. Evidently the circuit breakers on the main and secondary panels had been tripped by the impact of the torpedo hits, and, therefore, it appeared that there were no circuits, but this could have been corrected and even jury-rigged circuits could have been established without difficulty. What was needed was to reboard her with as many men as possible, then and there, and try to get her going again. On the other hand, with the threat of imminent air attack, who was going to do it? To get away from her was the safest thing to do. I can attest that we had no desire to see the RUSSELL tie up alongside her just at that moment.

Shortly after 5:00pm, Admiral Spruance sent a message to both Task Forces (Fletcher having relinquished Command following the first attack on the YORKTOWN), saying that, although we had sunk three enemy carriers and possibly the fourth, "the enemy was still coming on". Shortly thereafter, he ordered the Task Forces to retreat at high speed to the east. These messages seemed unrelated to things as we could see them. We had just learned from the snatches over the aviator's voice circuits that a successful attack had been carried out by our aircraft on the one remaining enemy carrier, and things were looking very good for us. Since we had radar and the Japanese did not, we could easily avoid a night action, just as we had done only a few weeks before at Coral Sea, and since we still had two healthy carriers, we would be ready to attack anything they might send in our direction early the next morning.

(In the intervening years there has been much discussion pro and con about whether Spruance's run to the east was justified. The historians of the Navy, however, have "conclusively" established that Spruance's run to the east was fully justified. For example, in "Victory at Midway", Gordon Prange states that it would have been "criminal folly" for Spruance not to have run to the east[28]. Prange and the other historians[29] excuse Spruance's decision on the basis that he did not have enough screening destroyers and, without more screen, could not have risked a night action. Neither Prange, however, nor any of the other historians, when discussing this incident, mention (1) Spruance's dominant position of air power, (2) his radar advantage, (3) the ability of the carriers to steam safely at high speed without a destroyer screen, especially at night.)

THE FINAL STAGES OF MIDWAY

In view of the order to retreat, we headed east leaving the YORKTOWN floating peacefully like a barn in a flood with a lone destroyer, the HUGHES, from our Squadron, to guard her, and with orders to sink her if the enemy showed up. By morning, the U.S. fleet was 150 miles to the east of the YORKTOWN[30], and, since the Japanese were simultaneously retreating in the opposite direction, the two fleets were about 350 miles apart. At this point, Spruance decided to start chasing them. He still had two healthy carriers and 80 operational aircraft (mostly dive bombers), easily enough to destroy the entire enemy fleet. The problem, however, was that he was too far behind. He only caught a few stragglers.

The RUSSELL did not head back west with the fleet at that time, but instead, transferred the YORKTOWN survivors to a cruiser and went further east.

During the Hughes' lonely night vigil with the YORKTOWN, they heard a shot fired from the YORKTOWN, and sent a boat with a party of men over to search her. The party found two wounded men. The irony was that the man who had managed to fire the shot, died. The other man lived. The men returning from the Hughes, however, reported several significant things. First, they reported that the YORKTOWN was in fairly good shape and recommended that an effort be made to salvage her. Second, they found that the communications people in the coding areas of the YORKTOWN and in the briefing rooms of the pilots, had left the safes open and the secret publications strewn around. (We heard this directly from the officers later, but reference is also found in diverse reports.[31]) The Captain of the HUGES reported these things to CincPac.

This shows additionally the state of mind of the men on the YORKTOWN at the time of the abandonment. Communications officers are trained to burn or sink all secret publications upon abandoning ship, and to treat it as a duty paramount to their lives.

THE YORKTOWN AND HAMMANN SINK

Although a fleet tug had tried unsuccessfully to tow the YORKTOWN, it was not until some 40 forty valuable hours had been lost before several destroyers returned to the YORKTOWN with a small salvage party of some 141 officers and men (mostly damage control people). Then, after another 12 hours, an enemy submarine finally located her and fired a spread of torpedoes at her from long range, i.e. over 12,000 yds. At that time, the HAMMANN, of our squadron, was alongside supplying electricity to the salvage crew on the YORKTOWN (thereby indicating that electricians mates and generator engineers had not been chosen to return so as to reactivate the YORKTOWN's still operational emergency generator). The torpedoes were sighted while still a long way out, but although several of the destroyers tried to disturb the run of the torpedoes by firing 5" shells at them, nothing effective could be done to stop them nor could the YORKTOWN and HAMMANN be moved out of the way in time. Both the HAMMANN and the YORKTOWN were hit, and when the HAMMANN sank, several of her depth charges went off further damaging the YORKTOWN. She too then sank early the next morning.

The HAMMANN was the second ship of our Squadron to be sunk. The loss of life, about 50 men, was due mainly to the depth charge explosions. Since we had already gone back to Pearl by that time, we did not witness the final hours of either the YORKTOWN or the HAMMANN.

USS Hammann (DD-412) sinking with stern high, after being torpedoed by Japanese submarine I-168 in the afternoon of 6 June 1942 – USN Ref: 80-G-32320

(I realize that describing the Japanese torpedoes as coming from a long distance, is not the way the Japanese submarine Captain has described it in his account of the sinking of the YORKTOWN[32]. I only repeat here what I heard and recorded immediately after the battle in the wardrooms of other ships of our Squadron, from officers who were there.)

MIDWAY IN RETROSPECT

In the aftermath of Midway, we felt exceedingly grateful. Every man in the fleet was well aware that, if the Japanese had won, America's task of defending Hawaii and keeping the sea lanes to Australia open would have been far more difficult. It would not have been "the end of the world", but we could see a much longer and harder war in store for us if we lost Midway. The victory at Midway, therefore, was received in the fleet with great jubilation.

The vast majority of the men in the fleet, however, had no idea of how strong the Japanese fleet had been, how close we came to defeat, or who really accounted for the things that made the difference between success and failure. The analysis of the critical factors which led to the victory shows that the cryptanalysts were initially highly responsible. There is no question but that our knowledge of the enemy's plans and the information our code breakers were able to gain during the battle were the all-important elements without which victory would have been impossible. The man most responsible for this was Lt. Cdr Joseph J Rochefort, and an associate of his, Lt Cdr.

Wesley Wright. The problem with Rochefort was that he had no interest in Naval protocol, and, in addition, due to his total dedication and concentration, he went without sleep both during the build-up and the battle. By the end he was totally exhausted. As a result, when the admirals at fleet headquarters gathered for an informal command celebration immediately after they knew that victory was assured, and invited him to attend, he showed up with a pipe in his mouth and wearing the same dirty purple and black smoking jacket and carpet slippers he normally wore when breaking codes. Unfortunately, but predictably, the admirals were offended. He was congratulated halfheartedly, but promptly passed over for promotion[33]. I am informed that in 1986, in long retrospect, Commander Rochefort's admirers succeeded in securing for him his much-deserved major award.

Next in line for kudos were the reconnaissance groups, i.e. the air search patrols, and the submarines. They too performed an invaluable service in locating the enemy. Many of the PBY's were shot down. In fact, the PBY which first sighted the Japanese carriers at 6:00am on June 4th, (the key contact report of the entire battle) was shot down by the Japanese very soon after he sent out his report. The submarines also provided important information, especially during the battle.

The air squadrons from Midway Island also made a valiant contribution. Immediately after receipt of the 6:00am contact report, the air squadrons on Midway took off to attack the enemy carriers (exactly as Fletcher too should have done). If Fletcher had launched his planes at the same time, despite the fact that the enemy ships were, at that time, beyond the out-and-back range of his fighters, Fletcher's attacking planes would have hit the enemy simultaneously with the attacks from Midway. This would have divided the enemy's fighter protection and have given all involved a better chance. As it was, the entire air group from Midway was shot down.

The same fate befell the torpedo bombers from the U.S. carriers. They had to make their runs without the simultaneous presence of the dive bombers attacking from overhead. This made it possible for the Japanese Zeros to come down to sea level and concentrate their full force on defending against the U.S. torpedo bombers. All but one was shot down, and he did not make it back to his carrier. No hits were scored.

These abortive attacks by the Midway Island and U.S. carrier-based bombers, however, at least took their toll of the enemy in terms of forcing them to expend their ammunition and energy. Also the final wave of U.S. torpedo bombers had drawn the Japanese fighters down to sea level. Thus, when the U.S. carrier-based dive bombers showed up, at 10:20am to be exact, the Japanese fighters were still in the process of regaining altitude after repelling the torpedo bombers. In addition, the lack of radar on the Japanese ships at the time figured importantly at this point in the battle, because, the Japanese were unaware of the two converging American air groups until a bare few minutes before the attack. Accordingly, the U.S. dive bombers had an unmolested shot at the enemy carriers, which they used to perfection. In the short span of three minutes, three out of the four enemy carriers were burning furiously with the aircraft on their flight decks, loaded with AVGAS and bombs, exploding everywhere. These three minutes were the minutes of destiny. They broke the back of the Japanese fleet, and the men who did it are the immortal heroes of Midway. They were, of course, joined in heroism several hours later by the aircrews who found and sank the lone remaining enemy carrier, the HIRYU.

4. GUADALCANAL TO SANTA CRUZ

"TOO EXPENSIVE TO SEND INTO THE WAR ZONE".

Although Midway had been a victory of major proportions for the United States , the Japanese Navy still held the upper hand. The United States only had four carriers left whereas the Japanese still had at least eight. In addition, the Japanese had the two largest (64,000 ton) and most powerful (9 x 18" guns and 24.5" armor belt) battleships afloat, the Yamato and the Musashi, and were comparable in support ships to the United States. Also, their planes were faster and more maneuverable, and had longer range than ours. Their torpedoes vastly outclassed ours. Therefore, despite the feelings of elation we had after Midway, everyone was aware that we still had a long, tough fight ahead.

On the other hand, regardless of the general bleakness of the prospects, a change for the better seemed to come over the RUSSELL by the time of Midway. We had travelled a long way together and had been through a great deal in a short time. We had survived the crucible of the North Atlantic, the U-boats, and the watch-in-three. We had beheld (and smelled) Pearl Harbor at its worst, before the clean-up, and we had seen the barbed wire on Waikiki. In addition, we had steamed 107 days consecutively, and had suffered the tensions of the close calls at both Coral Sea and Midway. In fact, our "passenger" list had already exceeded 1,500. We had stuck it out, and yet, we felt stronger every day.

The sailors of the RUSSELL had a lot to be proud of, but they were, by this time not just proud, they were both experienced and cocky. In fact, not long after Midway, while we were in Pearl Harbor, a group of RUSSELL sailors went over to the submarine base for recreation. It so happened that a few of the more ignorant submariners had intimated to the RUSSELL sailors that the submarines might be having something to do with the war effort, to which the RUSSELL sailors took sharp exception. The result was an unholy ruckus requiring the assistance of a large contingent of Marine sentries to quell it. Thereafter, the RUSSELL sailors were permanently banned from the sub base, which did not bother them—they did not want to go back there again anyway.

That kind of sticking together ashore, however, is a sign of a good ship. Captain Hartwig was extremely apologetic to the Submarine Command and vowed that proper punishment would be meted out to the guilty parties, but after he came back aboard all he wanted to do was hear more about it and laugh.

I, too, had undergone a personal transformation. It seemed to me as though I had scaled a mountain. I had coped with living in the confined maelstrom of a destroyer through the worst seas a ship will ever encounter. I had tackled a complicated technical job without any previous knowledge of it, and, in my eagerness to absorb it, had cut a swath of enmity across the ship. Beyond this, however, I had mastered the technology of the division, and even if I was not yet a mature officer, we had an excellent working organization. Then, of course, we had been through the first two battles in history between aircraft carriers—and, by the grace of God, we were still alive.

I have mentioned earlier that it was a time to grow up rapidly, but that is an understatement. There is no question but that the nine months between August 1941 and June 1942, not only turned me from a boy into a man, but gave me a degree of confidence which has lasted ever since and which I never could have gained by any other method. It is no wonder, therefore, that, when a new contingent of junior officers came aboard, they encountered a hardened and somewhat arrogant group of veterans.

At that time, two friends of mine in the class behind me at NROTC at Harvard, were assigned to the RUSSELL, i.e. Bill Wesselhoeft and Rog Tatton. In fact, this gave us four Harvard men on board and, after Mr. Pancake was transferred, we became (I believe) the only ship in the fleet with as many Harvard men aboard as Annapolis men (not that it did us any good!). Ridiculous as it now seems in retrospect, however, even though we were only a year apart in college, there was a long trail and a plethora of experience between our respective lives at that point.

This made it hard on them for a while. For example, we who had come out of the North Atlantic felt nothing from the meek motions of the ship encountered in the Pacific, and therefore, like as not on a day that others might consider rough, one of us might be inadvertently smoking a cigar on the windward side of the bridge, and receive a plaintive suggestion from the new officers that the health of the watch could be improved if one were to smoke it on the leeward wing.

Rog Tatton was assigned to me as assistant Communications Officer, and also, since the new contingent of Officers had exceeded the capacity of the Officer's quarters, extra bunks had to be installed in most of

RBR Lt Jg. June 1942 – RBR Personal Collection

the staterooms. The new officers were assigned to double-up, and Rog came in with me as my roommate. Rog was an excellent roommate. He announced when he first came into the room, "I never talk in the room!" I was taken aback somewhat by this at first, but, as time wore on, I began to appreciate the importance of Rog's policy. It insured a total lack of friction. Of course, we spoke often in the wardroom, or on the bridge.

During the first week or so after Midway, we were given recreation and relaxation. It was at this time that my promotion to Lieutenant Junior Grade came in. This promotion after less than one year of active duty, happened, not because of anything I had done, but because of the rapid expansion of the Navy. Even so, it was not well received by senior regular officers who had themselves spent several years as ensigns. Lt. Baylor, about whom I will be writing more presently, was especially hostile.

We remained in the Pearl area for several weeks firing torpedo and gunnery practice. At one point, we were sent out with three other destroyers to meet and escort to Pearl two of the new "fast" battleships, the North Carolina and the Washington. I remember standing on the wing of the bridge next to Crutchfield, the Chief Commissary Steward, when the two Battleships came into sight. Crutchfield was silent for a long time, just looking and thinking. Finally, he said, "Mighty expensive pieces of equipment to send out here in the war zone!"

Crutchfield was, unwittingly, expressing the actual view of the Naval Command about battleships in general even though outwardly, they still supported them. Thus, although the new battleship building program was continued at full speed, the sinkings of the old battleships by the Japanese airplanes at Pearl Harbor, and the sinkings of the British ships the Prince of Wales and Repulse, had so thoroughly demoralized the Naval Command about the battleships that they made very little use of them thereafter. For example, Admiral Nimitz refused to deploy them at Midway when there was a real chance that they might be needed, as has already been mentioned. Later, when battleships were again needed at Guadalcanal, they were not used (with one minor exception), and, in the only battle in the entire war in which battleships figured significantly, i.e. the battle of Surigao Strait, none of the newly built battleships was present, only the old ones. As will become apparent from the descriptions which follow of how the new battleships were actually used, the entire program of constructing some ten new fast battleships during World War II, was a colossal waste. This was obvious at the time to an objective observer such as Crutchfield, but the incredible thing is that no one on the decision-making level seemed capable of admitting it.

THE PHENOMENA OF THE SEA

I will digress now to speak of the phenomena of the sea which I observed during my four years at sea. I have already described the mammoth wave which we encountered off Boston in November 1941, the widely spreading phosphorous in the Gulf of Tehuantepec, and the seven simultaneous rainbows in the Gulf of Papua. Other phenomena were as follows:

The Green Flash of Dawn

I had enjoyed from an early age Kipling's poem, "Mandalay", but I never had any idea what the words "An' the dawn comes up like thunder, outer China 'crost the Bay" meant. Other than this possible hint of it in Kipling's poem, prior to my actually seeing the green flash of dawn, I had never heard or read about it.

I happened onto it through my interest in navigation. All Naval Officers are supposed to know how to do celestial navigation. I used to go up to the chart house in the evening and practice star-sights and computations, while the Navigation Officer was working out the ship's 8:00 o'clock position. The Navigator also was required to provide the Captain with the exact time and bearing of the sunrise, based on the ship's estimated position at sunrise. Having worked out the sunrise problem in the evening, I was curious to see how accurate I had been and watched constantly at dawn GQ. My technique was to align my binoculars (on the alidade) on the exact place where the sun was supposed to come up, and make sure that I was watching at the exact predicted time.

In the Pacific, however, even though the weather may be normally fabulous, there are almost always clouds on the horizon. I watched for literally hundreds of mornings to see the exact moment when the upper tip (called the "upper limb") of the sun would crest the horizon.

All in all, I was at sea for well over 1,000 days trying to catch the sun at the precise moment of breach. The first time I actually saw it was well after a year of trying. I saw a brief blue-green flash. I was amazed and told everyone about it, but no one else had seen it. It only lasts for about 1/10th of a second. It defies logic because instead of being red, it is blue or blue-green. It appears at the exact spot of the breach of the upper limb of the sun. Immediately thereafter, the sun comes up red. I saw it again two more times.

It was with great relief some twenty years later that I read an article in the Scientific American describing it and showing colored photographs of it. In addition, the article provided a technical explanation of it, which I cannot remember at this point.

The Bald Earth

One might not think that a completely cloudless sky is either rare or particularly interesting, I found the opposite on both counts.

A completely cloudless sky is almost never observed at sea. In New England, particularly on a cold day with the northwest wind blowing, a completely cloudless sky can be seen with reasonable frequency, say, a dozen times a year, cloudless that is, as close to the horizon as one can see. With the horizon completely exposed, however, the scope of vision is much expanded, and it is probable that many apparently cloudless days on land would not be really cloudless if the horizon could be seen.

Having noticed from my attempts to observe the sunrise that a clear horizon at dawn is rare, I began looking for it at other times, and found that it is extremely rare, even for brief moments of any day. I saw it only once, on one of the same mornings on which I saw the blue flash. It only lasted a few minutes.

The interesting thing about the totally clear sky and horizon is that one suddenly feels as though sitting on the top of a large round ball. As long as there are clouds (or trees) on the horizon, there is an optical illusion that the world is flat or even concave, but the complete removal of all obstruction reverses the impression.

If the sailors in the time of Columbus could have seen totally cloudless skies, they might not have been so convinced that the world was flat.

The Corposants or Saint Elmo's Fire

Much has been written about the phenomenon of Saint Elmo's Light or "Fire". It occurs when low lying clouds become positively charged. This draws electrons to the top of objects on earth. It can be demonstrated in a laboratory by what is called the "bush" experiment, in which a bush shaped object is made to glow from the accumulation of electrons.

The ancient Greeks wrote about it. Undoubtedly, the various flaming bushes and eerie incidents atop mountains described in the Bible were manifestations of the same phenomenon. It became known as the "corposants" (meaning "holy body"). In addition, since it was often observed on the masts of ships at sea, and Saint Elmo is the Patron Saint of Sailors, they regarded "Saint Elmo's Light", or "Saint Elmo's Fire" as evidence of his presence and therefore, a good omen. In Herman Melville's book "Moby Dick" Ahab takes it as an evil omen and, upon observing it, smashes his quadrant (navigation instrument) on the deck in defiance.

I was both prepared and eager to see the Corposants but had a long wait and even then, only saw them once. (I have since then seen them a number of times on trees).

The night I saw them during the War, we were convoying merchant ships to Guadalcanal around April 1943. The RUSSELL (at that time under the command of Captain McClain) was in charge of the screen and I had the deck. It was a very dark night with heavy low-lying clouds overhead. The Convoy's route brought us to within two miles of a certain island at which point the entire Convoy was to turn 90 degrees to the left. Shortly after the turn and while I was still anxiously checking to make sure that all ships made the turn properly, someone on the bridge yelled, "Hey, look!" I went out on the port wing and the lookout was pointing up. The radar antenna was covered with bunches of blue light, similar in color to phosphorous. It was the Corposants.

While I was looking straight at it, all of a sudden there was a brilliant flash of light. I winced expecting to hear a tremendous clap of thunder, but no noise at all ensued. The effect on my eyes, however, was to leave me totally night-blind for a few minutes. Thereafter, I did not dare look back at the Saint Elmo's Lights because I needed to be able to see, but there were two or three more similar silent bright flashes. I had never before (nor have I since) read about such silent bright flashes accompanying Saint Elmo's Lights, nor have I seen them again when witnessing Saint Elmo's Lights on trees.

Northern Lights

Perhaps the Aurora Borealis is too common to be called a phenomenon. The unexpected part for me was to find that it can be seen on almost any night. Often it is simply a large patch of pale light extending over a large area, resembling the Milky Way, but usually much less visible. Other times, it resembles a high cirrus cloud. At times, I have been looking at what I thought was atmospheric haze only to see it quickly move and change such that it could only be the Northern Lights. It often seems to be colorless, but close inspection usually reveals faint colors. Once in a while it is spectacular. I have never seen the bright colors often depicted in stories, but I did see a very brilliant display one night in the north Atlantic, in which a single strong vertical shaft of light, far brighter than the shaft of a searchlight could be, extended from about 45 degrees down to near the horizon.

The Animals of the Sea

There are many different types of flying fish, and these too vary depending upon where one is. For example, I remember that going north from Hawaii about 500 miles, the flying fish became large (i.e.., 12" to 16" long) and of brownish hue, whereas further south they were smaller (i.e., 6" to 8" long) and were dark steel blue (all have white bellies, of course). There also were different types of flying fish. For example, near the Equator, one will see little flying squids. Thor Heyerdahl observed them on the Kon-Tiki expedition. They are strange looking things. They do not have wings but instead have an enlarged portion at each end. I called them "flying dumb bells". Although I never had one in my hand to examine, I concluded that they were squids from the fact that, looking down on them from the bridge of the ship as they flew away from the ship in fright, they left a trail of black in the water. They were not good enough fliers to be blown up onto our decks. Another strange flying fish had fan-shaped wings and was small, i.e., about 2" in diameter. I called them "flying fans". Both the "fans" and the "dumb bells" shook their wings in their attempt to fly. I say shook because it describes what they did better than to say flap. The other, more conventional types of flying fish do not flap or shake their wings. They wiggle their tails laterally for propulsion as long as their tails remain in contact with the water, but once they are fully airborne, they only glide. Some have only one large pair of wings. Others have two sets of wings arranged fore and aft on the same level.

One of the most pleasing events at sea is when a school of porpoises decides to swim along with the ship for a while, usually far from land. They are so graceful and seem to be smiling perpetually. I always felt that they were somehow conveying good luck. Porpoises will rarely accompany a ship travelling over 20 kts., but one time a small dark-colored porpoise stayed with us at 27 kts. for a few minutes.

We often saw whale spouts in the distance, but since they swam very slowly and we were always on the move, we had little opportunity to observe the whales.

Although there is a great deal of interest in and talk about sharks, I can remember seeing only one in four years at sea. It happened during the recovery of a towed target after a target practice offshore near Pearl Harbor. One of the men handling the lines in the whale boat lost his balance and fell overboard. He was very quickly recovered, and there was no danger, but either by coincidence or by the cleverness of his pilot fish, within a few seconds, a very large white shark swam past the whale boat in a leisurely manner sending chills up the spines of us observers. Thus, although sharks were undoubtedly around, we did not see enough of them to determine what kinds populated what areas of the ocean.

The birds too vary depending upon where one is. The Albatross or "goony bird" is always in evidence when far from land. He is an amazing flier but very rarely flaps his wings. His flight is almost all gliding. In the upper latitudes, one sometimes sees the Stormy Petrel. Herring and Blackbacked Gulls will follow quite a way from land but when one sees Terns and the smaller gulls one knows that land is near at hand.

BATTLE OF SAVO ISLAND (AUGUST 9, 1942)

There was a brief lull after Midway but soon the Japanese started moving more troops and materials down the island chain in the Southwest Pacific toward Australia, and to intercept these, the U.S. took the offensive at Guadalcanal. The invasion of Guadalcanal started on August 7, 1942, and while the unloading of troops and supplies was still in progress, on the night of August 9th three Japanese heavy cruisers and three destroyers made a night attack on the much larger U.S. Naval Task Force protecting the landing. The U.S. forces included six heavy cruisers, two light cruisers, and eight destroyers. Admiral Fletcher was in charge of the carrier support group, but, to the great dismay of the cruiser group, he pulled away to the South on August 8th taking with him the North Carolina, the one battleship in the area. Fletcher has been criticized for withdrawing the carrier support[34] but not for his failure to send the battleship North Carolina to help the cruisers. The North Carolina was virtually useless with the carriers, whereas her presence with the cruisers would have made a tremendous difference.

As the enemy approached from the northwest, our cruisers (including the Australian cruiser, Canberra) were deployed in two groups patrolling inside the respective entrances to the bay. One destroyer was placed on patrol outside of each entrance. The problem with this disposition was that it did not permit our cruisers to make the most of their radar advantage. The two destroyers on the outer patrol had only SC-1 radars (the same radar as we had on the RUSSELL) which could not pick up ships reliably at over 10,000 yds., whereas a cruiser such as the CHICAGO, which by then had had radar for nearly two years[35] could have picked them up at over 30,000 yds. With our cruisers in the bay, however, the Japanese were able to sneak up in the radar "shadow" of Savo Island, and time their approach so as to dodge unnoticed behind the patrolling destroyers. Also, they came in close to Savo Island so as to confuse the radar picture. As a result, the American forces were taken completely by surprise. The enemy first capped the "T" on the southern group sinking the CANBERRA and damaging the CHICAGO. Then, they split and both crossed the "L" under the sterns of the northern group, sinking the QUINCY, ASTORIA, and VINCENNES. This was undoubtedly the most shocking defeat the U.S. Naval forces had ever experienced.

(Although the historians have discussed it at length, they have been inexplicably lenient with the Navy over the failure to use the one battleship in the area at the time. None of the histories cited in the Appendix of this book hints at it)

The invasion forces at Guadalcanal, after the defeat of our cruisers, could very likely have been totally destroyed if the Japanese had pressed their advantage. The enemy were not aware, however, that Fletcher with his carriers and battleship had withdrawn. Nor did they appreciate how totally they had defeated our remaining Naval protection. As a result, most of our men and equipment were successfully landed on Guadalcanal. Soon, the Marines were able to capture the airstrip. Then, although we could not prevent the enemy ships from bombarding at night or from landing troops on the northern end of the island, we were able to muster at least some air protection during the daytime even in the absence of Fletcher's Carriers.

BATTLE OF STUART ISLANDS (AUGUST 24, 1942)

In response to the urgent demands of the Marines on the island, the Carriers ENTERPRISE and SARATOGA were finally sent to their aid, and on August 24, 1942, they fought a battle northeast of Guadalcanal called the Battle of the Stuart Islands (Eastern Solomons). In this battle, the U.S. forces fared somewhat better, but the Enterprise was damaged and forced to return to Pearl Harbor for repairs. This left only the SARATOGA to provide air protection in the Coral Sea—Solomons area.

SITUATION TENSE WHEN HORNET JOINS

After our defeat at Savo Island and the temporary loss of the ENTERPRISE at Stuart Islands, the U.S. Naval protection in the South Pacific became both tentative and weak. In an attempt to fill the gap, the Carriers HORNET and WASP were being rushed to the scene, but for several weeks after the battle of the Stuart Islands, the "fort" in the Southwest Pacific was held only by the SARATOGA. At that time, the RUSSELL was in the HORNET's Task Force approaching Guadalcanal.

(6) SARATOGA TORPEDOED

After the HORNET arrived, the situation stabilized somewhat, but not long thereafter, we received messages from the shore-based radio direction finders that enemy submarines were congregating in the Coral Sea and in the approaches to Guadalcanal. Admiral Ghormely became area Naval Commander and after Fletcher had been criticized for his failure to support Guadalcanal, Ghormely adopted a policy of keeping the carriers at sea near enough to Guadalcanal to provide air support during daytime. The problem with this was that, in order for the sonars of the destroyers to be able to echo-range, which could not be done above 15 kts, and the command's notion that the carriers had to be screened by destroyers (rather than steaming at high speed, which they could easily do), the carrier Task Forces were limited to steaming at 15 kts. Also, since sonar in the South Pacific often had an effective range of less than 1000 yds, and the destroyers were spaced 3000 yds apart, the chance of detecting a submarine before he could fire a torpedo at the carrier was none too good, say less than 50%. As a result, the carriers were quite vulnerable. In my 1945 "diary" I wrote the following:

"One morning while I was in the Wardroom eating my two 'ripe' fried eggs with the red centers, the general alarm sounded. I was on the ladder in an instant, with people scrambling up ahead of me and pushing behind, amidst the noises of the blowers cutting off, watertight hatches slamming shut, ventilator and steam valves making a racket, gun mounts slewing out, ammunition hoists rattling and all of the other noises that you hear vaguely in the excitement. Coming onto the bridge, I heard someone yell, "There it goes," and as I looked, sure enough, there was a thin green line running diagonally across our bow. It was heading for the SARATOGA. We had warned her on the TBS voice circuit, and she was in a tight turn. But she was slow and heavy; we did not have much faith in her ability to dodge anything. We turned to the right and commenced running down the torpedo wake in hopes of finding the submarine, but rejoined after a fruitless search of an hour or two. (Later in the war, when there were more destroyers, we would have searched the area for at least a day before giving up.) When we got back, the old "SARA" was limping along at five knots. The torpedo had struck one of her screws."

WASP SUNK, NORTH CAROLINA, O'BRIEN TORPEDOED (SEPTEMBER 15th)

Next, after the SARATOGA, the WASP was torpedoed. She had just joined up with the HORNET, and we were steaming along in two groups, one with the WASP and the other with the HORNET about four miles apart.

In accordance with the usual practice during flight operations at the time, the WASP had separated from her Task Force screened by two destroyers, to launch aircraft, and was just returning when the first torpedo hit her. We went rapidly to GQ and I witnessed the explosion of the second torpedo. Immediately thereafter, with the RUSSELL in a hard right turn, I went onto the starboard wing and saw a torpedo hit the port side of the battleship NORTH CAROLINA. Next, the Task Force put on flank speed (25 kts.) to clear the area. I looked around, and the destroyer O'BRIEN (next behind us in the screen) was totally enveloped in a huge explosion. I thought she had been blown to bits, but when I looked back a moment later, there she was again as if nothing had happened. Actually, a torpedo had hit her within a few feet of her bow and had made a large hole below the anchor from the cutwater back to about 15'. (She was actually in no danger of sinking at that time and returned to Noumea under her own steam. Later on, the engineers at Noumea thought that the way to make her seaworthy for the trip back to the States was to pour concrete into her bilge. This created a rigid part in the middle of the ship which, due to its incompatibility with the surrounding more flexible steel stringers and plates, cause her plates to crack when she was at sea. As a result, when she was only part way home, she broke up and sank.)

The NORTH CAROLINA was in good shape. Despite her damage, she charged ahead at 27 kts. like a wounded boar, with fuel oil gushing out of her ruptured bunkers.

The WASP did not fare as well. Her hits developed into a fire which could not be controlled, and she sank.

Apart from the fact that the burning of the WASP showed again that our fire-fighting techniques were deficient, the sinking of the WASP and the previous torpedoing of the SARATOGA, disclosed a more fundamental problem, namely that for certain types of operations the Fleet was being needlessly tied to, and held down, by the destroyers. The sonars of the destroyers were only marginally effective above speeds of 10kts. and the upper limit was 15kts. Thus, although the destroyer's sonar screens were at least partially effective for slow speed operations such as fueling at sea which had to be performed at slow speed, at other times when the Task Force was steaming at 15kts, the destroyers had only about a 50% chance of detecting a submarine soon enough to prevent a torpedo attack. There is no question but that the large ships would have been safer steaming at high speed without the destroyers. Instead, the NORTH CAROLINA, the SARATOGA and the WASP were all torpedoed due to being tied down to the destroyer screen.

Battle of Santa Cruz Island. Task Force 17 on maneuvers with USS HORNET (CV-12) on left – USN Ref: 80-G-304510

The only historian who so much as hints at this is Blair. He does not say it directly, but he accomplishes much the same thing by criticizing the U.S. submarines for being afraid of the Japanese destroyer screens[36]. This is equivalent to acknowledging that, at the time, destroyers had little chance of sinking submarines and that a destroyer screen could be penetrated by an aggressively commanded submarine. Blair also provides support in a different and even more convincing way. He describes how the U.S. Submarine Command tried without success for the first three years of the war to make effective submarine attacks on the major Japanese fleet units. The failure was not attributed to the effectiveness of the screening of the enemy destroyers, but simply to the fact that the enemy fleet units moved too fast. These lessons learned in the Submarine Command, however, if known in the surface fleet, were not given credence. Although it may seem unbelievable now in long retrospect, it is a fact that the U.S. Surface Fleet Command was unable to learn either from these experiences of the submarines or from the well-known relative safety of the British "Queens", that it would have been far better to capitalize on the high speed capabilities of the large ships to minimize the hazard of submarine attack than to slow down the carriers to the destroyer's maximum sonar speed of 15 kts, at which speed the carriers were vulnerable to submarine attack. In addition, this failure to accurately evaluate the relative merits of safe high speed carrier operation without the destroyers versus vulnerable slow speed operation with a destroyer screen, did not merely result in the losses just described due to the enemy submarine action, but it also was the cause of costly command errors throughout the war. Fletcher's failure to attack at night between the halves of Coral Sea was justified by the command on the mistaken notion that he could not afford to weaken his destroyer screen. Spruance's run to the east at Midway was justified on the ground that he had an insufficient destroyer screen. This excuse for serious command error continued to be used later in the war, especially at Santa Cruz (October 24, 1942), and Philippine Sea (June 19, 1944), as will be described below. Remarkably, despite the clear technical fact that destroyer screens steaming at 15 kts were nowhere near as effective for anti-submarine protection as steaming at high speed, the Naval Command never acknowledged it either then or since, and, as far as this author is aware, no one else has brought this major omission to light.

PRELIMINARIES TO 2ND BATTLE OF SAVO ISLAND (sometimes referred to as the battle of CAPE ESPERANCE)

The sinking of the WASP and the disabling of the SARATOGA left only the HORNET. The enemy now started air raids from the Shortlands during the day and shelling the airfield at Guadalcanal as well as landing supplies at night. Guadalcanal was not a particularly important island in and of itself, but it became a focal point for the concentration of energy by both sides.

On October 11th, the HORNET Task Force was moved up to help defend against an attack by enemy cruisers which were reported approaching Guadalcanal from the north. During the day, the HORNET reached a position on the southwest side of Guadalcanal and began sending air strikes against the Japanese on the island and air searches to the north to locate the enemy attack force.

THE RUSSELL DEMONSTRATES HER PLANE-GUARD TECHNIQUES

This was the day on which the RUSSELL first established her reputation as the premier plane-guard destroyer of the fleet. The HORNET was continuously maneuvering to launch and recover aircraft for most of the day. These maneuvers required repeatedly turning into the wind to launch and recover and then reversing course to regain position. Our procedure was to drop back during the motion in one direction so as to be somewhat ahead of station when the HORNET reversed. Then, in the opposite direction, we would drop back again so as to be ahead of station when the HORNET turned again. In this way, relative to the rest of the Task Force, we were continuously steaming slower by about 1/2 kt. all day. Since these maneuvers were being done at high speed (i.e., 27 kts.), the difference in fuel consumption was significant.

In addition, we had become proficient in picking men up out of the water. All during the episodes previously described, there had been frequent ditchings of aircraft. They happened more often on strike days, when the aircraft would be fully loaded with both bombs and fuel. Under such conditions, the aircraft would move forward, leave the flight deck and lose altitude until they could pull in their landing gear, and with flaps down for maximum lift, try to gain enough altitude to permit pulling up the flaps, which was necessary before the aircraft could gain sufficient speed to become safely air-borne. Sometimes this process would take as much as ten minutes with the plane rising slowly and then skimming dangerously close to the water after pulling up the flaps. Ditchings on take-off occurred half-a-dozen times every strike day, and once or twice a week on ordinary days. Of course, ditchings also occurred when the aircraft returned from striking the enemy. Damaged aircraft were often ordered to ditch in order to avoid the risk of accident during landing. At other times, planes simply missed their landings or had some kind of engine failure on takeoff. Anyway, for many reasons, we were constantly having to pick up downed aviators.

I have already mentioned that bringing a survivor swimming in a life jacket, quickly to a ship is not easy. The Captain became quite good at stopping the ship within 50' of a survivor, but how to bring the survivor in from there was the problem. Lowering the boat was too slow, and further time would be lost because the boat would have to be picked up. Heaving lines (i.e., lines with a lead ball in a pouch attached to the end of the line called a "monkeyfist") could be easily thrown 50', but such lines sink too fast and there is also a danger of hitting the survivor on the head with the lead ball. In addition, the survivor might be too weak to be pulled to the ship with much force. In our first attempts to solve the problem, we made up heaving lines with a doughnut shaped pouch at the end that was light enough to float. This helped, but the best way, which was finally adopted as standard procedure, was to send out a naked, high speed swimmer with flippers on and with a line tied around his waist. By this method, as soon as the bow was about 50' to 75' from the survivor, the swimmer would dive from the bow of the ship and swim at high speed to him. Then, with the swimmer hanging firmly onto the survivor, the men on deck would pull both swimmer and the survivor rapidly to a cargo net where other men would be waiting to lift them both onto the deck. By this method, we were able to cut the time between aircraft splash-down and rescue, to less than one minute on occasion, and often to less than three minutes. Again, this resulted in fuel saving by reducing the time at high speed required for catching up to the Task Force.

CONCLUSION OF 2ND SAVO ISLAND BATTLE (SOMETIMES REFERRED TO AS THE BATTLE OF CAPE ESPERANCE)

During the day on October 11, 1942, the HORNET's search planes were unable to sight the enemy strike force, but the HORNET, being our only carrier in the area at the time, was nevertheless ordered to retire to the south taking along with her the only battleship in the area, while a cruiser Task Force was sent in to defend the forces on the island against the expected enemy Naval attack.

The enemy appeared around midnight and a second night battle was fought. This time, the U.S. heavy cruiser, HELENA taking station to the seaward of Savo Island, made radar contact at 30,000 yds.[37], and, thereby, was able to secure the advantage of surprise. Several instances of confusion on both sides thereafter, however, resulted in costly cease fires, and losses. In fact, the U.S. destroyer DUNCAN was sunk. Also, Cruiser BOISE was badly damaged but she managed to escape. The American fire control radar, however, proved to be highly effective. At least one Japanese cruiser was sunk and other enemy ships were damaged. Not only was this a victory for the U.S., but it confirmed that we were superior to the Japanese in a night battle in the open sea where we could make the most of our radar advantage. Again, however, the historians have been lenient with the Navy for leaving their lone battleship in the area with the carrier where the prospect of her being used was virtually nil, whereas her presence with the cruisers would have made a major difference.

THE BATTLE OF SANTA CRUZ (OCTOBER 24, 1942)

Build-up

After the 2nd Savo Island battle, the Japanese began moving ships and planes into Guadalcanal, bombarding the U.S. held airfield, and landing reinforcements more-or-less at will. The situation was becoming critical for the U.S. Marines on the island, and on about October 20th, a large U.S. Convoy of reinforcements was sent from Espiritu Santo.

The RUSSELL damages a sub

It was at this time that we made our one and only successful submarine depth charge attack. During all of these operations, the destroyers were making sonar contact with submarines (or suspected submarines) three or four times daily. When a contact was reported, the Task Force would immediately turn away and the destroyer which made the contact would pursue it initially to determine whether it was really a sub and, if so, to attack and remain in the area for an hour or so trying to score a depth charge hit on the sub. As I have explained, there was virtually no chance of actually sinking a sub by the astern form of depth charge attack. The principal usefulness of these attacks was to force the sub to submerge below periscope depth and thereby effectively to prevent the sub from firing its torpedoes. (Acoustic homing torpedoes were not yet available at that time.)

On this occasion, the RUSSELL reported a submarine contact and separated from the Task Force to make a depth charge attack. After the initial attack, which was negative, we lost contact with the sub for about 20 minutes. After regaining contact, we attacked again, still without results, but on this second attack the sonar echoes disappeared at about 800 yds. range. This indicated that the sub had gone to extreme depth.

Thereafter, when we regained contact with the sub a third time, we decided to set a standard pattern at a depth of 300′ plus one charge to be fired later by a K-gun to the side at the maximum depth of 600′. This latter charge was so deep that, when it went off, although we could hear it, no disturbance came to the surface. After the third attack, we were still trying to regain contact with the sub, when the Task Force Commander ordered us to rejoin the Task Force. Not long afterward, however, search planes from the Task Force reported a slowly moving oil slick in the area where we just had been. This slick was obviously emanating from a damaged sub. Long range air search planes were then called in from Espiritu Santo, the slick was followed for several days. The sub eventually had to surface, and it was sunk by air attack.

As far as I am aware, the RUSSELL never received any credit, or even an "assist", for this sinking.[38]

Preliminaries

The fact that a large U.S. convoy had been sent from Espiritu Santo to Guadalcanal stimulated increased enemy activity, and we began receiving reports from U.S. submarines that a Japanese carrier force was heading south from Truk Island. The ENTERPRISE rejoined the HORNET and we steamed north to meet them on the western side of the Santa Cruz Islands.

In my 1945 "diary", I wrote as follows:

"On the day before the battle, an enemy unit was reported, and an air strike was sent out, but contact was not made. That evening, following an attack scare at dusk, about thirty of our fighters were forced to make night landings on the carriers. It created a very tense moment, steaming along at night in submarine infested waters with our masthead lights burning and watching untrained pilots trying to make night landings. A number of them were, in fact, lost. After combing the water for several hours searching for them, the Task Force turned north and steamed towards the enemy fleet throughout the night."

The Taming of Chief Nally

At this point in the battle, a brief but memorable interlude took place. I have mentioned Schwarz, the Quartermaster striker, in several places in this narrative. I have not, however, mentioned Schwarz's boss, Chief Quartermaster Nally. Nally was a slightly built, lean, and cocky "fox-terrier" type of sailor. He had sharp features and a small neatly clipped mustache. Nally was imbued with a strong sense of his own importance. He was precise and generally scornful of anyone beneath him as well as of most of those above him. Nally was particularly curt with Schwarz at all times, not only because contumely was Nally's natural way, but also because a Quartermaster striker was about as low a form of humanity as one could find in Nally's sphere. Now it happened that, after we had turned north toward the enemy, we received a message indicating that the enemy force was large, that it was headed toward us at high speed, and that its position was only about 200 miles away. A simple calculation revealed that we would be engaged in a head-to-head night surface action with the enemy fleet by midnight. Everyone immediately grew tense. A few people froze. Some glanced around to see how their neighbors were reacting, and others put on dry grins or feigned nonchalance. The interlude to which I refer took place at this moment of realization that we were running slam into a night battle. As we were standing around immediately after receiving these messages, I observed Nally's hands fidgeting, nervously trying to pull a pack of cigarettes out of his pants pocket. He finally succeeded, dropped one on the floor, picked it up, put it in his mouth, and then handing the pack to Schwarz said, "Hey kid, have a cigarette!"

Very soon thereafter another message came in correcting the position of the enemy to 500 miles away from us instead of 200, i.e., well clear of night surface action range. Although this meant that we were headed for an aircraft carrier battle the next day, at least it relieved the tension enough for Nally to resume his normal truculence.

The Battle

After steaming toward the enemy all night, air searches were sent out at dawn. About an hour and a half later, the enemy was sighted within striking range to the northwest and an air strike was launched. The day was a beautiful tropical day with the sun beaming down upon an easy rolling, blue ocean. The RUSSELL had gone in to plane guard, and it was not long before the air attack force, heavily laden with bombs and torpedoes was winging its way towards the enemy.

The Task Force went into anti-aircraft formation, a close circle around the carrier, and commenced steaming back and forth awaiting developments. We had now been through two historic carrier battles, Coral Sea and Midway, and were familiar with the feelings of suspense and the knowledge of what might happen. We could well remember the great numbers of exhausted, oil soaked, and begrimed men we had picked up out of the water from both the LEXINGTON and the YORKTOWN, and how they had sat dejectedly in crowds on our cramped decks thinking of their buddies who had gone down, and of their little personal valuables still in their lockers, but there to remain forever under 2,000 fathoms of water. We also remembered the enemy planes streaking in, bursting into flames, but pressing home, anyway. These images filled our minds as we awaited the outcome of the day.

At around 10 o'clock, before our attack planes had returned, a large group of enemy planes located us. The ENTERPRISE and HORNET were in two separate groups at this time about ten miles apart, but plainly within sight of each other. This was a disadvantage, however, for the HORNET because the officer controlling the disposition of the fighters was on the ENTERPRISE and owing to our distance from her at the time, the HORNET did not receive the full benefit of the fighter protection.

In a few minutes the enemy was reported approaching our formation. We strained our eyes to locate them, but the small white clouds which might otherwise have been beautiful, were in the way. Suddenly a single shot rang out clear and alone. The SAN DIEGO had fired. Then we saw the burst, and near it was an enemy plane coming down in a steep dive on the HORNET. Then the cataclysm started. My job was to watch the carrier's radical maneuvers and keep us parallel to her. By this time, the Captain was letting me keep the con (i.e., direct the helm), so that he could pay more attention to directing the RUSSELL's anti-aircraft fire against the enemy attack, which attack, during this battle, was probably their fiercest of the war. Since I was extremely busy, I only remember bits of impression; enemy dive bombers coming down in numbers; torpedo planes careening in from all directions; the terrific, rhythmic din of the anti-aircraft guns; and the enemy planes crashing into the carrier or into the water near her. I remember once noticing that the water everywhere was covered with splashes and explosions of spent anti-aircraft shells. Another time, I caught a glimpse of an enemy torpedo plane which exploded just ahead of us, leaving a great burning patch of wreckage for us to pass through.

This was when Lee Pancake was killed. Before the battle he had been transferred to the Squadron Commander's staff on the Morris. One of the enemy torpedo planes which succeeded in penetrating the flak, passed over the MORRIS, and let go a burst of machine gun fire at her. Lee was standing in the open on the lookout platform. One of the bullets drilled him clean through the chin and out the back of his head. It was a freak hit. No one else on the MORRIS was hurt. We all liked Lee and knew his wife well. We were desolate at the news of his death.

Within ten minutes, this initial attack was over, and we could see that the HORNET was seriously damaged. She circled aimlessly for a few moments and then stopped completely, burning both amidships and forward. We formed around her in a protective circle. A call went out for two destroyers to come alongside and help her fight the fires. The RUSSELL was the nearest and went alongside taking position on the HORNET's port bow to fight the forward fire. The high over-hang of the carrier's flight deck crashed into the RUSSELL's bridge and did considerable superficial damage.

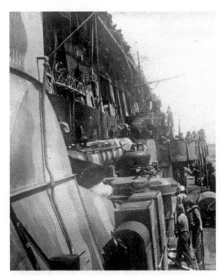

USS HORNET (CV-12) *seen from USS* RUSSELL (DD-414) USN *Ref*: 80-G-34106

The fire was in a forward storeroom on the port side and was spreading dangerously near to the 5" gunpowder magazine. All water mains on the carrier had been disabled and they were trying to fight this fire by bucket brigade. As soon as we could, we passed fire hoses from the RUSSELL over to them and began pumping water. Right next to the RUSSELL's bridge was a hawser hole on the HORNET, which led into the burning compartment and out of which smoke and flames were pouring. Terrill, the signalman, and I got a hose and as the ship would roll in against the HORNET, we would push the hose into this hole and spray it around. We were beginning to get the fire under control when suddenly, someone yelled, "Hit the deck", but before I was able to do so there was the loud roar of an airplane pulling out of a dive and scattered machine gun fire. An enemy plane had made a dive-bombing run on the carrier, but fortunately, for the RUSSELL, his bomb landed short on the starboard side. This was probably the time when the RUSSELL received the bullet holes in her stack. After this, having ascertained that the fire on the carrier was reasonably under control and after several orders from the Admiral to "haul out", because we were under attack, Captain Hartwig gave the order to resume our station in the screen.

In the meantime, the ENTERPRISE in the other Task Force had survived a severe attack. At the time we pulled away from the HORNET we could just barely make out the ENTERPRISE on the horizon, and the sky above her was speckled with the black puffs of anti-aircraft fire. The ENTERPRISE group had the benefit of the tremendous anti-aircraft batteries of the battleship SOUTH DAKOTA and also just prior to the attack, they had encountered a very well-placed local rainstorm. These things, coupled with the Fighter Director being on board the ENTERPRISE, gave her an advantage over our group and she managed to get through unscathed.

Battle of Santa Cruz Island. USS ENTERPRISE (CV-6) maneuvering with destroyers –
USN Ref 80-G-304520

It was not long before our own air strikes started to come back. The ENTER-
PRISE took on board as many of the HORNET's planes as she could and then
began pushing planes overboard to make room for the remainder. Some of
the returning planes had to make water landings and it was while picking up
one of these pilots that the PORTER, a destroyer in the other group, was sunk
by an enemy submarine which had been lurking in the vicinity (illustrating
another reason why the quickness of the pick-up procedure was so important).

Our Task Force remained in the circular formation around the HORNET, with
the destroyers patrolling assigned sectors. In our sector, we kept passing an
inflated life raft. Finally, Captain Hartwig told me to maneuver the ship to
pick it up. I was delighted to have a chance to "try my hand" at ship handling
and brought the RUSSELL around into the wind with the life raft dead ahead.
Just as I was slowing to 1/3 speed and getting my grapnel crew ready on the
fo'c'sle, one of the lookouts aft sang out, "Enemy torpedo planes".

My "moment" disappeared in a flash, and with all engines ahead full, we pivoted back into firing position.

In another few seconds, about a dozen enemy torpedo planes darted in
towards the stricken HORNET. One of the cruisers, I think it was the
NORTHHAMPTON, was towing the HORNET at the time, and tried to break
off. But the enemy raid was over before they could disengage. This time, the

enemy succeeded in putting a torpedo into the HORNET to permanently disable her engines.

After this second raid, we were again called alongside the HORNET, to take off the wounded. We took on board 109 stretcher cases, badly mutilated men.

USS RUSSELL (DDD-414) *alongside* USS HORNET (CV-12) – USN *Ref:* 80-G-304514

After that, we took on aviators and other key personnel. It was at this time that a second strafing attack occurred killing one of the men from the HORNET. It was another freak hit. He was in a group of men, none of whom were touched—apart from him. Among the survivors, there was a British Commander. I remember noticing his uniform. It was similar to a garage mechanic's suit with elastic at the ankles, gloves and a hood for flash protection. It was an ingenious rig which we might have done well to have copied. Probably far fewer men would have died of burns if they had been so clothed.

Small enemy attacks continued throughout the day until finally, at dusk, having received word that the enemy was approaching with surface ships, the Admiral ordered the Task Force to abandon the HORNET. This was unexpected and caused great confusion on the HORNET. Even though earlier we had come alongside to take off the wounded and others from the HORNET, this new order caused those remaining on the HORNET to take to the water immediately. Again, the destroyers had the problem of picking up men in the water. The Captain sent John Caster out in the whaleboat with a rope dragging astern, as at Midway, to gather the swimmers.

After the men had been picked up, there remained a question as to how to dispose of the HORNET if the Task Force were not going to defend her. She was floating peacefully with only about a 4 degree list. There was no evidence, however, of interest on the part of the Command to try to save her. Our orders were to destroy and leave her, and this is exactly what we did. One of the ships of our Squadron fired eight torpedoes at her, none of which exploded, and finally they set her on fire by firing several hundred 5" shells at her. The shell fire did not actually sink her, but she was unsalvageable when we left.

In this battle, the enemy showed us he had learned the lesson of Midway. He made our carriers his primary objective and having located them, he scattered his forces and attacked us from different directions. The result was that our air strikes were never able to find all of his carriers, but he found ours easily and attacked simultaneously from different directions which made interception difficult. We damaged but did not sink any of his carriers.

The enemy attack had been characteristically aggressive, but this very aggressiveness was the reason why he did not win a complete victory over us. Of the 120 to 160 enemy planes which made the initial attack, very few returned to their bases. Many of these were shot down by our antiaircraft batteries, but a large number seemed to attack too recklessly and almost throw their lives away. This loss of airplanes left the enemy powerless to annihilate us by any other means than closing with surface units. We were thankful that so many of the enemy pilots had gloriously joined their ancestors in the initial attack.

A STRANGER VISITS US AND THEN VANISHES

Bringing the wounded to the RUSSELL from the HORNET was slow because there were only 12 Stokes stretchers. This meant that the wounded had to be removed from the stretchers so that they could be returned for another patient. The Captain sent me down to take charge of the patient transfer operation and I began directing the men where to take each case as it came aboard with instructions to remove the patient from the stretcher, and return it to me promptly for passage back to the carrier. The only suitable place to send the patients was the Wardroom, and soon it began to fill up with the overflow going into the officer's staterooms. Finally, I was forced to remove some of the patients from the stretchers on the open deck of the fo'c'sle until room for them could be found below.

One of the wounded who had to be placed on deck was a patient who did not seem to be badly wounded, except that there was a small amount of blood oozing out of one ear. I asked him how he was, and he smiled and said he was OK. I then asked if he would mind if we took him off the stretcher for a few minutes until we could make room for him below and he said, "OK. No problem." Then, with the assistance of a couple of other fellows, I put him on deck as gently as I could, sent the stretcher back to the carrier, and went about my business. I learned later to my dismay that blood coming out of a patient's ear is the sign of a fractured skull, and that moving such a patient is very dangerous. The man died not long afterward. I felt sick at the time, and it continues to cause me remorse.

At one point, while all of this was going on, I went down to the Wardroom to see how many more we would be able to take, and found wounded men lying all around moaning and no one doing anything for them. The Doctor (Bob Schmidt) was, of course, extremely busy. I asked where the Chief Pharmacist's Mate was. His job was to take over treating the wounded, and when no one seemed to know, I sent a man to look for him, and went back up on deck. In a minute or so, the messenger came up and told me the Chief was in his bunk. I exploded, "In his bunk? How in the hell can he be in his bunk at a time like this?" and charged down to the Chief's quarters to correct the situation. I found the Chief flat on his back in his bunk staring with bald round cues straight up. I shook him. He was not dead, but showed no comprehension. (He actually had had a complete mental breakdown.) I then raced into the Wardroom, found Mess Attendant Bryant, got him released from his GQ station and put him to work tending the wounded. It was imperative to find help for our doctor and, back on deck, I inquired whether the HORNET had a doctor and possibly some pharmacists' mates they could send over to help us. Soon a doctor was lowered over from the HORNET and he went below. Eventually, all of the stretcher cases had been transferred, the RUSSELL pulled away from the HORNET.

Later I went back down into the Wardroom to see how things were going. There in the middle of the Wardroom was a slightly built, light complexioned man, who I presumed had been sent over from the carrier because I had never seen him before, helping our doctor, giving orders to Bryant and several other men from the RUSSELL. He had organized things with medical supplies arranged in orderly groups on the table and with the wounded men lying in neat rows with access in between. Each man's wounds had been assessed and a plan had been established as to what was going to be done. I asked where the doctor from the HORNET was, and they told me he had gone up to the Commodore's cabin. It turned out that he too had been wounded. He said he had diagnosed his problem as a collapsed lung and that he was sorry, but he simply was too weak to help. Back in the wardroom his small blond man was moving about from case to case telling the others what to do and how to do it. Our doctor had provided some blood plasma kits and this man was supervising administering blood plasma to several patients. Others were having tourniquets applied, wounds dressed, and fractures set with splints. A badly burned man was in Bargeloh's bunk. Under the small, blond man's direction, this burned man had been heavily dressed with Vaseline. I spoke to him. He was calm and lucid, but he wanted to get up and take a look at himself in the mirror. I tried to persuade him that his best chance was to lie quietly, but he insisted. After he had taken a look at himself, he went back to the bunk. I returned less than 15 minutes later, and he was dead.

Throughout all of this, the enemy air raids, although sparse, were still coming in and the ship was still at GQ, and after we pulled back out into the screen, I returned to the bridge and resumed my deck duties.

After the swimmers had been picked up and the HORNET disposed of, the remaining ships of our Task Force set off at high speed to the south in an effort to rejoin the ENTERPRISE Task Force which had already taken off to the south.

The next morning, the Captain and our new Executive officer, Lt Cdr. Leroy Taylor, conducted a burial service for the dead and we transferred the critically wounded to a cruiser.

Not long thereafter, the Captain called the Division Heads to the bridge and said he wanted to have recommendations from us for individuals deserving commendation. I right away said we ought to cite the small, blond man who had done such a terrific job helping Bob Schmidt with the wounded in the Wardroom. Everyone else agreed. Several other recommendations were made. A commendation for Mess Attendant Alonzo Bryant was proposed. The Captain said he would recommend one for Caster for his efforts in the boat rescue. Then the Captain asked us to find the small, blond man because he wanted to talk to him. The man was no longer in the wardroom. The man had been in the wardroom until the critically wounded had been transferred, but had not been seen since then. Only the critically wounded had been transferred to the cruiser, and, therefore, the man had to be still on board the RUSSELL. We went around the ship among both the crew of the RUSSELL and the survivors looking for him. No one had any information about him. I asked the doctor from the HORNET. He said he had seen the man, but assumed he was from the RUSSELL because he (the doctor) did not recognize him as a Pharmacist's Mate from the HORNET. Not being able to find the man, we spoke to all hands on the ship's P.A. system, explained that we wanted to find him to commend him and asked if he would identify himself. No one responded. While the remainder of HORNET's men were leaving us later in Noumea we looked at every man. He was not among them. In the end, we gave up. It was a complete mystery.

All through history, there have been reported supernatural visitations, some better documented than others. In this case, there is no question but that many people on the RUSSELL saw this man and can attest that he was directing the care of the wounded in the Wardroom. Also, we on the RUSSELL can attest that he was not a RUSSELL sailor. Although he may not have been a Pharmacist's Mate on the carrier, he still might have come from the carrier. He was not an officer (at least he wore no insignia), but he could have been an Aviation Mechanic because we took some of them on board. We questioned them, however, and they had no recollection of such a man. He had to have come on board early on, because he had already been working in the Wardroom for a while by the time we pulled away from the HORNET. Since the other AVMECS did not know him, it is not likely that he was an AVMEC. He could, however, have been an ordinary seaman or other rating on the HORNET, who came on board the RUSSELL posing as an AVMEC. But, if so, why we were unable to find him later? A destroyer is a small ship. I suppose it is remotely possible that desiring anonymity he could have avoided detection, but then how could he have left the ship unnoticed? When the HORNET's men left in launches in Noumea, I again watched carefully for him. There is no possibility in my opinion, that he could have disguised himself as critically wounded and have been sent to the cruiser. Could he have stowed away until much later and have left the ship while in port? Extremely unlikely.

In conclusion, although I wish to make no comment on the religious aspects of this incident, I do believe that the evidence supporting a case for a supernatural visitation is as strong as many of the more well documented and accepted incidents of same.

SIMILARITY BETWEEN THE DESERTIONS OF THE HORNET AND YORKTOWN

The desertion of the HORNET and our hasty retreat to the south bore a marked similarity to the desertion of the YORKTOWN at Midway. Admiral Kinkaid's decision to retreat to the South was, of course, the safest thing to do, but it totally disregarded the possibility of capitalizing on our radar advantage to defend and possibly to save the HORNET, which was vitally needed for the American war effort at the time. It should be noted that shortly prior to Santa Cruz, Admiral Ghormely had been replaced in Command of the Southwest Pacific area by Admiral Halsey. The curious part is that, although Halsey had been critical of the Fletcher-Spruance decision to abandon the YORKTOWN at Midway[39] when Kinkaid did likewise under Halsey's command at Santa Cruz, Halsey joined the chorus of praise. The fact that the SOUTH DAKOTA or the cruisers could have used their radar advantage to save the HORNET has been completely ignored by the historians. Of course, they all mention the retreat to the south, but none indicates that we had a good chance to save the HORNET which we turned down.

MR. BAYLOR RELIEVES THE DECK

After Santa Cruz and while steaming south with the Japanese on our heels, the following incident involving Lt. Baylor occurred. I was near exhaustion. The night before Santa Cruz, I had had the midwatch. Going off watch about 4:15 am, I had been able to grab an hour's sleep before going to dawn GQ during the day, From then on, the ship had remained at GQ while the events described were taking place and into the night because, as noted above, we were being pursued by surface ships. My next watch in the rotation was the 8 to 12 (i.e., 2000 to 2400), and, therefore, when the RUSSELL finally secured from GQ at around 8:30 pm, I simply remained on deck as OD. Thus, with only one hour's sleep in the past 24, and all of the exertion, I was very tired and had to whip myself to remain alert. Coffee, of course, helps, and I had found that cold coffee was the best. Cold coffee, however, in addition to keeping me awake, had the further effect on me of making me more irritable than normal.

Lt. Baylor was my relief, and per the usual procedure, I sent the messenger to wake him at 11:30. Mr. Baylor was the Gunnery Officer, and, of course, he too had spent a busy day. There were, however, three differences. He had had a full night's sleep before, three hours sleep since, and he had been seated in Gunnery Control for the entire day.

The messenger found him sleeping on the deck in his own stateroom, with a wounded man occupying his bed. Mr. Baylor did not appear at 11:45, the usual time, and I immediately sent the messenger again. Mr. Baylor had not gotten up. At 12:30, still no Baylor, and I sent the messenger again. At 12:40 Mr. Baylor appeared and started reading the night order book. There still might not have been an incident except that suddenly a bright flash of white light emanated from the wheelhouse. I was on the wing and shouted, "For Christ's sake, douse that light." and sprang to the door of the wheelhouse. It must be remembered that the Task Force was still fleeing from the pursuing enemy surface forces. Looking in the wheelhouse and seeing Mr. Baylor bending over the night order book with a flashlight in hand, I said, "Oh, excuse me Sir, no white light on the bridge, of course, Sir!" (A dim, red covered light was permissible because it cannot be seen at a distance and does not impair night vision.) I went back out on the wing. Next, the white light flashed again equally bright as before. I reacted instantaneously.

"Douse that light, Sir!"

"I will do as I like, I am reading the night orders!"

I had no alternative.

"As Officer of the Deck, I hereby order you to douse the light, and not to turn it on again!" Baylor froze, quietly said "Very well", took the book and retired into the enclosed chart house, for the next 15 minutes. Finally, he reappeared on deck, and saluted formally.

"I am now ready to relieve you." I returned his salute, said "OK" and started to leave. Baylor hesitated.

"Where are you going? I have not relieved you, and I will tell you when I have. What is the range and bearing to the nearest land?"

"What the hell difference does that make?"

"You seem to forget, Sir, that every officer of the Deck must be able to supply such information on to his relief."

I then took 10 to 15 minutes figuring it out and gave him an approximation. Next, he demanded the names and locations of all P.A.L.s (prisoners at large), the soundings of all peak tanks, the status of fuel on board, whether or not the mandatory 8:00 o'clock reports had been made to the Captain, and various other things. I went along with the gag, but was in the end unable to find the P.A.L.s amid the confusion of some 700 HORNET survivors sprawled all over the ship. I then stated that I had had enough of his joke, and that I would call the Exec. (Leroy at that time) unless he agreed to relieve the deck. He stated, "Very well, since you have clearly demonstrated your lack of fitness to stand top watch, I will relieve you in order to place a qualified officer on watch and I will have you removed henceforth from the watch list."

Fortunately for me, the Exec., and, of course, the Captain controlled the watch list. Baylor did lodge a formal complaint pointing out the facts that I had been unable to give an accurate range and bearing to the nearest land, and that I had been unable to locate the P.A.L.s as required by Naval regulations. By this time, the Captain and I had developed an excellent working relationship, and he was not about to remove me as OD at GQ. Mr. Baylor's complaint was simply ignored. The next morning, I was telling Caster about the incident with Mr. Baylor, and he said, "You should have told him that the range and bearing to the nearest land was 2000 fathoms straight down"

THE WHISPERS OF ANGEL'S WINGS

During the period of these Naval actions, we were frequently in port at Espiritu Santo.

The harbor at Espiritu Santo was excellent. It included an inner harbor which was large enough to accommodate an entire fleet, but its entrances were narrow providing reasonable safety from submarines. In addition, the entrances had been heavily mined. We had secret charts, of course, showing the safe path, through the mine fields.

The island was essentially a sleepy South-seas island occupied by the French and the main industry was coconut oil. Although it was not flat like an atoll, neither was it hilly like New Caledonia.

In accordance with my procedure of visiting the base communications offices to obtain the latest secret codes and to check the completeness of our Fox Schedules, I had an opportunity to go ashore frequently.

On one of my trips ashore, and this could have been earlier while we were still with the Hornet, I was in the U.S. Port Director's Office attempting to get a launch to take me back to the RUSSELL. Sounds of an argument were coming from the next room. I could overhear enough of it to realize that one of the combatants was French and the other American. I went in.

"Good morning Chief. I can talk a little 'frog language'. What seems to be the problem?"

"Nothing Sir. It's just this dumb Frenchman. He keeps running his boat over to the island over there at odd hours and without letting us know he's going to do it. So we're going crazy thinking it might be Japs trying to sneak in here. We just can't control him."

The Frenchman then explained to me in French that he saw no reason why they kept interfering with him, that all he was doing was bringing back his coconut crops.

"Let me ask you a question, Chief. Do you have any objection if he takes his boat over there at certain times of day and when you know about it beforehand?"

"None at all Sir, but he won't do it."

I then told the Frenchman that the Port Director had no objection to his taking his boat as long as he did it in daylight and provided the Port Director was given a schedule as to when he would leave and return, and where he would go, etc.; and further, provided he would stick to his schedule. The Frenchman was visibly relieved to know that the Port Director was at last speaking reasonably. At that point, all that needed to be done was to work out a way by which the Frenchman could accurately communicate to the Port Director what his trip schedule would be, and for the Frenchman to be able to understand any approvals or disapprovals they might have. I spent 15–20 minutes with him working out a kind of basic vocabulary of various words to use and how to present his trip schedule. The episode ended with the Frenchman all smiles, and the Port Director satisfied. Afterward, outside of the office, the Frenchman was very effusive, insisting that, the next time I was in port, I come to his house for dinner, meet the family, etc. He showed me where the house was about a mile down the road along the bay.

Several weeks later, we were back in Espiritu Santo and I persuaded Bill Wesselhoeft to go ashore with me and take up the Frenchman's invitation. It was in the late afternoon. We followed the Frenchman's directions and came to a distinctly French looking house. It was pale pink stucco on brick with cream trim. In front, it had a wrought iron fence surrounding a very formal garden. The windows, with all shutters fully closed, also had wrought iron railings and window-boxes for flowers. The level of the main floor was about four feet above ground level and a split pair of staircases joined at a central front door reminiscent of Fontainbleau, the whole setting was about as French-looking as a house can be.

Other than the fact that the flowers had obviously been recently tended by someone, there was no sign of life anywhere. Bill and I mounted the stairs and I knocked at the door. We heard nothing and waited for about a minute. Then, we knocked again, and I said to Bill, "I wonder if they're home." We waited and then gave a third knock, more or less out of desperation. At that point, the door opened about 1", a voice said loudly and firmly, "Non," and the door immediately shut again. This seemed to me the action a servant would take if the owners were not home, so I decided to leave a message. I then knocked again and said that I would like to leave a message for "Monsieur". The door cracked open again and I explained that, when Monsieur returned, they should tell him that the American officer who assisted him at the Port Director's Office had come to accept his invitation, and to say that we would come back another time. The door then closed but as Bill and I were about to turn around to leave, it flew wide open, and out stepped the Frenchman all smiles and apologies, flung his arms around us, and brought us into the house.

With the French, when the ice (which can be very thick) is broken, they (I can't resist it) go overboard. We were treated to a royal dinner with the whole family—fabulous food and wines, and on into the night regaling each other with yarns about homes, families, friends, mostly about France. Of course, we looked at photo albums, admired their antiques and knick-knacks, etc. Finally, at about 10:00 pm, Monsieur said, "And now, I am going to give you something to remember." He disappeared and a moment later returned with a very dust covered bottle.

Madame gasped an almost inaudible "Ah, non." Then Monsieur, placing a small liqueur glass in front of each of us, said, "It is my honor to share with you a drop from this bottle from the Emperor's own cellar". He then raised his glass to toast and said, "To your good fortune and safety in this war." We sipped.

It was without doubt the finest liqueur I had ever tasted. It qualified for Kipling's superlative as the "whispers of angels' wings." I have never tasted its equal again.

When Bill and I were ready to leave, I asked if there were anything they might want which I could get from the ships. I offered, in fact, to get them some of our most precious commodity, ice cream. To my surprise, they shrugged (in a Gallic way) at my suggestion of ice cream. Finally, Madame said "By any chance would you have any canned peaches?" Of course, we had canned peaches "running out of our ears", so much so, that the crew would complain loudly when peaches were served. Peaches were easy to obtain and I delivered them a case a few days later.

HORSE MANURE NAVY STYLE

While the Task Force was in Espiritu Santo, it was normal for a destroyer to be stationed on patrol outside of the channel entrance in order to provide continuous sonar coverage. A Japanese submarine had succeeded in entering Sydney Harbor, in Australia, and there was a real possibility that they might try it either at Espiritu Santo or Noumea. Captain Hartwig, being the Junior Commanding Officer in the Squadron, was usually assigned to this harbor entrance patrol duty. The result, of course, even though we were near land, was that the ship was in all respects at sea.

Soon after we first went on patrol at Espiritu Santo, we were on patrol one night at around 2:00am, a ship came in sight on our radar. We contacted the Flagship and were informed that it was a Liberty Ship named the Robert E. Peary coming into Espiritu Santo and not to worry about her. Shortly, thereafter, we flashed the recognition signal at her and received the correct response. All seemed to be in order. A little later, however, the Peary came back with a message which said, "Is harbor entrance mined?" We sent back, "Yes.". The Peary then sent, "Do not have minefield charts, must have pilot." I happened to have been asleep when all of this was taking place, the Captain had been called earlier, and since I had custody of the minefield charts, he called me on deck and told me to go over to the Peary with the charts, but not to let any civilians on the Peary see the charts. (Of course, the entire crew of the Peary were civilians.)

I then jumped into the whaleboat, charts in hand, and was lowered to the water with Meltzer at the tiller. We headed for the Robert E. Peary, which loomed as a large black shadow against the graying easterly sky, about 3000 yds. away, moving at about 4 kts. toward the harbor entrance. (Later in the war, I learned that the Robert E. Peary had been built at the Kaiser Works in Oakland California in four days, a record at that time for the construction of a complete ship).

Crossing under the stern of the Peary to make an approach on the starboard side (the usual gangway side), the air suddenly became suffocatingly laden with an overpowering stench resembling highly concentrated horse urine and feces. I could not believe it, at sea in the South Pacific!

Moving up alongside the Peary, the smell disappeared. As we approached where the gangway should be, nothing was there. I looked up at the bridge. The Captain had a megaphone.

"You the pilot?"

"Yes. How about lowering the gangway?"

"We haven't got a gangway!"

"Then lower a ladder or something!"

"OK"

He went off and a little while later, a couple of deck hands unrolled a rope ladder over side amidships. The Peary, however, was so lightly loaded and high in the water that the end of the rope ladder was still about six feet above the water level. I asked if they could lower it a bit more and was informed not. This left me with the challenge of mounting the ladder by grabbing the bottom rung and hoisting myself up by hands alone. In order to make this feasible I stuffed the charts under my belt, had Meltzer maneuver the whaleboat to a point where I could reach the bottom rung. I then grabbed the end of the ladder. Next, I was swinging in free air alongside the ship as the whaleboat pulled away. After struggling up a few inches, rapidly becoming exhausted, I decided to try pulling one foot up to hook it onto the bottom rung. This required me to tilt my body to a more-or-less horizontal position, and then while in that position, to my horror, the charts slipped out from under my belt and fell into the water. I finally got my feet hooked onto the bottom rung. This made me more secure against falling into the water, but now I had no charts. Luckily, Meltzer was still within range of my "hell's kitchen" wolf-whistle and came back. I told him to scan the ship's wake to see if he could find the charts floating. He went back, found the charts, and brought them up to me as I remained clinging to the bottom rung. Eventually, the comedy of errors ended, I mounted the ladder, and reported to the Captain of the Peary on the bridge.

The Captain's name was Look. He lived in Sausalito, California, and was 78 years old at the time. He was tall, lean, gaunt, and had a high standing shock of white hair. When I arrived on the bridge, I saluted him. Salutes, however, are not practiced in the Merchant Marine. He simply again asked me if I was the pilot, and upon my affirmance, he said, "OK, she's yours, I'm going down to breakfast." By this time, it had become quite light.

For Captain Look to leave the bridge like this, came to me both as a surprise and a shock. It so happens that, in the Merchant Marine, when a harbor pilot takes over, the Merchant skipper is relieved of responsibility. I did not know this at the time. The shock was that I had never taken responsibility for a ship entering a port, let alone guiding it through a crowded harbor or bringing it to anchor at an assigned location. Moreover, the minefield was a major worry. Only a few weeks earlier the USS Tucker, (DD 374), had strayed slightly in this same channel, and had been sunk by one of the mines. The maneuverability of the Liberty ship was an additional problem. Destroyers have two screws, plenty of power, and can be maneuvered, but Liberty Ships have only one screw, not much power and are slow to respond to the helm. Never having been on a Liberty Ship before, I had no idea of their turning characteristics or the response time to the rudder or to the engines. Nor was I familiar with anything else such as the engine room telegraph procedures, what kind of compass, etc.

So, as Captain Look disappeared down the companionway, I looked around and said to myself, "OK, you fool. Now get yourself out of this mess, if you can!"

What I had learned on my cruise on the Eagle boat (back during my ROTC days at Harvard) was very useful. The equipment on the bridge of the Peary was much the same. The Eagle too was single screwed. I was, therefore, familiar with the fact that single screwed ships back to port, except in a wind and then into the wind. Backing a single screwed ship should be avoided. Predicting which way they will turn is very difficult, especially when they are high in the water as was the Peary. I also knew that I had to keep her moving because there is no way a ship like that can be maneuvered unless she is making headway (preferably over 2 knots).

So, I laid out the soaking minefield charts (chart paper is wonderfully water resistant) and began trying to work out what course to take. Not having a gyro compass complicated the problem because, as I had learned on the Eagle boat, one cannot rely on bearings taken with a magnetic compass. My procedure on the Eagle boat had been to measure the angles between three prominent landmarks such as light houses, buoys, standpipes, jetties, beacons, etc., and to locate the position of the ship with a three-armed protractor using these angles. Captain Look had such a protractor in his chart house, so I started taking bearings. At that time, however, Espiritu Santo was relatively undeveloped and all I had to go by were the contours (tangents of shorelines) of the islands around the entrance. Using shorelines for navigation can be risky because they are affected by erosion and the tides. Also the cartographers are not as careful recording the shorelines as they are with the more usual navigational aids. While on the RUSSELL, however, I had used them to determine the RUSSELL's patrolling station. Therefore, using this method, I soon located our position on the chart. Then, as I headed the Peary around toward the channel entrance, I kept repeating my three-armed protractor exercise over and over simply to make sure. Rather than give the helmsman a compass course to steer (magnetic compasses swing back and forth), I located objects along the shore in the direction of the desired course and directed him to steer for them. The ship was steaming at about four knots, and as we headed into the channel, I took a quick look at the RUSSELL and thought, "Boy, if you guys knew what is going on over here!" They had no idea that the full responsibility of this maneuver had been thrust on me in this abrupt manner. Nor could they comprehend the apprehensions of a huge explosion, heaving decks, cascading wreckage, and hurtling bodies, visions of which crowded my mind and tightened my throat.

We headed in. The mine-free channel had two unmarked bends in it, one of 70 degrees right about 400 yds. in and the other of 90 degrees to the left about halfway through the minefield. When we reached the first bend, speaking softly to the helm in an attempt to avoid disclosure of the restriction of my vocal chords, I ordered him to come right and head for a prominent rock, which I had previously noticed as being on the correct line of the channel from the first bend. Then, with the tangent of one of the harbor islands directly abeam to port at the correct position of the second bend, I ordered the helmsman to bring her around to the left and steer for a Quonset hut on the far shore of the harbor. Then we headed down the remaining portion of the mine-free channel, out of the minefield and into the harbor. To be free of the minefield did wonders for my voice, but my problems were not over. I still had to obtain an anchorage assignment from the Port Director and bring the awkward and un-maneuverable Peary to the correct place through a harbor crowded with hundreds of ships of every description. I put the signalman to work on getting the berth assignment, by flashing light. Also, I contacted Captain Look, who by then had finished breakfast, and asked him to prepare to anchor. These things all went smoothly. Once I got the location of the anchorage, I headed the Peary in a zigzag path around several large ships and then directly to her assigned berth. With about 500 yds. to go I gave the order to stop engines. She moved steadily ahead and with about 50 yds. to go, still making about 1 kt., I ordered "All engines back one-third," forgetting for the moment that she had only one engine. Then, at the correct position, I told Captain Look that he should anchor. He ordered it, the anchor splashed, the chain rattled out, and we had made it without incident. My only mistake was that the ship was still moving forward. She, therefore, rode ahead about 30-40 yds. over the chain. A good seaman would frown on such a thing. Anyway, it did no harm. The Robert E. Peary was safely at anchor.

Captain Look offered me breakfast and we chatted. The mystery of the barn-yard smell was solved. The cargo of the Peary was 400 mules. On Guadal-canal, the Marines had found that mechanized equipment was useless on the steep and craggy hillsides. An urgent call had gone out for mules. The intensity of Meltzer's and my introduction to the aroma was due to our pass-ing under the stern of the Peary at the precise moment when the cowhands were hosing down the "green liquor" during morning chores.

Although my piloting experience had been loaded with tension and fear, it also had been exciting and interesting. So much so, in fact, that I did not breathe a word about it after my return to the RUSSELL. There is an old Greek saying, "Don't smile, the Gods may become jealous." In this case I was not so much afraid of the Gods as I was of the Regular Navy. If Hartwig had known that I had been given the full responsibility of piloting the Peary, he probably would have been afraid of being criticized for sending such a junior officer. The other officers would have been jealous and have put pressure on Hartwig to send them instead. In any event, I characterized it as an insuffer-able nuisance, and Hartwig let me continue doing it. Later in the war, I had the fun of piloting a number of additional ships into Espiritu Santo, including two large (20,000 ton) converted "President" liners, and, at Noumea, I piloted a division of YMS's (small mine-sweepers). The size of the President liners was somewhat appalling, but otherwise, the problem was always the same and not difficult. In every instance of piloting a merchant ship, the Captain would relinquish the con to me just as Captain Look had done. On the Navy ships, however, the Captains would follow what I suggested, but they kept the con.

I made what could have been a very serious mistake with the YMS Squadron in Noumea. In order to avoid the nuisance of taking the YMS's the whole way around the prison colony island (some 40 miles down and back, and about 5 hours), I thought it would be a good idea to take them across the shallow sand bar which separated the little ancient harbor from the head of the roadstead beyond. The Squadron Commander told me that the draft of these ships was only about two ½ feet. They were built all of wood and were designed for mine sweeping close to shore. Next, I looked at the chart and saw that the mean low water depth of water across the sand bar between the inner and outer harbors at Noumea was 2 fathoms, i.e., 12 feet. At least, I thought the soundings were fathoms because on the RUSSELL we had been working exclusively with charts showing fathoms. I then gave the order to enter the old harbor and head across the sand bar separating the old harbor from the open roadstead beyond, where the YMS's were supposed to go. Everything went well until after we, in the lead boat, were passing directly over the bar. The water looked a little bit lighter than I would have expected for a depth of 12 feet and so I took a second look at the chart. To my horror, the soundings were in feet. I did not know what to do. In fact, it was too late to do anything on the Flagship where I was. Nothing happened. We cleared the bar, by how many inches I will never know. I simply held my breath and tried to act nonchalant. The four remaining YMS's also passed over the bar without incident.

THE BATTLE OF GUADALCANAL (NOVEMBER 13TH TO 15TH 1942)

The RUSSELL returned to Noumea immediately after Santa Cruz. We had been hoping to be sent back to the U.S. for repairs, but the diametric opposite occurred. The Navy had moved so much equipment into Noumea that they quickly repaired us, and within a few days we found ourselves assigned to plane-guard duty in the ENTERPRISE's Task Force.

It was clear to us on the RUSSELL at the time that things were going very badly for the U.S. at that stage of the war. All of our big carriers, except the ENTERPRISE, had either been sunk or disabled, and although our cruisers had done well at long range in the open sea (at Cape Esperance), they had been trounced by the Japanese in night actions within the confined waters near Guadalcanal. As already noted, the Japanese torpedoes were far superior to ours, and their aircraft were faster and more maneuverable. So, now, with only the ENTERPRISE left and the Japanese raiding and bombarding Guadalcanal at night, virtually at will, things looked exceedingly grim. Two favorable things, however, should be mentioned. First, despite our defeat at Santa Cruz, the Navy had succeeded in landing reinforcements at Guadalcanal. Second, the Army had started making long-range bombing raids from Australia and New Caledonia on the Japanese island-held airfields and sending fighters and dive bombers to Guadalcanal. These measures successfully kept the enemy from attacking during daytime.

The ENTERPRISE's role was to provide as much air support as she could in order to hold the fort at Guadalcanal, but since it would be several months before new carriers, then under construction, would be available, it was questionable whether we had enough forces in the area to withstand the enemy.

Captain Hartwig and I were both very concerned when I began decoding secret reports in early November that the enemy was amassing ships for a major assault on Guadalcanal.

Although he undoubtedly kept the Exec informed, for security reasons, the Captain did not disseminate this type of secret information around the ship and only informed the Officers generally as might be necessary when action was imminent.

Around November 10th, a U.S. convoy of attack transports with 6,000 troops and large quantities of supplies was sent to Guadalcanal from Espiritu Santo. This convoy was guarded by a U.S. Task Force of 2 Heavy cruisers, 3 Light cruisers, and 8 destroyers. In the background, to the Southwest about 100 miles distant, the ENTERPRISE Task Force (where the RUSSELL was) prepared to offer air assistance.

The convoy arrived at Guadalcanal on the 13th and started unloading. At that same time, the enemy fleet was sighted approaching from the north with a strong force of 2 battleships, several Heavy cruisers, and about 14 destroy-ers. It will be understood that battleships are armor plated and carry 14" to 16" guns. An entire Task Force of cruisers and destroyers would not normally be a match for a single battleship, and the Japanese were bringing two. The U.S., however, had no choice but to fight. If the enemy ships were not turned back, Henderson Airfield on Guadalcanal and all of the supplies would be totally destroyed to say nothing of the loss of the transports, etc. Two mod-ern U.S. battleships, the WASHINGTON and SOUTH DAKOTA, were at that moment racing toward Guadalcanal from Noumea, but they would not be able to arrive before the 14th.

That these two new battleships were not already in position to defend the supply ships at Guadalcanal was hard to understand. It will be remembered that the SOUTH DAKOTA had been at Santa Cruz only three weeks earlier and, although damaged slightly, she still was in good enough shape to have been sent along with the cruisers to Guadalcanal to guard the convoy. Why she was not is curious. Everyone knew for at least a week before it happened, that a major enemy force was being gathered for an assault on Guadalcanal. It was inexplicable that the Navy having argued strenuously, over the span of many years, that the battleships should be built, now repeatedly showed a strange reluctance to send them into the only kind of situation in which they were really needed, but in which they might also be sunk. Instead, they sent in the cruisers and destroyers, which had substantially less chance of survival. There had been no reasonable excuse for not using the battleships earlier, but the need for them was particularly cogent at Guadalcanal on the night of November 13, 1942. The historians have either been unaware of this lapse or charitably forbearing.

We, on the RUSSELL, knew only that the prospects seemed extremely bad. All we could do was try to get some sleep and await the new day. In the morning, we heard the astonishing news that during the night, Admiral Callaghan had sent his cruiser force right into the middle of the Japanese battleship formation, that our ships had passed through the Japanese forma-tion, and in the confusion, the Japanese had ended up firing at each other. (The Japanese accounts of this battle deny that the Japanese ships fired at each other, but such reports must be viewed with the same skepticism as our own. We heard the opposite directly from people who were there, shortly after the event.) Most of the U.S. ships were heavily damaged and four destroyers (none from our Squadron) were sunk. The ATLANTA could not be salvaged. The important thing, however, was that, as at Savo Island, the Japanese had not recognized their advantage and had turned back without bombarding Henderson field. In addition, they left one battleship with disabled engines, drifting helplessly north of Savo Island. Therefore, even if our losses had been heavy, the cruisers had prevented the holocaust of a battleship bombardment of our forces on the island, and now the U.S. battleships WASHINGTON and SOUTH DAKOTA had joined the ENTERPRISE and were ready in case the Japanese tried another night attack on the 14th. During the day, reports began coming in that such a renewed attack was exactly what the enemy had in mind. In fact, on the afternoon of the 14th, dive bombers and torpedo planes from the ENTERPRISE were able to inflict severe damage to a large fleet of transports being sent in to supply the enemy on Guadalcanal. In the late afternoon, a message came in from Fleet Command, ordering the WASHINGTON and SOUTH DAKOTA to be detached along with four destroyers of our Squadron and to proceed at high speed to defend Guadalcanal against this renewed Japanese attack. The RUSSELL was not selected to join this new detached force. We, of course, cannot be sure of why the Admiral chose the others instead of us, but we always assumed that the RUSSELL was retained with the carrier because of her reputation for plane-guard excellence. In any event, the battleship Task Force went off into the night and we remained with the ENTERPRISE.

This was the only battle in the entire war in which any of the Navy's ten new fast battleships fired their main batteries in anger, and even at that, the SOUTH DAKOTA had a power failure and, as a result, she was unable to fire her guns[40]. All she did was take a pounding from the enemy. The WASHINGTON, however, made up for the SOUTH DAKOTA. Using her fire control radar, the WASHINGTON easily disposed of the enemy battleship KIRISHIMA and also sank a destroyer[41], but again, the U.S. destroyers suffered badly. The WALKE, BENHAM, and PRESTON (all from our Squadron) were sunk.

The success of the battleship WASHINGTON's radar-controlled gunnery, proved what these ships could do at night and showed how badly we had needed them, for example at Santa Cruz and around Guadalcanal at other times.

Although many of our ships had been sunk and others had been severely damaged, the battle of November 13th-15th was a major victory for the

U.S. which effectively assured us the capture of Guadalcanal. The RUSSELL remained with the ENTERPRISE patrolling off the southwest shore of Guadalcanal the next morning, while the ENTERPRISE launched air strikes to mop up the remnants of the enemy fleet and transports.

In the meantime, the crippled survivors of the U.S. cruiser Task Force started heading south from Guadalcanal toward Espiritu Santo. It was at this time, that the people on the bridge of the RUSSELL (I was below decks at the time) saw the cruiser JUNEAU blow up. She had been hit during the night of the 13th, and was limping back, south of Guadalcanal when a Japanese submarine torpedoed her. Terrill, the Signalman, told me that he had been looking at the JUNEAU through his telescope, that he looked away, heard a tremendous explosion, and then when he looked back, nothing was there. Apparently, one of the JUNEAU's magazines had been hit. She was literally blown to bits. Only a handful of men survived.

BLACK JAZZ

In my 1945 diary I wrote.

"I remember the night we came back to Espirito Santo after the Battle of Guadalcanal. It was a good feeling to see the big bombers, and torpedo planes taking off from the island airfield, but we were not happy. The old SAN FRANCISCO, and HELENA were there with bullet holes all through them. Three ships from our Squadron, the WALKE, BENHAM and PRESTON had just been sunk, and other destroyers we knew had been sunk also. That night in Espiritu Santo, when we nested with our ships, our hearts were low with thoughts of many the faces missing, and each one of us was thankful to be afloat. That was the time the Captain brought a band of Black jazz musicians out to the ship. I don't know where he found them, but along about 9:00 pm a large band came out to the ship in a launch. We had been sitting there as I say, in the dumps, a long time out and a long way from home, but boy, when those "Darktown Strutters" tore into that music, it was really good. It seemed so out of place to have them on board, but their music was so catching and joyful that our spirits were buoyed, and we laughed and sang until late that night."

THEN WAS WHEN THE CAPTAIN HAD TO BE A "SONOVABITCH"

We had been expecting to be sent home ever since the summer before, but every time they were just about to send us back, the Japs would sink more destroyers, and we would have to stay. The long months wore on in the blasted heat. New ships would come, join the Fleet for a few days and be blown to bits. The BARTON had moored alongside us in Noumea. She had just arrived from the Atlantic and had flags painted all over her bridge to indicate the number of subs and planes she claimed as victims. She was sunk less than a week later, blown up in the battle of Guadalcanal. The DEHAVEN had moored near us, a fine new Fletcher class, with the latest equipment. She was hit by dive bombers a few weeks later off the coast of Guadalcanal and sank in a matter of seconds. Somehow the RUSSELL was lucky. She was in and out with all the rest, but never at the wrong time. She had picked up survivors from the LEXINGTON, YORKTOWN, and HORNET and had seen the SARATOGA, WASP, NORTH CAROLINA, and O'BRIEN torpedoed. Being superstitious is human, but it seems especially strong among sailors. Some of us on the RUSSELL began to wonder if we were bringing bad luck, especially to the carriers, and felt uneasy when the orders came out assigning the RUSSELL to screen the ENTERPRISE. The ENTERPRISE, however, survived without further mishap, to our great relief.

It was at such times that the value of blind discipline became apparent. One simply had to keep going, standing watches, training the men, and repairing the ship to keep her in fighting trim, and all the while in those hot latitudes, with one's pep gone, and home a long way off. The more one thought about it, the worse it became. One simply had to stop thinking. When the mail came in, it was what we wanted, but to read it only made the pain worse. Then was when the Captain had to be a "sonovabitch". He had to keep driving or else pretty soon the men would have time to stop and think, think of home, children growing up and parents growing older, all out of touch with each other, and then think about the chances of being sunk. Thinking is fatal. As in Kipling's poem, "there's no discharge in the war"; there is no way out. Every man slogged on like an automaton, looking, staring with dull uninterested eyes at the unreal, incongruous beauty of the tropical surroundings.

4TH BATTLE OF SAVO ISLAND (NOVEMBER 30TH) (SOMETIMES CALLED "TASSAFARONGA")

After the Battle of Guadalcanal, something happened which changed the character of the war in the Guadalcanal area.

Although the Japanese had been turned back at least temporarily, they kept making nightly destroyer attacks on Guadalcanal, and there was still a real possibility that they might try another major assault. The U.S., therefore, continued to send a steady stream of transports up to Guadalcanal to build up the U.S. forces there.

During this period, the RUSSELL was still assigned to screen the ENTER-PRISE which was occupied with patrolling in the Coral Sea and providing air support where needed. In an effort to put an end to the nightly enemy attacks, on November 30th the U.S. sent a Task Force of five heavy cruisers and six destroyers into "Iron Bottom Bay", as the bay between Guadalcanal and Tulagi had by then become known, to deal with a squadron of six Japanese destroyers, which had been sighted earlier in the day approaching Guadalcanal.

The problem was that the U.S. cruisers forgot the lessons previously learned, that, in order to capitalize on our radar advantage, it was necessary to move outside of the bay into the open sea. For example, inside the bay we had suffered heavily (e.g., August 9th and November 13th), whereas outside, at long range, we had prevailed (e.g., October 11th and November 14th). On November 30th, the cruisers waited until midnight and then steamed into the bay in a nice, perfectly spaced column; in fact, a perfect target. The Japanese destroyers had previously entered the bay under cover of darkness and unbeknownst to our cruisers, were deployed so close to the shore of the Island that the radars on the cruisers were unable to detect them apart from the land. When the cruisers came into range of the Japanese torpe-does, which, it will be remembered was far greater than ours, the Japan-ese fired their torpedoes, and started moving away along the coast, still undetected. The enemy torpedoes were very accurately aimed. They sank the cruiser NORTHHAMPTON, and badly damaged the cruisers PENSACOLA, NEW ORLEANS, and MINNEAPOLIS. The U.S. destroyers claimed to have sunk an enemy destroyer with gunfire (this claim is subject to some question). Also, they fired torpedoes in the direction of the Japanese but scored no hits. The one remaining healthy U.S. cruiser, the HONOLULU, then under the tactical command of Admiral Tisdale, circled tentatively to the north (where no enemy ships had been sighted), while the enemy escaped to the west.

LET THE PT BOATS DO IT

After the defeat of our cruisers by the Japanese destroyers on November 30th, being convinced that the U.S. ships could not cope with the Japanese torpedoes within the confines of "Iron Bottom Bay", the U.S. Fleet Command decided to defend Guadalcanal from these nightly raids in a different manner. The larger ships were withdrawn. The island airfields were expanded and large quantities of shore-based aircraft were moved up. PT boats were brought in as a deterrent if not a cure.

This change permitted the ENTERPRISE to be drawn further to the rear, and owing to the shortage of destroyers, the RUSSELL was finally tabbed for duty convoying supplies to Guadalcanal. Then, after arriving at Guadalcanal, the RUSSELL was assigned to duty patrolling the enemy held coastline and bombarding enemy installations during the daytime under the direction of U.S. artillery observers on the island. At night we would withdraw across "Iron Bottom Bay" into Tulagi Harbor and leave the PT boats to do what they could to break up the enemy's destroyer raids.

U.S. PT BOATS VS. JAPANESE DESTROYERS

In my 1945 diary I recorded the following incident:

"One night, swinging at our moorings in Tulagi Harbor, we had occasion to watch three of our little PT boats fight it out with a division of enemy destroyers. It was painful to watch. We had four destroyers sitting peacefully in the harbor, each with eight torpedoes, and a main battery of 5" guns, but the combined commands had concluded that it was more important to keep the destroyers available for shore bombardment (rooting out Japanese resistance pockets on Guadalcanal) than to risk our being sunk by the superior Japanese torpedoes. So, our orders were simply to "Stay put". We went to General Quarters and got steam up, in case the enemy should decide to come over and attack us. Then we just had to sit there tearing our hair and grimacing with hatred while the enemy destroyers chased our little PT boats around, sinking several of them. Undoubtedly the discretion of the Command at that time was "the better part of valor." Also, although we would have gladly gone out there with the PT boats to do what we could, no one on the RUSSELL was unmindful of the fact that it was safer for us personally to remain where we were. Accordingly, as we steamed out of Tulagi harbor the next morning and waved at the surviving PT boats, we could not suppress a certain feeling of chagrin and admiration that these small and unprotected heroes had fought a battle which, by all rights, was ours and which we would have fought but for the superiority of the Japanese torpedoes."

Since I do not know the exact date of this incident involving the PT boats which we witnessed and heard on the voice radio, I cannot tell whether it was when Jack Kennedy's PT boat was shot up by Japanese destroyers, but from the accounts I have read, Jack Kennedy's story matches fairly well with the time and results of the one I recorded in 1945:

After the enemy destroyers had retired around 1:00am, the remaining PT boats picked up the survivors, and while they were limping back into Tulagi, we heard the following over the voice radio:

"Hey Joe!"

"Yeah?"

"Have any pickles left?"

"Only one, and I'm saving it for Josephine!"

BOGESS LOOSES HIS TEETH

One morning after returning to Espiritu Santo, the Captain and I went ashore together in the gig. I, for my routine call on the shore-based Communications Office, and he for the purpose of finding some beer for a beach party he was planning for the crew. We went our separate ways. I returned, and around 11:00 o'clock the Captain came back dejectedly. He said he had been everywhere and could not locate any beer. While I had been at the Communications Office, however, I had seen a Marine truck on the main road carrying some boxes covered with a tarpaulin and the boxes were very much the same size and shape as beer cases. I told the Captain I thought I had seen some beer being trucked and asked if he would let me go over and have a "shot" at getting some. He agreed and I went back over to the island. After landing, I walked up to the main road, and hitched a ride heading east. As we were going along, I noticed coming toward us another of the same kind of Marine truck I had seen before with the tarpaulin covered boxes, which resembled beer cases, so I asked to be let off. Next, I waited by the roadside and not long afterward, still another truck similar to the previous ones carrying the curious tarpaulin-covered boxes, showed up. I stepped into the road and more-or-less demanded a hitch. The Marine driver stopped reluctantly and let me come aboard. We then drove past the landing and continued west for another mile or so. Finally, the truck stopped, and the driver yelled at me that this was where they turned, and I would have to get off. I, of course, complied, but in the meantime had been able to peek at the boxes under a corner of the tarpaulin and had confirmed that they were, indeed, beer. Therefore, I started out on foot to follow the truck. The road was sandy and continued through a palm tree grove. After 400 yds. or so, I saw a small Quonset hut and near it a long line of tarpaulin covered beer cases piled about 6' high, about 12' across, and easily 150' long. Also, there was a Marine Sentry with a rifle at each end of the line of covered boxes. I felt the same way Howard Carter must have felt when he opened the door of Tutankhamen's tomb and beheld a room full of gold. Here I was looking at a tremendous cache of a commodity worth far more than mere gold; I had cracked probably the most securely held secret on the island

The next problem, however, was how to get some of it, which problem was compounded by the fact that the Marines were in possession of it. The Army, the Navy, the Air Force—any other branch of the services can be cajoled, bribed, or tricked, but the Marines are something else again. I learned early in the war that no one fools with a Marine sentry. The difference between a Navy Sentry and a Marine sentry is significant. Not only are the sentries hard, but the same strength and discipline extends throughout the Marine Corps.

I approached one of the sentries.

"Any way a guy can get access to some of that beer?"

"Forget it. If you don't believe me, go over there to the Quonset Hut and ask."

I went over to the hut, and as I entered, I was astounded to see the famous movie actor Robert Montgomery (an Officer on one of the Cruisers) coming out. I then approached the desk and spoke to the Yeoman.

"Morning. Did my eyes deceive me or was that Robert Montgomery?"

"Yeah. That was him all right. Yeah, the CO just gave him the bum's rush.'"

"Oh, is that so. I just came in to see if there is any way a guy might get a bit of that beer for his ship."

"Nope. I can tell you this. If Robert Montgomery can't, you sure as hell can't."

I had nothing to lose, so I kept on.

"I expect you are right, but can I ask the C.O. anyway?"

The Yeoman then grunted disgustedly.

"What's your name and the name of your ship? I'll put it on a note and hand it in to the CO."

"Lt. (jg) Russell of the Russell."

This stopped him briefly and he made me repeat it to be sure. He then put it down on a piece of paper and went in to the C.O. I waited a while. The C.O. came to the door.

"What's the Russell?"

"It's a tin can, Sir. We are nested with the Mustin, another tin can."

"OK, you come in here. I want to talk to you." Shutting the door behind him, he put his face directly into mine.

"How many men you got on those two ships?" "About 320 men each, Sir!" "Mmm—- mmm—- OK, Goddammit you've got 100 cases, but there are two conditions. First, you get the hell out of here and never come back, and second, if you breathe a word about this to anyone, the Marines will find you and make you pay with blood!"

I then went out. The C.O. ordered 100 cases to be put on a truck for me, fully covered, of course, and they took me and the beer back to the landing. At the Port Director's Office, I sent a flashing light message for two boats to be sent immediately for "very precious cargo". Still with maximum precaution to avoid being seen, the cases were loaded into the boats and taken to the Russell.

We immediately set up a party to be held on a nearby beach. Roasted weenies, and four bottles of beer were rationed to each man of both ships.

We had a man named Bogess in the Paymaster's office on the Russell. Bogess was very old, that is, he was about 45. Also, he had a full set of false teeth, both top and bottom. Poor Bogess. Either it was the weenies or the four bottles of beer or both. Anyway, after he returned to the ship he threw up and lost his false teeth overside.

I have no adequate explanation why the Marine CO gave us the beer. I just took it and ran!

(Editors Note: Other histories of the RUSSELL such as Robert Robinson's The Invincible Russell recount a much more colorful tale of how Bogess lost his teeth – "escaping" from a phantom shark while swimming outside the netted safe area.)

SYDNEY? AH, SYDNEY!

New Destroyers began arriving, and the RUSSELL rejoined the ENTERPRISE for the customary plane-guard duty. This continued for about a month. Orders then came in for the RUSSELL to proceed to Sydney, Australia for 10 days of recreation. This was the definite high point of the war for the men on the RUSSELL. Today, every time I see any of them (I saw Wesselhoeft last year), they still talk mostly about Sydney. If you mention Sydney, the answer is always, "Sydney? Ah, Sydney" and they kind of stare into space.

RBR second from left – RBR Personal Collection

The trip to Sydney was truly a summer cruise. On the way, we broke out the small arms and had fun shooting at the flying fish. Everyone forgot his gripes. It was a happy-go-lucky band of tired sailors.

We entered Sydney at a narrow, gated entrance, flanked by submarine nets, near Manly at the northeast end of the Bay. Sydney Harbor is a large expanse of water, perhaps 5 miles long by 3 miles wide, which, toward the west is spanned by a large black cantilever arched bridge resembling the bridge over the Firth of Forth in Scotland. The harbor can be described as a beautiful lake bordered by the city on the south and west, and by the suburbs of Sydney elsewhere. Hundreds of sailboats were in evidence. Ferries moved across the bay. Many ships were at anchor and others at docks. The RUSSELL was ordered to dock in a slip at the foot of the city, called Woolloomooloo. Across from the dock in Woolloomooloo was a park full of trees, having a high bare ridge running down the center of the park parallel to the ship. As we approached, I heard Terrill yell, "Hey! There's a gal who knows sema-phore." (Semaphore is another way of communication between ships. Certain positions of the hands holding semaphore flags, indicate letters. The flags are used to make the positions of the hands visible at a distance. Semaphore can, of course, be done with the hands alone at short range. A message can be transmitted faster by semaphore than by blinker.) In fact, there were at least a dozen girls on the ridge all fluent in semaphore, and within a short time, most of the Signalmen and Quartermasters had arranged dates.

A leave schedule was worked out with a small skeleton crew and the entire engineering plant shut down for the first time in years. 250 happy men hit the beach for 9 days each.

A simple mathematical computation revealed the principal problem. The population of Australia at the time was about 10,000,000. They had about 1,000,000 men under arms (a very high percentage of mobilization compared to ours), and about 500,000 of them were overseas. Even in the pre-penicillin era, with Victorianism still far from dead, one would expect at least half of the women left behind to be susceptible, half of those to be willing, and a half of those to be ravenous. This would leave over 60,000 in the final category, of whom at least 10,000 were in Sydney; quite enough for the 320 men of the Russell, even counting their own most exaggerated opinion of their male prowess.

I made this computation and, knowing that I have little, if any, character, became alarmed. Lib had come to California with little Bobby (then about nine months old) and anticipating that the RUSSELL might come in, had set up a little home in Oakland. I had her very much in mind, but knew that I had to do something like Ulysses did when he made his men lash him to the mast, and put wax in their ears when passing the sirens. A solution for me came in the mail, which was delivered to the ship upon arrival. It was an engraved invitation to the Officers of the RUSSELL to present their cards to the Hon. Sec. of the Imperial Services Club of Sydney and be accepted for temporary membership. As I have stated, I was an anglophile, and had always admired all of the British Armed Services. Therefore, when first ashore, I went immediately with my card to the Hon. Sec. and became a temporary member of the Imperial Services Club.

I then proceeded to the bar, of course, and ordered myself a drink, and equally of course, started to pay for it. A firm, large hand gripped my arm like a vice, and a deep voice said, "No." I looked around into a large face with a huge jutting chin, and a fine small, clipped mustache.

"This one is on me!"

The timbre and cast of the voice left no doubt that his wishes were to be obeyed. I then introduced myself and we spoke. I told about the RUSSELL, soon was introduced around, and I became the center of discussion. They, (most of whom were retired officers), wanted to know all about Coral Sea, Midway, Santa Cruz, Guadalcanal, etc., and I held forth with all of the details, including I am sure, some things which actually did take place. Thereafter, I made the ISC my headquarters, and for the remainder of my stay, I never was allowed to buy a drink.

I was surprised to learn that I was the first U.S. Naval Officer to accept their invitation, although by then, many U.S. Navy ships had moored in Sydney. The members of the club were curious to learn why this should be. All I could say was that young Americans are more oriented toward movies and honky tonks. I pointed out that the Americans were missing a very good thing, and that I really had no adequate explanation.

While I was confident that I had chosen a safe haven at the ISC sheltered from temptation, my plan contained a flaw for which I was not prepared. In accordance with my custom, on the first morning in Sydney, I went over to the Central Communications Officer of the Australian Navy to check on the latest code changes and Fox Schedules. While in the office, and after introducing myself to the Commanding Officer and establishing my credentials, the C.O. started showing me around the communications facility. In the course of this tour, he brought me into a room where half-a-dozen Australian WRENs (female officers) decoding messages. I looked down the line and my eyes came to rest on a girl who utterly stunned me. She was a very English type, about 5'6" tall and slim. She had light brown hair, blue eyes, clear, mildly aquiline features along the lines of Greta Garbo, and lightly colored pink cheeks. The other WRENs in the room were also attractive, but when the Commander introduced me, I must have betrayed what had happened to me because this particular girl was also uneasy and blushed. I went away in a trance. From then on, I returned frequently to the Australian Communications Office.

On my next visit, I asked her to lunch and she came. It happened that she was engaged to an Officer in the Australian Navy. I showed her my photographs of Lib and Bobby and asked her if she would show me the sights of Sydney. She agreed.

Then commenced for me an indelible ten days. I managed, by my communications excuse, to see her at some point nearly every day, and on the two weekends we were there, she and I went to the zoo, we went tea dancing, we bicycled, we took a picnic to Manly, we went to the movies, we dined, we laughed, we teased; in a word, I was very much in love with her. I also thought that she was in love with me, but we never talked about it. It was for both of us one of those "roads not taken". I do not agree with Robert Frost. The roads that I have taken in my life have been fabulous. In fact, I cannot believe I am as lucky as I am, but I would not want to desecrate the memories by saying that I am sure that not taking some of the other roads "made all the difference". When the Russell left Sydney, I had my binoculars focused on the Communications Office. She came to the balcony and we waved. I watched her until we rounded the point at Manly miles away.

My uncle John Russell was in Sydney at that time, and during one of the times when my friend was on duty, I looked him up. He took me to lunch at the Royal Australian Club. He was a very sad guy, extremely homesick, and he told me, "I'm not like you younger guys. I can't think of anything but home. Anyone but Hortense."

The gang at the ISC also took me around. On one occasion they arranged for me to play golf at a club north of Manly, up on a hill. During my round of golf, a crow-like bird stole my golf-ball. I was all alone and was prepared not to be believed any more than if I had said I had scored a hole in one. On the contrary, they were used to the bird story. They said that the birds are a nuisance and steal the balls frequently. On another occasion, they drove me out to one of the "Stations" (i.e., ranches). On the night out at the Station, I had a good deal too much to drink, but in the morning, they showered me, propped me up, and got me back bleary-eyed to the ship just in time to stand my in-port O.D. watch.

Gasoline, of course, was in very short supply and rationed. Therefore, nearly every car had mounted on its rear bumper a charcoal burner with a rig which would permit feeding the CO (carbon monoxide) to the carburetor. In this way, after once starting with gasoline, they could continue on a level road quite well using very little gasoline and mostly CO. It was not very useful for climbing hills or rapid acceleration, but adequate for locomotion.

The other Officers returned to the ship full of yarns. Caster told about being in a movie house and overhearing a conversation between a girl and a sailor in the seats in front of him, and the girl was saying, "I've never been out with a sailor before, but this is 4.0." There were also tales of fights, intrigue, brushes with the Shore Patrol and the police, as well as fantastic orgies.

The trip back to the fleet was still a summer cruise and we were still a happy-go-lucky band of men, but instead of being merely tired, we were exhausted.

5. CONCLUSION IN THE SOUTHWEST PACIFIC

THE FIRST DESTROYER CIC

After Tassafaronga, but probably before the trip to Sydney, the RUSSELL continued with her customary duties as plane-guard for the ENTERPRISE. The ENTERPRISE was not, at that time, being called upon for heavy combat duty, but we made several swings through the Coral Sea and launched air strikes against targets in the Solomons and Shortlands.

On one occasion, an aircraft from the ENTERPRISE had been damaged by Japanese anti-aircraft gunfire and had been forced to ditch near Rossel Island on the southeastern end of the New Guinea chain. The pilot and his crew had, in fact, been sighted by U.S. patrol planes, waving to them from the beach of Rossel Island. The RUSSELL was sent off on a solo mission to rescue this stranded air crew.

They say that if things can go wrong, they will, and I can attest to the truth of the statement. Not long after the RUSSELL had started on this detached duty, I was in my little "telephone booth" decoding a message on the ECM, when, all of a sudden, the ECM went "clunk". Thereafter, nothing I could do would make it continue. This was an emergency. Here we were, on detached duty, at which time the need to be able to receive coded dispatches was particularly critical. Beyond this, the problem was that no one on the ship knew anything about the ECM. It was not like the radar or sonar for which we had trained enlisted personnel. The ECM was top secret. Only I had access to it, and I knew absolutely nothing about it.

I took out the instruction manuals and started trying to figure things out. While I was fumbling around, trying to identify parts, I noticed a little metal thing in the back lying on the deck at the bottom of the case. I fished it out, and from one of its ends I could see that it had broken off of something else in the machine. I then took the cover of the machine off and, looking around the back, found another piece of broken metal which matched the little piece

I had found. Now I had located the thing which had broken, but what to do about it was another question. Trying to glue, solder or weld it seemed as remote as Peter Pan trying to attach his shadow to his foot with soap. I fiddled around and, in the course of pushing things, all of a sudden, I heard another "clunk". I looked around and a new letter had been printed. I then depressed the proper next key on the keyboard, went around to the back, found the thing I had pressed before, pressed it, and again "clunk". A further letter had been printed. Then, following this procedure, albeit laboriously, I decoded the message.

In this manner, we survived the breakdown of the ECM, but we had other problems. We were on detached duty and in an area which was not only routinely covered by enemy patrol planes, but also within reach of enemy bombers from Rabaul. For this reason, the Admiral on the ENTERPRISE provided us with a "fighter cover" comprising four fighter aircraft. This was fine in concept, but the fighters needed direction from ship-based radars if they were to be able to do us any good, and we were the only ship in this detached area with radar. We, therefore, set up what is believed to have been the first CIC (Combat Information Center) on a Destroyer in the U.S. Navy.

On the RUSSELL, the radar was located in a little room on the port side of the bridge aft of the Chartroom. This small room may have, in times past, been an emergency bunkroom for the Division Commander. In any event, the radar was located in it at this time. The room was too small and the radar console too large to allow for anyone else other than the operator in the room. The room did, however, have a port hole. So the way we set up our CIC was to open the port hole, and for me to sit outside on a chair with a mooring (otherwise referred to as a maneuvering) board in my lap. We had developed technique employing a clear plastic sheet which had been roughened with steel wool (to make the markings stick) covering the mooring board, on which we made markings with grease pencil. In this way, the markings rendered obsolete by the motion of the plane could be quickly rubbed out as the situation changed.

The way it worked was for the radar operator continuously to sing out the range and bearing of the "friendlies" or "bogies", as the case might be and for me, sitting outside, with the mooring board in my lap, to plot them, and, with the microphone for transmission on the aircraft voice radio circuit on a long lead, to direct the fighters.

The radar on the RUSSELL was not capable of determining the altitude of the contacts but at least it did show where they were sufficiently to permit us to tell the fighter pilots the direction where to look. Then by scanning up and down in that direction, they could spot the enemy. It was a bit rough, but it worked. We had three or four scares involving enemy search planes to the north, but were able to vector the fighters onto them and drive them off.

In between times, the pilots would chat or sing. Once, one of them burst out in the following song, "Ten thousand dollars going home to the folks." (Note: all GI's were automatically given a $10,000 life insurance policy.)

It happened that before the RUSSELL was able to reach Rossel Island, a U.S. submarine surfaced near the downed aviators, and rescued them.

HARTWIG GETS HIS ORDERS

By this time, the industrial power of the U.S. was beginning to be felt, and large quantities of supplies, ships and aircraft began appearing. The tide had definitely turned. The ENTERPRISE (and we with her) was patrolling the Coral Sea, and the U.S. was starting to move up the island chain.

It was around this time that Captain Hartwig was relieved from the Command of the RUSSELL and ordered to a new ship, then under construction in the States.

On the day the message came in detaching him, I happened to be within earshot of the Radio Shack, heard the commotion, and went in to see what it was all about. Next, when the message was complete, I took it off the typewriter and charged up the ladder to find him. He was not on the bridge, but I found him asleep on a cot on the open deck aft of the Commodore's cabin. I shook him and said, "Captain, look at this!" He rolled over, groggily came up to a sitting position, and read it slowly. Then all of a sudden, he snapped his head toward me with a fierce scowl.

"You sonovabitch, this is a hoax isn't it?"

I was shocked.

"Well, you sonovabitch, if you think I'd pull a trick like that on anyone, then—you."

I turned and walked away. It was a sad moment. He and I had come a long way together from Mersigs and greasy food in the North Atlantic. We had survived the Yellow Peril, the red snappers, Samoa, and Pearl. We had raced elbow-to-elbow around the bridge of the RUSSELL through the Coral Sea, Midway, and Santa Cruz battles, and had agonized nightly over the dispatches through the frightening saga of Guadalcanal wondering if we would be chosen next. It was I, more than anyone else (because I was O.D. at GQ) who had put into practice his fuel conservation concepts, which made us so good as a plane-guard and which probably saved our lives. He and I, if not buddies, were, and, in fact, remained good friends both later in the war and afterward. He even selected me out of all of the Junior Officers he knew, to be his Operations Officer, i.e. Chief of Staff, when he became a Squadron Commander. It was simply an unfortunate moment, obviously caused by the long times at sea and the tensions.

MICKEY MOUSE TAKES OVER

OUR NEXT COMMANDING OFFICER WAS LT. Cdr. W.H. McClain. He was small, red-haired (receding at the temples), poor on technology, and quintessentially Southern. He was affectionately called "Mickey Mouse", by one and all, except that, even though he was not an imposing person, the "Mickey Mouse" sobriquet was not used in his presence.

On our first trip at sea with him as captain, the invasion of Rennell Island (January 29, 1943), we were again assigned to accompany the ENTERPRISE. This time, however, the entire screen was made up of new Destroyers. We were the only ship of our class present. As soon as the Task Force had cleared the channel, the signal went up for the RUSSELL to assume her customary station as plane-guard and the "shapes" went up. I informed Captain McClain and told him that this was the time to head immediately for the calculated plane-guard station. He balked and said "How come? The shapes have not been executed." (i.e. hauled down). I said, "This is the way we do it Captain, it saves fuel." He would have none of it. Next thing, the ENTERPRISE executed the shapes and turned away from us, leaving us about 4000 yds. astern. "Mickey Mouse" went up to 30 kts. but was still 2000 yds. out of station when the flight operations were over. I then told him to start back again immediately, and again he demurred only to find himself racing a second time to regain station in the screen. We took plane-guard station three times more that day and continued to do it "Mickey Mouse's" way. That night after the fuel reports had gone in and it became known that the RUSSELL had expended a full day's run of fuel, more than any of the other ships, the RUSSELL was immediately moved up in the screen to a station not used for plane-guard duty. Directly after that particular Task Force operation, the RUSSELL was ordered to join the Destroyer pool at Noumea and we commenced convoying Liberty Ships to Guadalcanal, a duty which we continued to do until eventually moving north again to Pearl Harbor in May. Nothing could have proved more convincingly the value of Hartwig's procedures.

This relegation of the RUSSELL to the demeaning job of convoying Liberty Ships was not only humiliating, but it took us away from the interesting part of the war and into total boredom. My morale dropped considerably, and for the first time, I began hoping desperately for a transfer.

"FISTICUFFS"

At around the time "Mickey Mouse" came on board, the RUSSELL also received a contingent of new officers among whom was an Ensign Toivo Pulkinen. He could be described as a typical American Midwestern college grad, well-built, handsome, happy-go-lucky, smart, and fancied himself as a "lady killer". He stood JOD watches under me on various occasions, and we became good friends. Around mid-April 1943 after the RUSSELL had returned to Espiritu Santo from Guadalcanal, a group of us, including Pulkinen, went over to the island one night for some drinks at the newly established Officers' Club. It was a rollicking party with everyone yelling and laughing and horsing around. In the midst of the discussion, I was bragging about piloting Zadie Langhorne's Stinson 105 back from Nantucket to Hyannis at an air speed of 110 mph. Pulkinen said, "Hey, wait a minute. What'd you say?" I replied that I had flown Zadie's Stinson 105 from Nantucket to Hyannis at an air speed of 110 mph. He said, "A Stinson 105 can't fly at 110 mph." I said, "I flew a Stinson 105 at 110 mph!" He said, "It will not fly that fast!" I said, "Listen you sonovabitch, if you don't think a Stinson 105 will fly at 110 mph, then just step outside here and I'll show you!"

I should interject here that I had been a very placid child. In fact, throughout my entire boyhood, I had been in only one fist fight. It happened at a time when a friend of mine was being beaten up by an older boy bully. I had flown into a rage and had beaten up the bully. That was, however, the only fight I was ever in. The war, however, changed many people, including me. At this point in my career, my temper was on a "hair trigger" and the idea of wading in with fists flying was not merely acceptable, I was hungry for it.

Within seconds, Pulkinen and I were bashing away at each other outside of the club. He knew more about the "gentlemanly art of self-defense" than I, and soon my nose was gushing blood. I grappled with him, and since my legs were stronger, I threw him to the ground. We were then tumbling around on the ground when someone grabbed me from behind. At that point, Pulkinen took a pretty good shot at me. This infuriated me. Up until then, I had been merely bull-mad but not infuriated. I then swung around on this third party, and, the amazing thing is that Pulkinen did too, and we together lit into this third party, knocking him flat, and then turned back again to our own fight. I was no match for Pulkinen in boxing, but eventually I held my own with him in the wrestling department to the point where we both became exhausted and called it a draw. Then we got up laughing and went back down to the dock.

Neither Pulkinen nor I was aware of it at the time, but the man whom we had beaten up in the middle of our fight was the commanding officer of the base. In addition, somehow, he was able to obtain our names. I will write more about this later.

RUSSELL DETACHED FROM THE RUSSELL

The RUSSELL put to sea the next morning with a small Task Force to screen a convoy headed back to Pearl Harbor.

Pulkinen's and my black eyes and swollen noses soon healed, and we became even better friends than before. The RUSSELL steamed peacefully and, I should say happily, back to Pearl Harbor.

The entrance to Pearl Harbor comprises a long narrow channel which extends in a straight line about 1 ½ miles due west to Ford Island, where it splits, and ships can either turn north and proceed directly to the shipyard or continue west by a longer route around Ford Island. At this stage of the war, while salvage operations were still in progress in the area of the direct route, the Destroyers were usually sent the longer route around Ford Island. The Central Communications Office, however, is at the Navy Yard and, therefore, blinker messages could be sent from the signal tower to ships from the moment the ships started in the channel.

On May 9, 1943, as the RUSSELL nosed into the channel at Pearl Harbor, I was on the bridge, the blinker at the Navy Yard tower came on and we started to receive the following message: "DD414—LT. ROBERT B. RUSSELL DVG USNR HEREBY DETACHED...... This was the moment I had been hoping for. I let out a whoop and bolted from the bridge. There were a lot of details to attend to. My orders had to be typed up. My pay records had to be transferred. I had to pack, of course, and I had to turn over not only the custody of the secret publications, and the Mess Treasurer's books, receipts and cash, but also the title "B" equipment (equipment for which an officer must take personal responsibility). All I can say is that I flew. Luckily, Rog Tatton and I had very recently cited the publications and the title "B" equipment. Since he obviously would be the one to take over these duties from me, they presented no problem. Wesselhoeft had already taken over the Mess Treasurer's duties. The Yeoman typed up my orders, and the paymaster took the details and agreed to transfer my pay records "in due course". On top of all this, my promotion to full Lieutenant had come in and further paperwork was needed to complete it.

By the time the ship had rounded Ford Island, most of the foregoing details were either done or nearing completion, and I was stuffing my things into a cruise-box. The RUSSELL then proceeded directly into the Navy Yard where she tied up alongside a pier. I brought my orders, and promotion papers to the Captain at the same time as he came down from the bridge after docking the ship. He was a bit surprised by the speed, but obliged by signing both my transfer orders and my promotion, and I returned below to get my things, and bid good-bye to Bargeloh, Caster, Brown, Woodman, Wesselhoeft, Tatton, Hart, Silberman (Baylor, and Toivonen had already been transferred) and the others. These were hasty farewells with "Best of luck" and "See you at Armageddon". No time for sentiment.

Then Bryant and Warmsby took my cruise-box. On the way out, I went into the Radio Shack, said good-bye to Austin, Bass and the gang, went to the Bridge, shook hands with those who remained of the old gang Free, White, Nally, and Terrill, (Schwarz and Barrow had long since been transferred), proceeded up the gangway, and after a look back to fix her in my memory, turned away from the ship which had been my home for the previous 21 months.

Before departing from the subject of the USS RUSSELL—DD414, I should say a few words about her remarkable record. Many other ships have been given accolades by the press or awards by the Navy. The naval awards are often given in the form of Presidential Unit citations or by way of having subsequent ships named after them. Usually, however, this form of special recognition is reserved for ships which were either sunk or severely damaged. The RUSSELL was never so fortunate, or unfortunate, depending on how one looks at it, and, so far, she has received no recognition of any sort for her unusual accomplishments. Although she was never damaged seriously by enemy gunfire, she had many near misses, and torpedoes passed close by on a number of occasions. Her entire fo'c'sle was bent up 10" by a mammoth wave which could easily have capsized her if it had not hit her from straight ahead. At Santa Cruz, her bridge was smashed and she was strafed by an enemy aircraft. As for her accomplishments, she was just about first in everything. She is credited with the fastest test speed of any destroyer, 39.6 kts. She won the "E" for engineering excellence in her class for 1940. Her involvement in the war was not surpassed by any ship in the fleet. Thus, she was patrolling in one end of the Denmark Strait (between Iceland and Greenland) in September 1941 in search of the German pocket battleship VON TIRPITZ. She was at sea near the GREER at the time of the first confrontation between Germany and the United States—when the real war started. She was in the destroyer pool for convoy duty when the KEARNEY was torpedoed, and in a nearby convoy when the REUBEN JAMES was sunk. The RUSSELL was the first U.S. destroyer to be fitted with the British sound recorder in the fall of 1941, and then among the first to be fitted with radar in December of 1941. She escorted the first Marines to Samoa and the Army to New

Caledonia after the start of the war and was the first ship of the Pacific Fleet to fire a shot in anger at a Japanese aircraft after Pearl Harbor. She was in the first three major aircraft carrier battles in history; she rescued survivors from the LEXINGTON; she was the first to go in to pick up survivors from the YORKTOWN at Midway; and the first to go alongside the HORNET to fight the fires and take off the wounded at Santa Cruz. In addition she was the premier plane guard destroyer of the fleet in that, by her combined engineering and ship handling excellence, she was able to do the plane guard job without extra expenditure of fuel, whereas none of the other destroyers could do it. She was the first destroyer of the fleet to vector fighters by radar against enemy targets. Subsequent to the incidents described above in this book, she participated in the Aleutians campaign and in virtually the entire remainder of the war. At Tarawa she was the first destroyer to move in close to the beach to bombard and strafe the defending Japanese pill boxes and thereafter she returned frequently to that assignment until the landing was eventually secured. She helped cover MacArthur's move west along the New Guinea coast to Hollandia and then through Western New Guinea ending up at the landings at Morotai. Thereafter she advanced through the Philippines as part of "MacArthur's Navy" and took part in the battle of Leyte Gulf (the greatest naval battle in history in terms of fire power on each side). After that she was in the Luzon operation followed by the Manila–Subic Bay battles. At the end she served her turn on the picket line at Okinawa when the Kamikaze put 131 U.S. destroyers out of action in the short span of three months. Since the Subic Bay incident was the final battle in which surface ships of the U.S. fleet engaged surface ships of the Japanese fleet, not only did the RUSSELL fire the first shots by a ship of the Pacific Fleet at the Japanese after Pearl Harbor, but she fired the last shots between surface ships. In total, the RUSSELL was awarded 16, battle stars, ranking her amongst the most decorated US ships of WWII.[42]

PULKINEN'S REWARD

As I was going up the gangway, down were coming three burly fellows carrying sacks of mail. I hesitated for a moment, and then thought, "What the hell! I'm going to be home in a little while and I will see with my own eyes and hear with my own ears how things are, so what good will it do to read letters that will be anywhere from 3 to 8 weeks stale." (Letters came to us via very diverse routes and were often out of sequence by months), so I simply continued on. What I did not know was that, contained in the mail coming down the gangway as I went up, was a reprimand from Admiral Halsey's Staff to Pulkinen and me. By the time the personal mail was segregated and passed around, and the official mail was sorted out, distributed and catalogued, I had long since disappeared.

I will tell later about how the reprimand caught up with me. The reprimand was written in typically stilted Navy language. I regret not being able to quote it verbatim because at a later date, unbeknownst to me and being ashamed of it, Lib threw it away.

It was addressed to the Commanding Officer of the RUSSELL and listed various references to Navy Regulations by letters (a), (b) and (c). Next after "subject" came "Lt. (jg) Robert B. Russell, Ensign Toivo Pulkinen: Conduct of: Unbecoming of an Officer and a Gentleman." The text which followed was classic. It stated that subject Officers had been observed conducting fisticuffs at the Officers' Club at Espiritu Santo, had assaulted a Senior Officer, had been insubordinate, and had resisted arrest. It then went on to urge the C.O. of subject Officers to point out to subject Officers that such conduct was in violation of references (a), (b) and (c). It concluded by saying that the C.O. should issue a reprimand to subject Officers and take such disciplinary action as, in his discretion, he deemed appropriate.

Poor Pulkinen, he was at the mercy of "Mickey Mouse", who, being the cautious type, would obviously mete out the maximum penalty, simply to avoid the risk of criticism from Officers above him. Pulkinen was placed on "Hack". This meant that he had to "present his sword" to the Captain, a formality which was equivalent to temporarily relinquishing one's commission and remain in "house arrest" in the Wardroom for ten days; a very stiff sentence, considering that Pulkinen had been at sea for about five months and would be returning shortly to extended sea duty.

HITCHHIKING TO 'FRISCO

My orders did not provide for air travel, but I was able to wangle a ride in the cargo area of a PBM (2 motored flying boat) and arrived back in the States on May 14, 1943.

This was the time that I was in the line to get aboard a plane at the Honolulu airport, but missed it by only several numbers. I then succeeded in getting on board the next one. The one I missed crashed into the mountains across San Francisco Bay, killing all on board.

6. NEW CONSTRUCTION

Home on leave with Lib and RBR Jr. – RBR Personal Collection

LEAVE AND SHORE DUTY

Next for me was a period of leave and shore duty. It was wonderful to be home, to see Lib, and the family, and to meet Bobby, then 14 months old (he took his first steps after I arrived). The period, however, was also difficult, particularly for Bobby. He had heard a lot about me and had been shown photographs, but he knew nothing real. As far as he was concerned, I was an intruder who was taking a lot of his mother's attention away from him. We had 20 days leave, left Bobby with a baby-sitter, and went to Yosemite (and stayed at the Awahnee Hotel) for a week. Also, my parents came out West, and there was friction between my mother and Lib for my time, and conflict over how to manage my life. Beyond this, I was like TNT, and easily detonated; definitely a changed person from the boy who had had cups of Java with the men in Casco Bay, and who had had the ketchup spilled on his dress whites in Panama. Therefore, while it was wonderful to be home, it was also a trying time.

As I had done earlier, I did not wait out my full leave, but reported to Bethlehem Shipyard where my new ship, the destroyer OWEN (DD-536) was under construction. Bethlehem had assigned several offices on shore for use by the OWEN, and two or three of the Chief Petty Officers assigned to the ship had already arrived and were sorting things out when I came "on board".

Home on leave, 1943 – RBR Personal Collection

Copies of the orders of all of the officers who had been assigned to the OWEN were there, and from the dates of their orders, and the amount of leave each had been granted, I could see that I would be Senior Officer in charge of the OWEN for at least another two weeks.

At about that same time or shortly thereafter, while opening the morning official mail of the OWEN, I found a letter which had been forwarded from the RUSSELL to the Commanding Officer of the OWEN, on the subject of "Lt. (jg) Robert B. Russell, Ensign Toivo Pulkinen; Conduct ... etc." I, of course, had been previously unaware either of the letter or of Pulkinen's punishment (I heard about the latter later).

I studied the letter carefully, since I was then in command of the OWEN detail, and after deciding that a serious offense had been committed, I soundly slapped both of my own wrists, and slid the letter into my pocket.

THE BEST OF BOTH WORLDS

My greatest desire as a Naval Officer was to command a ship. I think it is accurate to say that I was obsessed with the idea. I was aware, however, that a reserve officer whose naval career was solely in communications would never be considered for a command. It was, therefore, imperative to me to get out of communications and into another job such as 1st Lieutenant (in charge of the deck crews, ships maintenance, damage control, etc.) or Gunnery. Gunnery, however, was out of the question because a Senior Gunnery Officer had already been assigned to the OWEN. My only chance for change was to try for 1st Lieutenant for which there was no clearly assigned officer. Another obstacle to my becoming 1st Lieutenant was that I had been assigned to the OWEN specifically as Communications Officer, and, if I were to be 1st Lieutenant, someone else would have to be found for Communications.

I immediately started studying the ship in great detail. My idea was to become so completely familiar with everything about the ship that I would become an authority, and the Captain, the Exec., and other Senior Officers would regard me as a logical choice for the 1st Lieutenant. As for a replacement for me in Communications, I decided to offer to coach and assist a Junior Officer, on the administrative side of the Communications job, and to take over as O.D. at G.Q., a job which I very much liked anyway. In this way, I could offer the benefits of my communications experience on the bridge during emergencies, but otherwise, hold down the job of 1st Lieutenant, while generally supervising communications.

I then got out all of the ship's plans and with them in hand, inspected every nook-and-cranny on the ship, which was then about 80% complete. It was excellent to be able to see it in the partially assembled state because many things were then visible which would be covered up later.

I also started studying the Standard Ship's Organization Book for destroyers and conferring with other Officers on ships ahead of us in the assembly line to see what they were doing about the Organization Book. They were, in fact, doing nothing, i.e., merely adopting the standard form as it was. I read the book, however, and found that it applied to Naval conditions of twenty years earlier in peace time.

USS OWEN (DD-536) USN *Ref:* NH 107249

Large parts of the book, particularly those parts dealing with emergency procedures, were totally obsolete. In the peace time Navy, all emergency situations such as fire, collision, man overboard, etc., were handled by various special groups of men and the rest of the ship would go to "quarters". During war time, however, the ship needed to be in readiness to fight, and, therefore, total confusion would result if a special detail were fighting a fire, the rest of the crew at quarters and the ship had to go to G.Q.

On the RUSSELL we had long since totally forgotten about the Ship's Organization Book. We would go to G.Q. for any special situation whether it be fire, collision, fueling at sea, etc. Therefore, I got the idea of rewriting the Ship's Organization Book to make it fit the needs of a ship at war.

This was, of course, while I was living ashore. It was not so nice for Lib, because I brought it home and spent my evenings typing.

By the time the Captain (Lt. Cdr. R. W. "Stuffy" Wood) and the Exec. (Lt. Frank Whelan) reported on board several weeks later, I had assimilated virtually every detail of the ship, and had completed and fully mimeographed a revised Ship's Organization Book all neatly bound in official looking covers.

R. W. "Stuffy" Wood was the son of a service officer and his wife also had been a service child. In fact, Stuffy's father had not risen to as high a rank as his wife's father, and this made her act as though she had some sort of special status. Another factor of tension in the background was that Stuffy (according to rumor) had been passed over once. As I said earlier, being passed over is a major trauma. Being passed over once, however, is not the end of everything. There is an old saying in the Navy, "Once fallen, not always a harlot", which is often repeated to console those who have been passed over once. The logical extension of this concept, however, does not follow. In other words, twice passed over is always the end of a Naval career, whereas twice fallen is not always a harlot, at least, not in my book.

As I indicated previously, passed over officers tend to be excessively "regulation" and cautious. It was, therefore, surprising that when Stuffy reported on board, examined what I had done, and heard my explanations, he was delighted. He adopted my procedures verbatim. His cautiousness, however, did keep him from gaining the credit. He said nothing about it to the Command. The reason was that the new Organization had not been approved by the command and doing anything which had not been approved was risky. It was better simply do it and tell no one. Then if others do it too, the blame will be spread. In this case the other ships which followed us in the assembly line, adopted our ship's Organization Book verbatim which they could afford to do by using as an excuse that, because we had done it, they assumed that it had been approved by the command.

After three of four ships down the line from us had adopted it, it was promulgated as standard for the fleet destroyers. As far as this author is aware, no one was given credit for making this beneficial change.

The important thing, however, from my point of view, was that not only did Stuffy accept my new organizational changes, but he also agreed to make me 1st Lieutenant, to let me coach and assist another officer for Communications, and to let me be O.D. at G.Q. I was, therefore, launched in my new ship with what appeared to me to be the best of both worlds.

STUFFY'S BUNKING PLAN

Stuffy got the idea that, consistent with my idea that the ship should always be ready to fight, every man should have his bunk as near to his battle station as possible. Being 1st Lieutenant, I was the person detailed to carry out his plan. The concept is not difficult. One starts with the ship at G.Q. and assigns a billet number to each battle station assignment. Then, one assigns a bunk to each billet number as near as possible to that battle station. Then, when the men report on board, they are given billet numbers from which they can tell both where they are to bunk and where their battle station is.

Such a plan ought to work without a hitch, but it does not. The problem is one of control and discipline in the living compartments. Men must have a leader and a control hierarchy in a compartment. Otherwise, the place becomes a mess, fights ensue, and discontentment is rife. What having everyone bunk near his G.Q. station does is break up the continuity of a compartment. It makes gunners, radiomen, mess attendants, engineers, etc., all live more-or-less side-by-side, without any defined hierarchy and no one in a leadership role. Moreover, battle station assignments are continuously being changed, and under Stuffy's plan, the men had to be continuously shifting their bunks. No place was "home".

We put Stuffy's plan to practice later when the OWEN was commissioned and I worked very hard to make it succeed, but finally, gave up. He was extremely intent on it, however, and adamant.

One night I went into his cabin and told him I would no longer support his plan. An angry exchange ensued. Neither of us would back down. Having come to an impasse, I simply turned and walked out.

I would not be honest if I tried to pretend that I was not worried, but, as I said, I was like TNT with a short fuse. I was aware that I might be court-martialled, but the threat of having a big hassle over it did not deter me in the slightest. I went to bed.

About an hour later, a messenger came down and woke me. "Captain wants to see you, Sir, in his cabin." I dressed, went up not knowing what to expect, and entered. After shutting the door, the Captain paused for a while and then said, "OK, Russ, now what do we do?"

We then bunked the crew according to a modified "Stuffy Wood" plan, splitting the divisions so that half of each division would bunk forward and the other half aft. In this way, a hit forward or aft would not wipe out all of any specialty. Some diversification was accomplished, but the necessary leadership in the compartments was maintained. It worked.

FIRE FIGHTERS

They had an installation at Mare Island (at the north end of San Francisco Bay), for teaching fire-fighting techniques. Since I was to be 1st Lieutenant, I thought I would profit by taking the course. It was a one-day affair. One learned about various types of fires, bilge fires, oil fires, aviation gasoline fires, deep-rooted fires, and various types of procedures, flash clothing, gas masks, CO_2 extinguishers, foam, water sprayed from various types of nozzles and the use of gasoline driven "handi-billies" for water pumping in case of damage to the ship's fire mains. Every man taking the course was just like everyone else, be he an Admiral or an ordinary Seaman. They put appropriate clothes on you and made you actually fight every type of fire, not merely observe it. Most of the fires were easy to fight, but two were fairly hair-raising. They had a simulation of a ship's hull and would start an oil fire in the bilges. Bilge fires can be fought rather easily with foam, but in case foam is not available, they taught you how to do it with water. In this latter exercise, you were given a hose with a spray nozzle on it and told to go down into the hold and fight the fire. They would, of course, make you wait until the fire was hot so that putting it out would not be too easy. The spray nozzle gives one quite good protection. It cools things down ahead of you as you proceed, and it also knocks out the fire ahead. The problem is that the fire sneaks around and the next thing you know, flames are coming up behind you. (This has been in a recurring nightmare of mine ever since.) You have to keep batting it down and working quickly from side-to-side to keep it from sneaking around. The amazing thing, however, is that you can do it. You actually can put the fire out. The second type of difficult fire was the AVGAS fire. For this, they had a thing they called a "Christmas Tree" comprising a large vertical central pipe as the trunk with smaller pipes branching off as limbs, and still smaller pipes branching from the limbs. This was mounted inside a big box. They would then pipe in 100 octane AVGAS under pressure, torch it off, give you a spray nozzle and tell you to put out the fire. This took guts. Even from a distance of 30-40 feet the heat of the flames on your face was fierce. What you had to do was to move in with the spray nozzle ahead of you. It would effectively shield you, and you would simply attack the fire with the spray nozzle. As with the bilge fire, you had to keep batting it down everywhere, but again, amazingly, you actually could put it out.

The course was highly intriguing for many reasons. First, we had seen the LEXINGTON and WASP burn up and had seen and heard a great deal about the paint and other types of fires on the cruisers and destroyers that had been hit in the Guadalcanal actions. In fact, orders had been issued by the Fleet Command to chip off all multi-layered paint on all ships. The Fire School, however, taught us that paint fires should be easy to put out, and, in fact, all types of fires should be extinguishable if one knew what to do and had the right equipment, and that even if the fire mains were hit, one could do it with a little gasoline driven "handibilly". I was therefore keen that everyone in the damage control detail on the OWEN would go to the school.

The course, however, yielded other dividends. It was a great confidence builder. I also wanted to take my own men personally through the course because I wanted no man to think I was afraid to do anything that I expected him to do. I issued an order that every man in the deck divisions (I had two divisions with about 90 men in each) had to take the Fire Fighter's Course. I arranged for this in groups of 30-40 men each and went through the course again myself with each group.

We never had any fires on the OWEN to test whether or not the education which the men received in firefighting paid off, but the pay-off in morale was clearly significant.

COSTIGAN

As the ships at Bethlehem were nearing commissioning, the standard procedure was to put them in dry dock, scrape off the barnacles, seaweed, etc., on their bottoms and apply an anti-fouling plastic coating. In addition, since the crews for the ships would by then be fully assembled and in barracks at the Naval facilities on Treasure Island (in the middle of San Francisco Bay), the procedure was to make up a working party of the entire deck divisions, bring them across the harbor in motor launches to the Bishop's Point dry-dock and have them scrape the bottom of their own ship.

Scraping the bottom of a ship is a dirty and exhausting task. It is done either with scrapers mounted on long poles, with air hammer scrapers, or with air driven rotary wire brushes. Scaffolding is rigged so that the men can be as near to the ship's hull as possible. The whole area, of course, is dripping with water, and as soon as the men start removing the fouling, the whole area becomes a dirty mess, and everyone becomes covered in wet filth.

The crew were not exactly pleased to be given this task as their first introduction to the OWEN, but it was a job that had to be done.

I was in charge. I assigned the 1st Division to one side and the 2nd Division to the other, with a Boatswain's Mate 1st Class in charge of each. The Chief Boatswain's Mate Hinton, and I assumed general supervisory positions. The ship was brought into the dry-dock, the water pumped out, the scaffolding rigged, and the men started to mount the scaffolding with their scrapers by around 10:00 am.

We learned the hard way that a ship in a dry-dock must be electrically grounded, because the first man to touch the bottom of the ship received a healthy shock which knocked him down. He recovered all right, but it was a disconcerting way to start the day.

The 1st Class in charge of the men on the Starboard side was named Costigan. Costigan was a very fine seaman. He was smart, knew everything about his job and could do it well. He was of Irish descent, tall, broad, strong as an ox and pug-faced. He did, however, suffer from the same malady as Pop Barrow of the Russell; namely, he could not stand shore duty because there was liquor on shore and liquor and Costigan did not mix well. Thus, while Costigan was a very able seaman, he never could get ahead unless they kept him at sea.

During the morning at the dry-dock, we were making good headway, and, at the noon break, the Chief and I figured we would be done by around 4:00 pm. After sandwiches and coffee, we started in again around 1:00 o'clock.

Things were going along well when around 2:00, while I was standing under the ship on the port side talking to the Chief, I noticed that not much noise was coming from the starboard side, and went around to starboard to see how they were doing. No one was there at all—completely vanished. I vaulted up the ladder. No one was on the dock. I ran down to where the launch was supposed to be tied up and it was gone. In the distance, I could see the launch with Costigan and all of the men from the starboard side headed for Treasure Island. I whistled. No one looked back.

So, I went back to the ship, assembled the men, told them what had happened, and said that we had no choice but to complete the job with the remaining men. We then split them into two groups, with me on one side, and the Chief the other, and continued on. Finally, with everyone exhausted, we finished the job under flood lights at around 8:00 pm.

In the interest of discipline, it was imperative to report the incident and have Costigan sentenced at a Deck Court. He was broken to 2nd Class, and we obtained another 1st Class to head up Costigan's division.

In cases like this the man who has been demoted is often sent to another ship as were Bleyer and Costa on the RUSSELL. Costigan, however, remained on the OWEN and one can imagine that there continued to be a deep coldness between Costigan and me. Later on, however, a switch occurred in our relationship.

It occurred after the OWEN had been commissioned and had been at sea for a month or two. We were fueling at sea. In fueling at sea operations, the destroyer steams parallel to the tanker (or other large ship) at the same speed. The tanker shoots over a line-throwing gun projectile to send a small messenger line to the destroyer. The messenger line is then used to pull a heavier hose-supporting line over. The hose-supporting line is passed through a snatch-block secured to a pad-eye at a high point on the destroyer's after deck house and serves to support the mid-section of a fuel hose which is then sent over. The fuel hose is large, i.e., about 6" to 8" in diameter. The pumping is done at high pressure, and a tremendous amount of fuel is delivered rapidly through it, once the hose has been properly inserted into the destroyer's fuel trunk leading to the fuel tanks. As the ships proceed, waves cresting between the ships will, every so often, slap against the fuel hose and swing it back and forth. In addition, the distance between the ships will vary, and in order to minimize the slapping action and to keep the fuel hose at the appropriate height above the water despite changes in the distance between the ships, a crew of 8 to 10 men is stationed up the deck to keep the correct tension on the hose-supporting line and to play it in or out as the distance between the ships varies.

On this particular day, fueling at sea, I was O.D. The Captain had the con. The lines and hose had been sent over. The fuel hose had been securely inserted in the fuel trunk, and fuel pumping had been commenced, all properly without incident. Suddenly, the peak of a wave slapped vigorously against the hose. The force must have been very strong because it pulled the pad-eye holding the hose supporting line right off of the after-deck house bulkhead. The mid-section of the fuel hose then tumbled into the water, the force of which pulled the end of the house out of the fuel trunk, and oil was gushing at full force all over everything. The only thing to do was for some men to follow down the hose-supporting line, take it again and hook it over something located at a high point on the after deckhouse and then have some other men pull on it to lift the fuel hose clear of the water. I asked the Captain, "OK to go fix it, Sir?" He said, "OK!" I then ran down on deck, called to the men standing there, "Come on!", and started down the hose supporting line right into the gushing oil. I did not look back, but I could feel someone right behind me.

We continued down to where we had the fuel supporting line at about the right place and then started lifting it across the deck towards the after deckhouse. We were, of course, in a sea of fuel oil slipping, falling, and scrambling. As we started to gain on it, I noticed that I had only one man with me and it was Costigan. Together, each helping the other, we muscled the hose-supporting line up a ladder on the side of the deckhouse and hooked the line around a stanchion post. The gang on the end of the line then pulled, and the fuel hose came up out of the water. By then the Tanker had stopped pumping. The fuel hose was reinserted in the fuel trunk and fueling was recommenced. It did, of course, take quite a while to clean up the OWEN, to say nothing of ourselves.

Thereafter, Costigan and I became good friends. He recovered his rating. A fine man and a superb sailor, that is as long as you could keep him at sea!

THE BEST SHALL BE THE FIRST TO GO

We had on board a sailor named Holloway. Holloway was a full-blooded Native American, I think from Oklahoma. He was extremely deft at handling lines. He wore gloves when he did it. No one else wore gloves, but I tried it several times and think it was Holloway's secret. It permits one to grip and pull harder. A good line handler can be very important on a destroyer for the special task of mooring the ship at a mooring buoy. This is done by bringing the ship up to the buoy. (Mooring buoys are huge buoys, i.e., about 10' in diameter, and have a great heavy ring in the center to which the destroyer hawser is secured or to which the anchor chain is shackled.) When mooring, the Captain will bring the bow of the ship up to the buoy, a messenger is then passed from the ship through the ring on the buoy, and back up on deck. The men on deck then pull on the messenger which leads a hawser down to the buoy through the ring and back up on deck. Until the hawser is safely cleated back on deck, the destroyer cannot relax.

Destroyers have high bows and much superstructure forward. As a result, the wind will rapidly blow the bow of a drifting destroyer. Thus, when the Captain brings the ship up to the buoy, everything must happen very rapidly, or else the ship will be blown too far from the buoy to complete the mooring. This can be dangerous if one is mooring near to shore with an onshore wind (as for example, along the north side of Ford Island in Pearl Harbor). Even when conditions are not dangerous, it is a fact that everyone in port will have "half-an-eye" on any ship making a mooring. Any Captain who has to take two or three passes at a mooring will be ribbed about it at the Officers' Club; and who is to say that a Senior Officer who might be on a future selection board, might not also see it and remember? Great tension, therefore, exists at mooring time, and the speed of line handling is at a premium. Holloway was the best. He was like a cat on the buoy. The lines fairly hummed when he did it.

In addition, Holloway was an excellent citizen. Clean, smart, willing, he did everything well. Undoubtedly the A-1 sailor in the deck divisions.

It so happened that while I was on the RUSSELL, there had been one policy of Captain Hartwig's which had a very negative effect on morale. Whenever orders came in from Fleet Headquarters for the RUSSELL to transfer certain ratings back to the States for new construction, Hartwig would transfer only the malcontents and troublemakers while holding onto the better sailors. Such a policy might seem to be the way to end up with all good men, but I had seen it work the other way. Thus, if the only way to get to new construction (i.e., to see one's loved ones and to remove one's self from the war for a while), was to be a dumb malcontent, then a good man would tend to lose interest in maintaining his reputation for excellence. It was, therefore, clear to me that the way to improve morale and develop excellence was to transfer the best men first.

When the OWEN's ship's company was first fully gathered at Treasure Island, I went over, assembled the 1st and 2nd Divisions, introduced myself as their Division Officer and told them about my policies, such as (a) no advancement without full completion of training courses and passing the exams, (b) clean compartments, (c) no obscenities in my presence, (d) contribution of any gambling pot to ship's service welfare fund policies and I included my new policy, i.e., the best shall be the first to go. I told it to everyone. No one believed me, but I was, in fact, dead serious about it.

The OWEN went through commissioning and underway trials, and a cruise to San Diego, all the while mooring frequently and with Holloway gaining great favor in the eyes of the Captain. Then, after the OWEN had been sent to Pearl Harbor where again Holloway executed a deft mooring at one of the difficult buoys north of Ford Island (this was about 3 months after commissioning), the OWEN received a draft order to release certain ratings for new construction among which was a call for a Boatswain's mate 2nd Class, Holloway's rating.

I naturally, immediately filled in Holloway's name. No one on the ship would deny that he was clearly the best.

Within a few minutes, I heard a thumping in the direction of the Captain's cabin and down came a messenger informing me that the Captain wanted to see me in his cabin.

This was one of those classic confrontations similar to the one I described above about the bunk assignment plan. I simply said that I had published this policy. I told him why I had done it. I said that we had other good men. But most important, I said, that if the Captain wanted to destroy me as a leader of my men, he could, and that such would be the result if Holloway was not transferred.

Stuffy wavered, but, to his credit and my great relief, eventually agreed to the transfer of Holloway.

THE JEWEL OF THE FLEET

I have mentioned my ambition to obtain a command. Part of my plan was to have a noticeably good-looking and clean ship. I also have mentioned that the Fire School had shown me that there was really no reason for the hysteria over paint fires. I, therefore, totally disregarded the Fleet directive that restricted the amount of paint a destroyer could take to sea to some ridiculously small amount such as 5 gallons. I had the paint locker loaded to the brims with gray side paint, black boot topping, black tar for the side rail nettings, red paint for the firefighting equipment, gripdeck (abrasive) paint for the walk paths along the deck, etc. I think it is not an exaggeration to say that we had on board 200 gallons of paint when we left the States.

In addition, the two 1st Class Boatswains mates were both formerly battleship sailors. This means that they were trained in many fancy things, such as reeving and parceling the lifelines, turk's heads for stanchion tops, canopies, varnished hand rails and white duck scat covers for the Captain's gig, and many other fancy Navy things seldom seen on destroyers.

Thus, after the news came around that Holloway was really going to be transferred, the 1st and 2nd Divisions seemed to take on new life. For one thing, I started having a steady stream of seamen asking for the course materials and to be examined. I had been tough on some of the men for obscenities, but now I heard none of it. Also, much activity started on deck. The men spontaneously transformed the little dirty whaleboat we used for the Commodore's (the OWEN was also the Squadron Flagship) or Captain's gig into a classy little imitation of an Admiral's barge with a white canopy having plastic port holes, a white tasseled fringe, white duck covered scats, and Coxswain's railing all reeved and parceled and with turk's heads on the posts as well as on the tiller.

Also without any specific prompting from me, the firefighting equipment on the main deck bulkheads was painted red, all the lifelines were reeved, parceled and turk's headed, with tarred netting along the deck line and neatly painted grip-deck, paths appropriately located on the main deck.

At about this same time, I instituted a policy in the Deck Divisions that the first thing we would do whenever the ship entered port, moored or anchored after having been at sea for an extended period, would be for everyone in both divisions to go down the sides on scaffolds and cut in the waterline with black boot topping.

I stuck to this policy with firmness. In fact, on Christmas Day 1943, we came into port and I ordered the men over the side to cut in the waterline. I never heard the end of it.

The result was truly remarkable. All of the rest of the Fleet would steam into port covered with rust streaks, with no waterline visible, and dingy-looking, and then here would come the OWEN looking like a Christmas toy.

Some of the men griped, some scoffed, others thought it was great. In any event, they all went along with it, because without exception, each was trying to be the best man in the Division. After Holloway left, and due to the circumstances under which he left, we soon had five men as good as he, to replace him.

I will relate later how these things had an affect opposite to the one I intended and eliminated all possibility of my ever being assigned to the command of a ship.

NOT ONLY "PUTTY, BRASS AND PAINT"

My relationship with the men on the OWEN was quite different than on the RUSSELL. The start was completely different. I was a veteran of Coral Sea, Midway, Santa Cruz, and Guadalcanal. By then, I had learned a great deal both about the equipment, and about the men, and knew better what not to do. I had studied the ship in great detail and had personally gone through the firefighter's school with every man in my division. In addition, they had seen me go down the hose-supporting line into the fuel oil with Costigan.

I dealt with the men only through the Chief Boatswain's Mate, and usually only asked him questions. I made him the boss and, of course, the bastard when tough action was necessary. (I did, however, take full responsibility for, and the brunt of, my policy of always cutting in the waterline upon entering port.) My method was to be personally on deck whenever the men were ordered to "turn to", not to give orders but simply so they would know I was not dozing comfortably in my bunk while they were sweating out a dirty job. Also, I now started talking to the men, small talk about home, etc., never about their work. That was the Chief's or their own more immediate Supervisor's business. I mentioned above that the men started coming to me for training courses, but they also started bringing me their personal problems. I became a kind of father-confessor-advisor.

My relationship with the Officers too was different. With them, I also had a head start, and was already in a prominent position and highly knowledgeable of practically everything on the ship before they came on board. Also, I knew better how to act with them as well. I was not flaunting my knowledge to anyone—merely answering questions and using my knowledge when required.

Things also worked well on the OWEN and morale was high in all divisions. Stuffy Wood was clearly an able Officer as was Frank Whelan, "Tibby" Tibbets, Zimmerman and many others. The crew was studded with strong, competent sailors. Thus, while I have described the OWEN as being as neat, clean and pretty as a Christmas Toy, she was not only "putty, brass and paint". She was a strong and well-run ship.

HOW TO PURLOIN AN ANCHOR

The OWEN was commissioned on September 20, 1943 at Bethlehem Shipyard in San Francisco and departed promptly for anti-submarine training in San Diego.

For some time before the scheduled commissioning I had been concerned that the OWEN's anchor and anchor chain had not yet been put on board, and I asked around the shipyard where it was. No one seemed to know, and the disturbing part was that no one was doing anything about it either. In my wanderings around the yard, however, I found three sets of anchors and chains back from the dock. I then asked what those anchors were for and was told that they were assigned to the three ships behind us in the assembly line (i.e., the TINGEY, the POTTER and THE SULLIVANS). I told the Chief about it. He took the hint and shortly before commissioning, with one of the 1st Class's and some men, he went to one of the yard crane operators saying he had "orders to take one of those anchor and chain sets back there and put it on the OWEN." The crane operator obliged, and the OWEN had an anchor.

Later I inquired of the 1st Lieutenant of THE SULLIVANS (she was in our Squadron) how they got their anchor. He said he had had a lot of trouble and finally had to steal the one from the next ship after them!

We always wondered what happened to the last ship they built at Bethlehem.

"AND THEN THERE WAS ONE"

In the Navy, the Officers on a ship, when she is commissioned, call themselves "plank owners". I do not know the derivation, undoubtedly something out of the days of John Paul Jones. In any event, at the commissioning party, we "plank owners" were talking and cracking jokes, and someone said, "Hey, I've got an idea. What do you say we all put $20 into a pot and the last plank owner to remain assigned to the ship gets it all?" Everyone thought it was a terrific idea. I collected the money and had the Carpenter's Mate make us a nice plaque out of wood about 25" long by 15" high, with a rope border. We put all of the $20 bills on it in a fan shape (as one holds a handful of playing cards), and above the bills in neat lettering, we put the names of the 18 Officers in order of seniority. Then above the names and in larger letters running across the top, we put "USS OWEN D536 PLANK OWNERS", and above that in even larger letters, "AND THEN THERE WAS ONE". Finally, the plaque was covered with a clear plastic and sealed around the edges. We hung it in the Wardroom in a prominent place.

Every Officer on the OWEN coveted that plaque. I had a secret resolve that, if ever the OWEN was hit, and was sinking, and I had a chance, before she went down, I would sneak into the Wardroom and take the plaque with me. Later, I shared this secret with another Officer and found he had the same idea. If we ever had been hit, there would have been a traffic jam in the Wardroom to get the plaque.

Of all the mementos of World War II I would have cherished in my study today, that plaque, along with my reprimand from Admiral Halsey, and my napkin ring (about which I will write later), would have given me the greatest pleasure. I was, however, transferred from the OWEN long before the last plank owner. Later, I heard that the most junior plank owner, Ensign Paris ended up in command of the OWEN when she was decommissioned. Unless the plaque was stolen in the interim, he must have it.

7. AMERICA TAKES THE OFFENSIVE

SIMULATED TORPEDO ATTACK

When the OWEN and the rest of the Squadron (DesRon 52) were ready for sea in the fall of 1943, we set off for Pearl Harbor screening a Task Force of two new battleships, the IOWA and the NEW JERSEY.

The OWEN was the Flagship of the Squadron and Captain G. R. Cooper, the Squadron Commander, was stationed on the OWEN together with his staff of three Officers and 10 enlisted men (Yeomen and Signalmen).

The OWEN did, of course, have to carry out the directives of the Squadron Commander (referred to as the Commodore) just as any other ship of the Squadron, but even though existing side-by-side on the same ship, the Squadron staff and the ship's company were completely separate entities. In general, ships preferred not to be selected as Flagship because the staff took up room and contributed nothing to the running of the ship. Also, the Commodore would usually preempt one of the whaleboats while in port, to the great inconvenience of the ship's company. There were advantages, however, such as never being selected for harbor entrance patrol, and other elements of preferred status due to the presence of the Commodore on board.

DesRon52 was made up of entirely newly commissioned ships and, although the key positions on all ships were manned by experienced sailors, many of the supporting cast were new recruits. One of the places where the inexperience showed up prominently was in the inability of the engineers to perform the engine room-fireroom sequence of changing speed without emitting smoke. Thus, as we put to sea under the critical eyes of the battleship Admiral, all ships of the Squadron were constantly emitting large puffs of smoke, to the great consternation of Commodore Cooper. In order to do everything possible to stop it, he sent out a directive that all ships would station a man at all times on every bridge, with a headset on, in communication on the IJV Circuit with a man in each fireroom, also constantly monitoring on the IJV

Circuit. The man on the bridge had orders to tell the appropriate fireroom immediately when any smoke issued from either stack.

I have already explained that if, in the ratio of the air-fuel mixture, there was too much air, the smoke would be white; if there was too little air, the smoke would be black. Therefore, the man on the bridge was constantly saying to one-or-the-other of the firerooms "You are making black smoke!" or "...making white smoke!"

One day, as we proceeded westward, the Admiral thought it would be a good idea for our Squadron to put on a simulated destroyer torpedo attack.

A destroyer torpedo attack involves the destroyers approaching the battleships in a line at high speed with the destroyers aligned in such a way with respect to the wind that the leading destroyer can lay down a heavy smoke screen to provide cover for the remaining ships, thereby (in pre-radar days) making it more difficult for the battleship's guns to hit the destroyers. The leading destroyer would, of course, be exposed to the gunfire, but it was hoped that the Squadron could be close enough, before the leader was sunk, to launch their torpedoes.

In order to put on such a simulated attack, then, the Commodore ordered the Squadron to steam away from the battleships, make a wide circle ahead, split into two divisions and come in from ahead on each side of the battleship formation at 30 kts.

As we approached, the MILLER was the leading ship of the 2nd Division. The Commodore in the 1st Division hoisted the flag signal "W" (which means "MAKE SMOKE"). On the MILLER, the signal "W" was hoisted, and everyone waited anxiously for the execution of the signal as the Division raced into torpedo attack position. The Commodore then ordered "W" to be executed. On the MILLER, Captain Kobey reacted instantaneously, ran into the wheelhouse, grabbed the IJV Circuit hand phone and bellowed,

"Make Smoke!"

The fireman striker at the other end of the phone who had no knowledge of the simulated torpedo attack and who had just spent all of his watches for the past month telling the firerooms not to make smoke, was stunned.

"Make smoke? What the hell do you mean, 'Make Smoke'?"

"This is the Captain. I SAID MAKE SMOKE!"

"OK Captain, but what color?"

"HOLY JESUS! — GREEN — GODDAMMIT!"

REORIENTING AS OUR FATHERS DID

There is an old story in the Navy about how, at the time when the Marine Corps was originally formed, the first Marine to be enlisted reported on board, went aft, put down his bag, sat down, and started cleaning his rifle. After a while, the second Marine to be enlisted reported on board, went aft, put down his bag, sat down, and started cleaning his rifle. So they sat there together for a while and finally the first Marine said to the second, "Things are really going to hell. It was never like this in the old Marine Corps."

This was very similar to my reaction when the OWEN joined the Fleet. Everything was different. The Task Forces were huge. We had at least a dozen Essex Class carriers, split into many Task Groups comprising at least two carriers, two battleships, and a Squadron of nine destroyers for each Group. No longer did the carriers hoist the "shapes" or turn without warning. Everything was done by signal and only when directed. In many ways, it was not like the "old Navy" that I was used to, and I, a veteran aged 25, tended to scoff at it. I was, however, pleased that DesRon 52 was selected to screen the Fast carriers. This was the type of duty I liked and knew most about.

(Apropos only of cracks involving Marines, it is said that when they gave the Marine Corps to the Navy, the Army was jealous, so that in order to give the Army something equivalent to the Marines, they gave the Army the mules. It is also said that when the founding fathers were passing things out at the inception of the armed forces, they gave the Army the work, the Navy the play, and the Marines the uniforms. The Marines counter with a jingle about how "ten thousand gobs laid down their swabs to lick one sick Marine", and how, when MacArthur invaded the Philippines, he did it "with God's help and a few Marines").

Having nine destroyers for each Task Group was a luxury. It permitted the screen to be stationed on a circle 6,000 yds. from the center of the formation, and, with the standard 3,000 yd. spacing between ships on the screen, to cover both the van of the group and the sides back to 30 degrees "abaft the beam" (i.e., 120 degrees back on each side).

Since the OWEN was also the Flagship of the Squadron (commanded by Captain G. R. Cooper), the OWEN would generally occupy the center position in the van in order to facilitate the dissemination of flaghoist signals or blinker or semaphore messages simultaneously to each side. As a result, however, of occupying this position, the OWEN rarely was called upon to do plane-guard duty.

The former practice of having the carrier and two destroyers perform the flight operations apart from the rest of the formation was discontinued, and the entire Task Group would turn into the wind and remain with the carrier. Therefore, the fuel saving technique for plane guard duty which we had practiced on the RUSSELL was not feasible.

The screening procedure was seriously inefficient. Since the wind direction would often be from astern or on the quarter, when the carriers would turn into the wind to conduct flight operations, there would be no destroyers covering the new van. In order to correct this condition, the screen would be ordered to "REORIENT" meaning that the entire screen would rotate around the formation. This would require the ships on the outside of the turn to speed up and those on the inside to slow down.

I explained earlier about how the fuel expenditure for a destroyer skyrockets at speeds above 25 kts., and since a speed differential of 10 kts. would be about the best one could do, even steaming at 30 kts, a simple calculation shows that it would take 18 minutes merely to move up two stations. A move of three or four stations, however, was often required. Of course, the ships on the inside of the turn could move quickly back to their new stations, but this created a problem because it left big gaps in the new van until the ships on the outside could reach their new stations. Also, since flight operations were usually over in 20 minutes, the formation was never properly screened during the flight operations, or thereafter, for another 20 minutes, while the reverse process was taking place. The expenditure of fuel by the ships steaming at 30 kts. to catch up (be they on the outside at the beginning or on the outside at the end of the exercise) was far greater than any small amount saved by the ones which slowed down. The end result was that all of the destroyers were seriously wasting fuel, in addition to which the carriers were not being properly screened during flight operations. Also, while the problem was most noticeable during flight operations, the same occurred every time the formation changed course, which was quite frequently. The Reorientation method was a hold-over from WWI when it was used for screening very slow convoys for which Reorientation was suitable. It was also used in WWII for slow convoys in the North Atlantic. For the reasons I have given however, reorientation was completely unsuitable for Fast Carrier Operations. At the same time, there was no other screening plan in the book.

The OWEN joined the Fast Carriers in late November 1943 after the invasion of the Gilbert Islands, and it was at about that time, after witnessing these very ragged, and fuel-expensive Reorientation maneuvers, that I devised a way to solve the problem. My proposal was to establish 12 fixed stations around the formation on a circle 6,000 yds. from the center with the stations starting at true north and continuing around with a station every 30 degrees. The idea was for the ships to move up and respectively to occupy consecutive stations in the van and stay there. Then, if, due to a course change, one side of the screen became lopsided, that is, with more stations occupied on one side of the formation than the other, the destroyers in the stations abaft the beam of the formation on the new course would move across the rear and fill the vacant stations on the weak side, while the other destroyers remained put. In this way, only the rear destroyers would have to move, and they would not have to use high speed. According to my proposal, if the Task Force were to reverse course, the destroyer screen would split and both sides would move back so as to assume the vacant stations in the new van. I also provided a way to resolve the case where two ships might be heading for the same station. Another feature of my plan was to have the screen start these maneuvers immediately and not wait for the carriers to turn. The idea was to accomplish what we had done on the Russell, i.e, to have the ships which had to move do so by slowing down if possible. The objective was both to save fuel and to provide continuous full anti-submarine coverage for the carriers.

Initially, I called it the "Fixed Station" screening method and talked about it among the Officers. At that time, while I knew the Commodore well because I was O.D. at G.Q. and, therefore, had frequent contact with him on the bridge,

I was not under his direct command. I mentioned my idea to him several times. He was instinctively negative to it. As I stated, there was no other screening plan in the book, and we continued to REORIENT as our grandfathers had done. I will describe later what became of the "Fixed Station" screening method.

WALTZING MATILDA WITH THE INTREPID

The next step in America's offensive was the invasion of the Marshall Islands on January 30th to February 2nd, 1944. The OWEN was screening two Essex Class carriers, the BUNKER HILL and the INTREPID and also the battleships Iowa and New Jersey.

The Fleet was large. America had also come a long way in many other departments. We now had a new fighter plane, the Grumman F6F, which was at least as fast and, in many ways, better than the Japanese Zero. We had new dive bombers and torpedo planes which were also better than the enemy's. The problems we had had earlier with our torpedo warheads had been solved. The anti-aircraft guns were much improved, and we now had shells with "proximity fuses" (i.e., shells which were detonated by microwave detection when they came near to an aircraft), which were substantially more effective against air attack than previously.

Therefore, to us on the ships, things seemed very optimistic and secure—a far cry from the tenuous and frightening days of Guadalcanal.

Although the enemy had inflicted heavy damage on the landing forces at Tarawa in the Gilberts, there was very little resistance in the Marshalls. We, in the Fleet, had little to do beyond typical routine operations.

After the invasion of the Marshall's, the Task Force was sent to raid the Japanese mid-Pacific bastion, Truk Island, on February 16-17, 1944. Although most of the enemy aircraft on Truk had been destroyed during the raid, in the evening, after the raid, while we were still in the area, several of the remaining enemy planes came out and one of them succeeded in torpedoing the INTREPID.

Japanese Cargo Ship hit by aerial torpedo 17 February 1944 – USN Ref 80-G-271624

The OWEN was on the starboard side of the formation when it happened, tracking an enemy aircraft on radar out about five miles. The night was very dark, moonless and overcast. The possibility that an enemy aircraft could make a successful attack seemed extremely remote. We did, of course, continue to track the plane on our radar. Pretty soon, it came in and flew directly over the OWEN. I remember that its motor seemed unusually quiet. The INTREPID, of course, had been warned and was attempting to maneuver radically. She could not do it radically enough, however, and the enemy succeeded in planting a torpedo in her rudder (suggesting an acoustic homing torpedo?). This caused the INTREPID to shear out of station and start careening wildly, while they tried to steer her by use of the engines. The OWEN was nearest to the INTREPID, and naturally took over screening her. We were, of course, still in submarine infested waters and it was vital to provide as much anti-submarine protection to the damaged INTREPID as possible. I had the con at the time, and my training on the RUSSELL all came together at this one moment, i.e., the night vision techniques, the binocular steadying techniques, the technique of how to detect when a carrier starts turning the split second it takes place without any signal and in the black of an overcast night. I had my eyes glued as much as possible to the INTREPID while racing from one wing of the bridge to the other and back. As the INTREPID waltzed unpredictably, we matched her every move. This continued without break from around 11 PM until dawn and was very exhausting. By dawn, the INTREPID was becoming better at steering by her engines alone and the problem abated.

The INTREPID returned to Pearl Harbor to be fixed, and the OWEN was sent along as her anti-submarine screen.

While we were gone, the Fast Carriers made a raid on Saipan (February 21, 1944).

CLAUSTROPHOBIA AND HOW TO CURE IT

After the OWEN had been at sea a month or so, she began leaking around the rudder post, and a man had to be stationed in the steering engine room to mop up the water continuously. The plans for the packing arrangement for the rudder post bearing showed that the lower bearings in contact with the water were made of lignum vitae (iron wood), the upper bearings were of babbitt-metal, and there was a narrow annular space for grease in between. We could see the babbitt-metal and it appeared to be OK. There was no way we could check the lignum vitae, and so we examined the grease packing arrangement. The grease was introduced into the bearing by means of a copper tube communicating from the deck of the steering engine room adjacent to the steering column through the double bottom of the ship to a low point near the lignum vitae bearing. The tube was equipped with an Alemite fitting at the deck level, and a grease gun was used to force the grease into the tube. We pumped in several quarts of grease and, since the space for the grease packing could not hold that much, we concluded that either the grease was running out through the lower bearing, or that the copper tube had become detached from the lower connection to the sleeve surrounding the column.

The only way to check this was to enter the double bottom of the ship through a hatch in the after-crew's compartment and to crawl aft through four honeycomb sections to where the steering column was located.

I decided to try it, took a flashlight, some wrenches, pliers, etc., entered the double bottom and was just wiggling into the first honeycomb section (through an 18" diameter hole) when claustrophobia began to set in. The double bottom had no ventilation, and the thought of suffocation became overpowering. Just then, it happened that a submarine alert was signaled, and the OWEN went to G.Q. I came close to panic, wiggled my way out as fast as I could, came back on deck and closed the hatch.

Later, I tried it again but was unable to make myself enter the first honey-comb. We had on board a small gasoline driven air blower with a long canvas air hose having metal rings lining it to keep it from collapsing. The electricians and engineers used it to provide ventilation when they were working in the double bottom, and they suggested that I try it.

It worked wonders. I took the hose into the double bottom with me, and as long as I kept the air blowing directly into my face, I felt no claustrophobia.

The lower fitting of the copper tube had, indeed, come adrift. I put it back on, tightened it up, and the leak was cured.

DISASTER STRIKES

On March 20, 1944, while we were in Pearl Harbor with the INTREPID, I learned by a message which came over the Fox Schedule that our daughter Victoria (then known as Tory) had been born in Oakland, California and that mother and daughter were doing well. We were preparing to rejoin the Fast carriers and I was sitting in my cabin bringing my Current Ship's Maintenance Book up to date, when a messenger knocked and said, "Mr. Russell, I have a letter for you, it's your orders." and he handed me a paper. It was a letter from Captain Cooper, Com DesRon 52 on the OWEN, ordering the OWEN to detach me, and for me to report to DesRon 52 for duty on Captain Cooper's staff.

This came as a horrible shock. A Reserve Officer who is put into staff duty has, from then on, virtually no chance ever to obtain a command. The reason is that Staff Officers are regarded as being specialists and paper-work people, not trained for leadership of men or command. Moreover, it came as a bolt out of the blue. No one had consulted me. I had no warning, no time to prepare a defense or alternative. Stuffy Wood was surprised too. It was totally Captain Cooper's doing. Beyond this, the staff was more-or-less hated by the ship. They took up room and contributed nothing. I was effectively being ordered to join the enemy.

I immediately went up to the Commodore's cabin and asked him how come. He simply said that he had been very impressed with me, that he needed me as Operations Officer (a job which at that time was equivalent to the peace-time job of Chief of Staff). I told him that it was the last thing I wanted to do, and that it would kill any chance I would ever have for a command. I pleaded. He simply said no, that I was in the Navy, and that I would carry out my orders. He was low pressure but completely firm, and unlike some of the other times when I defied authority, I saw no justification for defiance. I just went below, thought about it and eventually decided there was no way out. I went back up and said, "OK Commodore, I'm on board."

It was evident that I had over-done my efforts to become an outstanding officer in hopes of being assigned a command. All it had done was bring me to the attention of the Commodore and make him want me for his staff.

OPERATIONS OFFICER OF A DESTROYER SQUADRON

There were compensating features, however, of my new job. If I had succeeded in obtaining command of a ship, at best it would have been a DE. Such a command would have been fun, but most likely, far away from the action, doing things such as convoying transports, harbor patrols, etc. Being an Operations Officer, however, of a destroyer Squadron, with the Fast carrier Task Forces, I would be in the thick of the action. Moreover, it was a responsible position, and, at least, from a job point of view, it was on a par with the Captains of the ships of the Squadron. I would be dealing directly with the Captains as an equal by virtue of the Commodore's delegation of authority to me, even though my rank was lower. Thus, I was in a position to make a more significant contribution. In fact, my opportunity was greater than that of any of the Captains of the Squadron.

Being on staff, however, meant that I would no longer be standing watches or be O.D. at G.Q. Although that might have been deemed an advantage by some Officers, it was not to me. I liked standing watch, at least on a watch-in-four basis, and I reveled in being O.D. at G.Q.

In long retrospect, I should say that it was a fine promotion for me. The Commodore had paid me a very sincere compliment, and I should have been more grateful.

RUNNING A DESTROYER SQUADRON

There are two aspects to running a destroyer Squadron, one administrative and the other tactical, both totally separate. On the administrative side, the Squadron staff is not concerned with the internal administrations of the respective ships but is responsible for providing the ships with what they need, such as training, ammunition, provisions, fuel, replacements, repairs, the installation of new equipment, or weapons, etc. All of these things have to be arranged for and scheduled so that the ships will obtain what they need in an efficient manner. I mentioned earlier my Current Ship's Maintenance Book when I was still 1st Lieutenant of the OWEN. The Squadron administrative staff has to follow similar procedures for all ships of the Squadron in all of the above listed categories, so that arrangements can be made to fulfill those needs. The Squadron Staff also has to submit activity or war reports, and, of course, fill out the fitness reports of the Commanding Officers of the ships of the Squadron.

On the tactical side, the demands on the Staff are simpler. All that is required is to direct the ships to go where they should go and do what needs to be done. Understanding these needs in the context of the larger picture of the Fleet maneuvers may not be too easy. The rest is very simple.

In the Navy, these things tend to become needlessly complicated. A peace-time destroyer Squadron Staff will have five or so Officers and 10 men in it. We found that the job can be done with the Commodore, the Operations Officer, a Signalman, and a Yeoman. We had additional Officers and enlisted personnel assigned to duty on the Staff, but we turned them over to the OWEN's ship's company and let them help out in that way. An added advantage of the small Staff was that the Commodore and I and the two men could move quickly and easily to any other ship of the Squadron and we frequently did.

The Operations Officer's job at sea was simply to be "on call" at all times. He had to be on deck whenever any maneuvers were taking place as well as to know if ships were out of station, or to read any messages that could affect the Squadron. Otherwise, he had plenty of time to work on the administrative side. He handled all of the communications involving the ships' immediate needs by blinker-light messages and whenever we were in port, he would go around to all of the ships and bring up to date his books on the current status of their needs. Once these things were up to date, arranging for the neediest ships to obtain what they needed was a simple task involving working it out with the Staff s of the Fleet or the Base.

WESTWARD THROUGH THE ISLANDS

The next Task Force operations involved raids by the Fast carriers on Palau, Yap, Ulithi, and Wolei (islands in the approaches to the Philippines). This represented a very deep penetration into enemy waters considering that the Japanese still held Truk. On the other hand, our Fleet was very much larger by then than the Japanese, and our weapons and aircraft were now better than theirs. In addition, the Japanese opposition was weak, and we on the destroyers had little to do on the Palau raid. Of strictly topical interest, we passed over the famous "Barrows Deep", one of the deepest parts of the ocean, deeper than Mt. Everest is high. Another moment of interest came when we passed through an area of practically no wind, like Coleridge's "Rime of the Ancient Mariner" ("Day after day, day after day/We stuck, nor breath nor motion;/As idle as a painted ship/Upon a painted ocean"). Without any movement of air, the carriers had to steam at their top speed of 33 kts. in order to launch and recover aircraft. The destroyers simply could not keep up with them. This was the only time I can recall, in the Pacific, in which there was no wind at all. In a sailing ship, it would have been hell.

REORIENTATION CONTINUES

After the Palau raid, the fast carriers (and we with them) were sent to cover MacArthur's invasion of Hollandia on the Northern Coast of New Guinea, and then on a second raid on Truck. After that, DesRon 52 was sent on detached duty to bombard enemy installations on Ponape Island (April 28, 1944).

Throughout all of these operations, the destroyers continued the Reorientation maneuver. The fuel consumption was tremendous (destroyers had to be refueled every 4th day, limiting Fleet operations), and the coverage of the carriers was extremely sloppy. I again broached my "Fixed Station" Screening Method to the Commodore, and described it in substantially more detail. He was, however, dead set against it for various reasons. First, he thought the Squadron Commander should always be in the center of the screen for reasons of communication (i.e., be able to send messages simultaneously down each side of the screen by flag hoist, semaphore, or blinker). The Navy was no longer using those methods of communication for urgent tactical messages. All critical messages at that time were being sent by the TBS, a short range, VHF voice radio tranceiving circuit. It made no important difference where the Commodore was in the screen because all ships would hear the message simultaneously, regardless of the Flagship's location. Routine messages would be slower by my proposal, but being routine, it would not matter. He also was against my suggestion to start the maneuver of splitting the van before the carriers had turned. He felt that it would be risky, in addition to being very disconcerting to the Admiral. On the other hand, it was clear from the geometry of the problem that, even if the screen were to split before the carriers turned, the carriers would themselves turn long before reaching waters which the destroyer had not screened. In addition, by the reorientation method, the carriers were repeatedly going into unscreened waters due to the absence of antisubmarine protection in the new van and that was caused by the high speed which the destroyers on the outside of the turns had to put on, i.e. 30 kts. at which speed their sonars were useless. Captain Cooper also did not like the feature of my plan whereby the screen would often not be balanced perfectly on each side of the base course of the Task Force. This seemed to me to be of minor importance as long as the coverage was adequate on each side. He remained adamant. He did not want to argue. His position was that my proposal had no official approval, he had no way available to him at that time to have it evaluated and approved officially, and that he would not do anything that did not have official approval. We continued to reorient exactly as the Navy had done in WW I.

THE DOCTOR OF THE BUNKER HILL TAKES ONE GIANT STEP

One morning when we were screening the fast carriers after the Palau raid, shortly after the call of dawn G.Q., I came to the bridge, took up my binoculars and went to the alidade checking the positions of the various ships of the Task Group. The OWEN, at that time, was on the port quarter of the BUNKER HILL, and I was just in the process of checking the BUNKER HILL's bearing when the TBS came on. "This is Lucky (the BUNKER HILL's call sign). Our lookouts have just reported a man overboard on the port side amidships." I took the BUNKER HILL's bearing instantaneously and shouted to the O.D. to come to the course of that bearing. He gave the order and we started turning to that course. In a moment, Stuffy Wood came on the bridge and took the con. We discussed it and decided that the delay of the turn would put the ship ahead of a direct line to the man on the bearing I had observed when they sent the message. Therefore, when we approached the wake of the BUNKER HILL, we calculated that the thing to do was to turn right and proceed back down the wake looking for him. As we picked up the slick of the carrier's wake, Stuffy made the turn and stopped all engines, and the OWEN headed back down the wake, gradually slowing down. Within a few seconds, we heard a whistle. The man was right near our starboard bow. A swimmer dove for him, and we had him on board only moments later. It was a very prompt pick-up. Probably under five minutes from the time the man fell into the water.

Later, we talked to him. He was the Medical Officer of the BUNKER HILL. He explained his usual practice at dawn G.Q. was to leave his stateroom, go forward to the athwartships passage, turn right, go to the starboard ladder, mount it, come out of the door to the flight deck on the starboard side, turn left, and walk aft along the flight deck to where he then would enter the door leading to the sick bay. On this particular morning, for some unexplained reason, he turned left at the athwartships passageway. He then mounted the ladder and, in accordance with his custom, he turned left and started walking along the flight deck, actually walking forward on the port side but thinking he was walking aft on the starboard side. It was, of course, still quite dark and his eyes were not ready for night vision. He then continued to walk expecting soon to see the door of the sick bay, when, all of a sudden, he took a step, and nothing was there. Down he fell, right into the port bow wave of the BUNKER HILL.

There is a commonly shared apprehension about swimmers being run down by ships. The apprehension is valid for speedboats, but it is a fallacy for ships. Unless, by a freak, a man in the water is hit flush by a ship's cutwater (an occurrence he should be able to avoid by a mere couple of swimming strokes), the man is perfectly safe. The bow wave of a ship merely dumps the man to one side, but otherwise leaving him perfectly safe. The propellers do not suck the man in as he passes the stern. A man can be sucked in by the propellers if he dives down and swims near to the side of a ship as the stern approaches, but no one in his right mind would do that. On the other hand, as long as the man stays on the surface, he will never be sucked in any more than any of the other flotsam and jetsam which pass down the side of a ship year-in-year-out and without being sucked in.

After the bow wave of the BUNKER HILL had tossed him aside, the Doctor simply bobbed along like a cork 10 or 15 feet out from the ship. In a few moments, one of the lower AA gun stations loomed up and he shouted to the crewmen, "Hey, tell the bridge I fell overboard.", they said, "OK." He also had time to ask them to throw him a life jacket, which they did. It was about then, that the word came to us via the TBS voice circuit.

Soon after dawn, we went alongside the BUNKER HILL and passed the Doctor back to them in a breeches buoy, and by breakfast time he was in his own Wardroom, undoubtedly bearing the brunt of a good deal of razzing.

IN SAIPAN, THE WIND BLOWS FROM THE EAST; 1ST BATTLE OF PHILIPPINE SEA

The next item on the agenda for the American offensive was to invade Saipan and Tinian. Such an invasion was predicted to be reasonably exciting because the enemy had airfields (unsinkable carriers) on both islands, close enough to Japan to have replacement aircraft flown in rapidly along the island chain. In addition, the location of Saipan gave the enemy a very important further advantage due to the fact that Saipan is in the tradewind belt. It blows, day-in day-out without fail at 17 kts. from the N.E. This means that, if the Japanese were to attack us from the west beyond the range of our carrier-based aircraft, there would be no way we could move closer to the enemy in order to attack him because flight operations would require our heading into the wind to the cast, i.e. away from the enemy.

As a Squadron Operations Officer, I attended briefing sessions prior to the invasion. The Command anticipated that the enemy would defend vigorously on land and also bring out their fleet for naval action. Our fleet was, however, given the limited objective of defending the invasion, and attacking the enemy fleet only to the extent necessary to "meet the requirements of safety of our forces on Saipan." The speakers at the briefing session exhibited a good deal of tension. An attack by enemy aircraft carriers was clearly something they dreaded.

Having seen what had happened to the LEXINGTON, YORKTOWN, and HORNET in the early battles, I too was tense. On the other hand, we were bringing a tremendous armada. The U.S. Fleet included 15 new fast carriers split into four task groups each of which groups was larger than our entire Fleet at Midway. It also included 7 new fast battleships, 11 cruisers and 36 destroyers. The invasion force included 333 large ships, 148 small ships, 7 old battleships, 11 escort carriers, and over 50 destroyers. This was probably the most powerful Naval force ever assembled up to that date. Also, our airplanes and other weapons had been vastly improved. In addition, we had learned how to fight fires. Personally, I had a very different attitude than in the lean days of Guadalcanal. The only thing that concerned me was the possibility that the enemy fleet might stand off beyond the range of our carrier-based aircraft and launch their attacks at us without our being able either to retaliate or to close the distance between our Fleet and theirs, due to the direction of the wind.

The invasion of Saipan started on June 10, 1944, with an initial bombardment by the Old battleships, and from what we could gather, everything was going reasonably well on land.

I wrote in my 1945 diary as follows:

"This was evidently the big moment the enemy had waited for. Many times, they had boasted that they would defeat us if we ever came within their island chain. And now our submarines reported large numbers of enemy ships on the move from widely separated places. On the night of June 16th our submarines reported a task force including battleships and carriers exiting from San Bernardino Strait in the Philippines, and also a battleship force off Mindanao heading northeast. Spruance took steps temporarily to protect his rear by bombing the enemy airfields as far north as Iwo Jima, sending two of the carrier Task Groups north for that purpose, but, in view of the reports of enemy activity, he refueled his ships on June 17th and commenced concentrating near Saipan. At this time Admiral Nimitz at Pearl Harbor sent a dispatch encouraging Spruance and the fleet upon the eve of battle and stating that he counted on a decisive victory. Several enemy carrier-based planes were shot down about 300 miles west of Guam on June 17th.

"On June 18th Spruance brought his carrier forces together and steamed slowly westward during the day. More enemy position reports came in. By 8:00 a.m. it became evident that the opposing fleets were about 500 miles apart and steaming toward each other. Under these circumstances, while search contact might have been made, it was not likely that either side could make air attacks on the other before dark. However, there was a definite possibility that the two fleets could come close enough for surface combat before dawn of the next day. With this in mind Admiral Mitscher who was in command of the carriers asked Admiral Lee, the battleship commander, if he desired a night engagement. Lee replied that he did not consider the fleet sufficiently well trained to enter a night engagement.

(Spector mentions this[43], but passes by it without comment. Elsewhere it is ignored by the historians. Why the historians have not chastised the Navy for it, is curious. How the Navy could have come so far with those ships, and then, at the one moment for which their existence might have been justified, beg off on the ground of lack of preparation, is inconceivable).

"After several exchanges of dispatches, Spruance gave the order to retire to the east during the night. The battleships were then stationed about 15 miles to the west of the carrier Task Groups. In such a detached position, they were essentially useless. After Spruance had shied away from the possibility of a night action, there was no possibility that the 16" guns of the battleships could be used for any purpose because, during daylight, if an enemy surface ship had ventured within 200 miles of us in daylight, our carrier-based aircraft would have sunk it. If the battleships had been kept with the carriers instead of sending them 15 miles to the west they could have at least contributed to the anti-aircraft protection of the carriers, but having been sent west, even that minor advantage of having them in the Fleet, was lost.

"Around 11:30pm Mitscher called Spruance on the voice radio recommending heading west again for the remainder of the night in order to be within air attack range of the enemy by dawn. After an hour or so, Spruance came back on the voice radio rejecting Mitscher's proposal on the ground that he (Spru-ance) was afraid of an "end run". These were voice communications which we on the bridges of the ships in the fleet all heard. It was extremely interesting to be hearing such historic deliberations. It also was disconcerting because we had already seen overcaution on the part of Spruance at Midway and other admirals (e.g. Fletcher at Coral Sea, and Kindaid at Santa Cruz). We, of course, had no voice in the matter, but were tacitly cheering for Mitcher and hoping that Spruance would take his advice.

"The Fleet remained on an easterly course away from the enemy. By 8 a.m. June 19 we were only about 150 miles from Saipan, and about 100 miles from Guam. At this time the enemy was about 420 miles to the west of us, out-side of air attack range of our aircraft, but with Guam still in Japanese hands and so near, the planes from the enemy fleet could easily attack us and then refuel at their own airfields at Guam before returning to their carriers. We could not go west to attack their fleet during the day because the wind was from the northeast as it always is in the Trade Wind Belt and, therefore, we had to head northeast to launch and recover aircraft. In the early days of the war, when the Japanese airplanes were superior to ours, such a tactical posi-tion would have given the Japanese a great victory. Accordingly, it was both embarrassing and harrowing on the morning of the 19th to realize that the enemy actually had us in the position we feared most."

The attacks began to come in during the morning. About 400 planes in all came in that day. They were formed into separate raids of about 20 to 30 planes each, and they came in at 25,000 feet altitude, at which height we could detect them on radar as far out as 150 miles. My note shows that the IOWA had a contact at over 200 miles. This permitted us to vector our fight-ers onto them while still a long way out, making contact and starting to attack them at over 100 miles in some cases.

As I have mentioned, by this time in the war we had the new F6Fs which were considerably faster and more maneuverable than our earlier planes, nearly as good as the Japanese Zero, but very much more durable. They were quite capable of handling themselves with the Zeros and could easily shoot down the Japanese Vals (dive bombers) and Kates (torpedo bombers). Also, during the time that our planes were improving, the Japanese planes had remained the same.

In addition, we were lucky that the Japanese had elected to attack at such a high altitude. If they had come in at low altitude and from different directions, we could not have detected them soon enough to have vectored the fighters onto them in time to prevent the attacks from reaching the ships.

(It is curious that the Japanese Navy which had been so smart at Pearl Harbor and at Santa Cruz, had made such crude and easily discernible errors at Midway and now again in the 1st Philippine Sea battle. There are, however, many indications that the Japanese Naval command, patterned after our own, made equally inexplicable mistakes. For example, even though some individuals in the Japanese Navy were the initial proponents of air power over battleships, and they had dramatically proven its success, the proponents of air power did not have sufficient voice to prevail over the majority. Japan still pursued the construction of battleships much the same as the U.S. Navy.

This was, of course, a costly mistake for both Navies. The same goes for submarine construction. In both Navies it was given low priority compared to surface ships. The U.S. built only 140 submarines in World War 11 as compared to some 800 destroyers, whereas to build a submarine was less expensive than a destroyer and the value of a submarine to the war effort was conservatively ten times that of a destroyer. The Japanese Navy was even less favorably disposed to submarines. They virtually terminated constructing them toward the end of the war.)

During the attacks, there was a high overcast in our area as well as scattered clouds in which the attackers could hide. Most of the time, the CAP was still able to locate them. A few of the enemy penetrated to the west of us and attacked the battleships. With our binoculars, we could see the black dots of the AA bursts, and occasionally an enemy plane careening in flames toward one of our ships.

Around noon, a group of enemy planes was detected on the radar, circling to the south of our group. The CAP was vectored out to intercept them but, this time, the enemy was able to hide in the overcast, and evade the fighters. Our radars showed them all as a "merged plot", but although they must have been close to each other, our fighters could not see them. Several times we could hear our fighters on the voice circuits saying that they saw one of them, but in the next instant that it had disappeared. We on the ships were all looking for them, and had our guns ready, but even though we knew approximately where they were and that they were near enough for us to hit them with AA, all we could do was wait. This appeared to be a fairly formidable attack. It is very difficult to stop an air attack unless one can spot it a long way out and start firing before they come in to close range.

Suddenly someone yelled, "There he goes on the carrier". I looked up. There he was, all right, streaking down on the BUNKER HILL, coming on in and no one firing at him. When he was halfway down, the machine gun batteries on the carrier finally opened up. Next the 5" guns from the surrounding ships, and with only about 1000 feet to go we finally started pouring the shells into him. Next there was a big puff of red flame, and he disintegrated into little pieces as a 5" shell caught him with a direct hit. The BUNKER HILL was in a tight turn, heeling way over. Another enemy plane started to dive. I could not see the carrier at that point. She was behind a cruiser, but I could see another Jap diving over in that direction. The BUNKER HILL again came visible. She was still straining and lumbering in her turn when a huge geyser went up on the far side of her flight deck. "Uh-oh they got her that time", I thought. The attack did not last very long. Only about half a dozen enemy planes had succeeded in penetrating the CAP. I looked around and took a deep breath. All ships were still OK. The explosion at the BUNKER HILL had been a near miss.

We steamed back and forth after that doing the regular routine, turning into the wind to launch and to recover aircraft, then going back down wind again. At one point just after the Task Force had made a turn, the ship ahead of us began blinking with her signal light. Our signalman jumped to the light and began receiving the message. "Believe we saw a man in the water on our starboard quarter." I heard the message coming in and fixed my binoculars on the water in the area of their starboard quarter. In a short time, I was lucky enough to pick up a little speck, which seemed to be a man's hand. Yes, it was. Then a head bobbed up for just an instant. I sang out, "Captain, I've got a man in the water, here." I could not risk taking my eyes from the glasses for fear of losing him, so I just kept saying, "Over here where I'm looking. Yes, it's a man. There he is again." The man was about a mile and a quarter away at that time. He was a pitiful sight, holding up one bare arm in the air in a frantic attempt to attract attention and to reach out for us. He was not yet aware that we saw him. All he knew was that the fleet had come close to him, and now was heading away to leave him alone in the burning salt water of the vast Pacific. Slowly the OWEN turned around and steadied on the bearing of the man. Only then did I take my eyes off of him. Within a few minutes we picked up a wet, frightened and exhausted, but happy man. I do not recall how he came to have been in the water.

By mid-afternoon the enemy attacks ceased. Again, Admiral Mitscher proposed to Admiral Spruance that the Fleet head west directly toward the enemy and steam at high speed. Admiral Spruance did not reply for a long time. We who heard Admiral Mitscher's proposal, knew that we were listening to another of these historic moments about which naval buffs would argue for years to come. Admiral Spruance had a choice, whether immediately to steam west and perhaps have a serious battle the next day (at which time the enemy might well not repeat its high altitude mistake, but instead scatter and come in low), or to stay to the east, and count on defending the next day again without being able to counter-attack, as he had done that day. He did as he had done at Midway, he remained to the east.

If Spruance had gone west, however, and the enemy had made the "end run" he so dreaded, the enemy would have been trapped, facing a force four times its size, with nowhere to go. Complete annihilation of the enemy fleet would have resulted. To head west, however, was not in the operation order, and to stay near Saipan was. Spruance could not go wrong if he did what the operation order said to do. As a result of these delays, the Fleet was still only about 200 miles west of Saipan on the morning of the 20th. At this late point, reminiscent of Midway, Admiral Spruance decided to attack the Japanese Fleet. As I explained before, however, the wind at Saipan is always from the east, and it was impossible due to the necessity to conduct flight operations constantly, to make much net distance to the west.

I wrote in my 1946 diary as follows:

"The next morning, the Fleet was still about 200 miles west of Saipan, but finding the area clear, and seeing that no "end runs" had been attempted, we began to steam northwest and search for the enemy Fleet. As things were, the enemy had not retired to any great extent, possibly hoping that some of their planes would come back as scheduled on the return trip from the islands. However, when their hopes for any success in this plan began to dwindle, since there were very few Japanese planes left to return, they began to retire to the north towards Japan. They must have commenced moving north at about the same time as we began to steam northwest, because the two Fleets were gradually closing each other, and, after searching all day, we finally picked them up late in the afternoon.

"A strike was ordered immediately. The enemy force was over 300 miles away, it was late in the afternoon, and the wind was easterly requiring us to launch and recover while headed away from the target, but the Admiral's decision was instantaneous. He may have missed his opportunities the two nights before, but he did not intend to miss his chance a third time.

"Our fliers did a fine job that night. We listened in on the radio circuits of the attacking planes. Their courage was superb. They were aware that many of them would not be able to make it back to their carriers because the enemy was beyond the range of their fuel supply, but there was never any question that the attack would be pressed home. When they finally sighted the enemy Fleet, it was split into several groups, and one of the main groups escaped without heavy attack. Our planes sank several Tankers and Fleet auxiliaries in one group, and in another, damaged a carrier and a battleship. The carrier was "possibly sunk".

"On the return trip, our planes began to run out of gas. Some fell in the water many miles from the Task Force, others made it the whole way back only to drop when they got there. The Task Force had steamed at its best speed towards them to shorten the distance, but when they began to come back, the Task Force carriers had to turn around to the east and head into the wind. All ships turned on their masthead lights, and one ship pointed her searchlight upwards. Another ship fired starshells into the air to help beacon the fliers home. Most of the fliers who did get back were not trained in night landings and because of this, there were many deck crashes, which caused long delays before landings could be resumed. Many landed in the water and destroyers were sent to pick up the crews. We had stationed destroyers astern of each carrier, and every time one of the planes went in, the nearest astern destroyer would proceed to the rescue, and we would send another in to take his place. Soon, there were only two destroyers in the screen.

"During the melee, the OWEN moved in to take its turn at the astern station. When we got in close to the carrier, a plane began circling, and making passes very close to our truck light. After he had made three passes at our light, he suddenly ran out of gas just ahead of us. We backed down as hard as we could to keep from passing him and with the aid of swimmers, soon rescued the aviator and his crew. He told us that he thought our light had been the Signal Officer on the carrier, and that he couldn't understand why they wouldn't wave him in. During that rescue, we dropped astern of the formation, and as we commenced rejoining, we kept seeing planes ditching, and went here and there picking up crews. Some of our ships had thrown life rafts with lights on them into the water in an attempt to aid crews that might not have been picked up. Unfortunately, all it did was cause trouble, forcing us to investigate dozens of empty life rafts. The OWEN picked up nine air crews that night, and many other ships did comparably.

"What a sight! Picture our huge Task Force 58 steaming through the night, 350 miles northwest of Saipan, in the Philippine Sea, all lights burning, starshells dropping their long silvery trails, and covering the whole scene with a weird pale light, searchlights waving in the sky, and destroyers dashing in every direction. The confusion was tremendous. It was almost impossible to put out orders on the voice circuits, so many ships had messages to send, that we literally jammed our own radios."

After the rescue, Spruance had to decide whether or not to pursue the enemy fleet and try to mop up the stragglers while they still remained outside of the range of enemy bombers from Formosa or the Philippines. Admiral Nelson had once said, "Had we taken ten sail, and then allowed the eleventh to escape, when it would have been possible to have gotten at her, I could never have called it well done." Spruance had his chance at this moment to make the job "well done" by Nelson's standard. On the other hand, although Spruance's carriers and battleships could have easily made a high speed foray in search of the enemy, and have been as safe so doing as they were steaming with the destroyers, and although they would have undoubtedly found some of the enemy fleet, we in the destroyers were very low on fuel. Some of the destroyers could do little more than make it back to Saipan. As he had done at Midway and acting on the erroneous belief that he could not proceed without the destroyer screen Spruance headed east.

THE MOVE TO THE SOUTH

Although, from the historical point of view, the Battle of the Philippine Sea was stunning victory for the US aviators and fighter director teams, with great credit being due to the American aircraft and ship building industries, it cannot be denied that the Navy had not capitalized on several opportunities. On the other hand, there were several things on the positive side of the ledger. First, on June 19th, while Spruance's Fleet lay to the east, unable to close toward the enemy, the U.S. submarines torpedoed and sank two of the large aircraft carriers in the Japanese attack fleet (while they were inadvisably steaming slowly, escorted by destroyers). Also, on the 20th when Spruance finally caught up to the enemy fleet, another smaller carrier was damaged by Spruance's carrier-based planes. Further, the U.S. submarines had previously sunk several other Japanese carriers. These sinkings by the U.S. submarines coupled with the Japanese loss of four large carriers at Midway, damage to others, and now the loss of 400 of their best carrier pilots and planes during the famous "turkey shoot" on June 19th, left the Japanese with only four large, five small carriers, and two converted battleships with small flight decks in place of their after gun mounts in their entire fleet, but without enough trained pilots or carrier based aircraft to man more than a fraction of these ships. This reduced the Japanese fleet to relative impotency. In addition, by now, the U.S. submarine force been increased to 140 highly trained and aggressive Fleet submarines deployed in Japanese waters. The problems which the U.S submarines had been experiencing with torpedoes had been solved, and, at long last, they had started employing highly effective wolf pack tactics on Japanese shipping. In 1944 alone, the U.S. Submarines reduced the Japanese merchant marine to a level at which the demands of the civilian economy could not be met, let alone the military. Thus, not only had the Japanese fleet been reduced to insignificance, but the supply line of materials and oil to Japan had been so strangled that they had no hope of replacing their losses.

We in the Fleet were aware of the tremendous turn of the balance of power in our favor and after Saipan and Tinian had been captured, and the invasions of Guam, Palau, Yap and Ulithi had been completed, we looked forward to the next move.

The best course seemed to be to proceed immediately up the island chain to

Iwo Jima and then to Okinawa, with Okinawa being the prime target because, from there we would be able to accomplish a final total blockade of Japan using both attack aircraft during the daytime and submarines at night. With Okinawa in the hands of the U.S. and us sitting on their supply lines, Japan could not have held out much longer. The Philippine Islands and other Japanese held territories to the South would have then fallen without a struggle.

The attractive feature of invading Okinawa was that it was far enough from Japan and Formosa for the U.S. fast carriers to be able to support an invasion there from a position outside of the range of attack aircraft from shore based airfields, and it was small enough for us to be able to obliterate its air strips by means of carrier based air attack.

At the time, we on the ships were totally unaware that an intense dogfight was going on in the upper levels of the Command over this very issue, and that President Roosevelt was being pressured by General MacArthur to let him invade the Philippines. The debate is described in various recent histories[44].

The issue being debated was not quite what we had in mind. They were trying to decide whether or not to invade Formosa first. The only one who favored Okinawa was Spruance[45] (This should be noted in Spruance's favor because he has otherwise been criticized in this account for lack of aggressiveness.). Nimitz, at one point, favored Formosa, but he grew soft and backed away. King continued to favor Formosa but eventually gave in. MacArthur is depicted as arguing vehemently and more-or-less snowing President Roosevelt under[46] Apparently, the main things which won out for MacArthur in the end were (a) his prediction that the Japanese in the Philippines would torture and starve the populace if the U.S. were to cut off supplies to the islands, and (b) that if the U.S. were to invade Formosa first, it would be taken by the Philippinos as an abandonment of them by the U.S. which would, thereby, negatively influence future U.S. relations with the Philippines. Also, invading Formosa was said to be riskier because of the impossibility of knocking out the numerous Japanese air strips there. This was a plausible argument, and it was the point which convinced Nimitz to back off. The advantage of Okinawa on this issue seems to have become lost in the shuffle.

When one considers the many thousands of men killed in the Philippine invasion, to say nothing of those lost later at Iwo and Okinawa due to our giving the Japanese time to fortify those two places, the decision (which was made largely pursuant to the vanity of one man, MacArthur) not to move north directly after taking Guam, but instead to invade the Philippines, has to be regarded as one of the major blunders of military history. In addition, its ill effects do not stop at the mere needless expenditure of lives and materials. If we had taken Okinawa in September or October of 1944, when we could have done so, we would have very likely strangled Japan into submission long before August 1945 and, thereby, have avoided the holocaust of firing the atom bomb at people (the long range negative impact of which on us and our descendants is hard to estimate).

LIFE AT AN ADVANCED BASE

After Saipan, the U.S. turned south, invaded Guam, Palau and Ulithi and began making preparations to invade the Philippines. Ulithi became an advanced base for the Fleet and we went there many times.

One time right after entering port and anchoring, the Commodore was called to the Task Force Flagship for a conference. I was preparing to make my rounds to the ships when an Admiral's barge came alongside, and six Officers came up the gangway, each with a suitcase and a briefcase. They asked to see the Staff Operations Officer. I introduced myself and the spokesman gave me a copy of his orders to report to our Squadron and said, "We are the new technology team, come to give your Squadron training in new techniques." The group included a specialist in each of the following techniques: (a) sonar, (b) radar, (c) gunnery, (d) torpedoes, and (e) visual recognition of aircraft. Each had recordings and graphic aids ready for presentations.

We went into the Wardroom and began trying to figure out what to do with them. The Fleet was to remain in port only for five days and all ships would be very hard pressed in that short time to do what needed to be done. Interference with the in-port activities was the last thing the ships wanted, and, besides, how to move these Officers around from ship to ship was a real problem due to the critical shortage of boats (Destroyers have only 2 motor whale boats, and these would be heavily occupied with routine missions, to say nothing of taking and getting liberty parties daily to nearby beaches and clubs). The spokesman of the group explained that they had been sent down from Pearl Harbor, that this was their first call, and that they had no idea how we could best use them, but that they were ours for the next five days to use as we could.

The procedure we devised was to send the group to a first ship, have them report to the Exec., who would then bring separate groups of specialists on the ships respectively with a corresponding one of these experts for two hours. The ship was to feed them and if the visit was in the morning, the ship would send them (using the ship's own motor whale boat) to the next ship on the list. The ships were listed in the order of anchorage proximity. If the visit was an afternoon session, the ship was to give them dinner, find bunks for them, give them breakfast and send them to the next ship on the list in the morning.

A Yeoman typed the schedule on a mimeograph stencil. It named each expert, described his subject, and set forth the full itinerary with the group ending up back on the OWEN on the last day. The program was mimeographed. I then gave the spokesman and each of the experts copies and sent them off in the motor whale boat to the first ship on the list. This took about two hours. A copy of the spokesman's orders and a copy of the program was then placed on the Commodore's desk.

Not long afterward, the Commodore returned to the ship, the messenger called me, and I went to the Commodore's cabin. He said that the Fleet was sending a technical team around and it was going to be a "helluva" nuisance but we would have to find a way to do something with them. I said, "Yes" and told him that I had already taken care of it. He said, "What? How could you do that?" I said, "I've done it, look on your desk." He sat down, picked up the orders and my program, glanced at them briefly and then said, "This isn't what I want at all! Get the leader of the group up here. I want to talk to him!" I said, "They've already gone, Sir. I can't get him." The Commodore was furious, sputtered around, asked how I could think I had authority to do such a thing, etc. Then, he read my program again, went quiet for a while and finally said, "OK, I guess it'll have to continue, but before the group leaves the Squadron, I want to see the group leader."

Thereafter, I asked some of the Execs. when I saw them at the Officers' Club how the new technology team was going. They said it was OK. They appreciated the limitation of the time of the lectures to two hours and the boat scheduling. They also thought that they had profited from it.

When the new technology team finally came back to the OWEN, they were all smiles. Everything had gone like clockwork. They all felt that they had accomplished what they came to do and were appreciated. Also, they felt they had been treated royally. The Commodore also seemed to have forgotten his disapproval. Typically, however, as with Hartwig and Stuffy Wood, Captain Cooper never breathed a word about it to the command. The reasons were the same, namely, that the program had not been approved by the command and doing anything which had not been approved was risky. Later on, in one of the Fleet Bulletins, we read that there was a new technology team for destroyers making the rounds, and that a good way for a destroyer Squadron to handle them had been suggested by another Squadron Commander. The Bulletin then quoted our program verbatim.

AN OFFICER "WALKS THE PLANK"

When the Fleet would put in to Ulithi, it was usual for several of the destroyers to nest together rather than anchoring separately. The advantages of nesting were that (a) only one ship had to anchor, (b) repair crews could operate more efficiently, (c) fueling, ammunitioning, provisioning, showing movies, and running liberty parties, all could be combined and simplified, and (d) the Officers and crews of the respective ships could intermingle and "see some new faces". The ships would be tied together with fenders between to keep the ships from bumping each other, and the people would pass between ships over 2" x 12" planks simply laid across the gunnels of adjacent ships.

One night in Ulithi, we were nested with the Miller and an Officer from the Miller joined us for dinner in the OWEN's Wardroom. After dinner, an announcement came over the ship's PA system that the movie was starting on the OWEN's fantail. Most of the OWEN's Officers then proceeded aft to see the movie. Our guest, however, declined the offer to see the movie, and after a second cup of coffee, he bid goodnight to several of us remaining in the OWEN's Wardroom and departed for the Miller. I decided to attend the movie and sauntered aft.

The movie lasted for about an hour and a half and after it was over and the men were leaving the fantail, someone yelled, "Hey, there's a man in the water over here!" Someone else shouted, "My God! Give me a hand. He's awful heavy!" In a few minutes, a very limp, wet, and totally exhausted Officer was pulled into the motor whaleboat which had been tied astern, and then carried up on deck. It turned out to be the same Officer from the Miller who had been our guest at dinner. He had missed his footing while crossing the gang plank and had fallen down between the ships. Then, due to the noise of the movie, no one could hear his shouts for help. By the time he had been able to make his way to the stern where the motor whaleboat was tied up, he had become too exhausted to pull himself up into the boat. All he could do at that point was hang on and hope that someone would spot him after the movie, which luckily happened.

NEVER OVERLOAD A WHALEBOAT

While in port, both motor whaleboats were kept extremely busy. They had a rated capacity of 22 passengers and two crew (a Coxswain and an Engineer). Since the ship's company for Fletcher class ships was about 360 men and the nearest recreational facilities were about 25 minutes away in the boat, it is a matter of simple mathematics that, if one half of the ship's company were to be given liberty, it would take four hours using both boats to take them ashore and four hours to bring them back. Controlling these operations at the ship was no problem because they would be under the supervision of the duty OOD. The problem was at the shore end of the trip where the men would be lined up to return and be apt to be unruly due to the consumption of beer. Also, no Officer was in charge at the shore end and the Coxswain alone was responsible for maintaining discipline in his own boat, which could be difficult, especially if Gunners mates, Engineers, or other ratings not used to taking orders from Coxswains, were involved.

Preventing overloading of the whaleboats on such occasions became a critical point and often an officer passenger would have to take charge or otherwise assist the Coxswain to make sure that proper loading procedures were carried out.

One night in Ulithi, a large unruly crowd had congregated at the dock and was clamoring for space in the boats, one of the coxswains allowed 26 passengers into his boat and no officer intervened to help him. On the trip back to the ship, the whaleboat was overtaken by an LCM and the bow-wave of the LCM swept over the stern of the whaleboat swamping and capsizing her. It still might not have been a tragedy except that three men were trapped under the canopy of the whaleboat and, being unable to get out, drowned. One of the Officers who had been a champion swimmer in college, tried to swim for help to a destroyer only 400 yards to windward. He made it, but due to the resistance of the choppy waves, he was so exhausted when he reached that ship, that he collapsed into a coma and was unable to tell them what had happened. Eventually, help arrived and all but the three previously mentioned were saved.

TYPHOON IN ULITHI

One time we came into Ulithi on a tight schedule with the ships low on both provisions and ammunition. It became important to accelerate the loading schedule and I went over to the Port Director's Office to obtain as many LCMs (Landing Craft Medium) as I could for the operation. He assigned me four and, with them, I took up headquarters on the provisioning ship where I could supervise the loading and direct the LCMs where to go next including to the nearby ammo ship and to the ships of the Squadron. A strong wind had sprung up, but not enough to interfere significantly with the loading which seemed to be going along quite well. At around midnight, I was becoming exhausted and, while several LCMs were loading, lay down under the provisioning ship's Wardroom table for a quick nap. I do not know how long I was asleep, but I was awakened by someone yelling, "The Fleet's getting under way, there's a typhoon coming." I jumped up, ran on deck, and saw the MILLER (of our Squadron) passing abeam of the provisioning ship. There was no way that I wanted to stay on a provisioning ship during a typhoon, and, therefore, I swung out on a rope on a cargo boom, down into one of the LCMs, and asked the Coxswain to "Take me over to that Tin Can!" He obliged, and within a few minutes I was on the MILLER steaming out of Ulithi into a typhoon. I should explain that in a typhoon it is far better to be at sea on any vessel than on a merchant ship in the bay of an atoll. In an atoll, there is no way one can run with the storm and thereby reduce the effect. One has to take the full brunt.

In any event, although a typhoon can be very severe and dangerous to a destroyer, if the ship can be maneuvered into the "navigable semi-circle" (the part of the storm in which the speed of the storm is subtracted from the rotational velocity of the wind around the storm center), a destroyer should be able to weather a typhoon without trouble. In the Pacific, the waves tend to be so large, and widely spaced that a destroyer is not badly disturbed by them. In fact, after I went on board the MILLER, I found a bunk and had a nice long sleep. The storm was not as uncomfortable as on a typical winter day in the North Atlantic.

The sad part was that I found later that two of the four LCM crews which had been loading for us were lost in the typhoon.

WOMBLE

Unbeknownst to us, from about the time of the 1st Philippine Sea battle (June 19, 1944), Captain Cooper's relief, Captain J. P. Womble, Jr., was riding a Cruiser in the Task Force as an observer. He had already received his orders to become ComDesRon 52, but, since he had, up until then, been on extended shore duty, he wanted to be at sea for a while and observe the destroyers before assuming command. The arrangement was that he would simply notify the Command when he was ready.

He took his time and it was around August 1944 when he reported on board the OWEN and relieved Captain Cooper.

Before telling about Captain Womble's policies and where they led us, I should say a word about him personally. He was about 45 years old, red-haired and very fair-skinned, so much so, that he had to stay out of the sun at all times. He also was tall (6'2"), lean, of aquiline features and eyes set fairly close together. He spoke with a thick North Carolina drawl. He was, from all superficial appearances, what one might call a "red neck", but not by attitude or actions. He had a "thing" about telling jokes and always, I mean always, had a new joke to tell in the Wardroom, and he always ate with us (Captain Cooper only ate with us on occasion). I do not know the source of his daily new joke. He must have had someone sending them to him in the mail. In any event, he never repeated one that I can remember.

Another problem for Womble was that he was allergic to shrimp. One time there was shrimp in the food, he ate some before he realized it, and burst out in a rash and swellings.

Still another quirk was his coffee habit. He drank more coffee than anyone I ever knew. We counted his cups and he averaged over 30 on a normal day. (I often have wondered whether there was some relationship between the coffee drinking and his premature death of a heart attack at age 54.)

He was not at all a friendly type in the sense of being a "buddy", but one felt that he was friendly. He always called me, "Russ". He always smiled whenever he addressed anyone.

I was apprehensive at first about how things would go with Captain Womble because he was not technically inclined and knew little about destroyers either from a technical point of view or operationally. He was not, however, like "Mickey Mouse" McClain because, when we first met, he frankly admitted his lack of knowledge and told me that he was relying heavily on me to tell him how things were done. In addition, when I told him how they were done, he accepted it.

He also said certain things that gave me immediate encouragement. First, he said he had tried to study Captain Cooper's Squadron Instructions, had had great difficulty understanding them, and that he wanted me to write up a one-page instruction for the Squadron. I was delighted because I, too, thought that the existing instructions which incidentally had been adopted verbatim from Standard destroyer Squadron Instructions of the Fleet were not only difficult to understand but obsolete. They had been written during peacetime and had been simply carried on into war without change.

Captain Womble also said that he had looked at the destroyer formations on the radar screen and he thought there must be something wrong with the destroyer Captains because they seemed to be out of station so much.

I found this encouraging because, of course, I too felt the formations were sloppy, and his comment gave me hope that he might not be so negative toward my "Fixed Station" screening proposal.

He also said he was disgusted by the ships of the Squadron asking for a repeat of a TBS message. He said he wanted to transmit messages very fast and only once, and for every ship to get it the first time, even if it took a team of ten men on each ship monitoring the circuit. He told me to convene a meeting of all Captains and Execs. of the Squadron in the Wardroom of the OWEN for the next day, and for me to have my one-page Squadron Instructions ready to hand out at the meeting.

I went to work immediately. I could have condensed the instructions to one page except that I wanted to incorporate my "Fixed Station" screening plan in them. Also, I had figured out a way for a coordinated destroyer torpedo attack, and I also wanted to put that attack plan in the instructions.

My torpedo attack plan discarded the idea of trying to protect the destroyers by a smoke screen. Radar "sees" through smoke, so the smoke screen idea of WWI was obsolete. It offered no practical protection. My idea was for the Squadron to spread out and then, from different directions, launch their torpedoes when each ship reached a given circle the center of which was at the plotted position the enemy would reach at the plotted time of arrival of the torpedoes. It was simple. It made it possible to fire the torpedoes at the enemy from many angles, and it spread the destroyers out so as to make it impossible to sink them all at once.

Writing the general instructions was easy. I included in them the Commodore's views about ragged looking screens and his warning that TBS messages would not be repeated.

When I came to writing up my "Fixed Station" screening method, I needed a flag hoist signal to initiate the formation of the screen. I then studied the "General Signal Book" in search of something suitable and found that there was a signal "TCW" (Tare Charlie William) which meant: "Form a screen of fixed stations based on 000 degrees (true) as the center of the screen."

I had not previously been aware of the signal, nor did I know what kind of screen it had in mind, but it fit my plan quite well. The only things that TCW did not say were what the spacing between the ships on the screen would be and how the ships were to change from one station to another to fill a gap in the van. I adopted the signal "TCW" to initiate my proposed screening method and decided to rely on the Squadron Instructions to inform the respective ships as to how to shift station when required. I planned to base the screen on true north and therefore the full signal to start the plan would be "TCW-000".

The write-up of both TCW and the torpedo attack method took only about two more pages, and my proposed Screening Instructions ended up with three and one-half pages.

I had it mimeographed and brought it to the Commodore. He asked about TCW. Since I was so convinced it would work, and wanted to avoid its being turned down again, I took a chance (potentially the most serious of my Naval career) and I said it was a new plan but that we had previously adopted it and it worked well. (Although the squadron had not adopted it, I had at least discussed it previously with some of the Execs. and Captains of the Squadron and had received favorable comment.) The Commodore was also interested in the Torpedo Attack plan, I explained it to him in detail, told him it was totally new, and that practice by the Squadron in a simulated attack exercise would be needed before we could use the plan.

He made a few corrections and said he thought it was fine. The next day we convened, the new instructions were handed out, the Commodore spoke, saying much the same things he had said to me, a few questions were asked but nothing about TCW, the meeting broke up, and the Squadron got underway not long afterward.

THE OKINAWA—FORMOSA RAID (OCTOBER 10-14, 1944)

During the initial period after Captain Womble assumed the command of DesRon 52, the fast carrier Task Forces were occupied with carrying out raids against enemy installations in the Philippines. Presumably owing to his newness as a Squadron Commander, Womble was not initially put in charge of the screen, but instead, a Squadron Commander on another ship was assigned to command the screen in our Task Group, and things went along exactly as they had before.

In early October, however, the fast carriers made a raid on Okinawa and Formosa. The objective was to bomb and otherwise harass the enemy's aircraft staging route to the Philippines, preparatory to MacArthur's invasion of the Philippines.

During this raid (on the Formosa part), enemy aircraft succeeded in damaging two of our Cruisers, and, as a consequence, the Cruisers had to be sent back for repairs. It then became necessary also to detach several destroyers to screen the damaged ships. The Squadron Commander in charge of our screen was selected, and this meant that Captain Womble was now to be the Screen Commander. He was delighted. I said, "OK Commodore, when the other Commodore's ship is detached, I will run up the TCW, and we will form the screen by our new method." He said, "OK. I'm going down to breakfast, let me know if there is anything unusual." I said, "Aye, Aye, Sir", and he went to breakfast.

Soon thereafter, the other Squadron Commander was detached, and I ran up "TCW-000" to initiate the new screening method. When all ships in the screen had it up, I executed the maneuver. Then the suspense began. The OWEN, of course, under my direction, moved promptly to the correct position of her new station. Gradually some of the other ships started. The ship next to us did not move, but I succeeded in telling her where to go by blinker. My problem was that there was a speaker for the TBS in the Commodore's Stateroom, and I could not use the TBS to tell the ships where to go without tipping the Commodore off to the fact that I was having trouble. Finally, I had been able by blinker messages to get all ships but one, on their correct stations, when the Commodore appeared on deck. At that time, I had the signalman trying desperately to raise the one ship still out of position, on the blinker. The Commodore walked around, looked at the screen, and looked at the radar, several times.

"Hey Russ, what's that ship doing? Aren't they out of position? Look at that big gap between them and the next ship forward. Get on the TBS to them and tell them 'POSIT'"

("POSIT" is the Navy way of saying, "You are out of position, you dummy, get into position immediately!").

So I went to the TBS, gave the ship's call sign and said "POSIT".

"POSIT AFFIRM" came back immediately (meaning "We are in position!")

"That doesn't make any sense Russ. What is this all about? How can they think they're in position?"

I was on the spot and had to tell him that the Squadron had not actually ever used TCW before. This was a tense moment. This time I really did fear a Court Martial because I knew I had no defense. In an effort to extract myself, I blurted out that the plan was perfectly simple, and all the ship had to do was move up to the nearest fixed station. The Commodore paused for a moment.

"Show me where's the place he is supposed to be." I complied. The Commodore then picked up the TBS, quickly told the ship where it should be, and hung up. Within a few minutes, the screen was perfect. It was not quite balanced to each side of the base course, but it was very symmetrical in terms of spacing between ships and distance from the center of the formation.

From then on, the plan worked smoothly. During the first flight operations after the inauguration of the system, one ship needed directing, but I was able to do it by blinker. The ships shifted across the back of the formation and otherwise remained fixed. No ship had to steam at more than 20 kts. and often ships slowed down. The van was always closed. We, on the Flagship, did not occupy the center of the screen, but the Commodore was not concerned about it.

INVESTIGATED FOR FALSIFICATION

After the Okinawa-Formosa raid, we put into port briefly to provision and take on ammunition before the invasion of the Philippines. Not long after anchoring, the watch reported an Admiral's barge approaching. We had no idea what it might be. A large delegation of high-ranking Officers (two Captains, two Commanders, one Lt. Cdr. and five Chiefs) came aboard, demanded immediately to see the Commodore in the Wardroom and dismissed from the room everyone else except the Commodore and me. They said that a very serious offense had been committed FALSIFICATION OF FUEL REPORTS, and that a Court Martial would ensue unless we could prove that there had been no falsification. The Commodore was astounded. He had no idea what they were talking about, all we had done was turn in the reports exactly as the ships had given them to us. I had all the messages to prove it. They said, however, that they did not believe the reports were accurate because all ships in our Squadron had at least one day's-run more fuel left than any destroyer in the other Task Groups of the fast carrier Force.

I knew what the answer was and asked the Commodore if I could speak. He said, "OK" and I explained how TCW avoided the high-speed requirements of the Reorientation Method and that we had proved something similar when I had been with Hartwig on the RUSSELL in the early battles.

They were not especially convinced and asked to visit the ships and check the soundings of the fuel tanks. We obliged, of course, and they did it. The soundings all jibed, and they went away shaking their heads.

TCW SUCCEEDS

The history of TCW thereafter was quite spectacular. Not long after we put to sea again, Admiral Bogan, in charge of the Task Group we were in, sent the Commodore a complimentary message in which he described our Squadron as "the Perfect Circle Piston Rings" (there was a well-known brand of piston ring sold under the trademark "Perfect Circle").

In several weeks' time, after the fuel reports of DesRon 52 continued to show spectacular improvement over the other Squadrons in the Fleet, we were asked to explain it, and it was promulgated as the standard screening method for all Squadrons of the fast carriers.

The saving in fuel was enormous. My calculations showed that the saving for all the fast carrier screening destroyers combined was over 5,000 tons of oil each week.

LEAVE IT TO THE PROS

While in port after the Okinawa-Formosa raid, since we had to take on ammunition in a hurry, we obtained some LCM'S, went to the ammunition ship and from there tried to raise some working parties from the other ships to help out with the loading on the ammunition ship. The destroyers of the Squadron had very few men to spare because all available working parties were already either working on provisioning or would be needed to unload the LCM's when they arrived at the destroyer. I looked around the ammo ship and found that all they had was a crew of eight professional longshore-men and their Sergeant, obviously not enough. After calling around to nearby ships, we finally located a battleship which was able to send us a working party of 75 men. This was exactly what we needed, and when they arrived, we put the longshoremen to work loading on one side of the ship and the 75 battleship sailors on the other. The battleship sailors came in full of good spirits, joking and wrestling each other. Once they started, they went to work loading furiously. The longshoremen did it in a completely different way. All eight of them were large, Black, strong, and moved very slowly. The never lifted a shell ¼" higher than necessary and rolled it (on the edge of the base of the shell) whenever they could. The part that disturbed me was that at any one time, only one half of them worked. They were split into two groups of four, one group in the boat and one in the hold, but at each place only two of them worked and the other two were lying down sleeping. I was furious and took it up with the Sergeant. He told me to mind my own business. The long-shoremen heard me and just stared at me disinterestedly. For the first hour or two, the battleship crew were way ahead. They kept on loading into the night. I went into the Wardroom, flaked out in my favorite place under the table, and slept for an hour or two. Then someone came in and said that the crane operator in the after hold had gone off watch without replacement. I got up, went out, looked around and found the battleship crew had slowed down to a walk. I tried to get them going again. The professionals were load-ing exactly as they had been before, no change. In addition, their total num-ber of loaded LCM's was now nearly the same as the battleships crew's.

I went aft and tried to obtain a crane operator, finally was unable to, and started doing it myself. After a little practice, I got the hang of it and contin-ued with it for an hour or so until a proper relief could be found.

By dawn, when we finally completed the job, the battleship crew was completely spent. The professionals were still loading exactly as before and had loaded more ammunition by a factor of 5 to 4.

THE BATTLE OF LEYTE GULF.

(For many of the details of the following account of the Battle of Leyte Gulf which took place in areas apart from the fast carriers with Halsey, major reliance is placed on Stuart Adrian's "Battle of Leyte Gulf").

After the Okinawa-Formosa raid, we went back to Ulithi for a few days to rearm and rest, and then set out toward the Philippines. The operations order made clear that we, in this case the 3rd Fleet (since Admiral Halsey was in command), would be used in support of MacArthur's invasion of the Philippines. There was a significant difference, however, in the operations order in this instance than the OpOrd for Saipan. It had been well known that Halsey had been scornful of Spruance's run to the east at Midway. Also, although Halsey had been somewhat silent about Kinkaid's desertion of the Hornet at Santa Cruz, Halsey had been vociferous in his criticism of Spruance's holding the fleet to the east at the 1st Philippine Sea Battle. I was totally in accord with these thoughts. The difference in the OpOrd this time was that Halsey had secured Nimitz's approval for the following wording to be added: "In case opportunity for destruction of major portion of enemy fleet is offered or can be created, such destruction becomes the primary task." This was just what Halsey wanted. Ever since his midshipman days and his study of Mahan at the academy, he had been convinced that the enemy's fleet, primarily carriers in World War II (i.e. the power to control transportation) was the only real objective, and that the elimination of the enemy carrier fleet had to supersede anything else. Thus, in contrast to Spruance's action when he had had the chance to eliminate the Japanese fleet at 1st Philippine Sea and had rejected it, Halsey was resolved that if he had the chance, he would not fail.

Captain Womble and I were temporarily on the TINGEY, in charge of the screen of Task Group 38.2 under Rear Admiral Bogan. Halsey's flag was on the NEW JERSEY, one of the largest new U.S. battleships, also in our Task Group.

The ensuing battle was without doubt the greatest battle in history in terms of fire power between the two sides. The battle of Salamis in ancient Greece, 480 BC, may still hold the record for number of participants (believed to be over 1,000,000 men on combatant ships), but at Leyte Gulf the fire power was many times that ever seen before in a naval battle.

The opposing fleets were massive. The U.S. had four fast carrier Task Groups totaling some 8 large (CV) and 8 small fast carriers (CVL) having on board some 1,152 aircraft of the latest design which had proven themselves to be superior to the Japanese at the 1st Philippine Sea Battle and again recently in the Okinawa-Formosa raid. In addition, in "MacArthur's Navy" (the ships under Kinkaid assigned to MacArthur for support), there were some 18 escort carriers (CVE) having on board a total of 235 fighters and 143 torpedo bombers. This totaled to about 1500 combat aircraft. Opposed to this, the Japanese fleet included four large fast carriers (CV), five small carriers (CVL), and two converted battleships (BBCVL) which had small flight decks on their sterns. The U.S. superiority of about 4 to 1 in carriers might seem serious enough for the Japanese but in addition, the difference in available aircraft not only in quality but also in numbers was major. At the 1st Philippine Sea Battle, the Japanese had seen the destruction of the cream of their air arm, some 400 of their best naval aircraft and senior naval pilots. Then during the Okinawa-Formosa raid of early October, they lost another 500 aircraft including some 150 additional, much needed naval air men and planes. Thus, while they had a few carriers, they did not have enough pilots or planes to come close to manning them. Also, since the U.S. submarines had at last started to hunt the Japanese merchant marine by the German wolf-pack technique, few tankers were making it to Japan, and the supply of fuel oil to Japan had become so restricted that it was less than that needed to sustain their civilian economy to say nothing of having any to spare for the Navy.

However, the Japanese were in desperate straits. They had to try to prevent the landings at Leyte because the loss of the Philippines would mean that the U.S. would have air and submarine bases capable of blocking sea travel from the south thereby forcing them to transport the necessary supplies across China. As pointed out above, the loss of Okinawa would have been far more embarrassing to them, but even the loss of the Philippines would mean the eventual loss of the war. They had to do what they could.

Besides having the more or less useless carriers already mentioned, the

Japanese had available 7 battleships (BB), 11 heavy cruisers (CA), 4 light cruisers (CL) and some 23 destroyers (DD). The battleships included the Yamato and Musashi, the two largest battleships afloat, 63,000 tons each and with 18.1" guns capable of firing at longer range than any other ship, and they also had thicker armor plates. As for battleships the U.S. fleet had 6 new fast battleships available, and six old battleships accompanying the invasion forces with MacArthur, under Admiral Kinkaid. It must be remembered, however, that, as Billy Mitchell had preached, and Pearl Harbor had shown (as well as the sinking of the Prince of Wales and the Repulse), battleships were meaningless. Nevertheless, if the occasion were to arise in which battleships actually could be used, as for instance in a night action, the U.S. outnumbered the Japanese nearly 2 to 1.

In submarines also, The U.S. had much the upper hand. Admiral Lockwood at Pearl Harbor, using a promotion procedure which rewarded aggressive and innovative individuals with promotion over the heads of their more reluctant and conservative seniors, had successfully molded the U.S. submarines into a highly efficient organization which had been sinking Japanese shipping at a rate far in excess of their power to replace. Thus, the submarines alone were bringing Japan to her knees. Although the Japanese were able to field 11 submarines in the Philippine Sea, the U.S. had over 50 in the approaches to the Philippines.

We in the Fleet felt relaxed. We were part of a tremendous armada which we knew far exceeded that of the Japanese. Kinkaid had embarked from New Guinea with a fleet of 738 ships including the battleships and CVE's already mentioned, and we in the 3rd fleet were without doubt the strongest strike force ever assembled. It appeared that there was little that the Japanese could do.

Several factors, however, were at work which had the effect of making things somewhat more favorable to the Japanese than we appreciated. First was the dominant compulsion of Admiral Halsey to engage in a major fleet action and the permission in the operations order for him to do it if he had or could create the opportunity. This should have worked to our favor but as things happened, it did not. Second was the split in the Command between the 3rd fleet under Halsey reporting to Nimitz at Hawaii, and the 7th fleet under Kinkaid reporting to MacArthur. The 7th fleet was intended for ASW patrol off-shore, for air cover over the transports, and for supporting the army on the beaches under MacArthur's direction, whereas the 3rd fleet under Halsey was to defend the invasion from attack by enemy fleet units, to provide air cover, and neutralize the enemy airfields on Luzon. The problem was that the split in the command structure meant that there would be little likelihood of effective coordination between the two fleets. The third factor favoring the Japanese was that there was a mild but yet perceptible enmity between the services which contributed further to slowness of communication and lack of interest in cooperation.

The invasion of the Philippines at Leyte started with preliminaries on October 17th, and the major landings on the 20th. In the meantime, the enemy's naval units were forming up, and after making sure that the Leyte operation was not a feint, they topped up their fuel tanks and left Northern Borneo on the 18th with the intention of attacking and hopefully repelling the invasion. Early on the 23rd, two U.S. submarines the Darter and the Dace, sighted a large enemy force steaming north on the western approaches of the Philippines, near Palawan Island. After reporting them, the subs attacked and succeeded in sinking one heavy cruiser and damaging another so severely that she had to retire. It happened that the one which sank had been the flagship of Japanese Admiral Kurita, in charge of a force of 5 BB, 10 CA, 2 CL and 15 DD. He was able to swim to safety and transferred his flag to the Yamato, one of the two Japanese superbattleships. Thereafter Kurita's forced continued with two less heavy cruisers and destroyers.

On the 24th various enemy units were sighted converging toward Leyte through the Philippine archipelago. The first to be sighted was Kurita's "central force", at 0746 by Lt Adams from the Intrepid. Shortly thereafter, Halsey ordered Task Groups 3 (Sherman) and 4 (Davidson) to concentrate toward San Bernardino Strait where Task Group 2 (Bogan) was at the time, and to launch attacks on the enemy. At that time, he ordered Task Group I (McCain) with his 5 carriers to retire to the east for refueling and to return to the scene as soon as possible. At 0900, on the 20th one of Davidson's search planes sighted another Japanese force containing 2 battleships one heavy cruiser and 4 destroyers to the south entering the Sulu sea. It was now apparent that the enemy was attacking with strong surface striking forces both through the center of the Philippines toward San Bernardino Strait and from the south toward Surigao Strait. In addition, troop transports and supply ships were sighted approaching the western side of Leyte guarded by destroyers.

At about this same time, Task Group 3 still to the north off Luzon successfully fended off an attack by a large number of land based aircraft, but shortly thereafter, a lone enemy bomber cleverly evaded the air cover and planted a well-aimed bomb on the CVL PRINCETON. This unfortunately started fires which could not be contained. Her escort vessels tried desperately to save her, but in the end were unable. Late in the day, the light cruiser BIRMINGHAM came alongside PRINCETON to help fight the fires, and just at that moment a tremendous explosion on PRINCETON blew apart a major portion of her stern and showered BIRMINGHAM with flame, debris, steel plates, gun mounts etc. killing several hundred men on the decks of the BIRMINGHAM. PRINCETON sank at around 1800 on the 24th.

During the day, Halsey's planes concentrated on the central force, inflicting heavy damage and eventually succeeding in sinking the Mushashi.

We were unaware of it at the time, but the Japanese had succeeded in putting to sea a large carrier force containing 6 carriers, (one large, three small and the two battleship-carriers previously mentioned), together with assorted cruisers and destroyers. This force, under Admiral Ozawa, was intended by them to attack from the northeast and serve as a decoy, to draw the 3rd Fleet to the north in order to give Kurita in the center and Nishimura in the south a chance to close a pincer movement onto the beaches at Leyte. Ozawa's force arrived in position about 200 miles northeast of Halsey in the early morning of the 24th.

Halsey, however, had not launched air searches to the northeast, and Ozawa went for several hours undetected. In order to attract attention, he had some of his search planes, who had already located Task Group 3, break radio silence, but it brought no reaction. Finally, around noon, becoming concerned that Halsey might not detect him, Ozawa sent an air strike against Task Group 3 comprising some 40 fighters, 28 dive bombers and 8 torpedo planes, nearly all of his remaining aircraft. This attack reached its target at around 1330 and by 1400 had been completely dispersed by the U.S. defenders without inflicting any damage on the U.S. forces.

In the meantime, Halsey, at last having begun to wonder where the enemy carriers might be, at 1155, ordered a search to the north and east. This search was delayed in take-off, but finally was airborne at 1405 after Ozawa's attack had made it obvious to anyone that enemy carriers were to the northeast. These belated searches soon located Ozawa's force and mis-reported the enemy as being 4 BB, 5 to 6 CV and 6 DD. A second report came in at 1640 indicating a force of 2 CV and 1 CVL sighted.

The presence of these large carrier forces to the northeast galvanized Halsey. Although he continued to send attacks against the central surface force of Kurita for a while, after hearing that he had sunk one of the Japanese superbattleships and damaged numerous other ships of Kurita's force and also after hearing at 1600 that Kurita had turned back, Halsey ordered the three carrier Task Groups to rendezvous and move to the northeast. Earlier, he had sent a signal that a battleship group to be called Task Force 34 would be formed. From the report of 4 BB and 6-7 CV to the northeast, he saw the possibility of a night surface action, and Task force 34 was to be used for that purpose. Task Force 34, however, was not actually formed up at that time, but instead the battleships remained in the carrier Task Groups. Although Halsey informed Kinkaid and Nimitz about the intention to form Task Force 34, he gave no details as to what he intended to do with it, nor did he let them know that it had not actually been formed. This is significant because others such as Kinkaid to the south and Nimitz at Pearl Harbor, thought that Task Force 34 was already a reality. Thus, at 2022 when Halsey sent a message to Kinkaid saying "Am proceeding north with three groups to attack enemy carrier force at dawn," both Kinkaid and Nimitz thought he was going north with the carriers only and leaving Task Force 34, the battleships, behind to cover San Bernardino.

Thereafter, Halsey received a number of good indications that Kurita had turned around and was again heading for San Bernardino Strait. One such indication came from a night search plane from the INDEPENDENCE at 2030, reporting Kurita off the middle of Burias Island heading for the Sibuyan sea (i.e., back in the direction of San Bernardino) making 20 kts. Again at 2110 another INDEPENDENCE night search plane sighted Kurita off Aguja Point headed for San Bernardino making 20 kts. This latter report did not reach Halsey until 2320 and even then, he did not pass it on to Kinkaid. Finally, the night search planes reported that the navigation lights which had been blacked out for the entire war, were burning brightly in San Bernardino Strait.

It cannot be denied that Halsey had before him ample evidence that Kurita was bent on taking his fleet through San Bernardino. This, however, did not in the least deter Halsey's interest in heading north. He kept on despite messages over the TBS, which we heard, from several of his Task Group commanders to dissuade him. At 2320, the INDEPENDENCE recalled her night fliers. It happened that Kurita sortied from San Bernardino shortly thereafter completely unopposed. Halsey had not even taken the precaution of leaving a destroyer there on picket. (There can be no dispute that Halsey should at least have done the latter. I would not have especially wanted to be on that destroyer, but the need for same was clear).

Whether or not Halsey should have gone north at the time has been the topic of much discussion, with very few agreeing with the decision. Having been there and having been privy to much of the above information, I can only say that I think that Halsey was right. At the battle of Philippine Sea, we had seen Spruance run from the possibility of a show-down battle with the Japanese carriers because he was afraid of an "end run". That possibility, however, which Spruance had so dreaded, would have been the best thing for us that could have happened because we would then have had the enemy fleet trapped and could have annihilated every last one of them. The same thing applied on the night of the 24th October as we headed north in chase of the enemy carriers. We had no notion that the northern force was a decoy, but it seemed possible that the Japanese might try to by-pass us in an attempt to aid the surface forces to the south. In any event, it was clear that for Halsey to sink one enemy carrier would be as good as his sinking four enemy battleships and, if carriers were to the north, there was where Halsey should make his attack. Also, if Kurita actually was able to pass through San Bernardino and after going around Samar, penetrate into Leyte Gulf, he would be in deep trouble because not only could the CVE's be used for attack if properly armed, but also some of the forces under Halsey could be sent back to take care of him. As far as the southern Japanese force was concerned, there was not much chance that an inferior enemy force could come through Surigao Strait. It seemed less likely to succeed than the "Charge of the Light Brigade".

We went north through the night. Eventually Halsey formed up Task Force 34 and sent it further to the north to defend against surface attack.

While we were going north, Kurita had passed through San Bernardino and was steaming down the eastern shore of Samar with his central force. In the south, Nishimura was approaching Surigao Strait through the Sulu Sea. The pincer appeared to be closing. Earlier at around 2230 PT boats which had been deployed well to the south of Surigao sighted Nishimura and tried to attack with torpedoes. The enemy's radar was far inferior to ours. They were unable to fire accurately by radar and were forced to turn on their search-lights, thereby helping the PT boats to identify them as well as to take aim. It did not help, however. In spite of tremendous efforts and heroism on the part of the PT boats, the enemy was able to thwart these attacks. None of the over 30 PT boat attacks scored any hits. After the enemy entered the strait, how-ever, Oldendorf sent his destroyers down each side of the strait to make tor-pedo attacks on the flanks of the advancing Japanese column coming up the middle. Curiously the enemy remained steaming on a straight course. Sev-eral of the torpedoes from the U.S. destroyers found their mark. Three tor-pedoes hit the battleship FUSO which stopped in her tracks and within a few minutes blew up. Shortly thereafter, at 0320, Nishimura's flagship the battle-ship YAMASHIRO was hit by torpedoes. Then Oldendorf ordered his battle-ships and cruisers to open fire. Within minutes they were making hits, and soon most of the enemy ships were burning. Only the heavy cruiser MOGAMI and one destroyer were able to escape from the Strait, but the MOGAMI was sunk the next day as she was trying to limp off. It only took Oldendorf's bat-tleships 18 minutes to deliver the coup de grace to the southern Japanese force.

In the north at dawn, we simultaneously launched air searches and an air strike since it was assumed that the air searches would soon find targets for the strike force. In fact, not long afterward several somewhat scattered enemy units were located, and the air strike force was sent after them. At 0710 an attack was made, and the pilots immediately reported that there were "scarcely any planes on their decks", and that the fighter protection was non-existent. This news apparently made no difference to Halsey. The rapid move to the north continued.

Meanwhile offshore at Leyte Gulf, the three CVE Task Groups were deployed on a north-south line, with the northernmost group, "Taffy 3", more or less even with the southern tip of Samar, "Taffy 2" was about 30 miles further south and "Taffy 1" was about 90 miles still further south. No one in the U.S.

fleet suspected Kurita's presence. The night fliers had missed him by a matter of minutes as he passed through San Bernardino. Other searches had not been made in the area because Kinkaid thought that Halsey was covering it. Kurita had been steaming at 20 kts and by 0640 was approaching Taffy 3 when one of Taffy 3's aircraft sighted Kurita's force, reported it and then tried to attack. Soon thereafter the enemy sighted the CVE's and started closing in. At around 0700 the enemy opened fire, while the CVE's headed east into the wind to launch their aircraft while under fire. In fact, the WHITE PLAINS was hit soon after the shelling commenced and temporarily lost steering control. Some of the planes just launched were able to attack the enemy and one landed a bomb on the heavy cruiser SUZUYA which also dropped astern and eventually sank. During this time, all ships in the Task Group were making smoke and turning here and there radically such that collision among themselves became an additional major hazard. At 0730 the JOHNSTON which had been able to duck under her own smoke screen, again came under attack. This time she was hit by 3 14" and 3 6" shells in rapid succession and reduced to a burning mass of wreckage. Somehow with the aid of a well-placed thunder shower, and fantastic courage of her men, she was able to put out the fires and return to action. The other destroyers also charged into the breach firing their 5" guns and torpedoes under the hail of the fire power of 4 BB and now 4 CA. The aircraft soon expended their bombs. Only two were equipped with torpedoes, but the others made attacks as though they were armed with torpedoes simply to induce the enemy to turn away. Any respite was welcome. Also, they strafed the enemy, which caused little damage to the armored ships except that it did disable some of their radars and range finders. Some of the planes also had depth charges and they tried dropping them close to the enemy ships in hopes of damaging them. The attack continued with the enemy gradually coming closer, and the CVE's desperately running to the southwest toward Leyte Gulf, dodging as best they could and "salvo chasing", i.e. turning toward the place where the last salvo landed, on the theory that the enemy would change their settings between salvos. As this was going on the two CVE's on the port quarter of the formation were unable to come under the protection of the smoke screens because the wind was from the north east. Being thus exposed, the enemy succeeded in scoring hits on them and one of them, the GAMBIER BAY eventually was forced to slow down by reason of being hit in the engine spaces. Then the enemy fell on her with their full fire power and she was blasted into a blazing inferno. Eventually she sank at 0910.

In the meantime, aircraft from Taffy 2 showed up at around 0830 and by attacking the enemy forced them to turn away momentarily. Finally, at 0911 Kurita ordered his ships to turn north and the ordeal of Taffy 3 came to an end. For some two hours this force, which had been taken by complete surprise and which was neither intended nor equipped for such a battle, held off a far superior, much faster force. The destroyers HOEL and JOHNSTON, the destroyer escort SAMUEL B. ROBERTS, and the escort carrier GAMBIER BAY were sunk, and other ships were damaged. In return, however, the US forces had sunk the enemy heavy cruisers CHIKUMA, SUZUYA and CHOKAI, and the destroyer HAYASHIMO. It was ironic that the United States Navy with all of its vaunted power was able to put only this ill equipped but valiant force of heroes into action against the Japanese off Samar.

Admiral Sprague, in charge of Taffy 3 reported "The failure of the enemy main body and encircling light forces to completely wipe out all vessels in this Task Unit can be attributed to our successful smoke screen, our torpedo counterattack, continuous harassment of the enemy by bomb, torpedo, and strafing air attacks, timely maneuvers, and the definite partiality of Almighty God."

We, on the TINGEY in Task Group 38.2 received word of Kurita's attack on the CVE's at 0745. It was a plain language message, "Am being attacked by large enemy force, including battleships, off Samar".

At this point, besides the immediate reaction of "Well I'll be damned!", everyone was wondering what Halsey was going to do. At that time, he was about 200 miles from San Bernardino. If he sent some of his force back immediately, he stood a good chance of arriving within air strike range of this enemy force within about three hours. This was the opportunity which Spruance did not have at 1st Philippine because Spruance had not given the enemy a chance to make such a risky dash. But Halsey, by his run to the north had laid the trap and now he had his chance to close back in and annihilate them. Moreover, he could do it without reducing his ability to mop up the northern force, which, by now he knew was without air cover. This meant that the job could be done in the north with but a fraction of Task Force 38.

Halsey did not merely wait. He did worse. He ordered Lee with his now formed Task Force 34 to move northeast to "close the enemy at 25 kts", the enemy in this instance being their northern force. Then for the next three-

and one-half hours Halsey continued with his entire force north thereby separating himself from San Bernardino by an additional 87 miles which would have to be retraced.

Finally, at 1115 he ordered the IOWA and the NEW JERSEY, four cruisers and our squadron to proceed at high speed back to San Bernardino. Our squadron, however, was short of fuel, and Halsey lost another hour fueling. Even this decision to fuel the destroyers is curious because the plan was to steam at 27 knots at which speed the sonars of the destroyers would be quite useless, and otherwise there would have been virtually no need for the destroyers to participate. By the time we arrived at San Bernardino, at around 2230, all that remained of the enemy fleet was a lone straggling enemy cruiser which our cruisers sank firing by radar over our heads. The enemy main body had passed through the strait only one hour before.

Halsey has borne the brunt of much criticism for his actions in the battle. Even Nimitz, who never criticized his commanders was reputed to be furious, but in the end, Nimitz would not let any official criticism be voiced. No one else has been as kind. It is my opinion that the run to the north was well conceived, with the exception of the failure to leave a picket outside of San Bernardino. Otherwise, it succeeded in doing exactly what Halsey wanted. It gave him the opportunity for which he had dreamed, the chance to nearly completely demolish the enemy fleet. Unfortunately, he did not seem to see it. As it was, much was accomplished. Halsey had sunk the MUSASHI on the 24th and he sank four of Ozawa's carriers on the 25th. In addition, Oldendorf had sunk most of Nishimura's southern group. The YAMATO and three other battleships and some six cruisers had escaped, but what was left of the Japanese fleet and naval air arm was not impressive. All they really had left was the Kamikaze, about which more later.

It appears that Halsey somehow lost his grip at the crucial moment of the battle, at 0745 on the 25th, when he had his chance to send part of his force back to intercept Kurita (or to help attack Kurita if Kurita had decided to make a suicide run toward MacArthur's beach heads). There is some evidence that the message which Nimitz sent him at around 1000 may have contributed to his loss of grip. Nimitz' message was "Where is, repeat, where is Task Force 34? RR the world wonders". The final phrase was not supposed to be part of the message but was inserted merely as a coding technique intended to interfere with the enemy's attempts to decipher it. Halsey apparently thought that it was part of the message and took it as a deliberate insult from his superior. The accounts say that he shut himself in his room for a substantial period after receiving it.

So ended the greatest naval battle in history in which the essentially weak, under-manned, and oil-starved Japanese fleet took on the richest and most powerful fleet of ships and aircraft ever assembled. But as the battle progressed the final chapter was written by the vastly underdog Japanese actually fighting in the reverse role of favorite against a minor, inadequate and unprepared portion of the mammoth U.S. fleet, with that small portion holding its own against the Japanese by dint of sheer guts and ingenuity, and with the Japanese then getting away with a good portion of their ships under the noses of the admirals of that great armada.

"SEND THEM TO THEIR ANCESTORS"

The next day, the 26th, we continued south off of Leyte Gulf in the area where the fighting had taken place on the 25th. Our purpose was to comb the area for survivors. We did, in fact, find quite a few Americans and many Japanese as well, from the sunken Cruisers. We, on the TINGEY, in fact, picked up a U.S. aviator swimming near to a large group of Japanese.

The TINGEY took on board about 12 Japanese prisoners. Previously, we had been much impressed by the stories of suicidal attempts by the Japanese P.O.W.'S. to attack their captors and, consequently, we put the P.O.W.'S up on the fo'c'sle, with guards on them with loaded rifles about 20 yds. from them. The guards were given orders to shoot to kill if any of the prisoners should move closer to them. Eventually we sent the prisoners to a Cruiser where they could be more securely locked up.

Later in the day, the OWEN, some miles distant from us came upon a group of Japanese in the water and asked for instructions from the Task Force Command. Orders came back for the OWEN to take them prisoner. After a while, the OWEN reported that they had taken a few prisoners, but the remainder had refused to come on board. Then came back an order which we all heard, "Send them to their ancestors!" At this point, the men on the OWEN fired at the men in the water with rifles. I was grateful not to have been there. Their action was legal according to the Geneva Convention, but is this really what Americans want? Besides being disgusting and craven, history shows that kind of thing to be counterproductive. Thus, the sinking of the Luisitania by the Germans during WWI, perfectly legal under the rules of International Law, was undoubtedly responsible for firing up the American populace to participate in WWI (and who knows what motivation for the Japanese people will result from the dropping of the atom bomb?)

ORDERS HOME BUT NO ORDERS HOME

Soon after the 2nd Philippine Sea Battle, orders came in for me to proceed home to new construction as Staff Operations Officer for a new Squadron of 2200 ton destroyers, DesRon 66. 1 did not know it at the time, but Captain Hartwig (formerly of the RUSSELL and promoted in the meantime) had been assigned a new Squadron and had prevailed on BuPers to transfer me to his new command. A Lt. John ("Judge") Langdale was ordered to DesRon 52 to relieve me, and my orders indicated that when Langdale reported on board, I would be free to go. In fact, "Judge" came on board not long thereafter, and I prepared to leave. Commodore Womble, however, said "No". I asked how come, and he cited a Naval Regulation which permits a Commanding Officer to refuse to let an Officer be relieved if in the view of the C.O., the release of the Officer would risk the safety of the Command.

Up to a point, I agreed. "Judge" Langdale might need some time to become fully familiar with what we were doing, but I did not think that my absence would endanger the command. My views, however, on this were not relevant. I had no choice in the matter. I stayed.

"DIVING ON YOU LUCKY!"

In the period following the 2nd Philippine Sea Battle, the fast carriers spent their time patrolling the Philippine Sea and launching air strikes against enemy installations, primarily on Luzon. The enemy was unable to mount any important air strikes against our forces but did achieve minor success with small raids and suicide bombings (Kamikaze—"divine/spirit wind").

Their technique was to approach by jumping from cloud to cloud so as to evade our fighter cover, then, when over a carrier, to come straight down in a suicide attack.

A typical instance of such an attack occurred in late November—early December 1944 when we were with the BUNKER HILL whose call sign at that time was "Lucky". An enemy plane had been detected by radar. The fighters were directed to intercept it, but it kept ducking in and out of clouds. Finally, the radar signal became merged with others on the radar from our own planes and no one knew where the enemy aircraft was. At least we knew it was near. I was concentrating on the clouds over the BUNKER HILL, the nearest carrier to us. Suddenly the plane appeared in a steep dive about 3,000 feet up. I leaped to the TBS and shouted, "Diving on you Lucky!" Then, for about 10 seconds, we watched it dive down. There was not time enough for my message to do any good. Only one Oerlikon gun on the carrier opened fire before the plane hit. The damage was serious enough to force the Bunker Hill to return to Pearl Harbor for repairs, but that was all.

40 DITCHES IN A ROW

One evening after the Third Fleet had spent the day sending air strikes against the enemy on Luzon, our Task Group ran into a heavy rain squall just as the last group of aircraft was returning. The squall continued for an unusually long time, and the planes were very low on fuel. It then became dark and still there was no possibility of landing. Finally, the aircraft were ordered to ditch ahead of the formation and told that we would comb back and forth through the area to pick them up. After that, we could hear them on the aircraft voice circuit, one after the other, saying, "OK, we're running out now, so here goes." or something similar. 40 aircraft ditched in all.

Next came the job for the destroyers to pick them up. The situation was similar to the night before Santa Cruz and on June 19th at Saipan, except that we did it without having to put on any lights from the ships. The principal problem was to receive the reports of sightings, to direct the nearest destroyer to make the rescue, to direct the remaining destroyers to new stations to close up the van, and to direct returning destroyers where to take station in the screen.

I had my frosted plastic covered mooring board and grease pencil technique from old RUSSELL days, and sat down between the radar and the TBS with the mooring board in my lap under a red light.

Some months earlier, Frank Whelan had been transferred to Admiral Bogan's staff, and as the transmissions from the carrier of the sightings started to come in, I recognized Frank's voice. I did not say anything then but merely started plotting the sightings and directing ships to the rescue. After an hour or so, the Commodore, who had been up since dawn G.Q., told me he was exhausted, and since I was doing it anyway, he was going to bed. Of course, I was to call him if anything unusual came up.

We then continued with the rescue. The ditched air crews were getting into their inflatable rafts and they were using little flashlights which helped us locate them. The process of sending ships out and changing the screen to meet the needs of the rescue was working very well. Finally, Frank and I began calling each other by our first names because it had become apparent that the Admiral on the carrier had also gone to bed.

Eventually, after four swings through the area, we had picked up all but one of the air crews. We combed the area twice again but still no sign, and at around 3am, gave up the search.

STARS ALL AROUND, SILVER AND BRONZE

When we put into Ulithi several days later, a message came for Captain Womble to report immediately to the Flagship. He called me into his cabin with obvious anxiety and asked me if had any idea what it could be about, whether we were up to date on all reports, etc. I had no idea what it could be.

He went over to the Flagship and, after a couple of hours, came back laughing, called me to his cabin and said to me, "Remember the other night when I went to bed and you handled the Squadron to pick up those aviators?" I said,

"Yes." He said, "Well, guess what? They gave me the Silver Star Medal for it!" Then he said right away, "So you've got to get a medal for it too! Bring me the instructions on how to do it!"

I looked over the definitions for the medals and came to the conclusion that even though they had given him the Silver Star for it, in fact, the Bronze Star more accurately fitted what I had done. Eventually, the Commodore worked out my citation and included in it not only the rescue incident, but my screening method (TCW), my torpedo attack plan, and the rescue incident of June 19th which Womble had actually witnessed from a Cruiser.

My citation read as follows:

CITATION

"For meritorious achievement while serving as Operations Officer on the Staff of Commander Destroyer Squadron Fifty-Two, in action against enemy Japanese forces in the Pacific War Area, from June 10 to November 27, 1944. Persevering and determined throughout numerous naval campaigns, Lieutenant Russell rapidly solved problems of changing screen formations during action despite the enemy's savage and unpredictable battle tactics. Working tirelessly and with resourceful initiative as his task unit ranged the vast expanses of the Pacific in determined offensive, he developed a new and highly satisfactory screening method for protection of the Fast Carrier Task Force units and, in addition, ingeniously contrived an extremely beneficial device for use in coordinating destroyer torpedo attacks. Consistently alert in his performance of duty, he aided in the rescue of several downed airman on the nights of June 19 and October 29, directing the nearest ships to the scene of crashes and maintaining effective screen in the van. By his unfaltering professional skill, cool decision and outstanding administrative ability, Lieutenant Russell contributed materially to the success of his squadron's dangerous assignments and his gallant conduct in the face of fanatic opposition upheld the highest traditions of the United States Naval Service."

Captain Womble's Silver Star along with the notoriety he gained from the success of DesRon 52's TCW screening method, brought him a spot promotion to the rank of full Commodore shortly after I was detached and he was placed in charge of all destroyers of the fast carrier Task Forces with a Light Cruiser as a Flagship.

THE COBRA OR "CAIN MUTINY" TYPHOON

Captain Womble's Silver Star along with the notoriety he gained from the success of DesRon 52's TCW screening method, brought him a spot promotion to the rank of full Commodore shortly after I was detached and he was placed in charge of all destroyers of the fast carrier Task Forces with a Light Cruiser as a Flagship.

Although I recognized that the Commodore and "Judge" Langdale could use my expertise, and I appreciated the compliment which the Commodore's contention that I was indispensable conveyed, there is something extremely frustrating about having one's orders home, having one's relief on board and not being allowed to go. I was as always eager to contribute to the war effort and would not have earned my Bronze Star medal but for Captain Womble's keeping me on board (it happened during the period after I had received my orders and prior to my release). Nevertheless, there was something disconcerting about becoming less needed while still exposed to danger.

Actually, Judge Langdale rapidly learned what he had to do, the Commodore also became less dependent on me, and as they became more adept, I became increasingly restless.

Earlier on, I had asked my dad to send me some good books. He had sent me Henderson's "Jackson" and Bryce's "The American Commonwealth", and in order to keep my sanity, I started reading those two books. It was, indeed, rewarding, but time wore on, week after week. Although the enemy was constantly attacking the fast carriers in a scattered manner as I have described, and submarine attack was also an ever-present worry, a further worry was also the weather during the typhoon season.

In fact, we lost three destroyers in one typhoon during this period while I was being retained on the OWEN. This was the particular typhoon which undoubtedly Herman Wouk had in mind for the film "Cain Mutiny". It did happen. We were in it. The following account is from both my contemporaneous notes and from direct recall.

It occurred on December 18-19, 1944. We had just been near Luzon with the Task Force giving air cover to the invasion of Mindoro and had withdrawn to the east to fuel the destroyers. The day before the storm, the weather stations at Palau had reported that a tropical front was passing Palau and that it was only a front not a typhoon. Since the destroyers were low on fuel, it was decided to fuel immediately. The fueling operation started in the morning and several destroyers completed fueling. The wind, however, was mounting. Around noon several destroyers reported they were having great difficulty staying alongside the Tankers, and after one of them broke away from the Tanker taking lines, hoses and all, the operation was called off. There had been no typhoon warning, and, therefore, it was supposed that the weather would abate enough to fuel the next morning. The HICKOX and SPENCE from our group were very low on fuel and were ordered to remain with the Tanker group while the other destroyers returned to their Task Groups. Thus, the picture during the night was as follows: three large carrier Task Groups on a north-south line about twelve miles apart and a Tanker Group further to the north and east. In order to conserve fuel, the destroyers were authorized to steam on one boiler. The whole force then steamed at slow speeds back and forth, remaining in roughly the same area, throughout the night, the plan being to fuel the destroyers in the morning and then return to the Philippines to provide air support for the land forces.

In the morning, the wind had not abated. In fact, it had greatly increased, and the seas were tremendous. It was very difficult to send a blinker message to the next ship in the screen because of the height of the waves. Since our signal light was also only visible to others about half the time even when we were on the crest, the time available for signaling was less than one quarter of the lapsed time. The Admiral ordered the MILLER in to see if fueling from a carrier were possible, but when she approached the carrier, they ordered her back into the screen.

At this time, the wind was from the northeast indicating that if it were a typhoon type, circular storm, the center would be to the southeast of us, and as the storms in the vicinity of the Philippines travel in a northwesterly direction, we would be right in the path of the storm center. Furthermore, as storms in the northern hemisphere rotate in a counterclockwise direction around their centers, the northeastern side of the storm is where the wind is strongest (called the "dangerous semicircle"). This is because the velocity of the wind in the northeastern side is the normal rotational velocity of the wind plus the movement of the storm center, while on the southwestern side, the velocity of the wind is the normal rotation velocity less the movement of the storm center. Therefore, to avoid the worst part of the storm, Halsey ordered the Task Force to steam south with the seas on our port quarter. Under these conditions, holding course became very difficult for the destroyers because as the crest of a wave would approach, the destroyer would start running down the wave (imagine a 2,100 ton, 350' long surfboard!), the rudder would come out of the water behind the crest, sometimes also the screws would come out and the whole ship would vibrate as they churned partly in the air. At those times, the ship would surfboard down the waves with no steerage control, turning unpredictably to one side or the other. Then while everyone held his breath, the rudder would finally catch as we approached the point of broaching. Broaching is dangerous because it greatly increases the forces tending to capsize the ship. This sequence of surfboarding and nearing the point of broaching occurred repeatedly while the helmsmen tried to anticipate it and compensate.

Actually, unbeknownst to us, a typhoon had formed west of Palau and was heading directly towards us. The change of course to the south, which the Task Force had taken, had been wise because if we had remained where we were, the storm would have passed just to the south of us, putting the whole Task Force in the northeastern (dangerous) semicircle. As it was, the entire Task Force was not able to enter the southwestern semi-circle. In fact, the storm center passed between us and the tanker group which was the next group to the northwest of us at that time thereby placing the tanker group in the dangerous semicircle.

Having expected to fuel in the morning, some of the destroyers in the tanker group had pumped out their water ballast to make room for fuel. Water ballast on a destroyer is important especially if the waves are running high. A destroyer fully ballasted, that is, with all tanks full either of fuel, or water, can take a maximum roll of about 72 degrees before the righting force of the ship (metacentric height) becomes zero; but with no ballast, the maximum roll is around 60 degrees, (not taking into account the adverse effect of topside weights not present at the time of the original inclining experiment) and at that, there is less force resisting the roll prior to reaching the 60 degree limit. It takes a heavy sea to make a destroyer roll 60 degrees, but it is not impossible. I saw the inclinometer of the Russell at 50 degrees several times. Many destroyers have reported rolls of 70 degrees some even more. Probably in the cases of rolls of over 70 degrees where the destroyer recovered, the individual ship's characteristics were such that the rolls were safe, or it could have been that a lucky wave righted them. However, inclining experiments show that as a general rule, 72 degrees ballasted, and 60 degrees unballasted is the maximum roll of a Fletcher class destroyer. Anything more and the ship will turn turtle.

USS SANTA FE (CL-60) *rolling in Typhoon Cobra* – USN *Ref 80-G-700024*

Another factor which proved bad for some of the destroyers was that they had only one boiler in operation. This was authorized for the purpose of conserving fuel but was hazardous because it meant that the destroyers would not have enough power for emergency maneuvers.

The destroyers hit worst were the HULL and MONAGHAN, HICKOX and SPENCE. The HICKOX and SPENCE, were from our Task Group, and, being low on fuel, had partially pumped ballast. They were steaming on only one boiler and were with the tanker group where the storm was the worst. The HULL and MONAGHAN were part of the permanent tanker group screen. I have no knowledge of their circumstances prior to the storm.

In our group, we rode fairly well. We had passed into the southern semi-circle, and although it was a severe storm, and we had the threat of broaching mentioned above, we were reasonably all right. The ships in our Task Group which had trouble were the CVL PRINCETON Class carriers, ships that had originally been planned as Cruisers and were later converted into carriers. Evidently their hull size and their period of roll was resonant with the size and frequency of the waves, because the ships of that class began to roll drastically, i.e., 35 degrees or more. For a destroyer, such a roll is not too bad, but for a carrier, it is dangerous not so much for fear of capsizing as the damage due to shifting gear. Most of the planes on their flight decks carried away and fell over the side. On the MONTEREY, the planes in the hanger deck also carried away, crashed into the bulkheads and into themselves, and then caught fire. The MONTEREY had a difficult time. The smoke went down her engine room vents forcing the engineers to abandon their spaces, and in turn, causing loss of pressure on their fire mains, and the loss of ship control. So, she dropped out of the formation and lay helplessly rolling in the trough of the huge waves. It so happened that in the trough, her roll was much less, again undoubtedly due to the frequency of the waves and the period of roll of the hull. Then, not rolling badly anymore, they regained control, put the fires out, and saved the ship. Thereafter, rather than risk taking those great rolls again, she lay in the trough throughout the remainder of the storm.

In our group, quite a few men fell overboard from the big ships. We tried to find them, but the waves were tremendous, the surface of the water was sheathed in a driven scud about two feet thick, and the visibility was sometimes below 100 yards. None were found or recovered in our group.

What happened in the tanker group was far more disastrous. The SPENCE, HULL and MONAGHAN sank, and the HICKOX had a very narrow escape. We never even heard that the SPENCE, MONAGHAN or HICKOX were in distress. The HULL was able to report that she was sinking, and ships were sent to her aid, a fact which accounted for the rescue of many more from her than from the other two. All that could be gathered about the SPENCE was that she went into the trough with full rudder on, broached and capsized in a single roll. Only a handful of men were rescued from her. The only officer was the paymaster. He had been below decks and had no idea of either what happened or how he got out.

The HULL and MONAGHAN were 9-year-old destroyers of the FARRAGUT, "stack-and-a-half" Class, and from what we could gather over the radio circuit, the HULL simply broke up. Evidently, stability was not the main problem with the HULL and MONAGHAN; they had been retrofitted with additional equipment and were top-heavy. They simply couldn't survive such a storm. The tanker group ordered several changes of course in order to find the least rigorous course for the tankers, and it could be that the HULL and MONAGHAN, while trying to maintain station on a course which was more suitable for larger ships, subjected themselves too severely to the force of the waves. This theory is substantiated by the fact that the DEWEY, another ship of that same class, survived the storm, but did not attempt to maintain station.

The HICKOX, following the Tanker group maneuver, went into the trough and commenced rolling dangerously, taking water in her engine room hatches and topside air vents. Realizing their danger, they attempted to get out of the trough, but with only one boiler, they were unable to make it. Then thinking that if they backed, their stern would swing towards the storm allowing them then to "kick" her ahead and get out of the trough, they tried backing. This might have worked for a large ship with a high counter, but destroyers have very low sterns. The huge seas crashed down on the HICKOX's fantail carrying away smoke screen generators and stanchions. And, as these uprooted, they took pieces of the deck with them, allowing water to enter the compartments below. The steering engine room was flooded, and the ship lost all steerage control. In the meantime, during the excitement, the engineers injected water from a tank containing sea water in it rather than fresh water while attempting to light it off. Salt water is harmful to a boiler and reduces its efficiency materially. She lay helplessly in the trough for some time rolling dangerously. Luckily, she was partly ballasted and did not go over. Finally, by heroic efforts, they regained control and saved her. All of her radio antennas, most of her topside gear and radars had carried away. Several days later, she came limping back to the Task Force, severely damaged and using hand steering.

In total, nearly 800 men were lost in the storm and the damages to the Fleet were tremendous.

YULETIDE MAGIC

While playing dice, when one wins once, and then wins again, and then again, the fear of rolling "snake eyes" or "box cars" or "crapping out" continuously mounts. In much the same way, each time I experienced a near miss my concern over when it might be my turn grew. The sinking of the SPENCE and the near loss of the HICKOX, under conditions which could easily have applied to us, only intensified my restlessness.

We arrived in Ulithi shortly before Christmas 1944 and on Christmas morning I arose early, went into the Wardroom pantry, had the Commodore's Mess Attendant give me the Commodore's coffee and juice, and at 8:00 o'clock (his hour of call) knocked on the Commodore's door, "Your coffee and juice, Sir!" "Russ, what the hell are you doing here?" "Merry Christmas Commodore! As a Christmas present, how about sending me home?" He laughed and said, "I guess you've got me Russ. I can't very well refuse that."

So I made a quick exit much the same as I had from the RUSSELL. I could not, however, take my cruise box with me. It eventually caught up with me in San Francisco.

In the shuffle, however, someone took my napkin ring. This was a minor tragedy for me. In the Navy, it is customary for the Officers of the Mess each to have his own napkin ring, and to have engraved thereon the names of the ships on which he has served. My ring was a nice heavy silver ferrule having a diameter of about 1 ½" and a rolled bead at each end. On it, I had engraved U.S.S. RUSSELL DD414, U.S.S. OWEN DD536, and DesRon 52. 1 was looking forward to putting many of the other ships and commands on which we had served on it too, and should I survive, I was anticipating having it as a war memento. The value of the silver was minuscule.

In any event, within two hours, I was away from the OWEN, my home for the past 18 months. On Ulithi, I caught a 12:30 flight (by DC-3) to Guam and on the way had a Christmas dinner of Army K-rations. In Guam, I caught a 4:30 pm plane to Kwajalein where I arrived at 2:00 am Christmas morning (due to crossing the International Date Line). There was a hold-up at Kwajalein and at mid-day, I had my second Christmas dinner at an Army base. This time, they gave me turkey, cranberry, stuffing, squash, candied yams, pumpkin pie, the works. After Kwajalein, I arrived at Pearl Harbor at 3:00 am on the 26th. Departed Pearl Harbor at 8:30 pm, and arrived in Oakland at 11:15 am on the 27th.

8. "LIFE IN THESE UNITED STATES"

FATHERED BY "AN ENTERPRISING BOY OF 14"

After returning to San Francisco, I learned that my new duty was to be as Operations Officer of Captain G. R. Hartwig's new destroyer Squadron, DesRon 66. This came as a surprise. It will be remembered that Hartwig's and my parting, when he left the RUSSELL, had not been particularly pleasant. On the other hand, time can be a good healer. For me, time had allowed me to see Hartwig from a distance and to compare him to others, from which comparison his image profited enormously. Something similar must have taken place with Hartwig vis-a-vis me, because he selected me for his staff and when we met again, it was with great mutual pleasure. Also, although for the entire time we had been on the RUSSELL, he had remained somewhat akin to unfriendly, now, in this new context, he was very friendly. We joined socially with our wives and had many fine times together.

At one of those social occasions, after we had had quite a few drinks and the party was in full swing, something came up which prompted Lib to say to Captain Hartwig that he was old enough to be her father. He came back immediately, "Well, Lib, if that is so, I would have had to be a very enterprising young boy of 14!"

TOO BUSY FEEDING GERMAN POW'S TO WARM UP A BABY'S BOTTLE

After Lib and I had settled down from the initial swirl of my returning home, and I had had a chance to meet my little daughter Tory (already 9 months old) and renew acquaintance with Bobby, Lib and I began long-range planning. I was fully aware of the staggering Naval and military advantages the U.S. had over the Japanese, and I was satisfied that the war was effectively over. Obviously, to defeat the Japanese totally would probably take a lot of time, lives, and money, but the end result was very clear. My estimate at the time was that it would take about 12 months. I also had thought a lot on the many long night watches and knew that I wanted a professional career, preferably as a lawyer. I was very keen as a Naval Officer, but I never contemplated the Navy as a career. It was quite clear to me that I could only survive in the Navy in war time, and that, by nature, I was too rebellious and abrasive to advance in the Navy in peace time. We concluded that Lib should move back to the East Coast and we should start planning ahead for the post war phase. I called my dad and he suggested that we come to New York, leave the babies with them, while Lib and I would go back to California to sell the house in Piedmont, ship the furniture East, and, after I had returned to the Fleet in the Pacific, Lib would return east. This plan was agreed promptly, and Lib, Bobby, Tory and I, set off from San Francisco on the transcontinental express train called "The Chief", a train that ran over the Rockies to Chicago.

Trains in those days were fun. We had a small compartment with an upper and lower bunk aligned athwartships, one window, and a pull-out wash-stand-toilet arrangement. The babies slept in the lower bunk and we crammed ourselves into the upper.

One part of the modus operandi was for me to take the baby's bottle up to the dining car to be warmed up. When I first tried to do this, I came to the dining car and found it totally full and a long line of people waiting. I by-passed these people and came to the head of the line, at which point an Army Sergeant stopped me. I told him that I was not "queue hopping" and all I wanted was to have my baby's bottle warmed up. He told me they were too busy. At about this same time, I overheard one of the people being served speaking German. I then asked if those were German war prisoners, and he said, "Yes". As I noted earlier, I was, in those days, pure TNT with virtually no fuse. Instantaneously a vision flashed through my mind of the millions of dead at Verdun, the battles in Europe, Africa and in the Pacific, the sweat, the gore, the burned-out wrecks, and all of this devastation and tragedy caused to a large extent by the Germans. I exploded in tones that everyone in that dining car, as well as the men in the kitchen, could hear. I informed the Sergeant that "my Goddamn bottle" was "going to be warmed up before any waiter in that car did another thing", or I was "going to personally rip up the joint". My bottle was immediately warmed up.

"OOK AT MY 'POTS"

In the morning of our departure from Oakland, Lib noticed a spot or two on Bobby's chest. After we were on board and rolling eastward, the spots came out elsewhere, and it was obvious that he had chicken pox. We were not particularly concerned. Chicken pox went the rounds every year at all schools. Bobby was uncomfortable, but not too bad. He was up and around and not so sick as to deter him from taking apart my razor and putting the blade in the little razor disposal slot one time when Lib and I were in the dining car. (I had an awful time trying to figure out how my razor blade had disappeared. I finally asked him, and he pointed to the slot. He was only 2 years, 10 months at the time.)

He also wanted to run around, and we let him go out into the corridor. The Pullman was split into two sections, one of which included the compartments and the other of which comprised lower and upper berths which were made up into seats during the day. Bobby went out into the seat area and became friendly with everyone. After a while, I also went out and began talking to some of them. As I was doing so, the conductor came by, and took up in conversation with Bobby in the midst of which Bobby pulled up his shirt to expose his chest and fat belly covered with chicken pox and said, "Ook at my 'pots".

The Conductor said, "Well now, little fellow, you certainly have some nice spots there. Looks kind of like chicken pox to me", and looking at me, "Are you the father?" I allowed as to how I was, and then the Conductor said, "Gosh, I don't know what to do. We have a regulation against carrying anyone on the train with a contagious disease." I tried to convince him that it was only hives, but he was skeptical. Finally, he said he would have a Doctor look at it. We were at the time rolling across the winter tundra of Wyoming or Nebraska, and the prospect of Lib and the babies being put out in the middle of the night in the snow to be quarantined in some tiny village until Bobby was cured, was appalling. After an hour or two, the train came to a stop. We looked out. It was quite dark. We were not at a town. All that could be seen was the expanse of the wintry prairies. Doors opened and shut; footsteps were heard. A knock came at our door. It was the Doctor with the Conductor behind him. "Well now, let's have a look at this little feller." He pulled out a flashlight and looked at Bobby, "Hmm, Conductor, that's one of the best cases of hives I've ever seen!"

"TEN BUCKS PLACED ON THE SIDE OF THE TICKET COUNTER WILL GET YOU A TICKET"

We arrived in Chicago late and the train on which we had reservations had already gone. Also, the next train was fully sold out. I asked around and was informed that the way to get on the train was to go up to the ticket counter when there was no queue, place a $10.00 bill on the counter over to the right, say nothing about the $10.00 but merely ask if they could get you a ticket on the train you wanted. According to my information, the ticket would then be issued, and you would depart "forgetting" to pick up the $10.00 bill on the counter.

I was repulsed by such an idea, but there we were sitting on our bags in the middle of the Chicago station with two sick kids (Tory had, by this time, also exhibited chicken pox). I wrestled with this proposition for a while and eventually it dawned on me that, if what I was told were true, there had to be free bunks on that train. So, I got Lib and the babies and we simply went down to the platform, boarded the train and found a place for Lib and the babies to sit down.

Luckily, the Conductor left us alone until the train was underway. Eventually, he came around and I explained the situation to him. Sure enough, he found a lower berth for the babies and an upper for us, and it did not require the payment of an extra $10.00.

9. OKINAWA

THE WEST COAST SHAKEDOWN OF DESRON 66

Leave in January 1945 was far different for me than before. For one thing, the nature of the war was different, or at least, so I thought, and I felt no compulsion to report to duty early. The ships of DesRon 66 were new 2,200-ton Destroyers equipped with new AA weapons, a fancy CIC (combat information center) and new types of radars. However, I rapidly assimilated these changes and otherwise I already had a working knowledge of everything I needed to know to run the Squadron as defacto Chief of Staff. In addition, although I still had not given up hope of obtaining a command, I was aware that my only chance was to find someone to pull strings for me back at BuPers, and not by doing however well as I might do as a Squadron Operations Officer. I was relaxed, and asked Captain Hartwig for, and received, an extra week's leave. We sold the house, sent everything back East for interim storage, and settled down for a little recreation.

The designated Squadron Flagship of DesRon 66 was the PUTNAM (DD757). The staff included three Officers besides the Commodore and me and some 10 enlisted men. We established the same kind of staff nucleus of four people, i.e., the Commodore, me, the Chief Signalman and Chief Yeoman, that we had in DesRon 52 with Captain Womble, to facilitate quick shifting of the Command from one ship to another, while leaving most of the staff on the Putnam.

USS PUTNAM (DD-757) USN *Ref*: 19-N-76730

The Commodore and I reported on board in late January 1945 and supervised shakedown training exercises offshore at San Diego. This was a leisurely period, steaming out for maneuvering exercises in the daytime, and usually returning at night, where our wives were staying at the Hotel Del Coronado.

In order to become more familiar with the Squadron, we shifted the Flag consecutively from the PUTNAM to the ZELLARS, the KEITH, the HADLEY and the STORMES. At the end of the shakedown, the Commodore and I went to Bremerton, Washington and shifted the Flag to the FOX, another ship of DesRon 66, while the rest of the Squadron was sent, with various convoys to join the Fleet.

WESTWARD, ONCE MORE, ACROSS THE PACIFIC

We left Bremerton aboard the FOX on March 15th for San Francisco where we picked up a convoy bound for Pearl Harbor on March 23rd, arriving at Pearl on April 3rd. We then were briefed at Pacific Fleet Headquarters on the invasion of Okinawa, which had started on March 27th, and informed that our Squadron would be used in support of that operation. The Commodore and I were ordered to shift the Flag to the COMPTON (DD704), to take command of the screen of a large convoy headed for Ulithi. From there we were to proceed to Okinawa also with a convoy, and, then to shift the Flag back to the PUTNAM, which would already be there when we arrived.

This type of convoy duty was more like the old North Atlantic days, than the fast carrier type of duty I had been used to. In fact, one of the signal books used by the convoy was MERSIGS, the book I had studied when I first came on board the RUSSELL, which to me by then, seemed a million years ago. It was not the North Atlantic, however, it was the beautiful Pacific, nor were we facing the German wolf-packs. In fact, the Japanese, so far, were not much in evidence. We had little to do. Until we went farther west, I would have to classify it as totally boring.

THE MYRIAD FACES OF THE SEA

By this time, I had crossed the Pacific east-west many times, and the Equator north-south more than 50 times. I had, in fact, totaled about 300,000 miles at sea. Formerly, before all of this sea duty, I had always thought that once one was at sea, out of sight of land, the sea was the sea, that is, more-or-less the same no matter where one was. As we went from place to place and back again, however, I gradually began to realize that the face of the sea is significantly different depending upon where one is, and I became convinced that an experienced sailor who had plied the Pacific many times could readily tell where he was within rough limits of, say, a 100 mile radius, anywhere in the Pacific, by simple observation of the sea, the stars, the smell and whatever else was around him. For example, the direction and velocities of the winds in the Pacific broadly identify the latitudes and hemispheres. These are well known (i.e., N/S trades, horse latitudes, and doldrums in each hemisphere) and need no elaboration. Also, the waves vary considerably depending upon where one is. For example, the tremendous north latitude transpacific swells I mentioned earlier, only occur north of the islands in the area of the north equatorial current. Similar swells but of shorter spacing appear elsewhere. In some places, they are small. The nature of the waves also changes depending on the nearness and bearing of the islands. The smell of the air changes particularly when one is downwind of land. Also, the smells will vary. For example, the smell of a tropical "rain forest" type island is quite different from than that of an atoll. The clouds too vary as to where one is. In the northeast trades, for example, one finds small puffy clouds studding the sky like a string of pearls, the whole way to the horizon. In other areas, one finds large lazy clouds, and distant thunderheads with incipient waterspouts streaming part way down. (We saw a few touch the water. They do not, of course, suck solid water up, but they do suck up the scud. Water spouts are, of course, tornadoes, and can be very dangerous to ships.) The stars, of course, immediately disclose one's latitude with accuracy. A good sailor can quickly fashion himself a crude instrument (using sticks) by which he can take his latitude, using Polaris, to within 1 degree accuracy (i.e., 60 miles) or by averaging sights on other stars such as the Southern Cross. The sailor will, of course, also know roughly the time of day, the date and the season, and he can use these together with the direction of the sunrise or sunset to arrive at a fair idea of his longitude. Finally all signs of life, from minute plankton to the larger animals previously mentioned vary depending on where one is—and thus an experienced sailor can be quite precise as to his location, as the face of the sea reveals her myriad expressions.

THE TENSION MOUNTS

Although convoy duty from San Francisco to Pearl Harbor was boring, things were taking place which soon transformed it into something different. When we had been briefed at Pearl, we had heard that two destroyers were sunk in the opening stages at Okinawa, but such sinkings during the opening days of an invasion seemed reasonably normal. We did not get the full flavor of Okinawa until we arrived at Ulithi on April 16th. By then, four destroyers had been sunk at Okinawa and over 30 destroyers had already been put out of action. This brought a new dimension to our thinking when, on April 20th, we received orders to take over the destroyer screen of a convoy, bound for Okinawa. The tension was accentuated by the realization that at Okinawa the destroyers would be more on their own and not near enough to the larger ships for the enemy to prefer hitting the larger targets instead of the destroyers.

On the way from Ulithi to Okinawa, we spent the first three days at sea conducting emergency drill procedures in order practice communications and to iron out flaws in evasive maneuvers in the event of submarine or air attack.

My notes for the Squadron war diary (which I kept with me after the war) for April 24th, 25th and 26th for the approach of Okinawa read as follows:

April 24th

"At dusk RALPH TALBOT made contact with a submarine close aboard. The convoy was maneuvered to the right, clear of the area. RALPH TALBOT's contact was evaluated as SUBMARINE and SCHLEY was ordered to support him. COMPTON and WINTERBERRY took stations as for two ships, and increased patrol speed differential to 5 kts. RALPH TALBOT reported that in his first attacks he had possibly damaged the submarine and requested permission for one ship to remain with the contact until the next evening. This plan was agreed to in part and RALPH TALBOT was directed to order one ship to rejoin the convoy after several hours, the other to remain, and if the contact still looked good, to open up on radio requesting assistance of HUNTER-KILLER group from TF51." (At this time, we were about 250 miles southeast of Okinawa.)

April 25th

"At 0430, passed HUNTER-KILLER group on reverse course, presumably proceeding to the assistance of RALPH TALBOT. SCHLEY having rejoined at 0725, the patrol speed differential was decreased to 3 kts., and screen adjusted for three ships. RALPH TALBOT rejoined in late afternoon, and the screen was returned to its former status."

April 26th

"Made approach to Okinawa and, after passing through outer anti-submarine patrol line, detached ADRIA to proceed to Kerama Retto (a small group of islands to the southwest of Okinawa where there was a relatively larger area of sheltered water and anchorage). The convoy was consolidated first into two columns and then into one column in order to provide adequate clearance in the channel for both our convoy and a large convoy that was coming in at the same time. Convoy was dissolved and ships proceeded independently to assigned anchorages. Reported to CTG 51.5 for duty and was immediately directed to proceed to Kerama Retto to shift pennant to PUTNAM. Hoisted pennant on PUTNAM at 1327 and duly reported to all concerned. Remained in Kerama Retto during the night."

THE LOOMING STORM

In the Navy, cribbage is a popular card game, and this is especially true on destroyers. In cribbage, the hands can score from 1 to 29 points (pegs) depending on the cards one gets, but due to an idiosyncrasy of the game, it is impossible to have a hand containing a score of 19. Thus, when one has the worst possible hand, i.e., one which has no score in it, and the pegger asks for one's score, one naturally replies "19". After Okinawa, in the destroyers, there was a significant change in cribbage. Thereafter, whenever one had the worst possible hand, i.e.., a hand with no score, one said "Okinawa" and everyone knew what it meant.

When we arrived in Kerama Retto, saw what was there and heard about it from the men on the PUTNAM, we were shocked almost as much as when we had first steamed into Pearl Harbor on February 2, 1942. What we saw lying at anchor in Kerama Retto, were the hulks of some 35 severely damaged and burned out destroyers, put out of action by Japanese Kamikaze suicide attacks. The shock was of a different nature, however, than the one we experienced earlier at Pearl Harbor, because at Pearl, we had had no thought of an imminent repeat of the enemy attack, whereas at Okinawa, while the U.S. occupation was by no means complete, Japanese air raids were coming in daily, the destroyer picket line was providing the radar warning, and the enemy was spearheading its air raids on the island with preliminary attacks directly against the destroyers in order to eliminate the radar warning. These enemy attacks would obviously continue, more destroyers would, of course, be sent to the picket line, and what we beheld in Kerama Retto was, therefore, only the start. In addition, ComDesRon 66 and the Putnam were assigned to the destroyer pool for picket line duty.

THE PICKET LINE—OKINAWA APRIL 26 TO MAY 18, 1945

My war diary notes for DesRon 66 show the following sequence for the PUTNAM from April 27th to May 13th.

April 27th

The day after we arrived, April 27th, a large enemy raid penetrated the screen and badly damaged destroyers ISHERWOOD, HUTCHINS and RALPH TALBOT. The RALPH TALBOT had, in fact, just been with us in the convoy from Ulithi. At the time of the raid on the 27th, we on the PUTNAM were on the inner screen at Hagushi anchorage the main anchorage for the transports.

April 28th

On the next day (i.e., the 28th), the destroyers DALY and TWIGGS were hit, and the latter badly damaged. The PUTNAM was still assigned to the AA screen around the transport area. Some of the enemy aircraft succeeded in penetrating the air cover in the inner area, but caused little damage where we were. One plane crashed into the water not far from us.

My jobs at these times were to handle the communications between the screen Commander and the ships under us, to monitor the radars, and fighter director activity, as it affected the Squadron, and to keep the Commodore informed.

April 29th

On the 29th, PUTNAM continued to provide AA screen for the transport area, and, late in the day, was sent to take over an antisubmarine screening station south of Kerama Retto. That evening many raids were reported coming in from the west. None came within range of the PUTNAM but the destroyers HAGGARD and HAZELWOOD to the north of us were badly damaged.

April 30th

On the 30th, PUTNAM was sent to the east of Okinawa to a picket station off of Nagasuku Wan with two other destroyers. No enemy activity was reported. I was kept busy with Squadron command activity, controlling the disposition of various ships under us.

May 1st

On May 1st we returned to Hagushi anchorage and were assigned, with another destroyer, to convoy several ships out of Okinawa in the direction of Ulithi.

May 2nd

Early in the morning of the 2nd, we were detached from that convoy and sent back to Okinawa in command of the screen of a new convoy which was just approaching Okinawa.

Ships in Kerama Retto anchorage spread an anti-kamikaze smoke screen 3 May 1945 –
USN Ref: 80-G-324629

May 3rd

On the 3rd, the new convoy entered Okinawa waters, was officially dissolved, as a convoy, and PUTNAM was sent back to Hagushi where she anchored and was given a one day "availability" for engine repairs.

May 4th

On May 4th, large enemy raids came in. MORRISON, LITTLE and LUCE and the DE OBERRENDER were sunk and the destroyer HUDSON was badly damaged on the picket line. One enemy plane penetrated the CAP (Combat Air Patrol) and crash dived the BIRMINGHAM (she having been repaired since Leyte Gulf). PUTNAM got underway with one engine only but soon returned to anchor.

May 5th

PUTNAM spent the day in Kerama Retto obtaining fuel and ammunition and returned to Hagushi in the evening.

May 6th

PUTNAM joined the AA screen at Hagushi to the seaward of the transports, and at 9:30 AM was ordered to proceed to radar picket station No. 9. This was the same picket station where on May 4th one of the destroyers listed above had been sunk. My notes do not say which one it was. We arrived at Picket Station No. 9 (Lat 26N, Long 126-53E) at 12:40 PM, took charge of the destroyer AMMEN and two LCS's (Nos. 117 and 89). These small landing craft had been equipped with automatic AA weapons, but they were assigned to the picket stations mainly for picking up survivors if the destroyers were sunk. Later in the day, two additional LCS's joined (Nos. 56 and 198). At around 7:00 PM an enemy aircraft was detected approaching from the west. PUTNAM performed the fighter director function, "vectored" the fighter cover onto the enemy plane, which shot it down, about 15 miles away from us.

May 7th

We continued normal radar picket station routine. DesRon 66 submitted fuel reports, maneuvered LCS's, as was necessary to maintain position. No enemy aircraft approached.

May 8th

Foul weather set in, no aircraft were seen on the radar screen, friendly or enemy.

May 9th

Destroyer W. D. PORTER relieved destroyer AMMEN at Picket Station No. 9. In the late afternoon, enemy aircraft were detected approaching from the west. At 6:25 PM, PUTNAM picked up a group of enemy aircraft and conducted an "interception" on them using the fighter aircraft covering the picket station. Three Val's (Japanese dive bombers) were "splashed". Later, at 8:50 PM, two enemy aircraft approached from the south and both PUTNAM and PORTER opened fire on them, increased speed to 25 kts. and maneuvered in the area adjacent to LCS patrol line. Enemy aircraft continued to skirt the area throughout the night but did not close within gunfire range again.

May 10th

We searched for a crashed U.S. aviator, no results, but did find the wreckage of a Japanese aircraft. At 8:00 AM, PUTNAM was relieved by destroyer BACHE, and proceeded back to Kerama Retto.

May 11th

On May 11th, PUTNAM at anchor at Hagushi. Many raids to the west. Destroyers HADLEY and EVANS badly damaged in the vicinity of IEE Shima. (HADLEY was from DesRon 66, our Squadron.)

May 12th

PUTNAM proceeded to Ie Shima (it was at about this time that famous war correspondent Ernie Pyle was killed on Ie Shima) to screen HADLEY and EVANS at anchor.

May 13th

May 13th, PUTNAM returned to Hagushi. Destroyer BACHE, the ship which had just relieved the PUTNAM, was badly damaged at Radar Picket Station No. 9.

THE NAVY'S MOST CLOSELY GUARDED SECRET

By May 13th, about 45 destroyers had been put out of action, the devastation continued for several months. Although only 14 destroyers were sunk, 131 were put out of action all told. The Navy was honest to the public about the sinkings, but nothing was published about the tremendous number of destroyers put out of action. This was one of the Navy's most closely guarded secrets.

THE DESTROYERS PAID THEIR WAY

Although the destroyers had tough times in the North Atlantic, and at Guadalcanal, for the most part they simply helped the carriers arrive at the place where they could launch air attacks, and then the aviators fought the war for us. At Okinawa that all changed. At Okinawa, the destroyers were a key element in the defense, and they were, consequently, a prime target. They did their best, but the humanly guided missile is a formidable weapon (and is so even today). We were no match for it. All we could do was come back with more destroyers. Destroyers may have taken a beating in night actions at Guadalcanal, but that was child's play compared to Okinawa. In fact, more destroyer men were killed or wounded at Okinawa (over 8,000), than the total number of casualties in all other Naval battles of the United States up until then including World War II, combined.

THE NUMBNESS

The initial reason for the secrecy given by the historians is that Admiral Nimitz was anxious not to let the Japanese know how effective their attacks had been[47]. There was, however, also another reason for keeping these heavy losses quiet, which becomes clear when one contemplates how the news of such carnage might have adversely affected public opinion of the Navy. Here was the Navy, sending ship after ship, day after day, effectively to slaughter, in desperation reminiscent of the way waves of men were sent day after day into the breech at Verdun in 1916 in World War I. This was something military leaders were supposed never to do again.

It is one thing to think of Verdun as ancient history and to assume that in the future, military leaders would never again close their minds to innovation while pouring waves of men to their deaths day after day in pursuit of an obviously failing method of warfare. But, it is quite another thing to find one's self actually caught in such a situation, as we were at Okinawa, with the leaders continuing with an obviously losing method, many men dying because of it, and all the Navy could think to do was cover it up and hope that the enemy might not realize how effective it was. The frustration was intensified by the fact that there actually was a better way to do the same job available at the time. The Navy could have equipped the LCI's with radars, and they could have used smoke screens during daylight as they were doing already at night.

I felt I had to do something about it not only for my own safety but also simply to try to stop the colossal waste and loss of life, and I went to Captain Hartwig with a proposal. My idea was to shift the fighter direction function to the LCI's (using portable radars from the Army) as soon as it could be done, and in the meantime cover the destroyers with smoke screens not only at night as we were already doing, but also whenever enemy aircraft were around during daytime. Hartwig exploded with indignation. To him, the implication that the destroyers could not do the job intended for them by the Command was unacceptable. Also, the idea that the LCIs could carry out the fighter direction was preposterous. The LCI's had no personnel trained for that purpose. (Of course, the trained personnel could have been easily transferred to them). Also, he objected on the ground that the LCI's had been built for an entirely different purpose (Of course, so had the RUSSELL, but we still performed effective fighter direction on her—without any previous training). These were only the superficial drawbacks of my proposal. The real block was that Hartwig knew that no one in the Command would be receptive to the idea and he could not risk differing from the view of the command. Hartwig was actually in the same bind he had been in when I had previously proposed the ahead-throwing antisubmarine weapon in 1941. There was no way that he could bring himself to back a proposal which might be ridiculed or more importantly, which might be interpreted as a challenge to either the ability of the destroyers to do the job assigned to them or to the wisdom of the Command. In addition, the last thing he was going to do was give anyone in the Command the idea that Hartwig himself might be afraid of the Kamikaze. My proposal involved overtones of all of these things. He flatly refused either to propose it or let me do so. This time I had no way to insist that it be transmitted, and it died at that point.

While these things were happening at Okinawa, I found myself falling into a kind of mental numbness exactly as I can imagine I would have experienced had I been at Verdun in 1916. Although it was disconcerting enough to know that every time one's ship was sent to the picket line, the chances of getting hit were 50%, and doubly disconcerting to realize that the job we were doing could be done with much less loss of life by the LCIS, one has no choice in war. One must carry on. One always hopes for smarter leaders, but, on the field of battle, all one can do is accept the leaders one has and assume that they are at least trying to do their best. Even if destruction may be imminent, all one can do is close one's mind, move up and man one's station.

It should be noted, however, that spirits among the destroyer sailors continued to be high. In all of my movements around the ships of the Squadron at the time, and in the Command, everyone I met was enthusiastic and determined. I, personally, was uneasier than many due to my duty assignment, my experience, my belief that a better way to do the job was available, and the frustration of not being able to get anyone to listen to it.

My stateroom on the PUTNAM was near a door leading onto the main deck, and when the G.Q. alarm would ring, my practice was to put on my pants over my pajamas, put on my shoes, grab my hat, move quickly through the door onto the main deck and then mount a vertical set of outside ladder rungs leading to the Bridge. It was a very fast way to get to the Bridge. My problem was that I was so mentally numb, that I had to whip myself to make myself do it fast.

The near misses that had dogged my footsteps ever since seeing that torpedo pass down the side of the RUSSELL in the North Atlantic bore heavily on my mind, and now they were happening at an ever increasing pace as though approaching a crescendo. Thus, RALPH TALBOT with whom we arrived at Okinawa was hit only one day later, and destroyers all around us were being sunk or hit. Then on May 9th, we went to radar picket Station No. 9 following a sinking there, and next BACHE who relieved us there was hit.

Japanese "Zero" fighter crashing very near USS ESSEX (CV-9) off Okinawa 15 May 1945 – USN Ref: 80-G-324120

The crescendo struck, but in a different way than I was expecting. It came in the form of my orders home on May 13, 1945.

DETACHED

Unknown to me, Captain Cooper had been pulling strings in Washington to have me transferred to serve as his assistant in his new post as Head of Enlisted Distribution at BuPers. My orders merely stated that I was to proceed to the U.S. and report for duty in BuPers in Washington, D.C. I found out later that Captain Cooper had requested it. While I had little interest in duty in BuPers, I did see it as an opportunity to circulate in the proper places and with luck, obtain the command of a ship.

My orders had been issued on March 28th and finally caught up with me on May 13th. After another several days on the inner picket line, while I was cleaning up my affairs and turning over to my relief, Captain Hartwig agreed that I could leave. He was somewhat peeved at me because of our disagreement over my proposal for handling the radar fighter direction on smaller ships and for being so eager to leave when he and I had just come together again, but he appreciated the amount of action I had seen and was sympathetic.

I left the Putnam on May 16th and went to the transportation office on the SS CRESCENT CITY for assignment to a ship headed back to the States. It will be understood that, while it was uncomfortable to be on the destroyers on the picket line, it was worse to be on a transport in the transport area because the transports were virtually defenseless and "sitting ducks", i.e. stationary targets. I remained on the SS CRESCENT CITY until the 18th when I was sent to the SS AMES VICTORY, an empty ammunition ship, which soon put to sea bound for San Francisco. Even this was not without its danger, as I will recount in the next chapter.

10. THE RETURN

THE AMES VICTORY

Victory Ships were modern, high speed (18 kts.) merchant ships of about 7,000 tons.

The Captain (Roy L. Stall), was undoubtedly the foulest mouthed person I ever met, and I can say that I have met many a foul-mouthed sailor. Not only was he foul-mouthed but also mean at heart. For example, not long after I came on board, I heard about how the ship's cook had had a pet dog on board. After the dog had defecated on the rug in the Captain's cabin, the dog had just disappeared. Beyond this, he was stupid. As I said, I was not particularly happy about being on a merchant ship in the central anchorage at Okinawa because of being an enemy target in that area, but, simply as a general proposition, I was not happy about being on a merchant ship, even an empty one, in the war zone at all. One good hit amidships and they are done. Moreover, we knew from our experiences of only a few weeks earlier in the convoy with the RALPH TALBOT, that enemy submarines were in the area south of Okinawa. Therefore, when Captain Stall headed out of Okinawa totally alone, and steering a straight course, without any zig-zagging, it seemed singularly stupid to me. I was, however, powerless to do anything about it. Captain Stall was arrogant and unapproachable.

TIME LOSES ALL SIGNIFICANCE

Along with me on the Ames Victory, were about 10 Army and Air Corps Officers on board for transportation. I had a stateroom to myself on the port side, and we all ate together in the ship's dining saloon.

I soon became friendly with the Chief Engineer, and he showed me around his engine room.

After we had safely cleared the Okinawa area, the Ames Victory steaming at

18 kts. headed back for Pearl Harbor by a route which took us south near Eniwetok and from there more-or-less directly to Hawaii. The weather, as always, was ideal, and apart from the ever-present danger of submarines, the war anxieties of Okinawa were fading in the distance with each mile travelled.

For some time, I had been thinking about recording my war experiences while they were still fresh in my mind (these are the recordings to which I refer herein as coming from my "1945 diary" which I actually started writing on the way out to Okinawa), and, now, as the hours drifted aimlessly by, it seemed an ideal time to work on it. I asked the Chief Engineer if there was a typewriter on board I might use. He said he had one in his office, which was seldom used, and I could use it whenever I wanted.

Then started perhaps one of the more ideal periods of my life. Time had no importance whatsoever. I slept until I awoke, typed until I was tired and slept again, regardless of the time of day.

SCHOFIELD BARRACKS, THE ULTIMATE POKER GAME

One of the other passengers on the Ames Victory was a Carey Langhorne "Lang" Washborne. He was a long-range search plane pilot, who, like me, had been released for shore duty. He and I hit it off very well and started a practice of playing cards for a few minutes after each meal. One thing led to another and in order to enliven things a little, we started putting up a little money on the games. Eventually I introduced Lang to a game I had learned in Hawaii from "Gillie" Gillman called "Schofield Barracks" (named after an Army barracks upland on Oahu). The game involves first an ante. Each player is then given 5 cards, and the dealer starts by making a bet to open. The next player can raise it, meet it, or pass. If he passes, he forfeits the ante. If he raises, the opening bets keep on until met. When openers are met, players discard at their selection and draw new cards. Now the players expose one card each and bet. After that round of betting is met, another card is laid down and betting resumes. The final round of betting is reached when each player has but one card left in his hand. The game is exciting because one can see the possibilities of the importance of the final card unfolding as the game progresses.

Lang and I played it a few times with the usual wild cards, 25 cents maximum raise and maximum three raises, but we then got the idea that it might be fun to try "sky's the limit" on all bets with no restriction as to the number of raises. The game suddenly became totally different and extremely exciting even without wild card designations. We began working on each other by laughter, sarcasm, questioning, lying, etc. We complained and grimaced when good cards came into our hands and employed many other transparent ruses as our techniques for subterfuge and persuasion gained in proficiency. The pots (which, incidentally, were all simply recorded on paper) were not often large, the difference was that we felt as though we were playing with nitroglycerine on fulminate of mercury, which might detonate at any moment if disturbed. Once we had tasted the strong wine of Schofield Barracks with sky's the limit, we never went back to any other game. It became standard for one-half hour after each meal, including breakfast, and we kept a running tab. Our agreement was that the hand which was in process as we came under the Golden Gate Bridge would end the game. I will describe later how it came out. For the moment, it was this same intensive game, day after day, (with one or the other getting ahead by a thousand or so from time to time) and, in between times, with me typing in the Chief Engineer's cabin or sleeping in my bunk as the spirit moved.

THE LUCK FINALLY RUNS OUT

The Ames Victory surged steadily ahead on the homeward trail, passing Eniwetok on the seventh day, one day ahead of schedule. The excitement of approaching home began to set in. On the 13th day, we passed close by Pearl Harbor, Honolulu and Diamond Head. I stood out on deck while we went by and mentally revisited all the places I knew; Pearl Harbor, the Moana, Waikiki, Gillie's home, the Pali, Kailoua, etc. Eventually, with Oahu disappearing I turned away as the Ames Victory headed into the night—direction San Francisco.

At that time, although enemy submarines were still being reported in the area of Hawaii, due to the large number of ships approaching and leaving Hawaii, all ships were ordered to turn on their running lights when they came within a 50 mile radius of Diamond Head. Outside of that circle, the order was to steam with ships totally darkened. The Ames Victory passed Diamond Head at around 5:00 pm and figured to cross the 50-mile circle around 8:00 pm.

We had dinner. Lang and I finished our game of Schofield Barracks, and I went into the Chief Engineer's office to continue my typing. I was typing away happily at around 8:15 pm when I heard something slam, and then immediately the lights went out and simultaneously there was a tremendous "WHAM", while I was thrown backward onto the deck, crammed against the base of the chair with the typewriter and desk on top of me.

"What do you know!" I said to myself. "You come this whole Goddamn way through everything, and now you get torpedoed on a lousy merchant ship this close to home!"

Next, I felt myself. I was OK. I pushed the desk away. Left the papers where they were. I had rehearsed this in my mind many times. Take only the bare essentials. Pictures, mementos, letters—all of those things go by the boards—only take what one needs in order to survive, i.e., life jacket for floatation, hat to protect the head from the sun, sheath knife—that's it. I did, however, have one extra. I kept it in a pocket in my life jacket. It was a small round tin box of a hard candy they make in France in the Pyrenees called "Berlingots". I also had some vitamin capsules in the tin box under the misguided notion that vitamins might help me survive. In addition, I had rehearsed exactly where to go and could go there quickly even in total darkness. In war time, one soon schools oneself to learn this on any new ship. I got up, moved quickly along the passageway to my cabin, put on my life jacket and hat, returned through the passageway to the life boat on the starboard side, to which I was assigned for abandon ship, and, also according to prior rehearsal, looked down at the water line to make a mental note of where it was for later reference, to see if we were sinking.

It probably took me only about 20 seconds after the "WHAM" to reach my station at the starboard boat. At about the same time I arrived there, I heard the Captain stumbling down the ladder from the bridge uttering an unbroken string of obscenities. He reached the deck and lurched forward. Just then flames burst out forward, and it appeared that we might have been hit forward. This was fortunate, still some hope that she might not sink. Next, in the glow of the flame I could see something else. I ran forward to take a look, and there, next to our bow, was another ship.

We had run head-on—I mean cut-water to cut-water—into another ship on diametrically opposite courses. I went back and took another look at the water line. It was still the same—i.e., no danger. Also, since it had not been a submarine, there was no immediate fear of a second torpedo.

The crisis was over, and all that remained was to assess the damage and determine whether the Ames Victory could proceed to San Francisco or whether she would have to return to Pearl Harbor. A second consideration was the safety of the other ship. Accidents at sea are like automobile accidents. One cannot leave the scene of the accident unless it is appropriate to do so. Therefore, the Ames Victory and the other ship steamed on parallel courses together at very slow speed, assessing things. Captain Stall inspected below. The forward peak tank had been crushed in, and the bulkhead to the No. 1 hold had been cracked, flooding the No. 1 hold, but otherwise, everything was in good shape. The lights had gone off because the shock had tripped the circuit breaker on the main panel. Nothing had broken. Therefore, all that was needed was to throw the switch again. The engines were undamaged. The other ship also seemed to be OK, and so, after exchanging messages, the Ames Victory proceeded on her way to San Francisco, and the other ship headed for Pearl Harbor.

I would be unfaithful to the Guardian Angel who protected me to say as I have in the title of this subchapter that my luck had finally run out. She still protected me. All that had happened was that she gave me another story of a near miss to tell.

It turned out that the other ship was not actually in as good shape as her Captain originally thought. She started taking in water. They tried to get her quickly into a dry-dock before it was too late, but she sank in the harbor just as they were bringing her into the dry-dock. They could, of course, raise her from there, and she was effectively salvaged.

THE BATTERING RAMS

The Ames Victory resumed steaming at her customary 18 kts., and we went back to our respective routines, except that soon I began feeling the ship shudder every so often and hearing a deep booming sound. It was as though something might be adrift in the No. 1 hold. I went forward and took a look. It was very dark, and I had no flashlight, but I could hear something heavy sloshing around in the water in No. 1 hold as the ship pitched into the swells. There seemed to be several large floating timbers, and every so often these would ride back on a wave and crash like battering rams into the bulkhead separating No. 1 and No. 2 hold. This seemed to me to be exceedingly dangerous because flooding No. 2 hold could sink the ship. I went off, found the Chief Engineer and told him about it. He came up, took a look at it, agreed and then conferred with the Captain about it. The Captain wanted to ignore it, but the Chief Engineer insisted that speed be reduced to a few knots, and that the ship ride in the trough until morning. The Chief Engineer has nearly equal status with the Master of a merchant ship. He was the sole Officer who could have persuaded Captain Stall to do this. The next day, the deck hands lassoed the larger of the battering rams, and we went back up to 16 kts., not quite full speed, and the booming in No. 1 hold became minor.

THE GOLDEN GATE—THE FINAL HAND

As time wore on, I had gradually gained a fair ascendancy over Lang in the daily Schofield Barracks games. In fact, I had worked my advantage up to about $1,800, and now, we had passed the Farallons and were approaching the Golden Gate with the steep gray-green hills on the left and the buildings of the Presidium visible on the right. Lang and I sat down to the last hand. I had the deal. We fought at each turn betting up even on the openers. Lang discarded and drew two cards. I had two tens and two Queens, discarded the fifth card and, fantastically drew a third Queen. I need not say that a full house in poker with no wild cards is rare. I was excited. Then, we started putting the cards down and betting and raising each time.

The betting was unusually intense. Lang first put down two fours (in sequence, of course). I put down a Queen and a ten. Next, Lang put down a King and I a ten. Next, Lang put down a second King and I a second Queen. Now each of us only had one card left. Showing on my side were two tens and two Queens. On his side, two fours and two Kings. I did not, of course, know what his final card was, nor he mine. I could see one of three possibilities for him: (a) that he only had two pairs in which case I would win, (b) that he had a full house with three fours and two Kings in which case I would also win, and (c) that he had a full house with three Kings in which case I would lose. The question was which one it was, and whether I could discern from his manner some clue as to the answer. We started betting on the final card with the pot already at about $1,000, in other words, with me still ahead by $800 if I lost. We kept on. I thought he was bluffing—faking confidence to make me call. I knew I had a very strong hand, and that the odds against his drawing two cards to fill out the full house with three Kings were great. I kept on. The pot went to $1800. I kept on. Finally, when the pot reached $3,000, I began to feel that his confidence was too solid. I called. He had the other King! And I was $1200 in the hole.

I cannot remember if I paid it all off. I know I went around to his home while I was still in San Francisco and paid him a large part of it, but I have an idea that I still owe him some of it.

One final comment, the "blinding diamond and hell hearted ruby" quality of that game of sky's the limit poker forever-after reduced all other card games to "pale amethyst and mere jargoon" for me (Kipling, "Their Lawful Occasions"). I do not remember ever playing poker again, except maybe once or twice with my kids.

"WALKING DOWN MARKET STREET MINDING MY OWN BUSINESS"

In the Navy, at a Deck Court, the usual story goes, "Well, Captain, it was like this. There I was, walking down Market Street minding my own business, and up comes the Shore Patrol and grabs me!"

It so happened that after we landed in San Francisco and I was getting organized to go East, I was in the city one night walking down Market Street minding my own business. As I continued along by the pawn shops and juke box parlors, I heard running steps behind me, perhaps 50 yards away. I paid no attention. They drew closer, but still obviously unrelated to me. Then, all of a sudden, someone landed all over me. My first thought was that I was being mugged. Next, I heard, "Mr. Russell, you sonovabitch, how the hell are you?" I looked up, and to my amazement it was Austin, the radioman from the RUSSELL. You will recall that after a soft start I had transformed into an extremely "Reg" officer and had been unfriendly with and separated from the men on the RUSSELL. My relationship with them had improved as the cruise wore on, but it never came close to the quasi paternal relationship I had later with the men on the OWEN.

Austin and I threw our arms around each other and swaggered into the nearest bar. Then for an hour or so we drank and talked about the RUSSELL and a million and one things, the funny stories, Benny Cotton, the jazz in Espiritu Santo, etc. He had just been transferred from the RUSSELL to new construction. We reminisced about Midway and going out in the whale boat together and many other incidents. He told me about how Pulkinen had been put on hack, and I told him about my slapping my own wrists for the same offense. We finally got too drunk to do anything but laugh and insult each other. I was not only very happy to see Austin, but also relieved to know that my sins on the RUSSELL had not been indelible.

ASSIGNED AS CAPTAIN COOPER'S ASSISTANT IN THE BUPERS ENLISTED DISTRIBUTION DIVISION

Upon returning home, I learned that I would be assisting Captain G. R. Cooper (my former Squadron Commander), then head of Enlisted Distribution at the Bureau of Personnel (BuPers) in Washington, D.C. Lib and I rented a "Duplex" (they call them "Townhouses" now) at a housing project called The Fairlington, in Arlington, VA and had the furniture sent down from storage in Boston. I reported for duty in early July 1945. As with the Hartwigs, we had a very friendly reunion with the Coopers, and became close to the family, in fact, from then until the present day. Captain Cooper's son George Jr. lived with us when he went to MIT, and we remain close friends.

At BuPers, the Captain gave me a desk in his own air-conditioned office. By today's standards it may be hard to perceive, but in those days, there was no central air-conditioning. Only a few offices had it and all on an individual, window-unit basis. Therefore, since Washington is abominable in the summer, I was indeed privileged to be sharing the air-conditioned office with the Captain.

Captain Cooper was dark-haired as I was then, about an inch shorter than I, of virtually the same build, and we both had similar features. Also, we frequently went here-and-there in the department to meetings, etc., together. I had people repeatedly ask me whether we were related.

The Distribution Department had just installed an IBM card system, a forerunner of the modern computer. It was, of course, crude by today's standards, but it did, at least, provide a great increase in the speed of information retrieval over prior methods. Thus, if someone wanted, say, a guitar player, we could run the machine for the Washington area, and 18 cards would drop out from which we could make a selection.

Aboard ship, I was always hearing about the civilian cook who was made a Radioman in the Navy, and the civilian mechanic who was made a cook, etc., but after seeing what was done in Enlisted Distribution, I became convinced that errors of that sort must have occurred extremely rarely.

THE MEDALS SCANDAL

Shortly after my arrival at BuPers, my Bronze Star Medal (mentioned above) came through, and Captain Cooper also told me that he was arranging for me to be awarded the Commendation Ribbon. I asked why, and he told me that a survey had disclosed that of all the medals awarded by the Navy up to around July 1945, the ratio of medals awarded Annapolis graduates compared to medals awarded enlisted men and Reserve Officers was 17 to 1, and that the situation was becoming extremely embarrassing because the newspapers had "gotten hold" of it.

Bronze Star presentation ceremony – RBR Personal Collection

In order to correct the situation, all Commands were ordered immediately to start giving out medals to anyone they felt in the least deserving. This is how I obtained my Commendation Ribbon. About 30,000 such awards were literally shoveled out by the car-load. Of course, they were of the lowest level of award. But for a few upper level awards granted in this cover-up hysteria, the Navy Crosses and Silver Stars still went almost exclusively to the Annapolis graduates.

Of course, one must recognize that the award of a medal was extremely important to the career of a Regular Officer, whereas it was of only cosmetic significance to the Reserves. Something was false, however, about the system. A Naval Officer is expected to be a leader and courageous. (Here the word "expected" is more than an expression of a possibility in the future; it is used in the mandatory sense as when Nelson said that England "expected" every man to do his duty). Medals should not be given for merely doing what is expected. It would be more effective to have medals granted only posthumously, and to have them carry an annuity to the bereaved signifying grateful appreciation of the nation for the sacrifice of significant contributors. Such a medal system would be much less likely to be falsely applied and would stimulate contribution and heroism. It was used in England in the great days of the British Navy. Today's system in America only stimulates fraud and cynicism.

BUPERS REQUESTS RECOMMENDATIONS ON HOW TO REDUCE THE PERSONNEL REQUIREMENTS OF THE RESPECTIVE COMMANDS

While I was with Captain Cooper, at BuPers, a directive came around asking for recommendations on how to reduce the personnel requirements for the respective commands. This stimulated my keen interest because, while at sea, I had already come to the conclusion that the destroyers and destroyer Squadron Staffs were lavishly over-manned. I had stood "watch-in-three" in the North Atlantic, and I had operated destroyer Squadrons with a nucleus of four and I knew from experience that many things could be done with far fewer people than the personnel then assigned. In addition, I was fully familiar with the practice followed by a large majority of the commanding officers upon putting to sea, of submitting deficiency reports. The usual complaint was insufficiency of trained personnel to fight the ship. Many of the CO's under whom I served, did it habitually, and after I became a Squadron Operations Officer, I saw it frequently. The reason for submitting such reports was to establish an alibi to be used later in case the ship came under criticism. For this reason, they were universally exaggerated. Rarely, if ever, were they truly justified, but they gave an impression that the ships were constantly undermanned with trained personnel. Still another practice was "empire building". The more men an officer can gather under him, the more important he will appear. Therefore, requests for more personnel were standard procedure. These things led to overstaffing because, although the senior officers in over-all command were aware of these practices, having themselves done the same thing as junior officers, they had no incentive to crack down. In fact, they too still wanted to empire build. (The Battleship building program during World War II was a dramatic and massive example of useless empire building on the part of the Naval Command, especially in view of the fact that they practically never used those ships when the need for them arose. The same syndrome is being repeated again today in the Fleet's huge task groups built around the Nimitz class of nuclear carriers at $100 billion per group).

I saw much room for improvement, and, since destroyers were my specialty, I made a detailed outline of the personnel reduction possibilities for both destroyers and Squadron Staffs. By my recommendation, the job could be done with less than half of the presently assigned personnel. It took me about a week to complete my proposal (every billet, watch and battle station had to be analyzed), have it mimeographed, and bound for presentation. Captain Cooper was somewhat concerned. His reaction was not quite the same as Captain Hartwig's had been back in 1941, when I submitted my recommendation for an "ahead-throwing" anti-submarine weapon, because

Captain Cooper knew that I was an experienced officer at this stage and that I knew what I was talking about. He also knew, however, that many other Officers would violently disagree. Therefore, in keeping with the philosophy of avoiding controversy at all costs, he simply forwarded my proposal up the chain of command without comment.

The fate of my suggestion was essentially the same as that of my anti-submarine weapon proposal. It was attacked vigorously by virtually all of the Regular Navy Officers who were asked for comments. No one supported it.

The conclusion of the survey which was represented by the Navy to the public as being "unanimous" was that, at the present levels, the ships were undermanned.

DIVERSIFICATION AND MINIATURIZATION

In view of the extreme effectiveness of the humanly guided missile, and the comparative safety of the LCI's at Okinawa while the destroyers were being decimated, when I was working with Captain Cooper in BuPers, I had an urge to put in a recommendation for a reduction in the size of ships. My thinking was supported also by the experience around Guadalcanal where the only solution was to remove the large ships from the area and let the PT boats do the job. In addition, in view of my own experience with the operation of a one-man CIC, I knew that a two-man CIC can be effective. I therefore saw that the message for the future was diversification and miniaturization, and I submitted a proposal to that effect to the Navy.

My initial idea was to build large numbers of small microwave shielded ships. In particular, I had in mind building small, "invisible" submarines, and to build them in such numbers that they would become effectively an "infantry of the sea". By the end of World War II, there was sufficient technology to render it feasible. Thus, the Germans had already perfected microwave absorbers capable of making a submarine's snorkel radar-invisible. In addition, it was known that a thin, sharply pointed object, if aimed correctly, would not reflect sonar. This meant that a small sub shaped like a flat disc would be sonar-invisible if pointed toward the sound. Also, it was known that a submarine submerged below 100 ft. could not be seen and a small, largely plastic one cannot even be detected by other means at that depth from the air. Therefore, the "invisible" submarine was possible. Although the Japanese had tried using midget submarines and had achieved a minor success with them in Sydney, Australia, in early 1942, the Japanese design was crude and they eventually gave it up. The Japanese failure with the midget sub, however, did not prove lack of feasibility of the concept any more than the failure of the tank in World War I proved the lack of feasibility of tank warfare. Actually, while the concept of the small, invisible sub was feasible even at the end of World War II, with today's technologies, (see e.g. among others, the British robot search submarine called "SMARTIE") it can be done easily and cheaply. I believed then, and I believe today (1987) even more firmly that the small, invisible submarine is the Naval weapon of the future. To make it effective will require a completely different command structure and philosophy, but if done properly, it will render all large warships obsolete. I would like to see it done by us rather than by our future enemies, but, with the presently existing Naval command and its attitude, there is little likelihood of same.

As with my previous unconventional proposals, however, I heard nothing further from the Navy about it, and I have seen nothing since then suggesting that they are even considering it. Recent "inexplicable" submarine activity in the Baltic Sea makes one wonder if the Russians may be doing it instead.

THE ATOM BOMB

While I was with Captain Cooper, and, in view of my impression from Okinawa that the war might go on somewhat longer than I had originally thought, I began exploring how, in BuPers, I might find a way to "wrangle" a command. Also, because a transfer from the Reserves to the Regular Navy might help in this regard, I applied for and was offered a commission in the Regular Navy. I was not actually interested in a career in the Navy, but only thought that a Regular Navy Commission might help me obtain a command if the war were to continue.

On the other hand, I had worked hard, and was tired. The forecast of an intensification of the carnage we had witnessed at Okinawa for at least a brief period, if we were to invade Japan, was, to say the least, disquieting.

Therefore, the dropping of the atom bomb and the consequent ending of the war came as a relief. At the same time I believed we would have succeeded without the bomb, and it seemed to me unfortunate that we dropped the bomb in such a way as to leave an impression that we ourselves thought it had to be done in the most horrifying manner possible. While I was grateful that hostilities had ended, I thought at the time, that we should have dropped The Bomb in a rural district with plenty of warning, and that the way we did it was not only inhumane but shortsighted because it totally overlooked the effect which our doing it in that manner would have on the Japanese for generations to come.

DISCHARGED

After the dropping of the atom bomb, I became totally uninterested in the war and useless to Captain Cooper. I started spending my time in the archives pouring through war diaries to verify times, places, dates, etc., for the account of my war experiences on which I had been working.

Finally, in September after the surrender of Japan, the Navy issued a directive allowing the discharge of Reserves on the basis of a point system by which points were allowed for a wife, children, months of sea duty. As I remember it, one had to have 40 points in order to qualify for discharge. I had over 50 points, immediately requested discharge, and "reported for duty" at Harvard Law School on the 1st of October. My promotion to Lieutenant Commander came in November while I was on "terminal leave". My promotion to Commander came upon my retirement from the Reserves as a "tombstone" promotion, i.e., it was based on my Bronze Star award.

11. CONCLUSION

So ended World War II for me. The things that stood out were not only that America had accomplished a tremendous victory for all mankind, but also that the people did it with great spirit. To be there and feel the enthusiasm was a truly great experience. Whenever the American sailors were asked to sacrifice themselves, they responded unhesitatingly, even light-heartedly, and without question. Many things were not perfect. Much improvement could have been used, but no human endeavor is free of fault. The main thing was that we were fighting for a sacred cause, we never wavered, and we won.

I was proud of what America had done. I was grateful to have had the opportunity to play my part in it.

12. EPILOGUE

Captains Hartwig, Cooper and Womble all made it to Admiral (Cooper and Womble made it to Vice Admiral). I understand that several of the others also made it to Admiral. I have seen Tatton, Wesselhoeft and Woodman on various occasions, but very few of the others.

(Since writing the above, there have been two reunions of the RUSSELL which I attended. Many of the old shipmates have shown up including Hart, Woodman, Wesselhoeft, Terrill, Schwarz, Austin, and Stashkevich mentioned in my narrative, and many others. Caster, Bargeloh, and Tatton (just recently) have passed away. It is a great pleasure to get together with those who still survive. There is something about having been shipmates during those historic and trying times, which brings together a group like that and keeps them together.)

RETROSPECT AND RECOMMENDATIONS

As one looks back across the broad panorama of World War II, one sees that the true heroes were people like Lt. Cdr. Rochefort and the aviators at Midway, the fighters and the fighter directors at Philippine Sea, and Admiral Lockwood in the Submarines. Little has been written about them, yet much has been written about the true goats of the War such as MacArthur (for his needless invasion of the Philippines), the surface fleet command (for their continuation of the prewar misevaluations of the weapons, for their repeated rewarding of mediocre performance, and for their continuation of the holocaust of Okinawa without seeing, or seeking a better solution), and Truman (for his dropping the A-Bomb on a crowded city, which will plague America for generations to come), and all been given the accolades of the nation and enshrined in history as heroes.

The unfortunate aspect of this is not only that an injustice was done to the overlooked individuals, but that the incentive for excellence which rewarding the true heroes would have provided, was lost, and even more importantly, the naval system which caused the failures both before and during the war, escaped without criticism or reform. There would be no point in writing about these things at this late date but for the fact that the same system which produced, covered up for, and sanctified the wrong people, still exists today, and the type of naval leaders it produces still lead us today and will lead us again in the next war.

Now is the time to do something about it. Many people think that doing anything significant is impossible, but this author believes that a simple, small change, to be described below, is all that is needed. In order explain this in an understandable way, it is necessary to review certain case histories which illustrate the point.

The experiences of World War II such as the comparison between the methods of Admiral Lockwood in the submarines, and those of Admiral Nimitz in the surface fleet, and other case histories such as that of Commander Sims in the time of President Theodore Roosevelt mentioned above in the preface of this book, show that the source of the problem lies primarily in the promotion system of the officers.

The common denominator between the Commander Sims story, and that of Admiral Lockwood is that, in both cases, innovative junior officers were sought out and promoted out of turn over the heads of non-producing senior officers. In both cases periods of great activity and improvement in the Navy followed. Prior to the Sims case the Navy was essentially weak and complacent. After President Theodore Roosevelt adopted Sims' proposals and promoted him, the U. S. Navy rapidly became a major world force. In the Lockwood case similarly, the submarines were miserably inept and fraught with damaging misevaluations at the start of World War II. In fact, they remained that way for nearly two years. Then after Lockwood started promoting the aggressive and imaginative junior officers over the heads of their sluggish seniors, the submarine force suddenly became alive. It was only after Lockwood had instituted that policy that the submarines began using valuable methods which the Navy had previously scorned because they were either British or German, or which the conservative Navy hierarchy had thought to be impossible at the start of the war. The key to the success of Lockwood's policy was that it introduced the highly novel possibility of an officer being rewarded instead of reprimanded for disagreeing with a superior officer who might be following a nonsensical approach or rejecting a needed improvement. Suddenly, to play it safe and disturb no superior officer's feelings was no longer the sure way to promotion but instead, so doing might well result in removal from command and replacement by a more imaginative and aggressive junior. The result was that everyone except those who really were unfit for command, began doing their utmost to be aggressive and creative, and the previously service-wide fear of "ruffling the feathers" of senior officers in the course of demonstrating creativity or aggressiveness, virtually disappeared.

The important point was that Lockwood's policy capitalized on the most vital motivating factor in the officer's lives, to bring about improvement, whereas, as many of the incidents described in this book demonstrate, the normal promotion policy (which is still in existence today) worked in exactly the opposite way. Although the author's experience with the policy which he instituted on the OWEN (see above p. 254) that "the best shall be the first to go" was in a microscopic setting, it is relevant to the large picture because it achieved its objective in the same way Lockwood's did, i.e., by rewarding the best men first with the thing they desired most. In Lockwood's case it was promotion. In the author's, it was a transfer back to the States for new construction. In both cases it was the reward for excellence which stimulated excellence. The analogy is worth mentioning only because it is another live case history of a single small change in policy creating a major increase in the productivity of men.

The sudden burgeoning of the efficiency of the officer's corps in the submarines brought about by Lockwood's policy, occurred in the Navy only in that command, and it did not last beyond the war. In the surface fleet, the usual selection procedure remained in effect, and, as the foregoing account shows, the surface fleet remained shackled to its inept misconceptions throughout the war. This author has been able to find no significant instance in the surface fleet of an aggressive and imaginative junior officer being selected for an important command over the heads of more conservative but senior officers. In fact, all of the significant command assignments made in the surface fleet during the war were given to graduates of the Naval Academy classes of 1901 to 1905[48]. One negative result of this concentration of important command posts in highly senior officers (average age 61 years), which has not hitherto been given sufficient notice, is that those elderly gentlemen did not have a "feel for" the new technology, primarily radar, and neither knew how to use it nor how to capitalize on its advantages. Yet, despite these shortcomings, in no instance of which this author is aware, was an officer of the surface fleet reprimanded for being nonproductive or for failing to make the most of his equipment, or for failing to take aggressive action. Instead, many officers were praised and even decorated, despite their not using the equipment to its best advantage and losing major opportunities—numerous illustrations of which appear in the foregoing account, and conversely creative officers such as Commander Rochefort who broke the Japanese codes prior to Midway, were passed over if they committed the mortal sin of offending a senior officer.

The only case, known to this author of creativity being rewarded in the fleet, was Captain Womble's spot promotion to Commodore in charge of all destroyers in the fast carrier task groups. This promotion was given to Womble in recognition of the efficiency of his squadron as demonstrated by his nearly perfect recovery of 40 downed aviators on the night of November

27, 1944 and his revolutionizing the screening method of the destroyers by the introduction of the TCW method and its major fuel savings as describe above. Womble's promotion, however, did not serve as a stimulating factor for the officer's corps in general because Womble's name was already at the top of the list by virtue of his then seniority. His promotion was not a case of rewarding the creativity of a junior by promoting him over the heads of others more senior.

That in the cases both of Commander Sims during the Presidency of Theodore Roosevelt, and of Lockwood in World War 11, all branches of the Navy which came under the influence of the policy improved dramatically, is evidence of two things. First, it shows that the naval system is basically an excellent system because with only one apparently small change, the system was shown to be capable of functioning extremely well, and second, it showed that the key to the problem lies in adjustment of the promotion system because Lockwood's improvement resulted almost exclusively from his change in that one factor.

The reason why the beneficial effect did not last in those cases, is that, in both instances the policy could not have been put in effect without exceptional leadership, i.e., that of Theodore Roosevelt in the first instance, and that of Admiral Lockwood in the second. The U.S. naval promotion system is designed specifically to avoid the arbitrary exercise of judgment by one man on the issue of promotion. This feature of the system is intended to minimize the possibility of favoritism or bias, an obviously desirable aim. In fact, Roosevelt might have been accused of favoritism for promoting Sims. In any event, Roosevelt's action was a unique case which obviously cannot be taken as a model for the future. Lockwood's case was equally unusual. In fact, it is surprising that he was able to do it at all. Normally promotion is regulated by BuPers in Washington where the selection boards sit, and where they base their judgments on the fitness reports. That Lockwood got away with cutting across the usual lines of procedure is probably attributable to a combination of the facts that (a) the submarine command was somewhat isolated from the rest of the fleet, (b) his ships were much smaller, (c) most of the main body of the officer's corps had little interest in serving on submarines, and (d) there was a war in progress. Moreover, many of Lockwood's promotions were non-permanent, spot promotions which a local commander could make during wartime without the permission of BuPers. Spot promotions remained in effect only during the specific duty for which the spot promotion was necessary. Even so, spot promotions were eagerly sought after because they provide an excellent addition to one's record. What Lockwood did, therefore, does not apply to the Navy in general and would be feasible only in war time anyway. Accordingly, although the Sims and Lockwood case histories demonstrate that promoting creative junior officers out of turn over the heads of their superiors can do remarkable things to improve the Navy, neither case teaches a way to achieve the same effect in the peace-time system as it exists today.

Before discussing how this can be done, it will be useful to review the drawbacks of the present system. One of the problems is the natural human tendency of the officers on the selection boards to select for promotion persons "in one's own image". This means that persons who hold the same opinions on controversial subjects as the selection officer will be selected. This automatically results stagnation. Another problem is that the line between insubordination and creative thinking is a fine one. For example, no one in the Navy at the time of Sims agreed with him and, but for the intervention of the President, he would have been court martialed. Obviously, no board of naval officers at that time would have promoted him. But yet his contribution was both validly critical of the command and highly creative. In fact, it is curious but true that the more creative and revolutionary an idea is, the more likely it is that the idea will imply criticism of the command, and be generally rejected (an example of which is the author's suggestion outlined above on page 354 that the miniature, robot controlling, submarine is the naval weapon of the future). Another problem is that creativity is difficult to identify. This is a corollary of the problem of selecting in one's own image. If a candidate is proposing a radical change with which the selection officer disagrees, the selection officer will regard the candidate as stupid instead of creative. Another problem likewise a corollary of the "own image" syndrome is the natural psychological block against admitting that someone else is smarter. Thus, if a candidate has proposed or done a smart thing, experience shows that others will immediately say that they too had the same idea but that it is no good. In fact, it may well be true that they did have the idea and that they simply did not have the foresight, brashness and persistency required to bring it to the attention of others. The result, however, is that the selection officers will down-play the value of what the creative candidate has done and not classify it as creative.

These factors both explain why the present selection board system does not reward creativity, and why it cannot be expected to do so even if given rewarding same as a specific objective. From this it follows that a selection board which is controlled by active regular naval officers, especially senior officers, will not be able to achieve the objective of finding and promoting, out of turn, creative junior officers. What is needed is a special promotion board created for this purpose and kept entirely independent of the Navy.

On the other hand, there is little likelihood that a board of non-naval persons would have technical expertise sufficient to evaluate the issue of creativity in the naval context. This indicates that at least part of such a board will have to be made up of naval officers. In order, however, to prevent current naval thought from dominating the board, technically competent civilians also should be appointed to it. Since such a board will need to be independent of the Navy, the naval officers selected for it will have to be separated from the officer's corps. Also, in order to insulate the members from political or other types of outside pressure, the members will need to be given tenure and placed in a status similar to a judge. Also, in order to assure that such a board will be able to evaluate the latest technology, older and retired officers should not be selected for service on the board. The pay and status of members of such a board should be high enough to attract good young men.

There will be no need for such a board to replace the existing system. The two systems can operate concurrently.

More specifically, the present proposal is to establish such a board, to make it independent of the Navy with a membership (say 6 with the President being empowered to cast a vote in case of a tie) made up half of civilians and half of persons drawn from the naval officer's corps. They should be given life tenure and pay commensurate with Federal Judges except that an early retirement policy should be enforced to prevent the board from accumulating elderly members. The board will be given the task of seeking out a mandatory annual quota (say 20 per year) of creative officers and promoting them out of turn. It will be necessary to provide such a board with both the power and the budget to conduct investigations anywhere within the naval establishment, and to interview anyone they choose in order to find the true source of creative actions. In addition, the board will be specifically empowered to investigate the reasons why officers have been passed over by the regular promotion board, and to promote such officers when it appears that their sin has been to criticize the command when criticism was due.

One might question whether the significant expense of such a board would be worth it. The answer is that, if such a change in the promotion policy resulted in stimulating the Navy toward excellence, as experience shows that it would, the resulting saving of lives in the future would render the price of such a system indeed small.

Finally, it should be noted that there would be no point in consulting the Navy about the desirability or feasibility of such a special promotion board. Today's Navy considers that it is in an excellent state of preparedness, and that it is acting with full creativity and intelligence, there is no possibility that anyone in the Navy will support this proposal. If the benefits to be gained from it are to be realized, the institution of this special promotion board will have to be imposed on the Navy presumably by the executive or legislative branch of the government with legislative funding. The difficulty, however, of placing such a proposal before those branches of the government is that their usual practice is to rely on the Navy for advice on to how to proceed on such matters. So doing, however, would kill it. The only hope for the improvement promised by this proposal is for the executive and legislative branches to seek advice and support from other sources, as for example, retired regular officers and experienced reserves.
48

ACKNOWLEDGEMENTS

In the preparation of this book, I have received much help and encouragement from friends, former shipmates, and my patient, long-suffering wife Nancy.

AFTERWORD

To close where we began, here is my father's tall tale of the exploding bathtub. He was probably about eight or nine years old at the time:

"Well then there was the time when Danny Delmanzo and I were together on a rainy afternoon. My parents were in Europe and the Delmanzo's lived close to us on the Upper West Side. Their apartment was on the second floor, just over a drugstore called Freigen's. They served tea and things to eat there as well.

On this rainy afternoon, we thought we would play in the bathtub with our boats. I had a couple of ocean liners and a submarine. Danny had a sailboat. We would wind them up and they would go around the great big old tub. It had a fine, glazed surface that was crazed and not exactly white anymore, more like yellow. The boats went round the tub all in one direction, lest they bump into each other. We did this for a while, until we got bored. The boats kept going around and it was kind of dull.

After a while we thought it would be a good idea to have a battle between the boats with cannons. I had seen a movie called "Beau Geste" in which these toy boats staged a real battle, and I was very turned on by that, so we got to talking.

"You know firecrackers blow up under water?"

"No—really?"

"Yep, and I've got some in my drawer at home."

So I raced back to my family's apartment. In my drawer there were about twenty firecrackers. I got them all out and brought them back. There were about 15 2-inchers and three 5-inchers. I got some lead wire and we wrapped it around a couple of the 2-inchers, lit the fuse and put them in the water. They would sink down, blow up, and the water would go up in a nice little spout.

We did this a few times, then we started wiring two of the 2-inchers together—that made things a bit more interesting. Meanwhile, the old ladies downstairs at Freigen's were having tea and they probably thought there was some heavy construction going on upstairs at Delmanzo's.

We got down to where we were running out of 2-inchers and all we had were the 5-inchers. We wired the lead to one of the 5-inchers and lit the fuse. We retreated to the door and in a few seconds, she went KABOOM and the water went up to the ceiling in a nice little column.

So there we were. We only had two 5-inchers left. We decided to go for broke—that is to wire the remaining 5-inchers together, twist the fuses together and see what would happen. We attached the lead to the firecrackers, torched the fuse, dropped it into the water, and ran back to the door of the bathroom. Danny held on to one side of the doorframe and I the other. In a second, she went **KABOOOM!** The water hit the ceiling like a geyser and then the old tub just folded up and out towards us. The water surged towards us with tidal wave-like force while we stood gripping the door with our mouths hanging open.

Then I thought to myself, "Oh no! The water'll go through down to Feigen's and ruin their merchandise!" so I charged out of the apartment and down the stairs. As I walked past the windows of Feigen's I saw a couple of fellows running around knocking boxes off the top of cabinets and all the old ladies were standing outside the store. So I thought I better not say anything and, becoming very insignificant, I crept away.

The old tub was soon replaced, and everything was back to normal when my parents returned from their trip. But one day when I was in school, there was a note that came to the teacher—would Bobby Russell go to his father's office on his way home for lunch. I didn't know what it was about, but I had an idea.

When I went into my father's office and stood in front of his desk, he sat there without saying anything. Finally, he picked up a piece of paper and tossed it across the desk at me. I looked at the paper and it was a bill from the plumbers for one bathtub: $70.00.

And that was the last I ever heard of the blown-up bathtub."

REFERENCES

Barde. Robert E. "The Battle of Midway: A Study in Command", published PhD Dissertation, University of Maryland, 1971. 465p. [University Microfilms 72-2576) MIC 224-C.

"The Battle of Midway (As Released by the Navy Department on July 14 [1942]", O.N.I. WEEKLY, No. 25, 1942, pp. 37-44.

Bennett, Geoffrey. NAVAL BATTLES OF WORLD WAR II. Foreword by Admiral Arleigh Burke, USN. London: B.T. Batsford, 1975.

Blair, Clay. SILENT VICTORY, THE U.S. SUBMARINE WAR AGAINST JAPAN. New York: J.B. Lippincott Company.

Brown, David. CARRIER OPERATIONS IN WORLD WAR II. Vol. 2, THE PACIFIC NAVIES, DEC. 1941-FEB. 1943. London: Allan, 1974.

Buell, Thomas B. THE QUIET WARRIOR: A BIOLGRAPHY OF ADMIRAL RAY-MOND A.SPRUANCE. Boston: Little, Brown, 1974.

Costello, John. THE PACIFIC WAR. New York: Rawson, Wade, 1981.

Field, John. "The Life and Death of the USS 'Yorktown'", LIFE, Vol. 13, November 16, 1942.

Frank, Pat and Joseph D. Harrington. RENDEZVOUS AT MIDWAY:U.S.S. YORKTOWN AND THE JAPANESE CARRIER FLEET. Forewords by Admiral Frank Jack Fletcher and Yahachi Tanabe. New York: John Day, 1967.

"The Full Story of Midway", U.S. NAVAL INSTITUTE PROCEEDINGS, Vol. 68, No. 9, September 1942, pp. 1317-1321.

Hough, Richard A. THE BATTLE OF MIDWAY. New York: Macmillan, 1969.

Karig, Walter. BATTLE REPORT. VOL. 3, PACIFIC WAR: MIDDLE PHASE. New York: Rinehart, 1947.

King, Ernest J. U.S. NAVY AT WAR, 1941-1945; OFFICIAL REPORTS TO THE SECRETARY OF THE NAVY. Washington: Government Printing Off ice, 1946.

Lindley, John M. CARRIER VICTORY: THE AIR WAR IN THE PACIFIC. New York: Elsevier-Dutton, 1978. 184p.

Lord, Walter. INCREDIBLE VICTORY. New York: Harper & Row, 1967.

Middleton, Drew. CROSSROADS OF MODERN WARFARE. Garden City, N.Y.: Doubleday, 1983.

Morison, Samuel Eliot. CORAL SEA, MIDWAY AND SUBMARINE ACTIONS, MAY 1942—AUGUST 1942. Vol. 4 of HISTORY OF UNITED STATES NAVAL OPERATIONS IN WORLD WAR II. Boston: Little, Brown, 1949.

Potter, Elmer B. NIMITZ, Naval Institute Press, 1976.

Prang., Gordon W. MIRACLE AT MIDWAY, by Gordon W. Prang , Donald M. Goldstein and Katherine V. Dillon. New York: McGraw-Hill, 1982.

Pratt, Fletcher. "The Knockout at Midway" [Americans in Battle, No. 6], HARPER'S MAGAZINE, Vol. 187, No. 1119, August 1943, pp. 246-253.

Pratt, Fletcher. THE COMPACT HISTORY OF THE UNITED STATES NAVY, Hawthorn Books, Inc., New York, 1957.

Roscoe, Theodore. UNITED STATES DESTROYER OPERATIONS IN WORLD WAR II. Annapolis: U.S. Naval Institute, 1953.

Smith, Chester L. MIDWAY 4 JUNE 1942. Los Angeles: Bede Press, 1967.

Spector, Ronald H. EAGLE AGAINST THE SUN, Macmillan, 1985.

Stewart, Adrian, THE BATTLE OF LEYTE GULF, Charles Scribners Sons, New York, 1980.

U.S. Naval War College. THE BATTLE OF MIDWAY INCLUDING THE ALEUTIAN PHASE, JUNE 3 TO JUNE 14, 1942: STRATEGICAL AND TACTICAL ANALYSIS. (NAVPERS 91067). Newport, R.I.: U.S. Naval War College, 1948.(Cited herein as "War College '48".)

U.S. Navy. Commander-in-Chief, U.S. Fleet. BATTLE EXPERIENCE FROM PEARL HARBOR TO MIDWAY, DECEMBER 1941 TO JUNE 1942 INCLUDING MAKIN ISLAND RAID 17-18 AUGUST. (Secret Information Bulletin No. 1).

Washington, D.C.: U.S. Navy Department, 1943. (Cited herein as "Cominch 43".)

ENDNOTES

Frontmatter

1 Blair, <u>Silent Victory</u>, Lippincott, 1975 p. 30
2 Blair, <u>Silent Victory</u>, Lippincott, 1975 p.31
3 Fletcher Pratt, <u>Compact History of the United States Navy</u>, Hawthorne, NY 1957, p.194
4 Fletcher Pratt, <u>Compact History of the United States Navy</u>, Hawthorne, NY 1957, p.194
5 Blair, <u>Silent Victory</u>, Lippincott, 1975 p. 791
6 Scientific American, May 1983, Vol. 248, No. 5, pp. 53-61

Preliminaries

7 Spector, p. 217
8 Potter, p. 314
9 Potter, p. 193
10 Potter, p. 314
11 Blair, p. 80
12 Pratt, p. 256
13 Blair, p. 125
14 Blair, p. 791
15 Blair, p. 18
16 Blair pp. 281-282

Pearl Harbor to Coral Sea

17 Roscoe, p. 23
18 Spector, p. 14
19 Spector p. 191

20 Spector, p. 160
21 Potter, p. 77

Midway

22 Field, p. 160
23 War College 1948, p. 140, Bard p. 310
24 Costello, p. 301
25 Roscoe, p. 124
26 Lord, p. 223
27 Lord, p. 223
28 Prange, p. 302
29 War College 1948, p. 143, Prange. 327, Barde p. 327 and p. 336, Spector, p. 175
30 Lord, p. 267
31 Lord, p. 224, Barde, p. 345, Prange, p. 329
32 Lord, p. 275
33 Potter, p. 104

Guadal Canal to Santa Cruz

34 Spector, p. 191
35 Rosoc p. 23
36 Blair, pp. 18-20, 125, etc.
37 Bennett, p. 199
38 Actually....
39 Lord, p. 256
40 Spector, p. 212
41 Spector, supra, p. 212

Conclusion in the Southwest Pacific

42 https://en.wikipedia.org/wiki/USS_Russell_(DD-414)

America Takes the Offensive

43 Spector, p. 308
44 Spector, pp. 417-420, Potter, pp.314-324, Blair, pp.693-695
45 Potter, p. 322
46 Spector, p. 418

Okinawa

47 Potter, p. 371

Retrospect and References

48 Spector, p. 18 and Potter, p. 50

CPSIA information can be obtained
at www.ICGtesting.com
Printed in the USA
LVHW081750271221
707271LV00010B/69/J